THE CLASSICAL GUITAR

"The guitar is a wonderful instrument which is understood by few."
                                                    Schubert

"The instrument most complete and richest in its harmonic and polyphonic possibilities."
                                                    Manuel de Falla

"I love the guitar for its harmony; it is my constant companion in all my travels."
                                                    Nicolo Paganini

"Nothing is more beautiful than a guitar, save perhaps two."
                                                    Chopin

THE CLASSICAL GUITAR

ITS EVOLUTION

AND

ITS PLAYERS

SINCE 1800

BY

MAURICE J. SUMMERFIELD

First Edition 1982

Second Edition 1991

Third Edition 1992

Fourth Edition 1996

© ASHLEY MARK PUBLISHING COMPANY 1982, 1991, 1992, 1996

THE CLASSICAL GUITAR. ITS EVOLUTION AND ITS PLAYERS SINCE 1800. © 1982, 1991, 1992 and 1996 by Maurice Joseph Summerfield. All rights reserved. No part of this book may be used or reproduced in any manner whatsoever without written permission except in the case of brief quotations embodied in critical articles and reviews. For information write to Ashley Mark Publishing Co., Olsover House, 43 Sackville Road, Newcastle-upon-Tyne NE6 5TA, United Kingdom.

FIRST EDITION	MARCH 1982
SECOND EDITION	MAY 1991
THIRD EDITION	JULY 1992
FOURTH EDITION	NOVEMBER 1996

Typeset and printed in United Kingdom.

HARDBACK	1 872639 11 9
PAPERBACK	1 872639 16 X

THE CLASSICAL GUITAR

CONTENTS

Preface	5
Its Evolution	9
Its Players and Personalities	21
Its Duos, Trios, Quartets and more	267
Its Other Guitarists	287
Its Composers	293
Its Makers	327
Its Scholars	347
The Flamenco Guitar	363
Index	375
Sources of Information and Supply	378

To My Wife, Tricia

THE CLASSICAL GUITAR
PREFACE TO THE FIRST EDITION

I have long felt the need for a book dealing specifically with the classical guitar and its most important players and personalities since 1800. Those authors who have written books in past years about the history of the classical guitar have usually devoted a large section of their work to the lute, vihuela and early guitar. As a result in these books many important players and personalities, in particular contemporary classical guitarists, are not included or are given only a brief mention.

Since the publication of my first book, 'The Jazz Guitar – Its Evolution And Its Players' in 1978, it often occurred to me that the format I applied to this work would lend itself admirably to one on the classical guitar. Amongst the many enthusiastic letters I have received from guitarists all over the world about this first book, many of the writers supported this view. With their encouragement I began to write this book early in 1980. Originally I had hoped to complete the new work early in 1981 but the task proved much greater than I expected. The book was finally completed earlier this year and I am now satisfied that 'The Classical Guitar – Its Evolution and Its Players Since 1800' is currently the most complete and up-to-date work dealing with the modern classical guitar.

As with my book on the jazz guitar, one of the most important features of this new book is its very full listing of records, music and details of books and magazine articles. Most of the items detailed are still currently in production or print. Those which are not can be obtained with a little patience by using the Sources of Supply section at the back of the book. I have personally found that an advert placed in one or more of the specialist guitar magazines will often bring that elusive item. You will also be amazed, particularly if you live in a larger city, at what your local main library can offer. In regard to records you should remember that many items are available in different countries with different brands, sleeves and numbers, so be careful not to duplicate or be misled.

The collection of photographs in this book of classical guitarists, past and present, is I believe a unique one. It gives me really great pleasure to see such a collection under one cover and I wish to give special thanks to all those who have supplied them. Their contribution has been vital to the excellent illustration of this book.

I realise there is a possibility that some readers may feel that some other classical guitarists they know of and admire have been omitted. However, I have sincerely tried to include all those guitarists who I believe have made an impact on the evolution of the guitar in classical music since 1800. I have not included the many great guitarists who play the classical guitar but not classical music. Therefore Nashville stylists like Chet Atkins, Latin American virtuosos such as Baden Powell and Sebastião Tapajos, and jazz guitarists like Charlie Byrd and Lenny Breau are not included. I am aware that there are many fine classical guitarists throughout the world who may well deserve a place in future editions of this book but circumstances and events have not as yet allowed them to contribute in an effective way to the evolution of the classical guitar. Some of these guitarists that I have heard play in concert or on record, or know of, are illustrated in the appendix to the players' section of this book as a tribute to their ability and important contribution to the growth of today's classical guitar world.

Maurice J. Summerfield, June 1982

THE CLASSICAL GUITAR
PREFACE TO THE SECOND EDITION

The first edition of this book sold out within a few months of its publication in June 1982. My intention in 1983 was to correct the various errors in the first edition and release an updated second edition in the same year. My involvement in other matters, in particular the birth (in September 1982) and the subsequent monthly publication of Classical Guitar magazine, has meant that my original intention was delayed by about seven years. And what good job it was! In this relatively short period of time the classical guitar world has seen an explosion in the volume of world-class players emerging on the scene. Similarly the output of classical guitar scholarship and research, with its many publications and recordings, is unprecedented in the history of the instrument. As a result, this edition contains over one hundred and fifty new entries with all the original historical and other information updated on the evidence of the most recent research published by scholars all over the world. Also included in this edition is a chapter on the great flamenco guitarists of the twentieth century.

Without writing a book of encyclopaedic proportions it would be impossible for me to cover in any comprehensive way the enormous area now inhabited by the classical guitar. My selection has therefore been made according to my own feelings and beliefs, and to those who will inevitably criticise it on the grounds that certain (and no doubt numerous) names that have been omitted should have been included, I can only say that I agree wholeheartedly and wish that the book could have been big enough to encompass them all. Nevertheless I believe that it does give a clear outline of the classical guitar's development since 1800 in terms of its players, its composers, its constructors and the very many scholars and personalities who make up the history of this fascinating instrument.

My association with Classical Guitar magazine, now recognized internationally as the foremost magazine of its type, has of course helped me greatly in finalizing this second edition. In particular my special thanks must go to my friend and colleague Colin Cooper, the general editor of Classical Guitar magazine. Without his support, his many suggestions and encouragement, this new edition could not have been published in such a complete and accurate way.

Maurice J. Summerfield, March 1991

THE CLASSICAL GUITAR
PREFACE TO THE FOURTH EDITION

The prefaces to the first two editions of my book 'The Classical Guitar – Its Evolution, Players and Personalities since 1800', printed on the previous page, are still valid with the exception of the last sentence in the second paragraph of the first preface. It is this new, updated and much enlarged, edition which I now confidently believe is the most complete and up to date work dealing with the classical guitar since 1800.

Maurice J. Summerfield, November 1996

ACKNOWLEDGEMENTS

Arnaldur Arnarson

George M. Bowden

Prof. Jaques Chaîné
Classical Guitar Magazine
Colin Cooper

Françoise-Emmanuelle Denis
Decca Records
John W. Duarte
Deutsche Grammophon

EMI Records

Eduardo Falu
Bernard Fanning

Blanco R. Garcia
Izydor Geffner
Gendai Guitar (Japan)
Gramofon AB BIS (Sweden)
Guitar Review

Ole Halen

Dean Kamei

Andrew Liepins

Barry Mason
Jorge Morel
Musicmasters Records

Matanya Ophee

M. Perott
Polydor Classics
Philips Records

Radio France

Thérèse Wassily Saba
Sony Records
Richard Stover

Terence Whitenstall

All photographs are from the files of Classical Guitar magazine unless shown otherwise

THE CLASSICAL GUITAR

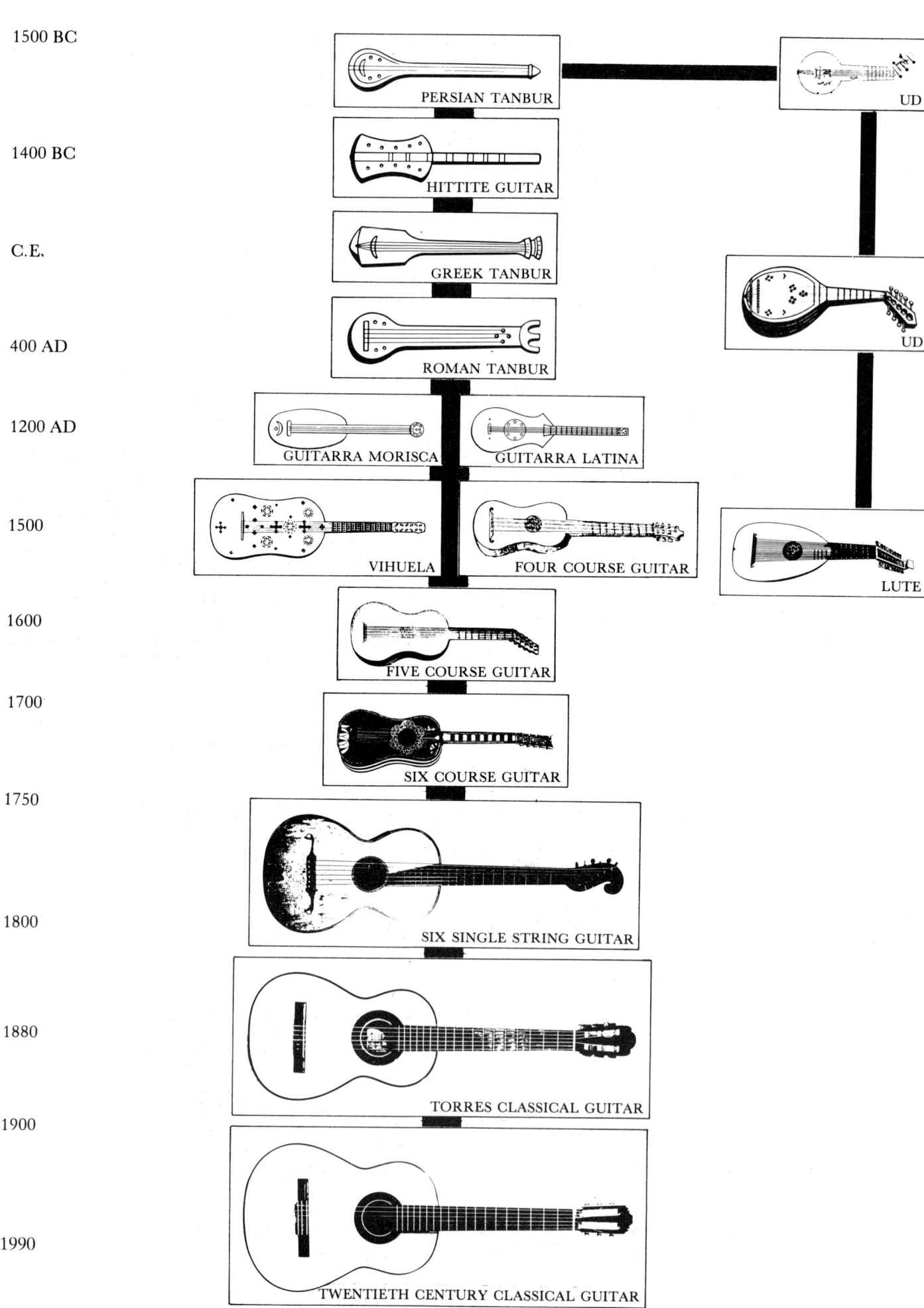

Chart showing the evolution of the classical guitar as an instrument from 1500 BC to the present day

THE CLASSICAL GUITAR
ITS EVOLUTION

This book deals with the evolution of the classical guitar since 1800. Many excellent books have been written in past years on the history of the guitar and its origins before that time. These are listed at the end of this chapter for those readers who wish to extend their research of this earlier period in greater detail. Nevertheless, as a start to this chapter I believe it necessary to make the reader briefly aware of the origins of the guitar before 1800.

For many years several guitar scholars and historians put forward the theory that the guitar's ancestor was the Persian ud. They claimed that the Spanish guitar gradually evolved from this lute-like instrument after the Moors brought the instrument to Spain when they invaded the Iberian peninsula around 711AD. However, more recent research has shown that the six-string classical guitar, as we know it today, evolved in a different manner.

The first guitar-like instrument on record is shown on a 1400BC archaeological object taken from the city gates of the new Hittite settlement at Alaja Huyuk. It shows a Hittite musician playing a long-necked guitar-shaped instrument rather than the more common tanbur. During this period of history the popular instrument of the region was the tanbur which, although having a fretted or marked neck, had a distinctive bowl-shaped body as opposed to the guitar shape of today. The word guitar itself is derived from two Persian words, tar – meaning string, and char – meaning four. Therefore char-tar stood for a four-stringed instrument. Many of these early stringed instruments originally had four strings. Over the years the name char-tar gradually evolved into the word guitarra in Spain and then into similar names throughout most of Europe. An exception was Portugal, where the word for a guitar has always been violão, derived from the Latin word fidicula (a small plucked fiddle-like instrument).

Illustration of four course guitar in 1551 music book

From these early tanburs/chartars emerged the Greek tanbur in 300BC. Later the Romans developed their own tanbur around 300AD. These instruments were both chartars, i.e. four-stringed instruments. It now seems absolutely certain that the Romans took their tanburs to the Iberian peninsula in 476AD, almost three centuries before the Moors' invasion of Spain, and it was this Roman tanbur that was later developed into the guitarra morisca and the guitarra latina. These were both guitar-like instruments, distinctly illustrated in the important historical document 'The Cantigas of Alfonso the Wise' in 1270AD. The guitarra latina had a flat back, as has the modern guitar, and the soundboard had one hole over which the strings passed. It was used for playing chords and was a forerunner of the vihuela. The guitarra morisca had a vaulted back, the fingerboard was large and the soundboard had several soundholes. It was used for the playing of melodies.

It was these instruments that later evolved into the aristocratic vihuela (a six double stringed instrument tuned GCFADG) which dominated the courts of Spain and Portugal during the sixteenth century. The four-course guitar (tuned CFAD – the same as the middle four strings of the vihuela) was used mainly by troubadours to accompany songs and dancing.

The ud, which had also evolved from early tanburs, eventually developed into the baroque lute (like the vihuela the original lutes were tuned GCFADG). This instrument became extremely popular in England, France, Italy and Germany during the seventeenth century. Although related to the early guitar, because of its similar origins, the lute really had little part in the evolution of the guitar. Nevertheless the technique required to play both fretted instruments had many similarities, with each instrument's strings laid out in courses (that is, pairs of strings tuned either in octaves or unison) and with similar tuning.

Both these instruments were fretted – fret is derived from the old French word ferreté, meaning 'banded with iron'. The frets on early instruments, unlike the metal frets of the modern guitar, were made of gut and tied around the neck. The lute and vihuela had ten or eleven frets, whereas the early guitar had between four and eight. The number was dependent on whether the guitar was to be used for melody or the strumming of chords. A great deal of the music originally written for the lute and vihuela in later years became successfully transcribed for the six-string classical guitar, and now forms a valuable part of its repertory.

The period of musical history from 1400BC to 1800AD saw a vast multitude of plucked string

Julian Bream playing a Renaissance lute

An interesting illustration from Pablo Minguet's "Modo de taner todos los instrumentos mejores" (Method of Playing All the Best Instruments) published in Madrid 1752

instruments evolving first in the Middle East, Asia and the Far East. Later, in Europe, the Greeks and Romans had, as well as their tanburs, the harp-like lyra and kithara. It seems likely that the kithara, originally a four-stringed hand harp, also derived its name from the Persian words char-tar. In India the sitar, surbahar and tampura were popular stringed instruments. The Chinese had their p'i p'a and the Japanese their samisen. There is little doubt that all these early instruments are distant relatives of the guitar, sharing with it their origin in the tanbur (sometimes mistakenly called the nefer). In the sixteenth century many versions of the lute also appeared. The chittarone and theorbo lutes were two of the more popular versions of this aristocratic descendant of the Persian ud. The citterne, a mixture of the lute and four-course guitar, also appeared in the sixteenth century, as did the first mandolins in Italy. Many of these had six courses of strings, but as the eighteenth century drew to a close the four-course mandolin, as it is known today, became established. As most of these early fretted string instruments fell into disuse and became museum pieces the mandolin remained one of the few to survive in the guitar-dominated nineteenth and twentieth centuries.

In Europe both the lute and the vihuela gradually fell into disuse towards the end of the seventeenth century. The lute suffered from the addition of more and more strings so that it became virtually impossible to master (and also to tune). When the tuning of the four-course guitar changed to DGBE and a fifth course (low A) was added, the vihuela began to lose its popularity. The addition of this fifth string on the four-course guitar is often accredited to the Spanish poet and musician Vicente Espinel (1551-1624). By the time the six-string guitar came into being towards the end of the eighteenth century the vihuela was extinct.

It is not known exactly when the sixth string was added to the guitar but most historians agree it happened around 1780, and probably almost simultaneously in Italy and Germany. (Some scholars now suggest it could have developed in France (the term chitarra francesca being employed by the Italians to speak of single-string instruments, regardless of the number of strings). The German luthier Jakob August Otto has often been credited to be the first person to make a six-string guitar, adding its lower E, around 1790. But it now seems probable that the first six-single-string guitars were being made in Italy a little after the middle of the eighteenth century.

By 1800 most countries of Europe had given up the five- and six-course guitar in favour of the six single-string guitar. In Russia a seven-string guitar was developed by the guitarist Andrei Ossipovitch Sychra (1772-1850). This was tuned DGBDGBD, and was to remain very popular for many years in that part of the world. The noted Italian composer Luigi Boccherini (1743-1805) had given the 'new'

Frontispiece of Luys Milan's "El Maestro", a collection of vihuela music, which was published in Valencia, Spain in 1535. It shows Orpheus playing a six course vihuela

would be a period of decline in the progress and popularity of the guitar as it became overshadowed by orchestral and keyboard instruments. It was again in Spain at the end of the nineteenth century that the evolution of the classical guitar would be given an enormous boost by the luthier Antonio de Torres Jurado and the virtuoso guitarist Francisco Tárrega.

Torres, inspired originally by the virtuoso guitarist Julián Arcas, had developed a larger bodied guitar with advanced fan strutting and a wider fingerboard. It was with this new version of the instrument that Francisco Tárrega developed a new playing technique which would eventually make musicians aware of the enormous potential of the guitar. His work was to be extended in the first half of the twentieth century by more Spanish guitarists, in particular Andrés Segovia. It was Segovia who, against extreme opposition, would embark upon a worldwide crusade lasting for almost eighty years to promote the instrument. This crusade was eventually to be successful, and today the guitar has become one of the most popular classical instruments, with a repertory of available music that approaches in quantity and in quality that of any other instrument.

Towards the end of the eighteenth century a well-known organist, Father Basilio, a monk of the Citeaux order, turned his full attention to the guitar. He developed a fine solo technique on the guitar its first taste of musical 'respectability' by adapting several of his finest quintets to include a part for guitar. This he did in Spain under the patronage of the Marquis de Benavente, an enthusiastic amateur guitarist, around 1790. By 1800 several virtuosos of the six-string classical guitar were beginning to emerge in various parts of Europe, and the first golden age of the classical guitar was about to begin.

This golden age of the guitar began simultaneously in Spain and Italy around 1775. The appearance of the first six-single-string guitars coincided at the beginning of the nineteenth century with another important development in the internal construction of the instrument, fan strutting. This is the term used for the strips of wood attached in a particular manner to the back of the soundboard of the guitar. These strips not only help to distribute the sound waves along the soundboard, but also reinforce the soundboard, enabling it to be thinner and so able to vibrate more freely. In time there would be many variations and extensions of fan strutting, but there is no doubt that even these early simplified versions were an important innovation. The years 1800 to 1980 were to see a gradual development of the instrument in three main areas. These were the guitarist's technique, the guitar's repertory and the construction of the instrument. These parallel developments began in Spain, and to a lesser exent in Italy, at the end of the eighteenth century. Towards the end of the nineteenth century there

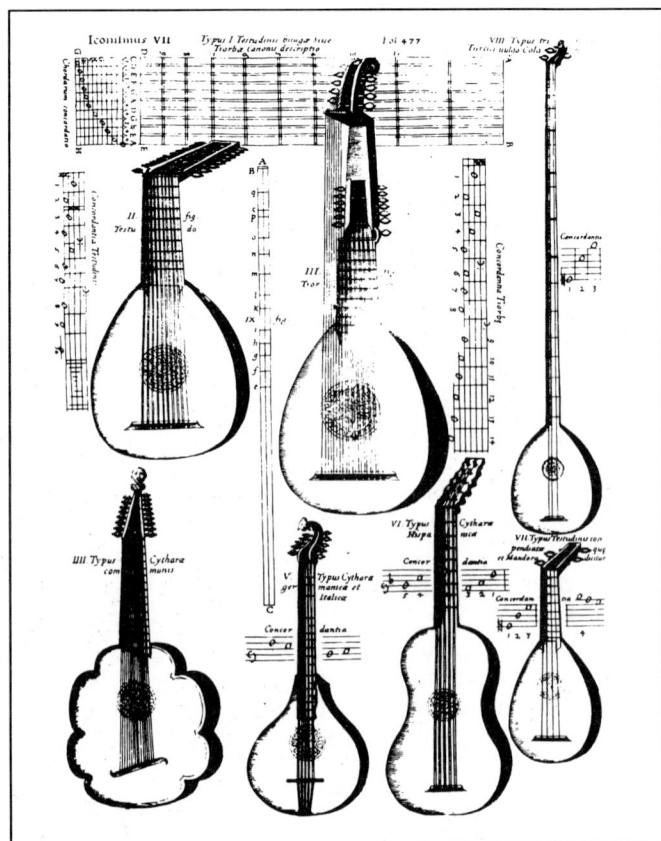

A variety of stringed instruments, including a five course guitar (named Cythara Hispanica), from Athanasius Kircher's "Musurgia Universalis" published in Rome 1650

instrument and his virtuosity became widely recognised in Spain. He was asked to play for Charles IV of Spain, and later he was to become tutor to Queen Marie Louise. Basilio, whose real name was Miguel Garcia, influenced two other important eighteenth century guitarists, Fernando Ferrandiere and Don Federico Moretti. In 1799 Ferrandiere published his method for the six-string guitar in modern notation, 'Arte de tocar la Guitarra Española', and Moretti published his 'Principios para tocar la guitarra de seis ordenes'. It has been suggested by some scholars that both these works drew upon an earlier work, published in 1780, 'Obra para Guitarra del sexsto orden, by the guitarist Antonio Ballesteros.

It was these men who laid the foundations in Spain for a nineteenth century revival of the guitar which would be completed by two of Spain's greatest exponents of the six-single-string guitar, Fernando Sor (1778-1839) and Dionisio Aguado (1784-1849). These two brilliant musicians led very active careers of concertizing and teaching. Both lived for a good part of their lives in Paris, then as now one of Europe's most important centres for music and the arts. Sor in fact died in Paris; Aguado returned to Spain to spend his last years in his native city Madrid. Both men were prolific composers and their music still remains an integral part of the twentieth century guitarist's repertoire.

Sor was the greater and more prolific composer of the two, but Aguado's books, in particular his New Guitar Method, made an unparalleled contribution to the learning of the guitar in the nineteenth century.

Dionisio Aguado was also the inventor of the tripodison, an unusual guitar accessory devised to hold the guitar rather than resting it on the right thigh. However, this invention did not achieve any lasting success. Both Sor and Aguado published important guitar methods which, over the years, were translated into several languages and are still used to this day.

It is interesting to note the variation in these two great guitarists' right-hand technique. Whilst both agreed on the 'tirando' stroke to pluck the strings (that is, the right-hand fingers rise after plucking the string as against 'apoyando' in which the fingers continue past the string to rest on the string below), Aguado advocated the use of the fingernails whereas Sor used the pads of his right-hand fingertips. Nineteenth century guitarists were divided on this matter, and the controversy has continued to the present day. At the beginning of the twentieth century Franciso Tárrega advocated the right-hand 'no nail' technique, and this method of plucking the strings was continued by Emilio Pujol among several other important guitarists. The vast majority of twentieth century players

Portrait of Francesco Corbetta on music "Varii Scherzi di Sonate Per La Chittara Spagnola" published Brussels, Belgium 1648

have followed the use of the nails as advocated by Andrés Segovia (and by Miguel Llobet) from the early 1920s.

The early part of the nineteenth century saw many fine guitarists, but two are regarded as being the most outstanding: Fernando Sor from Spain and, from Italy, Mauro Giuliani (1778-1829). Little is known of Giuliani's early musical background, but on his arrival in Vienna in 1806 musicians soon became aware that he was a guitarist/composer extraordinary. He associated with and became the friend of many other fine musicians in the Austrian capital, including Beethoven, Hummel, Diabelli, Moscheles and Mayseder. Giuliani has the distinction of having had the first guitar magazine in English, 'The Giulianiad', named in his honour. It was published in London in the early 1830s by the German-born guitarist Ferdinand Pelzer. Vienna, where Giuliani made his home, was one of the great European centres for the arts, music and the guitar at the beginning of the nineteenth century. It was also the home of several other important and influential guitarists including Simon Molitor (1766-1848) and Johann Kaspar Mertz (1806-1856) as well as guitar makers like Johann Staufer.

Two other important and influential Italian guitarists were Matteo Carcassi (1792-1853) and Ferdinando Carulli (1770-1841). Although not of the stature of Giuliani, Carcassi and Carulli were prolific composers and contributed greatly to the nineteenth century repertory for the guitar. All three Italian guitarists performed widely throughout Europe. Whereas Giuliani made Vienna his home and centre of work, Carulli and Carcassi chose Paris.

Other important nineteenth century guitarists were Giulio Regondi (1822-1872) and Napoléon Coste (1805-1883) from France, Luigi Legnani (1790-1877) and Zani de Ferranti (1802-1878) from Italy, and Don A. F. Huerta (1805-1875) and Julián Arcas (1832-1882) from Spain. In Russia Andreas O. Sychra (1772-1852) and Nicolas Makarov (1810-1890) were also important figures in the development of the guitar. The Italian violinist Nicoló Paganini (1782-1840) was also a virtuoso guitarist and composed several important pieces for the instrument.

An important feature of the evolution of the instrument in the early years of the nineteenth century, and one which has continued to this day, was the co-operation between the guitarist and the guitar maker in improving the quality of sound and volume of the instrument. Fernando Sor worked closely with René François Lacôte in France and Louis Panormo in London, Luigi Legnani worked with Staufer, and towards the end of the century Julián Arcas was instrumental in developing the larger-bodied classical guitar with Antonio de Torres Jurado in Spain.

Although after 1860 the guitar continued to have a few outstanding soloists, its acceptance in most musical circles as a serious musical instrument

Francisco Tárrega

began to decline. There were several reasons for this. Despite the large output of compositions by guitarists themselves, the instrument's repertory was limited because none of the great composers had written for it. Hector Berlioz (1803-1869) and Franz Schubert (1797-1828) were both guitarists, but with the exception of a few songs written with a guitar accompaniment by Schubert and a few simple studies by Berlioz, neither wrote for the guitar. Although Coste had begun to transcribe the baroque music of Robert de Visée in the 1830s, little of the excellent music of past centuries, written for the lute, vihuela and guitar had at that time been transcribed for the six-string instrument. With the exception of the compositions of Sor and Giuliani, the quality of most guitar music did not compare with the vast library of fine music available for other instruments. The use of the guitar in folk music, accompanying singers and dancers (as in flamenco), and in other popular forms of music lowered further the estimation of the guitar in the eyes of the vast majority of serious musicians and music teachers throughout Europe. These prejudices against the guitar lasted for many years and even today still linger on in some areas of the classical music world. The original nineteenth century small-bodied guitars also suffered from a lack of volume which hindered their use when played in company with other instruments.

It was the great Spanish guitarist Francisco Tárrega (1854-1909) who was to set the guitar back on an illustrious and firm course. Originally a talented pianist, he won first prize for harmony and composition at the Conservatory of Madrid. He began to play the guitar as a child and continued to develop his technique on the instrument throughout his conservatory career. It was Julián Arcas (1832-1882) who had originally encouraged the luthier Antonio Torres to make a wider-bodied guitar with a wider neck, and subsequently Torres developed and improved the pattern of fan strutting, also paying close attention to the type of bridge referred to by Aguado in his Escuela of 1825. Tárrega realised that to play this new guitar with its larger body and different shape, the techniques applied to the earlier and smaller guitars would have to be altered. Carulli and Molino were using footstools as early as 1810, but it was the custom to rest the instrument on the right thigh, with the right hand supported by placing the little finger on the table of the guitar between soundhole and bridge. Carulli and his fellow countryman Molino, who also lived in Paris, were advocates of this position, although we find Aguado in his Method saying that 'In no way will one rest the little finger on the table, or any other finger, because the hand must remain free and nimble'.

Guitarists of the period would also sometimes bring the thumb of their left hand over the edge of the neck to finger bass notes, and the strings seem to have been plucked more with the 'tirando' stroke than with the 'apoyando' stroke, although both strokes must be as old as the instrument itself.

Tárrega found that the larger-bodied Torres guitar needed to be rested on the left thigh, the player's leg slightly raised by the use of a footstool. The raised fingerboard made resting the little finger on the soundboard impracticable, and the abandonment of that particular technique paved the way for a closer examination of 'apoyando' technique. The wider neck meant firm rules for the placement of the fingers on the fingerboard.

Tárrega also made a significant contribution to the evolution of the modern classical guitar by extending its repertory. He not only composed a quantity of delightful original pieces and studies for the instrument, but also extended the art of transcribing for the guitar music originally written for other instruments, as Carulli, Matiegka, Giuliani, de Fossa, Heeser, Schuster and many others had done earlier in the nineteenth century. Tárrega's transcriptions of Bach, Beethoven, Mozart, Schubert, Haydn, Albéniz and Granados are a delight to hear and play. His many public performances of these transcriptions and original compositions did much to bring the guitar to prominence once again. Although he did give many concerts in several European countries,

A Nineteenth century cartoon of an imaginary 'battle' between supporters of Carulli and Molino

including France, Italy and England, he was not fond of travelling and preferred to stay in Spain. As a result his influence was not as great as it possibly could have been had he extended his public performances to more countries.

With the approach of the twentieth century the second and the greatest golden age of the classical guitar was beginning to dawn. As it had been Spain that had laid the foundation of the nineteenth century classical guitar, so it was Spain once again that contributed so greatly to the twentieth century guitar through the work of Tárrega, the founder of the modern guitar school, and Torres, the father of modern guitar construction.

Early in the twentieth century Emilio Pujol (1886-1980) and Miguel Llobet (1878-1938), two of Tárrega's pupils, travelled widely and gained new audiences for the guitar both in Europe and in America, yet it was to be another Spanish guitarist, Andrés Segovia (1893-1987), who would lead the classical guitar into its greatest years.

A self-taught guitarist, Andrés Segovia's great musical talent was recognized at an early age. He disregarded the advice of other Spanish classical musicians to change to a 'more serious' musical instrument and dedicated himself to establishing the guitar worldwide as an instrument equal to any other classical instrument. He decided that this could only be done by presenting the guitar in concert to as many audiences as possible and by extending its repertory. This he did with tireless energy for almost eighty years. Few would deny that his success in achieving these goals went far beyond his wildest dreams.

There are few countries in the world in which Segovia did not appear in concert. Everywhere his audiences were astounded not only by his incredible musicianship but also by the scope of the guitar in the hands of a master. It was in the early 1920s when Segovia began his campaign to encourage prominent composers to write for the guitar. His pleas were first answered by Joaquín Turina (1882-1949) and Federico Moreno Torroba (1891-1982) in 1924. In fact the first great composer of modern times to have written for the guitar was Manuel de Falla (1876-1946), who in 1920 composed Homenaje pour le tombeau de Claude Debussy, thus fulfilling an early promise to Miguel Llobet.

Segovia never let up in his campaign to enlarge the guitar's repertory. He also made many transcriptions of fine music originally written for other instruments. Within a relatively short period the guitar gained a vast library of original works. Other important composers who have written especially for the guitar as a direct result of Segovia's instigation are Joaquín Rodrigo (1901), Manuel Ponce (1886-1948), Mario Castelnuovo-Tedesco (1895-1968), Alexandre Tansman (1897-1986) and Heitor Villa-Lobos (1887-1959).

Segovia also continued the tradition of early nineteenth century guitarists by working with guitar makers to improve the quality of sound and the volume for the instrument. He worked first with the Ramirez family, and subsequently with Hauser and Fleta. He was also instrumental in the development of the nylon guitar string with the luthier Albert Augustine in 1947. This development was an enormous step forward in the evolution of the guitar.

The years from 1930 to 1996 have seen the rise of many outstanding guitarists in most countries of the world. Although there were variations in certain aspects of the technical approach, for example the 'no nail' technique versus nails, using the right-hand side of the nails or the left-hand side of the nails to pluck the strings, the great majority of guitarists have followed the technique of the instruments as developed by Tárrega and refined by Segovia.

In France, Ida Presti (1924-1967) was recognized as a child prodigy in the 1930s, and later with Alexandre Lagoya (1929) formed their guitar duo, undoubtedly one of the greatest of all time. Many great guitarists have also appeared in Spain after Pujol, Llobet and Segovia. Regino Sainz de la Maza in the 1930s was followed in more recent times by Narciso Yepes, José Tomás, Angel Romero and Pepe Romero.

In Britain two great guitarists appeared in the 1950s and 1960s. Julian Bream and John Williams both continued and extended the Segovia tradition

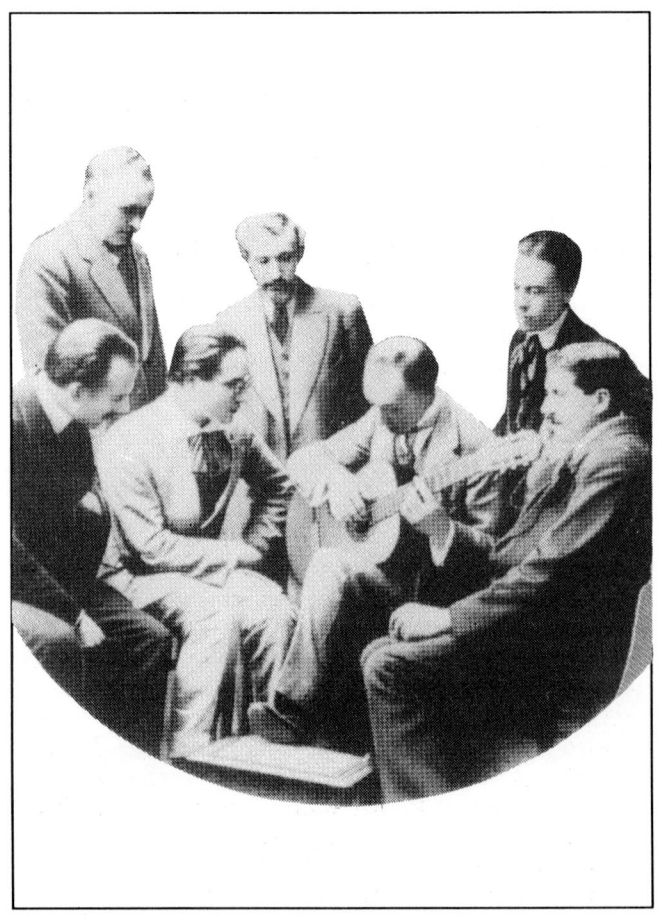

Miguel Llobet with admirers. Left to right, standing: Severino Garcia Fortea, unknown, Juan del Moral Parras. Seated: A son of Tàrrega, Andrés Segovia, Miguel Llobet, another of Tàrrega's sons.

Andrés Segovia, 1959

in a magnificent way, yet each has departed from it on occasion and in his own fashion: Julian Bream becoming a major figure in the revival of the Renaissance lute and its music; John Williams instigating a fusion of classical and rock music with his commercially successful group 'Sky'.

In South America during the 1920s and 1930s Agustín Barrios Mangoré was the outstanding guitar virtuoso and composer. Nevertheless Segovia still proved, after his various concert tours there, to be the most lasting influence on guitarists in more recent generations. Maria Luisa Anido, an early pupil of Miguel Llobet, continued this tradition and was the teacher to many of the great guitarists originating in South America in recent years. In more recent times the world has seen many more great guitarists emerge. Italy has produced Oscar Ghiglia. In the United States, Vahdah Olcott Bickford and William Foden were two of the most influential guitarists at the beginning of the twentieth century, and in more recent years Christopher Parkening, David Tanenbaum and Eliot Fisk. From Cuba Manuel Barrueco, Rey de la Torre and Leo Brouwer; from Austria Konrad Ragossnig; from Japan Akinobu Matsuda and Kazuhito Yamashita; from Czechoslovakia Vladimir Mikulka; from the Soviet Union Alexander Frauchi; from Scotland David Russell. These are only a few of the most outstanding players of the twentieth century. The chart on page 20 shows in detail the most important classical guitarists from 1800 to 1996.

Wherever he went Segovia not only encouraged prominent composers to write for the guitar but also made a point of approaching music conservatories, colleges and universities to establish a seat for the classical guitar. At the beginning of the twentieth century the guitar was not accepted in any of these institutions, although the Guildhall School of Music in London had appointed a professor of guitar as early as 1887 – Giulia Pelzer, sister of Madame Sidney Pratten. Today there are very few departments of music education which do not include the guitar in their curriculum and who do not have a professor of guitar.

Andrés Segovia was without doubt the most important classical guitar figure of the twentieth century. There is not a classical guitarist today who does not owe a direct debt to his almost superhuman efforts which, more than any others, have led to the establishment of the instrument worldwide.

The classical guitar currently rides on the crest of a wave of popularity and growth, but what of the future? The 1960s saw the development of the ten-string guitar played by Narciso Yepes, who also instigated its production. José Tomás plays and advocates an eight-string guitar, as does the Belgian guitarist Raphaëlla Smits, who has helped to promote the instrument through her recordings of music by Mertz and Coste. A seven-string guitar (with an extra string above the high E rather than a low D) has been developed. In Sweden, Göran Söllscher plays an alto guitar with eleven strings. Apart from the notable exception of Maurice Ohana, few modern composers have been tempted to write for these special instruments.

In past centuries, adding extra strings to stringed instruments usually in time spelt doom for the instrument. These current variants of the six-string guitar will no doubt linger on, but it seems certain that the standard six-string classical guitar will be dominant for many years to come. The number of talented players of the instrument, its general acceptance in all musical circles throughout the world, and the size of its repertory, all continue to grow at a staggering rate.

Narcisco Yepes with his ten-string guitar

Selected Reading

The Evolution of the Classical Guitar – Wilfrid M. Appleby (I.C.G.A. 1966).
La Guitare et les Guitaristes – José de Azpiazu (Editions Symphonia-Verlag AG, Bâle 1959).
The Illustrated History of the Guitar – Alexander Bellow (Franco-Colombo 1970).
The Segovia Technique – Vladimir Bobri (Macmillan 1972).
The Guitar and the Mandolin – Philip J. Bone (Schott 1914 and 1954)
Die Gitarre und Ihre Meister – Fritz Buek (Robert Lienan Normals Schlesinger 1926).
The Guitar in England 1800-1924 – Stuart Button (Garland Publishing Inc., New York 1989).
The Orphée Data base of Guitar Records. Compiled by Jacques Chaîné. Editions Orphée, Columbus, Ohio, 1990).
La Chitarra a cura di Ruggero Chiesa (EDT, Torino 1990).
Classical Guitar Magazine 1982 through 1996 (Newcastle upon Tyne).
Classical Guitar Music in Print – Mijndert Jape (Musicdata Inc., Philadelphia, 1989).
Guitars from Renaissance to Rock – Tom and Mary Evans (Paddington 1977).
La Guitarra: Sus Antecedentes Históricos y Biografías de Ejecutantes Celebres – Segundo N. Contreras (Buenos Aires 1927).
Den Klassika Gitarren – Martin Giertz (Norstedt & Söners, Stockholm, 1979).
Manuale di Storia della Chitarra – Vol.I, Mario Dell'Ara; Vol.II, Angelo Gilardino (Bèrben, 1988).
Guitares – Michel Foussard (Eurydice 1980).
Guitar Music Index, Volumes 1 and 2 – George Gilmore and Mark Pereira (Galliard 1976).
The Art and Times of the Guitar – Frederick V. Grunfeld (Macmillan 1969).
Guitar Review Magazine – 1946 through 1991 (New York).
Guitar Music in the Archives of G.F.A. – Thomas F. Heck (G.F.A. 1981).
The Guitar – History, Music, Players – Kozinn etc. (Columbus 1984).
Guitar and Vihuela Bibliography – Meredith Alice McCutcheon (Pendragon 1985).
Die Gitarre – Peter Päffgen (Schott, Mainz 1988).
Diccionario de Guitarras, Guitarristas y Guitarreros – Domingo Prat (Buenos Aires 1934, reprinted Editions Orphée 1986).
Classical Guitar, Lute and Vihuela Discography – Ronald C. Purcell (Belwin Mills 1976).
Handbuch der Gitarre und Laute – Konrad Ragnossnig (B. Schott's 1978).
La Guitarra Española – José Villar Rodríguez (Clivis, Barcelona 1985).
The Story of the Spanish Guitar – A.P.Sharpe (Clifford Essex 1954).
Guitarren-Lexicon – Josef Powrozniak (Verlag Neue Musik 1979).
Gitarre – Fred Seeger (Lied der Zeit Musikverlag, Berlin 1986).
Die Gitarre – Alexander Schmitz (Ellert & Richter Verlag, Germany 1988).
The Guitar From the Renaissance to the Present Day – Harvey Turnbull (Batsford 1974).
Traditions of the Classical Guitar – Graham Wade (John Calder 1981).
Handbuch des Laute und Gitarre – Josef Zuth (George Olms Verlag 1978 reprint).

THE GUITAR

DEFINITIONS BY CARL SANDBURG

A small friend weighing less than a newborn infant, ever responsive to all sincere efforts aimed at mutual respect, depth of affection or love gone off the deep end.

A device in the realm of harmonic creation where six silent strings have the sound potential of profound contemplation or happy go lucky whim.

A highly evolved contrivance whereby delicate melodic moments mingle with punctuation of silence bringing "the creative hush".

A vibratory implement under incessant practice and skilled cajolery giving out with serene maroon meditations, flame dancers in scarlet sashes, snow white acrobats plunging into black midnight pools, odd numbers in evening green waltzing with even numbers in dawn pink.

A chattel with a soul often in part owning its owner and tantalizing him with his lack of perfection.

An instrument of quaint form and quiet demeanor dedicated to the dulcet rather than the diapason.

A box of chosen wood having intimate accessories wherefrom sound may be measured and commanded to the interest of ears not lost to hammer crash or wind whisper.

A portable companion distinguished from the piano in that you can take it with you, neither horses nor motor truck being involved.

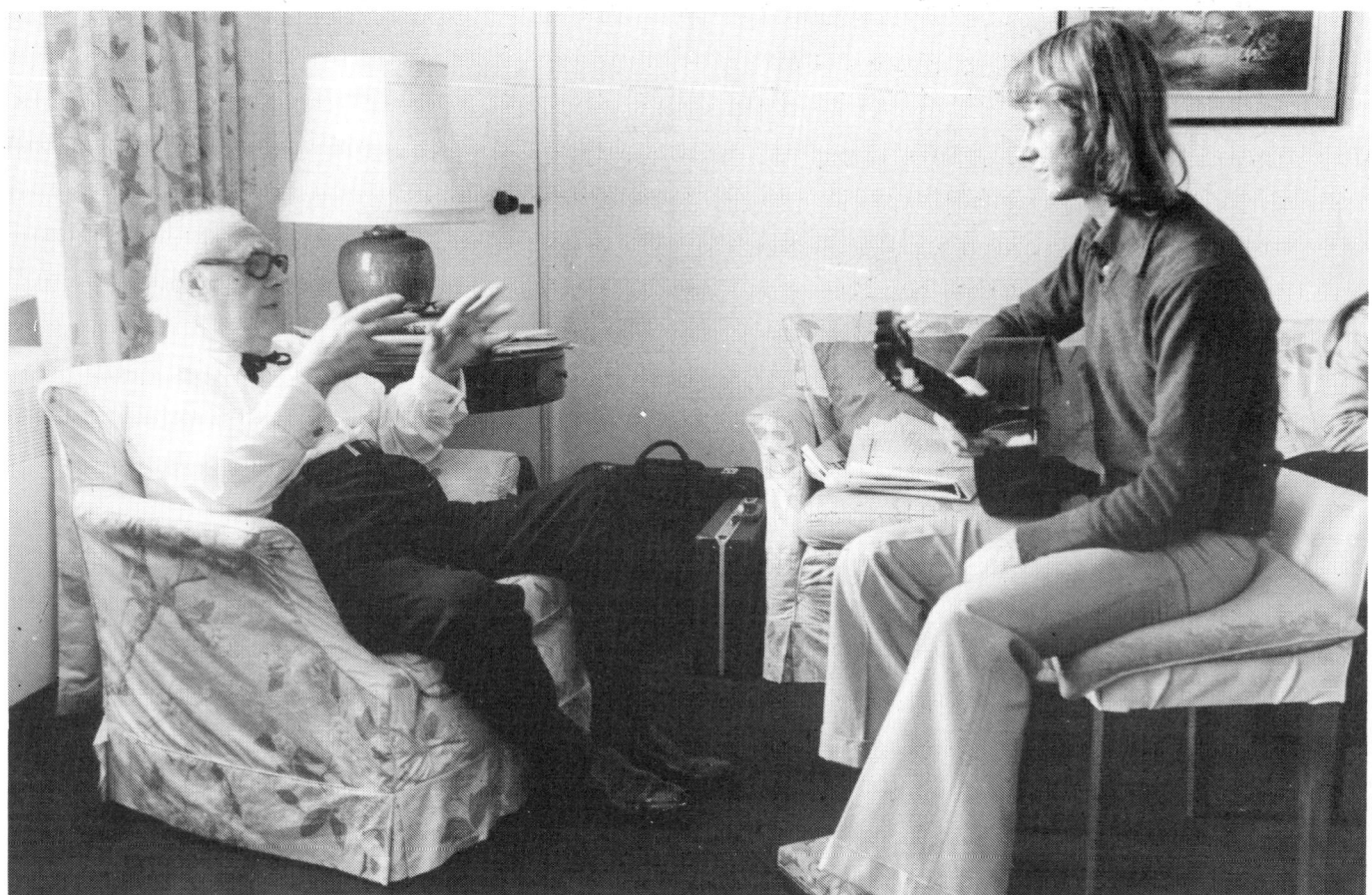

David Russell with Andrés Segovia

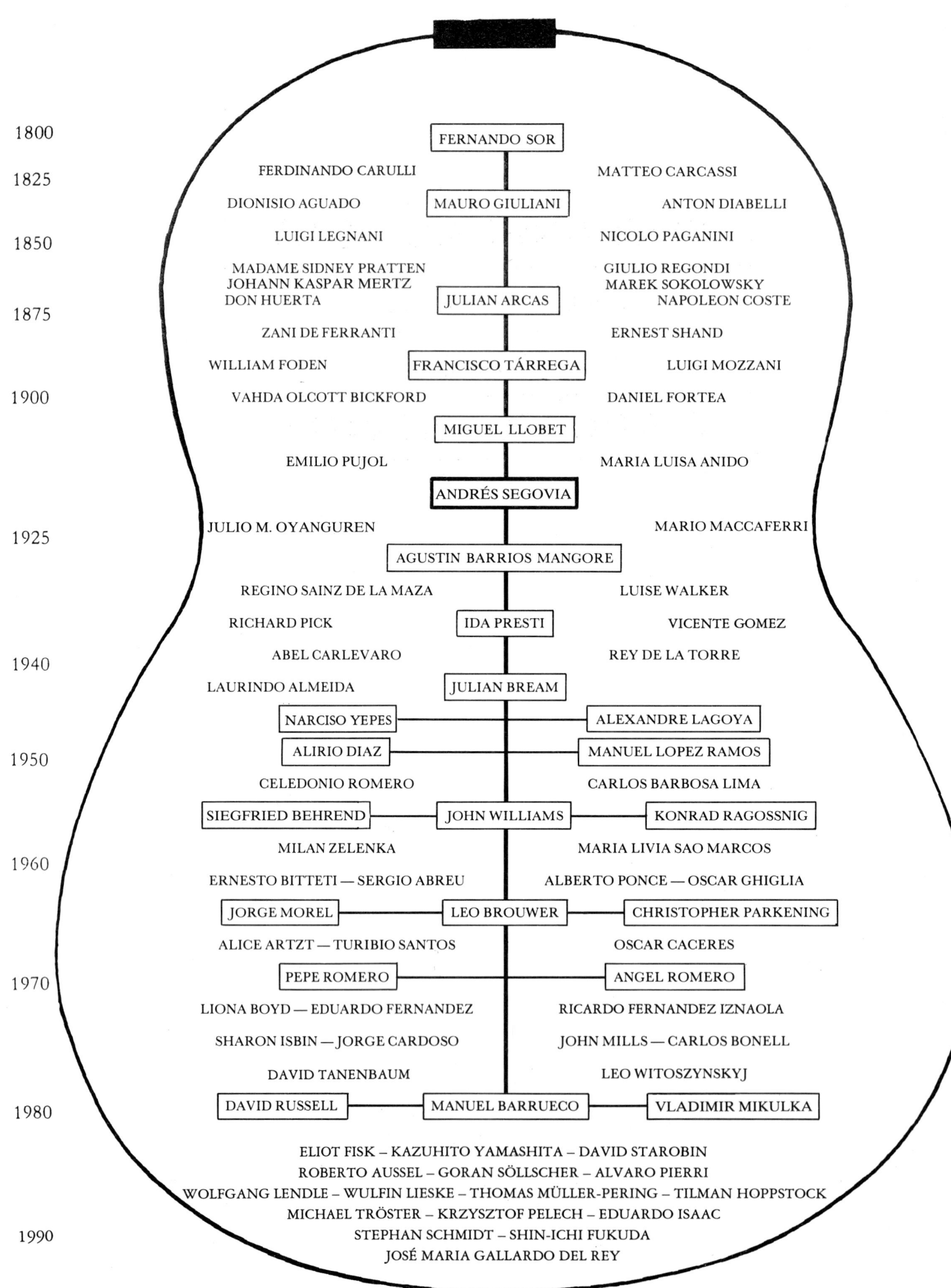

A general chart showing the most important classical guitarists since 1800.

THE CLASSICAL GUITAR
ITS PLAYERS
AND
ITS PERSONALITIES

CODE TO ABBREVIATIONS OF PUBLISHERS' NAMES IN SELECTED MUSIC COLUMNS

B	Broekmans en Van Poppel
B & B	Bote & Bock
B & H	Boosey & Hawkes
BA	Ricordi, Buenos Aires
BP	Brazilliance Music
CG	Carl Gerhmans
CHANT	Chanterelle
CO	Columbia Music Company
EMB	Editio Musica Budapest
EMM	Ediciones Musicales Madrid
EMT	Editions Musicales Transatlantiques
ESC	Editions Max Eschig
FC	Franco Colombo
GA	Guitar Archives – Schott
GSP	Guitar Solo
JWC	J & W Chester
MB	Mel Bay
N	C. F. Peters
RIC	Ricordi
SI	Belwin Mills
SY	Ricordi
SZ	Suvini Zerboni
UE	Universal Edition
UME	Union Musical Espanola
ZA	Zanibon
ZM	Musikverlag Zimmerman

NB. These abbreviations appeared in the First Edition. Additions to the further editions such as Bèrben, Guitarre und Laute, Editions Orphée, Sikorski and Tecla Editions are recorded in full.

MIGUEL ABLONIZ

Born – MICHEL AVLONITIS

Cairo, Egypt

29 May 1917

Miguel Ablóniz

The son of a Greek father and an Italian mother, Miguel Ablóniz now lives in Italy. He began to teach himself the guitar at the age of eight. Qualified teachers were not to be found in Cairo at that time, and for a period of five years the young guitarist used the methods of Carulli, Albert and Carcassi. Ablóniz then managed to correspond with prominent teachers in Europe who were able to send him new guitar books and music. In 1933 he made contact with the French guitarist André Verdier, a former pupil of Miguel Llobet. Verdier recommended the young guitarist to Emilio Pujol, who also began to correspond with Ablóniz.

During the second World War Miguel Ablóniz gained a lot of experience as a concert guitarist, both in recital and on the radio. Eventually he was to devote most of his time to teaching and transcribing, rather than playing in concert. In 1946 he went to the Escuela Municipal de Música in Barcelona, Spain, to study privately with Pujol. He continued his musical studies with Juan Parras del Morral. In 1945 he travelled to Great Britain to hear and meet Andrés Segovia.

In 1953 Miguel Ablóniz moved to Milan, Italy, where he established in his home a guitar school, still in existence today. He teaches at a number of Italian academies and colleges, and also spends some time each year visiting guitar courses abroad. These include one held at the Ithaca College in the USA, where he is the principal teacher.

Over the years Miguel Ablóniz has transcribed around one thousand works for the guitar. He is widely regarded as one of the instrument's foremost authorities and teachers.

SELECTED MUSIC

Arietta Medievale.	Bèrben
Bulería Gitana.	Ricordi
Capriccio Flamenco.	Bèrben
Chorinho.	Ricordi
Cowboy Melody — based on 'Colorado Trail'.	Ricordi
Four Preludes.	Ricordi
Four Recreational Pieces.	Ricordi
Guitar Chôro.	Bèrben
Improvisation – Homage to Villa-Lobos.	Ricordi
An Incorrigible Dreamer.	Bèrben
Moods.	Bèrben
Partita in E.	Ricordi
Polo.	Ricordi
Prelude and Guitar Bossa.	Bèrben
Sequential.	Bèrben
Tango Andaluz.	Ricordi
Tarantella Burlesca & Bossa Nova.	Bèrben
Three Gitanerías.	Ricordi
Two Ricercari Moderni.	Ricordi
Valsette and Marcetta.	Ricordi
Crab Fingering.	Bèrben
Essential Exercises for the Left Hand.	Bèrben
Fifty Arpeggios for the Right Hand.	Bèrben
Ten Melodic Studies.	Ricordi
The Twenty-Four Diatonic Scales.	Bèrben
Tuning and Fingerboard Rediscovered.	Bèrben

SELECTED READING

Article   Guitar Player, October 1977

SERGIO ABREU

Born – SERGIO REBELLO ABREU

Rio de Janeiro, Brazil

5 June 1948

Sergio Abreu

Sergio Abreu showed exceptional talent from early childhood. In 1961 he and his brother Eduardo (born 19 September 1949) played for the eminent Argentinian guitarist Adolfina Raitzin Tavora, a former pupil of Andrés Segovia. She was so impressed by the brothers' ability that she immediately decided to coach them in advanced technique and musical interpretation.

As a duo the Abreu brothers performed all over the world, achieving great success. In the eyes and ears of many critics they were the true successors to the throne of Ida Presti and Alexandre Lagoya. Life as a professional guitarist did not appeal to Eduardo, and Sergio turned his attention to the solo platform, achieving much success and high critical praise in his tours of the United States of America, Australia, the United Kingdom and most other European countries. He performed a duo with the violinist Yehudi Menuhin in the Windsor Festival, England, and also took part in the Guitar '81 Festival in Toronto, Canada, appearing as performer, judge and teacher.

In recent years Sergio Abreu has devoted most of his time to the construction of classical guitars of excellent quality, but he still remains a fine guitarist.

He is also active in arranging, particularly in the duo field in which he and his brother had been so prominent.

SELECTED RECORDINGS
The Guitars of Sergio and Eduardo Abreu   CBS 61262 LP
The Guitars of Sergio and Eduardo Abreu
                               Ace of Diamonds SDD219 LP
Two Concertos for Two Guitars   CBS 61469 LP
Sergio Abreu Interprets Paganini and Sor.   Ariola 201614 LP

SELECTED READING
Interview	Guitar, February 1978
Interview	Guitar, January 1979
Interview	Guitar Player, July 1980
Interview	Sound Board, Spring 1990
Interview	Guitar Review, Fall 1994

MARIO ABRIL

Born – Havana, Cuba,

26 February 1943

Mario Abril

Mario Abril spent his early years in the small city of Sagua La Grande where he studied music theory, music literature, piano, violin and the guitar under the guidance of his mother. In 1961 he took part in the ill-fated Bay of Pigs invasion of Cuba, and was captured. During his twenty-two months imprisonment he met the well-known Cuban guitarist Hector Garcia, who was also a prisoner. Garcia became Abril's teacher, and for several years after their release from prison the two musicians worked together in the United States of America.

Mario Abril earned a Bachelor's degree in guitar from the University of Albuquerque, New Mexico, and a Ph.D. degree in music theory from the Florida State University School of Music. For many years he performed extensively throughout North America as a guitar recitalist. He is currently an associate professor of guitar and music theory at the University of Tennessee, Chattanooga. He has written articles for several guitar magazines including Guitar Review, and has had many books of guitar solos and transcriptions published by Hansen House.

DIONISIO AGUADO

Born – DIONISIO AGUADO Y GARCIA

Madrid, Spain, 8 April 1784

Died – Madrid, 20 December 1849

Dionisio Aguado

Dionisio Aguado was the son of a prominent clergyman in Madrid. He showed an early aptitude for music and was taught the rudiments by a monk called Basilio in a Madrid college. But it was the renowned singer/guitarist Manuel García to whom Aguado owed his thorough grounding in both music and the guitar.

In 1803 Aguado moved to a small estate which had been left to him by his father, in the village of Fuenlabrada, near Aranjuez. There he was able to devote all his time to an intense study of the guitar and music. The end result was several volumes of studies for the guitar and finally his 'Method for Guitar' published in Madrid in 1825. Aguado took up residence once more in Madrid after the end of the French invasion. After the death of his mother he travelled in 1826 to Paris, where his works for guitar were already well known. He returned to Madrid in 1837. In Paris he met the great guitar virtuoso Fernando Sor. They developed a strong social and musical friendship, though their technical approach to the guitar was very different. (For instance, Aguado used his right-hand nails and dazzled his audiences with an amazing technique, in direct contrast to the 'no nails' technique of Sor.)

For a time they lived in the same house in Paris. A sign of the close friendship of these two virtuoso guitarists is Sor's duet for two guitarists, Les Deux Amis, which was dedicated to their association.

In late 1838 Aguado decided to return to his native Spain, and he took up residence once again in Madrid. Here he was to remain until his death in 1849 at the age of sixty-five.

The volume of Aguado's compositions was not as great as that of his friend and fellow countryman Fernando Sor, but there is no doubt of his genius and the lasting qualities of his music. Aguado was also the inventor of an unusual accessory for the guitar, called the tripodison. This was a three-legged stand on which the guitarist could rest his guitar whilst playing. Aguado claimed that his invention increased the volume of the guitar, and also made the guitar easier to play in concert. Despite support for this contraption from several players, including Sor, the tripodison did not gain wide support, becoming extinct within a short period of time.

SELECTED MUSIC
Allegro and Allegro Vivace.	GA301
Allegro brillante.	GA302
Easy Waltzes and Studies.	GA303
Fandango and Variations, ed. Tarrago.	UME
Selected Works.	ECH 400
Six Selected Pieces.	GA55
Thirty-one little Guitar Works.	N3212
New Guitar Method.	Tecla

SELECTED READING
The Tripodison Article. Guitar Review No.39, 1974
Dionisio Aguado the Man – José Romanillos.
 Guitar International, April 1984
Guitar Method of Dionisio Aguado – Erik Stentstadvold
 Classical Guitar, March & April, 1990

MIGUEL ALCAZAR

Born –

Mexico City, Mexico

26 April 1942

SELECTED RECORDINGS

Tablatura Mexicana para Guitarra Barroca.	EMI-Angel SAM 35029 LP
Paganini & Gragnani Sonatas (with Rudolf Werthen, violin)	EMI-Angel SAM 35035 LP
Música Barroca para Laud	EMI-Angel SAM 35039 LP
Ponce – 24 Preludes, Sonata de Paganini etc.	EMI-Angel ASM 77042 LP
Música Mexicana para Guitarra.	EMI-Angel SAM 35065 LP
Música Latinoamericana.	EMI-Angel SAM 35066 LP
Napoléon Coste Souvenirs.	Tritonus TTS 1003 LP
Música de Guitarra Barroca.	Tritonus TTS 1005 LP
Ponce – Obras Completas Vol.1.	Tritonus TTS 1008 LP
Vargas y Guzman Sonatas para Guitarra.	Tritonus TTS 1011 LP

SELECTED READING

Interview.　　　　　　　　　Classical Guitar, December 1984

Miguel Alcázar

Miguel Alcázar is one of Mexico's foremost players and teachers of the classical guitar. In 1963 he was awarded the first prize in the composition contest sponsored by the Mexican Guitar Associations. In 1964 he won the Beryl Rubinstein Scholarship for Composition at the Cleveland Institute of Music. His opera La Mujer y su Sombra won first prize in the Fundación Morales Estevez Contest and was premiered at the Fine Arts Palace in 1981.

Alcázar obtained his Masters Degree with honours from the National Conservatory of Music in Mexico in 1971. Since that time he has been a faculty member there and also at the Cleveland Institute of Music and the Universidad Veracruzana. He is also a prolific recording artist and music editor. His many editions of Mexican music have been published by Universidad Veracruzana, the Liga de Compositores de Mexico, Tecla Editions and Editions Orphée. His concert career has taken him throughout the USA and Europe.

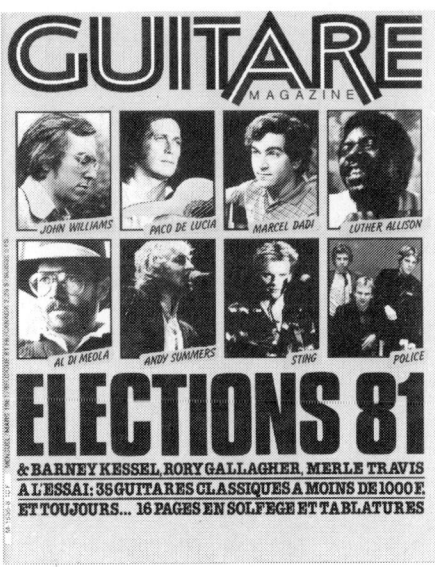

A selection of guitar magazines

Laurindo Almeida

LAURINDO ALMEIDA

Born – LAURINDO JOSÉ ALMEIDA NOBREGA NETO

Prainha, Santos, Brazil, 2 September 1917

Died – Los Angeles, USA, 26 July 1995

Laurindo Almeida was one of the most important guitarists of the 20th century. He was one of the few musicians to achieve great success in both the classical and jazz fields of music. He was the total musician, not only a brilliant soloist and accompanist, with a distinctive warm sound, but also an outstanding composer and arranger. His overall musical talent and original concepts gained him enormous international respect amongst his peers in the 60-plus years of a professional career.

Almeida received his early music tuition from his mother, who was a concert pianist. She hoped that he too would become a pianist, but Almeida fell in love with a guitar owned by his sister Maria. In a short time it was evident to all around him that he was on the way to being a master guitarist. In 1936 he signed on as guitarist on a Brazilian cruise liner, the 'Cuyaba'. During the voyage to Europe he absorbed a wide variety of musical styles including his first exposure to jazz. On a visit to Paris he heard the 'Hot Club of France' string quintet, starring the Gypsy virtuoso guitarist Django Reinhardt. This group made a great impression on him. On his return to Brazil he settled in Rio and took on the post of staff guitarist/arranger with Radio Mayrink Veiga. By 1944 Almeida had reached the heights of his profession in Brazil. In 1947 he decided to move to the USA, settling in Hollywood. Here he worked as a studio musician in films, and as a classical soloist with violinist Elizabeth Waldo. His interest in jazz helped him get the guitar seat in the famous Stan Kenton orchestra, which became a legend over the whole world for its innovations in jazz music. His most outstanding recordings with Kenton were his solo work in Pete Rugolo's *Lament,* and his own composition *Amazonia.* In 1950 Almeida left the Kenton orchestra to lead a more diverse musical career.

In 1953-54 Almeida joined forces with saxophonist Bud Shank and, with the addition of bass and drums, recorded three brilliant recordings entitled 'Brazilliance'. These recordings were the forerunners of bossa nova, mixing Brazilian rhythms with American jazz. Almeida's impeccable taste as a composer, arranger and guitarist shines through on all these recordings. It was during this time he made the first of many solo guitar albums of both classical and popular music for the Capitol and Decca labels. In 1963-64 he toured the world as a featured soloist with the Modern Jazz Quartet. This association originally began as a project for the 1963 Monterey Jazz Festival. In 1966 he made the American debut recordings of Radamés Gnattali's *Concerto de Copacabana* (Capital SP 8625), and the Villa-Lobos Guitar Concerto (Capital SP 8638). Throughout his career Almeida was years ahead of his peers in his promotion of the music of Barrios, Gnattali, Villa-Lobos and other outstanding South American composers. From the 1960s he performed, recorded and published (through his Brazilliance Publishing Company) the guitar works of these and other great South American composers.

In the 1970s Almeida once more gained great international popularity with his 'LA Four' quartet, which featured saxophonist Bud Shank, bassist Ray Brown and drummer Shelley Manne. This group was a direct continuation of his original Brazilliance quartet.

From the 1970s right up to the time of his death Laurindo Almeida remained one of the most popular and sought-after guitarist/composer/arrangers in Hollywood. He often concertised and recorded with his wife Deltra (Didi) Eamon, the talented Canadian soprano, whom he had married in 1971.

Laurindo Almeida won ten Grammy Awards and, as well as performing on the guitar, had a long list of film scores to his name including, amongst others, *Viva Zapata, The Godfather, A Star is Born, Camelot* and *The Agony and The Ecstasy.* He was a prolific composer. One of the Grammy Awards was for his composition *Discantus* which tied with Igor Stravinsky in 1961 for best contemporary composition. His many original works included concertos for guitar and orchestra (he recorded his first concerto on the Concord Concerto label – CC-2001 – in November 1979) and his recently finished guitar quintet. Almeida received an Oscar for composing the music to the animated fable *The Magic Tree.* In October 1977, he was awarded the Certificate of Appreciation from the American String Teachers Association for 'a lifetime of dedicated and distinguished service to the guitar in the United States'. He also published many valuable books of arrangements of classical and jazz standards for guitar, and an excellent tutor. These works are an enormous contribution to the 20th century repertoire of the guitar. He donated his unique collection of over 1000 items of music and original scores to the California State University at Northridge.

Laurindo Almeida was one of the busiest and most popular classical guitarists in the United States. There is no doubt that through his enormous output of records, publications and also his concert appearances, he was one of the most influential guitarists on the North American Scene for over forty years.

SELECTED RECORDINGS
Guitar Music of Spain.	Capitol P8295 LP
Guitar Music of Latin America.	Capitol P8321 LP
Vistas D'España.	Capitol P8367 LP
Danzas.	Capitol P8467 LP
Villa-Lobos.	Capitol P8497 LP
Spanish Guitars.	Capitol P8521 LP
From the Romantic Era.	Capitol DP8601 LP
Plays Radamés Gnattali.	Capitol SP8625 LP
Virtuosi (with Deltra Eamon).	Orion ORS7260 LP
Almeida Concerto for Guitar.	Concord 42001 CD

SELECTED READING
Interview	Guitar Player, August 1968
Interview	Guitar, July 1974
Interview	Guitar, November 1979
Interview	Frets, June 1979
Interview	Classical Guitar, April 1992
Interview	Acoustic Guitar, Sept/Oct 1993

SELECTED MUSIC
Chôro Para Olga.	BP25
English Air.	BP29
Gypsy Dance.	BP44
Gypsy Suite on Popular Motives, in 5 Movements.	BP26
Gypsy Suite, in 5 movements.	BP27
Insomnia.	BP23
Lament in Tremolo Form.	BP20
Mystified.	BP38
The One Minute Divertimento.	BP24
Pavana for Pancho.	BP28
Serenata in Memoriam to Garoto.	BP501
Soledad.	BP500
Sueño.	BP35
Two Spanish Folk Songs.	BP45

MARIA LUISA ANIDO

Born – ISABEL MARIO LUISA ANIDO

Moron, near Buenos Aires, Argentina, 26 January 1907

Died – Tarrogona, Spain, 4 June 1996

SELECTED RECORDINGS
Grande Dame de la Guitare — Erato STU70722 LP
Guitar Recital — Capital P18014 LP

SELECTED MUSIC
Impresiones Argentinas – Nine Compositions — Ricordi

SELECTED READING
Interview — Classical Guitar, August 1988
Article — Classical Guitar, February 1993

Maria Luisa Anido

Maria Luisa Anido's father, Don Juan Carlos Anido, was the publisher of 'La Guitarra', a magazine devoted to guitarists and guitar music. Encouraged by her father, she took up the guitar at an early age and studied first with Domingo Prat and then later with Miguel Llobet.

Maria Luisa Anido showed exceptional talent at an early age and made her concert debut at the age of ten on 7 May 1918 in Buenos Aires. From that time she continued to give concerts throughout the world. In 1925 she gave a series of duo concerts with her renowned teacher Llobet. Over the years she made many recordings and broadcasts, particularly in her native Argentina. She was made professor of the guitar in the National Conservatoire of Music in Buenos Aires, and for fifty years taught many of Argentina's finest classical guitarists.

In her 81st year she she took up residence in Havana at the invitation of the government of Cuba, where she continued to teach. In May 1988 she was made Doctoris Honoris Causa at the National Institute of Art, Havana.

Maria Luisa Anido as a child with her Torres guitar.

WILFRID APPLEBY

Born – WILFRID MORRISON APPLEBY

Brighton, England, 3 July 1892

Died – Cheltenham, England, 10 December 1987

Wilfrid Appleby

For many years Wilfrid Appleby was one of the leading personalities on the British guitar scene. As editor of 'Guitar News' he kept British guitarists informed on international and British guitar events and personalities for over twenty years, following the end of World War II.

Together with his wife Kay, Wilfrid Appleby originally decided to take up the study of the guitar to fill the time created by the wartime curtailment of his international Esperanto activities. After a period of intense study of books from the public library, and also music obtained through friends in Spain and Argentina, he became a proficient player and teacher. As an acknowledged authority on the guitar, he was invited by A.P.Sharpe, the editor of the long-established fretted instrument magazine B.M.G., to write a monthly column on the classical guitar. In a period of over five years he wrote almost 80 articles.

Appleby then took an active part in the revived Philharmonic Society of Guitarists. He was also very much involved in his own local guitar society in Cheltenham, formed in 1946. Together with Boris M. Perott, he helped to promote the talents of the young guitar prodigy Julian Bream.

In 1951 he decided that B.M.G. ('Banjo, Mandolin, Guitar') did not cater enough for the classical guitar lover. Together with his wife Kay and a few friends he formed the International Classical Association (I.C.G.A.). He also produced the first copies of 'Guitar News', which was to provide an excellent service to its readers all over the world until it ceased publication in 1973. Wilfrid Appleby also gave occasional recitals on the guitar, and was often called upon to give lectures about the instrument. All his work for the guitar was a labour of love, both the Guitar Society and 'Guitar News' being run on a non-profit basis.

From his home in Cheltenham, Wilfrid Appleby continued a very active life until his death at the age of 95. Throughout his long life he put his many talents to various uses, becoming in addition to a guitarist a poet, a writer, an Esperanto expert, a philatelist, a herpetologist, and a painter good enough to have his work hung in the West of England Academy of Art.

SELECTED READING

B.M.G.	Regular articles
Guitar News.	Regular articles
Guitar Review.	Various articles
The Evolution of the Classical Guitar –	Wilfrid M. Appleby. I.C.G.A. (1966)

JULIAN ARCAS

Born – Mariá, Almería, Spain – 25 October 1832

**Died – Antequera, Málaga, Spain
16 February 1882**

Julián Arcas

Julián Arcas, a virtuoso guitarist, was one of the most important figures in Spanish music of the nineteenth century. The music he performed was based mainly on traditional Spanish folk and flamenco melodies.

During the years 1860-70 Arcas was at the height of his career as a recitalist. He made lengthy and highly successful concert tours of Spain and the rest of Europe. In 1862 he performed for the British royal family in Brighton, England.

In 1864 he made his name in Barcelona, Spain, and then appeared in several concerts throughout Spain with a young pianist called Patanas. By 1870 he was tired of travelling and settled once again in his native city of Almería. There he established a business in the Calle Granada.

He then became very interested in guitar construction, and co-operated with the famed maker Antonio Torres of Seville in developing the instrument. After ten years in business in Almería, he retired to Antequera, Málaga, where he died soon after, at the age of fifty, in 1882.

One of Spain's great nineteenth century guitar virtuosos, Julián Arcas was also a highly respected and prolific composer and arranger for the guitar of national melodies and dances.

SELECTED RECORDING
The Music of Julian Arcas – Maria Esther Guzman.
Almaviva DSI 0103 CD

SELECTED MUSIC
El Delirio – Fantasía.	UME
El Fagot – Waltz (Oliva).	Ricordi
Jota Aragonesa.	Ricordi
Los Panaderos – Bolero.	Ricordi
Soleá de Concierto.	Ricordi
Spanish Guitar Music, ed. Benkö.	EMB

ALICE ARTZT

Born –

New York, USA

16 March 1943

Alice Artzt

Alice Artzt showed exceptional musical talent from an early age. After studying the piano and flute, she turned to the classical guitar at the age of thirteen. Her first important teacher was Alexander Bellow in New York. She later studied with Ida Presti and Alexandre Lagoya in France, and with Julian Bream in England. She also studied composition with Darius Milhaud at Aspen, Colorado, and has done graduate work in composition and musicology at Barnard College, Columbia University, earning her B.A. there in 1965.

Alice Artzt made her European debut in London in 1969. Since then she has toured Europe extensively and performed throughout North and South America and most other parts of the world. She has had works dedicated to her by several well-known composers, including John W. Duarte and Guido Santórsola. She has been featured on many television and radio programmes, including a special recital produced and broadcast by the BBC in London in honour of the 75th birthday of Sir Lennox Berkeley. The author of a popular guitar technique book, The Art of Practising, she is also a prominent member of the Board of Directors of the Guitar Foundation of America, and also an authority on the comedian Charlie Chaplin.

SELECTED RECORDINGS

Classic Guitar	Gemini. GME 1018 LP
Original Works.	Gemini GME 1019 LP
Bach & his Friends.	Klavier KS 555 LP
Music by Fernando Sor.	Meridian E77 066 LP
Music by Tárrega.	Meridian E77 026 LP
English Guitar Music.	Meridian E77 037 LP
Romantic Virtuoso Guitar Music.	Hyperion A66040 LP
Glory of the Guitar.	AVM1007 LP
	(Reissue of Gemini GME 1018)
Musical Tributes.	Hyperion A66146 LP
Variations and Chaconnes.	Hyperion Helios CDH 88026
American Stage Music – Alice Artzt Trio.	
	Bay Cities BCD 1042

SELECTED READING

Interview.	Guitar, August 1973
Interview.	Guitar, November 1977
Article.	Guitar Player, May 1979
Interview.	Classical Guitar, Jan/Feb 1984

ROBERTO AUSSEL

Born –

Buenos Aires, Argentina

13 July 1954

Roberto Aussel

Roberto Aussel began his guitar studies at the age of seven and gave his first recital at the age of thirteen. His principal teacher was Jorge Martínez Zarate. In 1975 and 1976 he was awarded first prize in three of the most important international guitar competitions, the Radio France Competition in Paris, the Alirio Diaz Prize in Caracas, Venezuela, and the International Competition in Porto Alegre, Brazil.

Since that time Roberto Aussel has established himself as one of the world's finest classical guitarists, giving concerts throughout Europe and the Americas. Several composers have dedicated works to him, including Marius Constant, Francis Kleynjans, Astor Piazzolla, Francis Schwartz, Jose Luis Campana and Raúl Maldonado. In 1980 he was made a Master of the Bordeaux International Guitar Seminary. He has been editor of guitar music for the publishers Henri Lemoine, Paris, since 1983.

Roberto Aussel lives in Paris.

SELECTED RECORDINGS
Recital de Guitare	Vol.1. Adda CIR 822 LP
Recital de Guitare	Vol.2. Adda CIR 825 LP
Bondon Guitar Concerto.	Cybelia CY 655 LP
Roberto Aussel.	GHA 5256002 LP
Latin American Music	Circe 87 101 LD CD
Guitare Plus Vol.1 – Mandala	Man 4802 CD
Guitare Plus Vol.4 – Mandala	Man 4814 CD
Guitare Plus Vol.8 – Mandala	Man 4827 CD
Baroque Music	GHA 126 024 CD

SELECTED READING
Interview.	Classical Guitar, March/April 1984
Interview.	Classical Guitar, April 1985
Interview.	Soundboard, Winter 1992
Interview.	Guitar Review, Fall 1995

JOSE DE AZPIAZU

Born – Onante, Spain – 26 May 1912

Died – Geneva, Switzerland

28 December 1986

Born in the Basque region of Spain, José de Azpiazu began to study the guitar at the age of thirteen. His first teacher was his uncle. When still a teenager, Azpiazu was asked to give recitals at the festivals in San Sebastián. He met with considerable success as a guitarist at these recitals, but still decided to devote most of his spare time to his other talent, painting. He won the first prize for designing and painting at the School of Modern Arts in San Sebastián in 1929. He was also active in the Basque Folklore Society.

It was not until, at the age of twenty-four years, Azpiazu made his debut on Radio Bilbao that he started his professional career as a guitarist. He soon gave up his other activities, devoting all his time to his career as a concert guitarist. He toured Spain extensively for many years but, owing to to World War II, it was not until 1950 that he performed abroad. He had a very successful concert tour of Switzerland which included several radio broadcasts.

While in Geneva he became friendly with painter Andrés Segovia junior, who introduced the guitarist to his father. Segovia was so impressed that on his recommendation the professorship of guitar at the College of Music in Geneva was bestowed upon José de Azpiazu.

José de Azpiazu

Azpiazu was a prolific arranger and composer of guitar music. His Suite in C won first prize in the 1954 International Competition held in Modena, Italy.

SELECTED MUSIC
Cachucha.	Ricordi
Cubana.	Ricordi
Fandanguillo de Huelva.	Ricordi
Five Iberian Miniatures for Guitar.	Ricordi
Jota on popular themes.	Ricordi
Minué del Baztán Errimina – Nostalgie.	Ricordi
Six Children's Stories.	Ricordi
Theme with Variations – Homage to Sor.	Ricordi
Tonadilla – Homage to Granados.	Ricordi

SELECTED READING
La Guitare et les Guitaristes des origines aux temps modernes.   Edition Symphonia-Verlag AG. Bâle, 1959.

CRISTINA AZUMA
Born -
São Paulo, Brazil
12 November 1964

Cristina Azuma

Cristina Azuma began to play the guitar at the age of fourteen. Her first teachers included Hugo Luiz, Paulo Porte Alegre, and Edelton Gloeden. She went on to study music at the University of São Paulo, from where she graduated.

Since 1981 Azuma has given many solo guitar recitals in Brazil and abroad. She has also worked in various enembles including the Opus 12 guitar trio, and the early music group Confraria Ensemble. She has also worked in guitar duos with Paulo Bellinati, and Celso Machado. She made the first of several recordings at the age of twenty-one. A prolific composer, she won prizes for two of her compositions at the 8th Carrefour Mondial de la Guitare held in 1988 in Martinique.

Cristina Azuma was invited to play at many international festivals including the 1990 Havana and Martinique festivals, and the 1992 Cordoba and Tokyo festivals.

In March 1993 Azuma played at the inaugral concert of the Palacio de la Guitarra in Tsukuba, Japan - a theatre and museum dedicated to the guitar. She continues to appear in concert throughout South America, Europe and the Far East.

Since 1990 Azuma has lived in Paris where, attracted by the baroque movement in France, she is preparing for her Doctorate in Musicology at the Sorbonne. At the same time she maintains a busy career as a teacher and recitalist.

SELECTED RECORDINGS
Cristina Azuma	RCA 803.391 LP
E de Lei	LOCO 9107 CD
Contatos	GSP 1009 CD

SELECTED MUSIC
3 Pieces for Two Guitars	Guitar Solo Publications

CARLOS BARBOSA-LIMA

Born – ANTONIO CARLOS BARBOSA-LIMA

São Paulo, Brazil

17 December 1944

Carlos Barbosa-Lima

Carlos Barbosa-Lima began to play the guitar at the age of nine. His teachers were Isaias Savio and B. Moreira. By the time he was thirteen years old he was regarded as a child prodigy, and had already made a successful recording in Brazil.

At the age of twelve Carlos Barbosa-Lima had made his concert debuts in São Paulo and Rio de Janeiro. He then went to the USA, making his New York concert debut at the Alice Tully Hall in March 1972. Following this success the young guitarist made extensive concert tours of the North and South Americas and Europe. In March 1974 he made his debut in Paris at the International Week of the Guitar, and in June 1979 he was the first guitarist to participate in the 'Festival Casal' in Puerto Rico.

In recent years Barbosa-Lima has lived in New York, leading a busy life as an international concert guitarist and recording artist. He is active as a transcriber, and his work has resulted in many excellent transcriptions for the guitar of music by Scarlatti, Bach, Handel and modern South American composers. He has had works written for and dedicated to him by many well-known composers including Francisco Mignone, Leonardo Balada, Guido Santórsola, Albert Harris and John W. Duarte. In 1976 he commissioned Alberto Ginastera to write a work; the resulting Sonata Op.47, dedicated to Barbosa-Lima, is now regarded as one of the outstanding twentieth-century compositions for guitar.

SELECTED RECORDINGS

Dez Dedos Magicos Num Violão de Ouro.	Chant CLP-1001 LP
O Menino e o Violão.	Chantecler CMG 1004 LP
Musicas de J.O. Queiroz.	Chantecler CMG-2434 LP
Album de Modinhas.	Chantecler 2 08 404 079 LP
Imortal Catullo.	Continental 1-35-404-020 LP
Brasil e Violão.	Chantecler 2-10 407-250 LP
Scarlatti Guitar Recital.	ABC Dunhill ABC/ATS 20005 LP
Mignone – 12 Guitar Studies.	Philips (Brazil) 6598-312 LP
Scott Joplin Works.	Concord Concerto CCD-42006
Jobim & Gershwin.	Concord Concerto CCD-42005
Music of Cole Porter and Bonfa.	Concord Concerto CCD-42008
Impressions.	Concord Concerto CCD-42009
Brazil, With Love (Duet with Sharon Isbin).	Concord Picante CCD-4320
Rhapsody in Blue; West Side Story (Duo).	Concord Concerto CCD-2012
Music of the Americas.	Concord Picante CCD-4461
Charts of the Chief.	Concord Picante CCD-44 89
Ginastera/Gnattali/Almeida.	Concord CCD-42015
Twilight in Rio.	Concord CCD-42017

SELECTED READING

Interview.	Guitar, July 1983
Interview.	Guitar International, May 1984
Interview.	Guitar Player, April 1983
Gentle Genius of the Guitar.	Americas Magazine, July/August 1987
Interview.	Classical Guitar, May/June 1983
Profile.	Soundboard, Summer 1994

SELECTED MUSIC

Contemporary Etudes, Preludes & Pieces.	Mel Bay Publications
Guitar Scales.	Mel Bay Publications
Arpeggio Studies.	Mel Bay Publications
Elements of Technique.	Mel Bay Publications
Brazilian Music for Guitar.	Mel Bay Publications
More Brazilian Music for Guitar.	Mel Bay Publications

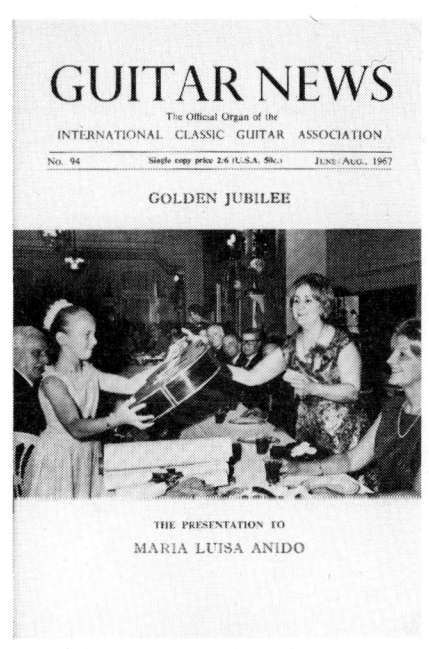

A selection of 'Guitar News' which ceased publication in 1973

Augustín Barrios Mangoré

AGUSTÍN PIO BARRIOS MANGORÉ

Born – San Juan Bautista de las Misiones, Paraguay

5 May 1885

Died – San Salvador, El Salvador – 7 August 1944

Almost fifty years after his death, full recognition is finally being given to the genius of the Paraguayan guitar virtuoso Agustín Barrios Mangoré.

One of eight children, Barrios was born into a musical family. He began to play the guitar at an early age and was able to use the instrument to study harmony at his school. His first formal teacher was Gustavo Sosa Escalda, who introduced the young guitarist to the music of Sor, Tárrega, Aguado and other composers of the established guitar repertoire. By the time he was thirteen years old, Barrios was recognized as a prodigy. He was awarded a scholarship to the Colegio Nacional in Asunción. There he studied calligraphy (he was a fine graphic artist) and also achieved high results in mathematics, journalism and literature.

In 1910 Barrios, already established as a guitar virtuoso, left Paraguay and went to Argentina. Over the next thirty-four years he toured the South American continent, giving concerts in the major cities and towns of Argentina, Uruguay, Brazil, Venezuela, Costa Rica and El Salvador. He also visited Chile, Mexico, Guatemala, Honduras, Panama, Columbia, Cuba and Haiti. Between 1934 and 1936 he also visited Europe, playing in Spain, Germany and Belgium.

It was in 1932 that Barrios began to call himself 'Nitsuga Mangoré – the Paganini of the guitar', Nitsuga being Agustín spelt backwards and Mangoré the name of a legendary Guarani chieftain.

By the mid-1930s Barrios was suffering from a bad heart condition and could not continue to undertake long and strenuous concert tours. He lived his last years in El Salvador, teaching, composing and giving occasional guitar recitals.

As well as being an outstanding player, Barrios was a composer of over three hundred works for the guitar, many of which are now accepted as some of the finest guitar solos ever written.

SELECTED RECORDINGS
Agustín Barrios – Historical Recordings.	Chanterelle CHR 011. 012, 013 CD
Agustín Barrios Mangoré – Original Recordings (2 LPs).	El Maestro EM8002
Agustín Barrios Recordings – Vol.3.	El Maestro EM8002 V3 LP
Gentil Montana plays Barrios.	Leguiz 67-368 LP
John Williams plays Barrios.	CBS 76662 LP
Jesús Benites plays Barrios (2 LPs).	Globo 402-403 LP
La Catedral – Wulfin Lieske.	Saphir INT 830.846 LP
Barrios Vol.1 – Philippe Lemaigre.	RIC 148130 CD
Barrios – Enno Voorhost.	Sony SMK 6480 CD
Barrios – Jesus Castro Balbi.	Opus 111 OPS49-9209
Barrios – John Williams.	Sony SK64396 CD
Barrios – David Russell.	Telarc 80373 CD
Barrios – Wolfgang Lendle.	Opus 91-Z405 2 CD

SELECTED READING
Agustín Barrios.	Guitar, July 1974
Agustín Barrios.	Guitar Player, January 1978
Agustín Barrios – Illustrated biography.	Richard Stover (with El Maestro record set EM 8002)
Appreciation.	Classical Guitar, August 1994
'Six Silver Moonbeams' – Biography of Agustin Barrios –	Richard Stover. Querico. 1992
Genio de la Guitarra – José Cándido Morales	CUI Editions, El Salvador 1994

SELECTED MUSIC
Barrios – 4 Volumes.	Zen-On
Barrios – 4 Volumes ed. Stover.	Belwin Mills
Barrios – 7 Volumes	Barrios Anniversary Edition
Barrios ed. Stover.	Mel Bay Publications

Manuel Barrueco

MANUEL BARRUECO

Born –

Santiago, Cuba

16 December 1952

Manuel Barrueco began his guitar studies at the age of eight in Cuba, under the tutelage of Manuel Puig. His talent showed immediately and he was enrolled in the Esteban Salas Conservatory to extend his early musical training.

In 1967 Barrueco's family moved to the United States, where the young guitarist continued his studies with Juan Mercadal in Miami and Rey de la Torre in New York. In 1971 he entered the Peabody Conservatory in Baltimore, where he was a full-scholarship student (studying under Aaron Shearer), a soloist with the Peabody Orchestra and a winner of the Peabody competition – the first guitarist to achieve these three honours.

In 1974 Barrueco won the Concert Artist Guild Award, and in the same year made his New York debut at the Carnegie Recital Hall. Success followed success, and Manuel Barrueco is now recognised as one of the finest classical guitarists of the twentieth century. He has given highly acclaimed concerts in most parts of the world and has made several outstanding recordings, first for the Vox-Turnabout label and currently with EMI.

Since 1975 Manuel Barrueco has been on the faculty of the Manhattan School of Music, where he is one of the co-founders of the guitar department. In 1990 he was appointed to the faculty of the Peabody Institute, Baltimore.

SELECTED RECORDINGS
Villa-Lobos, Guarnieri, Chavez. Vox Turnabout TV34676 LP
Albéniz, Granados – Spanish Dances.
                                    Vox Turnabout TV34738 LP
Scarlatti, Paganini, Giuliani, Paganini.   Vox Turnabout TV34770 LP
Bach Lute Suites Nos. 2, 4.   Vox Cum Laude VCL 9023 LP
Falla, Ponce, Rodrigo.   Angel/EMI CDC 7 49228 2
Mozart and Sor.   Angel/EMI CDC 7 49368 2
Bach, De Visée.   Angel EMI CDC 7 49980 2
Villa-Lobos, Orbón, Brouwer.   Angel/EMI CDC 7 497102
Mozart Flute/Guitar Duos.   EMI CDC 7 54102-2
Albeniz & Turina.   EMI CDC 754382-2
Sometime Ago.   Angel/EMI CDC 7243 5 55039
Portrait.   EMI CDC 724 5 55315

SELECTED READING
Interview.	Guitar, April 1973
Interview.	Guitar, June 1979
Interview.	Guitar Player, October 1980
Interview.	Guitar & Lute, January 1981
Interview.	Classical Guitar, May 1986
Interview.	Classical Guitar, July 1989
Interview.	Soundboard, Summer 1989
Interview.	Classical Guitar, January 1993
Interview.	Classical Guitar, October 1994
Interview.	Guitar Review, Winter 1996

RENE BARTOLI

Born –

Marseilles, France

1941

René Bartoli

The guitar was an established feature of the Bartoli household, and René Bartoli began his studies on the instrument at an early age. His first tutor was an uncle, and Bartoli made such progress that he decided to make the guitar his career.

In 1959 he won the Concours International de Guitare competition organized by ORTF (French radio and television). Following this success, he was able to study with Andrés Segovia, Ida Presti and Alexandre Lagoya.

In 1960 René Bartoli gave his first recital in his native town, Marseilles. Over the next few years he was to give many guitar recitals throughout France, but was rarely heard in concert in other countries. He was appointed Professor of Guitar at the Marseilles Conservatoire in 1965, a position he still holds.

Bartoli has made several recordings for the French record company Harmonia Mundi, and is one of France's most influential guitarists. In recent years he has been closely associated with the annual Festival of Arles.

SELECTED RECORDS
René Bartoli.	RCA LSB4032 LP
Guitare 1.	Harmonia Mundi HMV572 LP
Guitare 2.	Harmonia Mundi HMV583 LP
Guitare 3.	Harmonia Mundi HMV751 LP
Music for Flute and Guitar.	Odyssey 321 60218 LP

BILL BAY

Born – William Alan Bay

Pacific, Missouri, USA

25 April 1945

Bill Bay

Bill Bay is currently Vice President of Mel Bay Publications Inc founded by his father in 1947. In recent years Bay has taken over the management and product development of the company. As a result the company has one of the most extensive catalogues of classical guitar music books and methods. Mel Bay Publications are also major sponsors of classical guitar events including the annual GFA Festival held in the USA.

Bill Bay began playing the trumpet at the age of seven. By the time he was eleven he was playing with a number of jazz bands throughout the St Louis area and soloing with a number of symphonic bands. In his teens he fronted a thirteen piece jazz band which included several notable musicians including saxophonist David Sanborn. Bay took up the guitar whilst at college and soon took an active interest in the many facets of the instrument. After completing his master's degree he joined the family publishing company. At that time the company had 25 books in print. Today it has over 2000 products including videos and audio recordings.

Bill Bay's close personal association with guitarists such as Aaron Shearer, David Grimes, Carlos Barbosa-Lima, Russel Brazzel, Richard Pick, Keith Calmes and flamenco guitarist Juan Serrano has led to the publication by Mel Bay Publications of many important classical guitar music books and methods. Bay's endeavours in recent years have made a most valuable contribution to the classical guitar world.

SELECTED MUSIC
Editiones Classicae	Series	Mel Bay Publications

SIEGFRIED BEHREND

Born – Berlin, Germany – 19 November 1933

Died – Hausham, Bavaria, Germany

20 September 1990

Siegfried Behrend

Siegfried Behrend's father was a guitarist who taught at a conservatory in Berlin. As a student at the age of sixteen, Behrend entered the same conservatory to study the piano, composition and conducting. While there the young musician began to take a close interest in the guitar. His father recommended him to a guitar teacher, and within a year Siegfried Behrend had given his first public concert.

He decided to gain experience and knowledge of his instrument by embarking on an extensive concert tour of Germany. At the age of twenty-one he toured throughout Italy and two years later throughout Spain. From that time Siegfried Behrend gave concerts in most countries, including the Soviet Union.

Siegfried Behrend recorded extensively for the Deutsche Grammophon label, and has had many of his original compositions and transcriptions published. He took a particular interest in avant-garde music for the classical guitar, and was regarded very highly as a teacher of his chosen instrument.

SELECTED RECORDINGS

Two Guitar Concertos – Rodrigo/Tedesco.
Deutsche Grammophon 139 166 LP
Siegfriend Behrend, Guitar.
Deutsche Grammophon 139 167 LP
Deutsche Gitarren Musik.   Deutsche Grammophon 139 377 LP
Alitalienische Gitarren Konzerte.
Deutsche Grammophon 139 417 LP
Guitar and Percussion. Deutsche Grammophon 2530 034 LP
English Guitar Music.   Deutsche Grammophon 2530 079 LP
Chitarra Italiana.   Deutsche Grammophon 2530 561 LP
Treasures for Guitar.   Supraphon 50 780 LP
Guitarra Olé.   EMI Electrola SHZE 383 LP
Meister Werke für Zwei Gitarren
(with Martin Kruger)   Acanta DC 23 098 LP
Sinfonische Folklore.   Colosseum SM 570 LP
Requiem AVF Hiroshima   Thorofon CTH 2026 CD
In Memoriam.   Thorofon CTH 2201/2 CD
Behrend and Friends.   Thorofon CTH 2070 CD

SELECTED MUSIC

Fantasía Malagueñita.	JWC
Granadina de la Rambla.	JWC
Postkarten – Suite No.1 (7 easy pieces).	ZM 1896
Six Monodien (1974) (Modern).	ZM 1907
Three Spanish Dances.	ZM 1802
Zorongo para Murao.	JWC

SELECTED READING

Interview in 'My Fifty Fretting Years' –   Ivor Mairants.
Ashley Mark, 1980.
Interview.   Guitar International, June 1984.

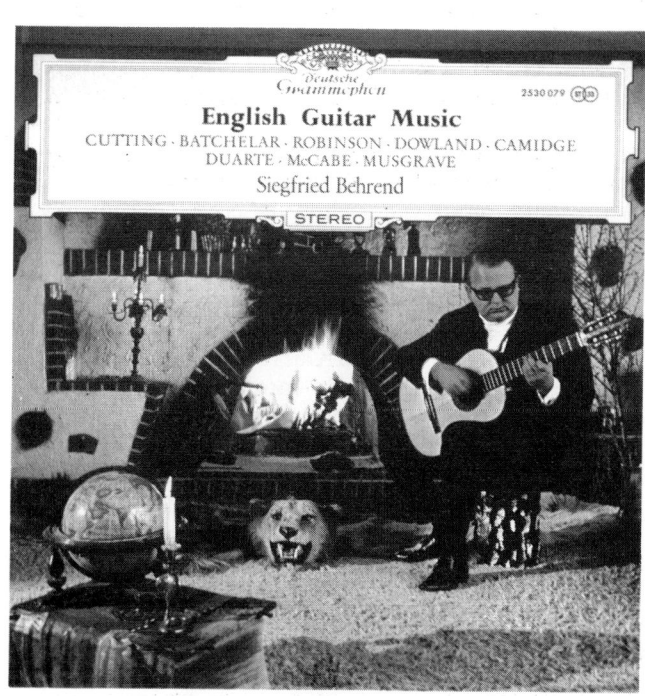

PAULO BELLINATI
Born - São Paulo,
Brazil
22 September 1950

Paulo Bellinati

Paulo Bellinati first played the guitar under the tutelage of his father at the age of eleven. At the age of seventeen he began to study classical guitar with Isaias Savio at the Conservatory 'Dramatico e Musical' in São Paulo. After graduating from this conservatory he won two scholarships. These enabled him to go to Switzerland for six years where he continued his music studies at the Conservatory of Geneva, and also taught at the Conservatory of Lausanne.

In 1988 Bellinati won first prize for his solo guitar piece 'Jongo', at the 8th Carrefour Mondial de la Guitare` in Martinique. He continued to lead a busy career in Brazil, performing and recording with many important Brazilian musicians including Gal Costa, Leila Pinheiro, Caetano Veloso, Edu Lobo, Chico Buarque and his group Pau Brasil. In 1994 Bellinati won Brazil's equivalent of a Grammy, 'Premio Sharp', for his arranging of Gal Costa's CD recording 'O Sorriso do Gato de Alice'.

Bellinati spent many years researching the music of the brilliant Brazilian guitarist/composer Annibal Agusto Sardinha (Garôto). Garôto is generally accepted a the 'father' of bossa-nova. The result was two volumes of music of Garôto's guitar solos edited by Bellinati, who also released a highly praised ecording of these works. A virtuoso guitarist, Paulo Bellinati has established himself as a most important figure in the international classical guitar world.

SELECTED MUSIC
Guitar Works of Garôto (Two Volumes)
	Guitar Solo Publications
Jongo	Guitar Solo Publications
Modinha	Guitar Solo Publications
Suite Contatos	Guitar Solo Publications
Valsa Brilhante	Guitar Solo Publications

SELECTED RECORDINGS
Guitar Works of Garôto	GSP 1002CD
Gitares du Bresil	GHA 126-015 CD
Serenata	GSP 1005 CD
Afro Sambas	GSP 1015CD
Lira Brasileira	GSP 1016 CD

SELECTED READING
Profile	Guitar Review, Winter 1992
Interview	Classical Guitar, January 1992

ALEXANDER BELLOW

Born – Moscow, Russia, 1912

Died – Sherman, Connecticut, USA

12 March 1976

Alexander Bellow

Alexander Bellow was a Russian-born, naturalised American citizen. A graduate of the Moscow Conservatory, he majored in composition and conducting, and was awarded the degree of Doctor of Music with honours. He also studied painting and engineering. During World War II he was imprisoned by the Germans in a concentration camp. He managed to survive, and emigrated to the United States of America in 1949 with his wife Mura and daughter Natasha.

As a classical guitarist, Bellow performed in the United States and abroad both as a solo recitalist and as part of a chamber group. On the advice of Andrés Segovia he decided to devote his musical talents to teaching. Alexander Bellow's greatest contribution to the guitar was as a teacher, and also as a transcriber of many early guitar compositions from the original tablature. Almost one hundred of his original compositions were published. He was also instrumental in forming the first USA guitar orchestra in New York.

Alexander Bellow's book 'The Illustrated History of the Guitar' is now accepted as one of the standard works for the study of the instrument, and is highly recommended reading for the guitar enthusiast.

SELECTED MUSIC

Arpeggiato.	Kerby
Cavatina.	Hansen
Preludio e Toccata.	Kerby
Prelude, Scherzetto and Fugue.	Hansen
Scherzando.	Kerby
Sonata for Guitar.	FC 2794
Sonata II for Guitar.	Kerby
Sonatina II.	Hansen
Suite Provençale.	Hansen
Tales of the Alhambra – As told by Washington Irving.	Kerby
Variations on a theme of Mudarra.	Kerby

SELECTED READING

The Illustrated History of the Guitar – Bellow.	Franco Colombo Inc. 1970

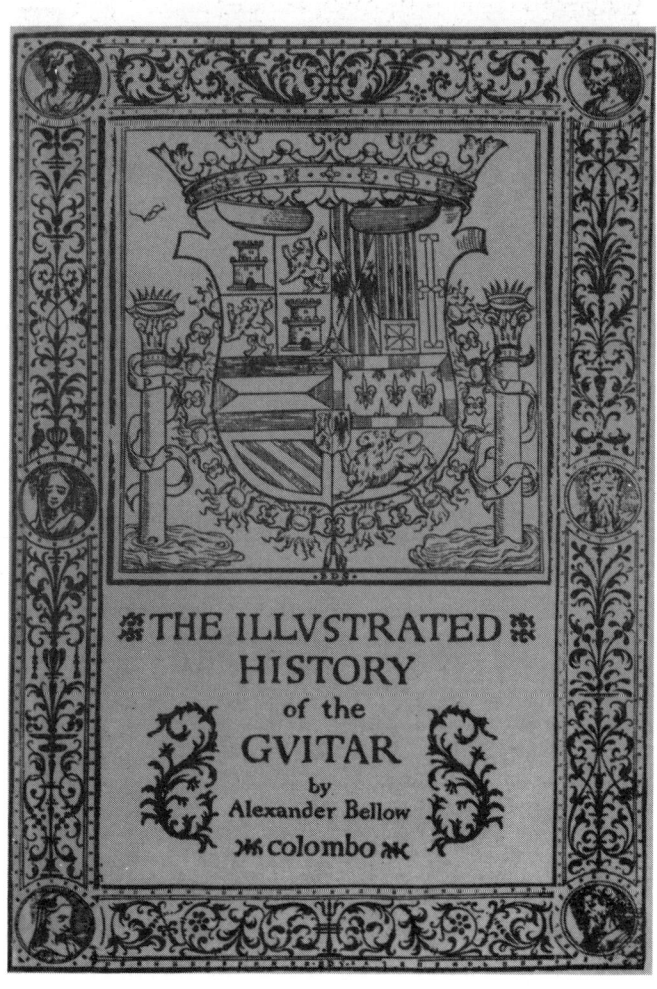

BALTAZAR BENITEZ

Born –

Durazno, Uruguay

31 July 1944

Baltazar Benitez

Baltazar Benitez began to play the guitar at the age of twelve, studying with Pedro Machin. He later studied with Abel Carlevaro at the National Conservatory of Montevideo. In 1968 he was chosen by the Jeunesses Musicales of Uruguay to tour his nation, since when he has won many of his country's most important musical awards. In 1970 he received a grant from the Spanish Cultural Institute to study in Santiago de Compostela with Andrés Segovia and José Tomás. In 1971 he won first prize at the International Guitar Competition held in Santiago de Compostela, and in 1973 won first prize at the Tárrega Competition in Benicasim, Spain.

Baltazar Benitez has also studied the lute and the harpsichord. Since 1972 he has led a busy life as a concert and recording artist and has held the teaching post for classical guitar in Tilburg, Holland.

SELECTED RECORDINGS
Latin-American Music.	Nonesuch H-71349 LP
Bach & Scarlatti.	Nonesuch H-71404 LP
The Guitar Music of Astor Piazzolla.	Canal Grande CG 9322 CD
Tango – An Anthology.	Channel Crossing CCS 5393 CD

DANIEL BENKO

Born –

Budapest, Hungary

1947

Daniel Benkö

Daniel Benkö's first instrument was the violin, which he studied from the age of six. He became interested in the guitar at the age of fifteen when he joined a pop group. His interest in classical music revived, and he joined the Bela Bartók Conservatory in Budapest to study classical guitar. After qualifying there, he went on to the Ferenc Liszt Academy of Music in Budapest, where he earned his degree in guitar at the age of twenty-four.

During his time at the Liszt Academy, Benkö became interested in the lute. He went to England to study the instrument with Diana Poulton, and also to Holland to study with Eugen M. Dombois. His interest in early music extended, and he also played in his concerts other early fretted instruments including the orpharion, the vihuela and the baroque guitar.

In 1972 Daniel Benkö founded the Bakfark Consort, and a few years later the Benkö Consort. With these groups he played music from Eastern and Western Europe, from the thirteenth to the nineteenth century.

Benkö has given concerts in many countries as a solo and ensemble artist, and is a prolific recording artist on both guitar and lute. Established as one of

Hungary's foremost guitarists, he also teaches lute at the Ferenc Liszt Academy.

SELECTED RECORDINGS
Romantische Ungarische Gitarrenmusik.
    Telefunken 6.42809 AZ LP
Balint Bakfark Complete Lute Music.
    Hungaraton SLPX 12771-75 LP
Guitar Serenade.   Hungaraton SLPX 12661 LP
Vivaldi Lute Concertos & Trios. Hungaraton SLPX 11978 LP
Dance Music from Hungary. Telefunken 6.42782 AZ LP
Spanish Romance. Hungaraton SLPD 12895 LP

MATS BERGSTRÖM
Born - Gavle,

Sweden

7 March 1961

Mats Bergström

Mats Bergström is a graduate of the Royal College of Music in Stockholm, where he studied with Rolf la Fleur. He went on to study with Sharon Isbin at the Juilliard School in New York. Bergström won first prize in the 1983 John Mills Competition, held in Surrey near London. He made his debut recital in 1983 at the Wigmore Hall, London. In 1992 he won the silver medal at the Radio France Competition, Paris.

In recent years Mats Bergström has become a much sought-after chamber musician and accompanist. He has arranged many songs and instrumental works for guitar. His work on Swedish poets Carl Michael Bellman, Birger Sjoberg and Evert Taube, together with singer/actor Mikael Samuelson, has attracted particular attention.

SELECTED RECORDINGS
16th, 17th & 20th c. English Music   Polar POLS 406 LP
Villa-Lobos   Proprius PRCD 9021
Après un Rêve w. Annika Skoglund   Proprius PRCD 9996
Songs for Frida w. Mikael Samuelson
    Musica Sveciae MSCD 625
Carl Michael Bellman w. Mikael Samuelson
    Artemis Arte 7128
Castelnuovo-Tedesco Chamber Works Proprius PRCD 9124
A Little Help from My Friends   Areco 20011
Die schöne Müllerin w. Olle Persson
    Vanguard Classics 99133 CD

HECTOR BERLIOZ

Born – La Côte Saint André, near Grenoble, France

11 December 1803

Died – Paris, 8 March 1869

Hector Berlioz

The popularity of the music of the great nineteenth century composer and orchestrator of genius Hector Berlioz continues to grow, yet it is amazing how few musicians and music lovers, even today, realize that the guitar and the flute were the only two instruments on which he could play.

Berlioz's father encouraged him in his music studies from an early age, first on the flute and flageolet, and then the guitar. He studied, together with his elder sister, with a teacher named Dorant. At the age of eighteen Berlioz was sent by his parents to Paris to study medicine. He soon discovered that medicine was not for him, and decided to make music his life. The decision upset his father, who promptly stopped his maintenance. Berlioz was therefore forced to earn his living teaching the guitar, as well as the flute. He wrote several studies and variations for the guitar, and these were published by Aulagnier in Paris during this period.

In 1830 Berlioz won the Prix de Rome at the Conservatoire of Music, where he studied under Lesueur. This success earned him a government grant for three years' further study in Rome.

The following years saw the full development of Berlioz the composer. He became friendly with Mendelssohn and Paganini amongst many other fine musicians and composers. His very distinctive style of composition and orchestration has been attributed by some authorities to his ability to play the guitar and the flute to the exclusion of other instruments.

In his famous Treatise on Instrumentation and Orchestration, five pages are devoted to the guitar and mandolin. Berlioz's last guitar is now in the museum of the National Conservatoire of Music in Paris. Made by Grobert of Mirecourt (1794-1869), it was originally owned by Nicoló Paganini, and bears the signature of both its famous owners.

SELECTED MUSIC
25 Romances.   Chanterelle

SELECTED READING
Memoirs – 1865 (translated Gollancz 1969)   Hector Berlioz
Treatise on Instrumentation and Orchestration
                                             Hector Berlioz
Hector Berlioz – Biography – Robert Clarson-Leach
                                         Omnibus Press, 1987

Portrait of Hector Berlioz with his guitar on a French ten franc banknote

GILBERT BIBERIAN

Born –

Istanbul, Turkey

19 February 1944

Gilbert Biberian

Gilbert Biberian was brought up and educated in England, where his Greek/Armenian family had come to live. He studied the guitar and composition at Trinity College of Music in London, graduating in 1968. In 1965 a French government grant took him to France to study with Ida Presti and Alexandre Lagoya. He continued his work with this legendary guitar duo until Ida Presti's untimely death in 1967.

After leaving Trinity College, Biberian studied interpretation with the pianist Anthony Kinsella for three years. Following a successful debut in the Wigmore Hall, he was invited to work with the London Sinfonietta and Pierre Boulez, Luciano Berio, the Nash Ensemble, the BBC Symphony Orchestra and many others. Biberian has also played at the Proms and at Covent Garden (where he played the guitar part in Tippett's King Priam) and has performed concertos and solo recitals on numerous other occasions.

While continuing his solo work, Gilbert Biberian created and directed two guitar ensembles, the Omega Players and the Omega Guitar Quartet. Both groups stimulated much original composition and made a substantial contribution to contemporary music in the 1970s and 1980s. Elisabeth Lutyens and Reginald Smith Brindle were two of the prominent composers who wrote works for these ensembles.

A highly sought-after teacher, Gilbert Biberian has taught and lectured extensively, and has directed guitar workshops and masterclasses in the UK, Canada, USA and Europe. In 1975 and 1978 he was invited to teach at the International Guitar Festival, Toronto, Canada, and to be on the jury of the International Guitar Competition in 1978. He has taught summer schools in New Zealand in 1979 and lectured in Venezuela. In addition to numerous visits to the USA he was Artist in Residence of the Wisconsin Conservatory of Music, Milwaukee in Spring of 1984. In the same year he was Guest Artist at the First International Guitar Festival at the University of Lamont in Denver, Colorado. In 1985 he gave several recitals in Norway and was broadcast on Norwegian Radio. He has been Professor of Guitar at Trinity College of Music from 1988-1996.

Biberian studied composition with James Patten, Elisabeth Lutyens and Hans Keller. Since 1965 he has produced well over one hundred compositions, not only for solo and ensemble guitar but also for the voice and for various combinations of other instruments, including a concerto, two song cycles and a sonata for flute and guitar. His guitar compositions are finding their way into the standard repertoire and are being performed widely. His works have been published in England, Italy, Holland and the USA.

He was Vice-Chairman of EGTA (UK) in 1994; a Trustee of the World Youth Music Foundation, and has been a member of the Management Committee of the Cheltenham International Festival of Music between 1993 and 1996.

SELECTED MUSIC
Greek Suite	Broekmans B1140
Monogram.	Waterloo
Prelude & Fugue.	Novello
Sonata No.3.	Chanterelle
Eight Valses.	CPP/Belwin
Colombine.	Chester
Intermezzo.	Ricordi
Pierrot (for 2 Guitars).	Chester
24 Preludes (2 Volumes)	Editions Orphee

SELECTED RECORDINGS
Omega Guitar Quartet (Stravinsky & Biberian).
President PTLS 1066 LP
Monogram (with Ponce, J. McGuire etc.)
John Holmquist. Cavata CV 5001 LP
Sonata No.3 – F. Henderson Musical New Services G121 LP
Eight Bagatelles for Cello and Guitar – Heurtefeux/Flachot Duo Circe 87121 CD
Four Waltzes – Tetra Quartet. CD DB 2

SELECTED READING
Gilbert Biberian.	Guitar, August 1972
Gilbert Biberian.	Guitar, December 1976
Contradicting the Unexpected – Interview.	Classical Guitar May/June 1983
Gilbert Biberian's Rhythm Workshop.	Classical Guitar March/April 1983
What's New about Teaching? – Biberian.	Classical Guitar
Interview.	Guitar Review, Summer 1992

VAHDA OLCOTT BICKFORD

Born – ETHYL LUCRETIA OLCOTT
Norwalk, Ohio, USA, 17 October 1885
Died – Los Angeles, USA, 18 May 1980

Vahda Olcott Bickford

As a child Vahda Olcott Bickford lived in Los Angeles, where she showed an early gift for music. She began her study of the guitar at the age of eight and became one of the last pupils of the renowned teacher Manuel Ferrer (1828-1904). She proved to be an outstanding pupil and was to give many successful concerts throughout the United States of America.

She went to New York in 1914 and soon became known through her concerts and teaching of the guitar. By invitation she lived for a time with the famous Vanderbilt family at Biltmore. There she taught Mrs Vanderbilt and her daughter Cornelia to play the guitar. It was while she was in New York that Olcott became associated with the famous astrologer Evangeline Adams, and was her only assistant for nine years, adopting her new name of Vahda.

In 1915 she married another outstanding North American musician, the guitarist/mandolinist Zarh Myron Bickford. They lived and worked together in New York, finally moving to Los Angeles in 1923. During her stay on the East Coast, Vahda Olcott Bickford established herself as an outstanding guitar soloist and teacher.

In 1923 she was instrumental in founding the American Guitar Society in Los Angeles. There is little doubt that through her promotional efforts and her transcriptions of music for the guitar, she was one of the most influential figures in the North American classical guitar scene during the first fifty years of this century.

Vahda Olcott Bickford died at the age of ninety-four in 1980. Still devoted to the guitar, she spent her last years teaching and giving her expert advice to musicologists and historians of the guitar. She continued to give concerts with her husband Zarh until his death in 1961. Bickford continued as a solo artist until her last concert at an American Guitar Society meeting in 1977. Her second husband, Robert Revere, died in 1980.

SELECTED MUSIC
Olcott Bickford – Method for Guitar.
Oliver Ditson, Philadelphia 1921

SELECTED READING
Vahdah Olcott Bickford.   Guitar and Lute No.14, 1980

1993 Spanish stamp honouring Andrés Segovia

ERNESTO BITETTI

Born – ERNESTO GUILLERMO BITETTI

Rosario, Argentina

20 July 1943

Ernesto Bitetti

Ernesto Bitetti began his studies at the age of five in his native Argentina. He continued his musical education at the Instituto Superior de la Musica Universidad Nacional del Litoral, from which he graduated with the highest honours in 1964. In 1961 he was awarded First Prize in the 18th Concurso de la Sociedad Hebraica Argentina de Buenos Aires for stringed instrument playing, and in 1962 he reached the finals of the Coupe International de Guitare in Paris, France. In addition to the guitar, Bitetti has studied conducting, choral music, piano, flute and composition.

Since his initial and immediate success, Bitetti has continued to tour annually throughout Europe, the Soviet Union, Central and South America, the United States, Canada, Japan, Israel, New Zealand, India, the Far East and South Africa.

He has appeared as soloist with leading orchestras including the English, Israel and Munich Chamber Orchestras, and also with leading symphony orchestras throughout Europe, the Far East, North and South American, Australia and South Africa. He has given joint recitals with Teresa Berganza in Vienna, and appeared at the festivals of Edinburgh and Aix-en-Provence. During his 1980-81 United States tour, he played in concerts and recitals coast to coast, including a performance at the Kennedy Centre for the Performing Arts.

Many prominent composers have written works expressly for Bitetti, including Mario Castelnuovo-Tedesco, Joaquín Rodrigo, John W. Duarte, Federico Moreno Torroba, José Buenagu, Anton García Abril and Angelo Gilardino. With the St Louis Symphony Orchestra, Bitetti premiered the Concierto para la Guitarra Criolla by Waldove de los Rios, and in New York City's Town Hall he appeared with the violinist Ruggiero Ricci in the first performance of Duo Concerto No.2, written specifically for the occasion by the Spanish composer Tomás Marco.

Ernesto Bitetti is a major recording artist for Hispavox. Since 1989 he has been head of the Guitar Department at Indiana University School of Music, Bloomington, USA, and currently divides his time between that country and Spain, where he lives in Madrid.

SELECTED RECORDINGS

Música Contemporanea.	Hispavox HHS 10-304 LP
Bach/Weiss Suites.	Hispavox HHS 10-331 LP
Rodrigo Concierto.	Hispavox HHS 10-335 LP
Músicos Españoles en la Guitarra.	Hispavox HHS 10-344 LP
Four Centuries of Spanish Guitar Music.	Hispavox HHS 10-365 LP
Four Centuries of Italian Guitar Music.	Hispavox HHS 10-400 LP
Halffter Concerto.	Hispavox HHS 10-420 LP
Waldove de los Rios Concerto.	Hispavox HHS 10-429 LP
Encores.	Hispavox HHS 10-450 LP
Albéniz.	Hispavox HHS 10-460 LP
Paganini Guitar/Violin Works (with R.Ricci).	Hispavox HHS 10-473 LP
Grandes Exitos.	Hispavox HHS S-60-135 LP
Rodrigo Concierto de Aranjuez.	Hispavox HHS S-60-157 LP
Manuel de Falla.	Hispavox HHS S-60-207 LP
Ernesto Bitetti plays Vivaldi.	Hispavox HHS S-60-687 LP
One Guitar for Two Worlds.	Deutsche Grammophon DGG 435 288 2 CD
Antologia De La Guitarra Clasica. (2 CDs).	EMI Classics CMS 7 646142 CD
Vivaldi Concertos/Bach/Weiss. (2 CDs).	EMI 7 64682 CD
Four Centuries Italian Music.	EMI CDM 7-64683-2

SELECTED READING

Interview.	Classical Guitar, May & June 1987

VLADISLAV BLAHA

Born - Brno,
Czech Republic
22 August 1957

Vladislav Blaha

Vladislav Blaha studied at the Brno Conservatory with Arnost Sadlik. He went on to study with Roland Zimmer at the Liszt College of Music in Weimar, Germany. He graduated from this college and went on to study with Gordon Crosskey and John W. Duarte in England.

Blaha gained international recognition after winning prizes in various competitions, including Volos, Greece (1978), Esztergom, Hungary (1979), Kutná Hora, Czech Republic (1980), Markneukirchen, Germany (1981), and Radio France in Paris (1983). Since that time he has given concerts in many parts of Europe, Asia, and South America. He is currently Professor of guitar at the Bruno Conservatory. Blaha is also president of the Czech Classical Guitar Society, and director of the Rychnov International Guitar Festival and Summer School.

SELECTED RECORDINGS
Concertos for Guitar and Orchestra	Panton 81 0679 LP
Blaha Plays Bach & Weiss Suites	Pronto 0-008CD
The Spanish Guitar Vladislav Blaha	Pehy CD PY 0003-2231

SELECTED READING
Interview	Classical Guitar, October 1989
Profile	Classical Guitar, June 1993

DIEGO BLANCO

Born –
Palma de Mallorca, Spain
2 June 1951

Diego Blanco

Diego Blanco started to learn the guitar at the age of eight with his uncle. Later he studied with the guitarist and teacher Dan Grenholm, a pupil of Emilio Pujol and Andrés Segovia.

Whilst learning the guitar Blanco was also taught the piano and the theory and history of music, by the Spanish composer and pianist Lorenso Galmes. At the age of eleven Blanco gave a series of concerts throughout Spain, but his real debut as a recitalist of importance was in Stockholm, Sweden, in 1968, where he enjoyed enormous success.

Diego Blanco has subsequently given many concerts in Scandinavia, Spain, Italy, England, Eastern Europe and the Soviet Union, and has appeared in numerous television and radio programmes in these countries. Several composers have dedicated works to him, including Koch, Karkoff, Rautavaara, Santórsola and Saeverud.

In 1979 Diego Blanco won the important Queen Sofia's International Guitar Competition in Madrid. He has made several recordings for the Swedish company BIS.

SELECTED RECORDINGS
Blanco Plays Ponce/Sojo/Lauro/Barrios.	BIS LP33
Blanco Plays Fernando Sor.	BIS LP133
Guitarra Española.	RCA (Spain) LSC16359 LP
Music for Flute & Guitar with Gunilla von Bahr Vol.1.	BIS-LP 30
Music for Flute & Guitar with Gunilla von Bahr Vol.2.	BIS-LP 60
Music for Flute & Guitar with Gunilla von Bahr Vol.3.	BIS-LP 90
Popular Guitar Music.	BIS-133 CD

VLADIMIR BOBRI

Born – VLADIMIR BOBRITZKY

Kharkov, Ukraine, 13 May 1898

Died – New York, USA, 3 November 1986

Vladimir Bobri with Andrés Segovia

Vladimir Bobri was brought up in a family atmosphere of culture and scholarship, and he acquired an adventurous attitude towards life and art. He was a graduate of the Imperial Art School of Kharkov, where he became interested in the theatre and in early icon painting. He studied scenic design by apprenticeship at the State Dramatic Theatre. Because of the turbulent events of the Revolution, Bobri fled from Russia in 1917, leaving his homeland for ever.

In Constantinople (Istanbul), Vladimir Bobri designed sets and costumes for the Russian ballet, produced movie posters and painted ikons in a monastery; in Anatolia (Turkey) he engaged in archaeological work. Then, in 1921, he went to the USA and settled in New York, where he became known for his imaginative murals, advertising art and book illustrations.

Although Bobri was a painter, he had a secondary, almost equal love for music, especially the music of the guitar. In 1936 he was a founding member of The Society of the Classic Guitar, an organisation that was to have far-reaching influences on the growth of interest in the guitar in this country.

From 1948 to 1986 he was the editor and art director of Guitar Review. He was the author of many essays on subjects related to the classical guitar, and composed a number of works for the instrument.

On 31 August 1972, Bobri was named 'Puntius Counselor at Large Efficientior' to 'Música en Compostela', a unique organization devoted to the study and interpretation of the music of Spain, located in Santiago de Compostela. The honour, in the form of an illustrated parchment, was given in consideration of his outstanding contribution to the appreciation of the classical guitar through his presidency of The Society of the Classic Guitar and his work as editor of Guitar Review.

On 10 January 1973, Vladimir Bobri was decorated with the Cross of Isabel la Católica with the rank of Knight-Commander (Comendador). This important decoration was bestowed in recognition of his lifelong achievements as a designer, painter, art director, composer and writer, and for his utilization of these talents to make others more keenly aware of the richness of Spanish culture. Presentation of the cross was made by H.E. Alberto Lopez Herce, Consul General of Spain in New York, at a ceremony attended by Spanish dignitaries, including Andrés Segovia.

Vladimir Bobri was without doubt one of the most important guitar personalities of the twentieth century.

SELECTED READING
Guitar Review – regular contributor and editor
Article.   Guitar Review, Winter 1987

SELECTED MUSIC
Very Easy Pieces.   FC
Complete Study of Tremolo.   FC3046
Eight Melodic Exercises.   NY2604
130 Daily Studies for the Classical Guitar.   FCS2605
Tango in A (1936) dedicated to Oyanguren.
                                                 Celesta Music, New York

DUSAN BOGDANOVIC

Born -
Beograd, Yugoslavia
11 February 1955

Dusan Bogdanovic

Dusan Bogdanovic first became interested in music through his father, a well-known physics professor who also played the violin and guitar. Bogdanovic began to play the guitar at the age of twelve, studying and playing with his father. His early musical interest was in rock, pop, jazz and South American music. He began to play the classical guitar after hearing recordings of the music of J.S. Bach, Debussy, and Ravel.

Bogdanovic entered music school at the age of sixteen. At the same time he studied architecture. In 1975 he won third prize in the Barcelona International Guitar Competition, and first prize at the Concours Internationale d'Execution Musicale held in Geneva, Switzerland. He studied composition and orchestration with Alberto Ginastera and Pierre Wissmer, as well as the guitar with Maria Livia Sao Marcos, at the Conservatory of Music in Geneva. Bogdanovic went on to win several more international competitions, including the Orchestration Medal from the Geneva conservatory in 1976, and made his USA debut at the Carnegie Recital Hall, New York, in 1977. From 1977 to 1980 he was a professor of guitar at the Geneva Conservatory of Music.

Bogdanovic began to develop an interest in improvised music and in African and Indian ethnic music. In the late 1970s he moved to the USA and settled in Los Angeles. He began an association with various jazz musicians. He was a member of the fusion group 'Lingua Franca'. He also recorded with bassist Charlie Haden, and flautist James Newton. At the same time he concertised and recorded with the Falla Classical Guitar Trio.

Dusan Bogdanovic now lives in San Francisco, where he has taught at the Conservatory of Music since 1989, concentrating on the instruction of guitar performance and improvisational techniques. A prolific composer, performer and recording artist, he is one of the most distinctive voices in the contemporary world of the classical guitar.

SELECTED RECORDINGS
Guitar and cello Duets w/ Valter Despalj
    PGP/RTB 530050LP
Bach with Pluck Guitar and Harpsichord	ESSAY 1023 CD
Falla Guitar Trio	Concord Concerto CC 2011 CD
Falla Guitar Trio	Concord Concerto CC 2013 CD
Worlds	MA Recordings M009A CD
Levantine Tales	MA Recordings M013A CD
Mysterious Habits	GSP 1014 CD

SELECTED READING
Interview	Seicorde, January/February 1993
Article	Guitar Review, Spring 1996

SELECTED MUSIC
Counterpoint for Guitar	Berben
Polyrhythmic and Polymetric Studies	Berben
Jazz Sonata	GSP
Jazz Sonatina	GSP
Little Cafe Suite	GSP
My Eternal Green Plant	GSP
Sharon's Songdance	GSP
Six Balkan Miniatures	GSP
Mysterious Habitats	GSP
A Fairytale with Variations	GSP
Omar's Fancy	GSP

PHILIP JAMES BONE

Born –
Luton, England, 29 January 1873

Died – Luton, 17 June 1964

Philip J. Bone

One of the leading personalities on the fretted instrument scene of Great Britain for many years, Philip James Bone, FRSA, MRST, was educated and trained for the scholastic profession. It was during his early days as a teacher that he became attracted to the mandolin and guitar. At first he played as a pastime, with no serious intent, but his interest in these instruments developed into a passion and he came to London to study under G.B. Marchiso, Professor of Mandolin and Guitar at Trinity College of Music. His progress was phenomenal, and he was chosen to give the first performance in England of two of Beethoven's compositions for mandolin and piano, Sonata and Adagio, at Trinity College in London.

He was awarded the Medal of the Royal Society of Arts for mandolin playing, and then followed one of the longest and most distinguished careers in the history of fretted instruments. He was founder and conductor of the Luton Mandolin Orchestra for forty years. Under his direction the orchestra gained high honours in the international sphere and was probably the first British mandolin orchestra to play on the mainland of Europe. He conducted 'The Trocadero' by request before the President of France in Paris in 1909.

His publication 'The Guitar and Mandolin – Biographies of Celebrated Composers and Players' is world renowned, and he made contributions to Cadenza, Keynotes, B.M.G. and other music journals. The numerous honours conferred on him included election to Fellowship of the Royal Society of Arts and membership of the Royal Society of Teachers.

In 1951 the British Federation of Banjoists, Mandolinist and Guitarists, then in its 22nd year, elected him its president, an office he held for thirteen years.

SELECTED READING
The Guitar and Mandolin
Philip J. Bone. Schott (1914, rev. 1954)
Philip J. Bone – A Bone of Contention.
Classical Guitar, May/June 1984

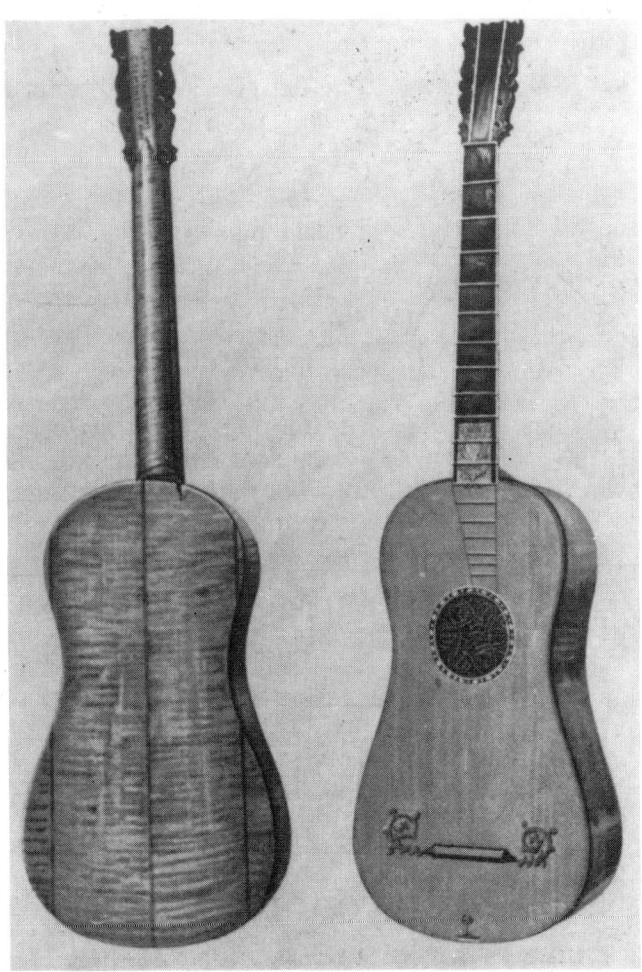

A Stradivarius guitar – Cremona c.1680

CARLOS BONELL

Born – CARLOS ANTONIO BONELL

London, England

23 July 1949

Carlos Bonell

Born in London of Spanish parents, Carlos Bonell began to play the guitar at the age of five. His first interest was Spanish folk music, but by the age of seven he had already decided firmly on the classical repertoire – by studying both guitar and violin. His first teacher was his father, a keen amateur guitarist. His first public appearance was as a guitarist at the age of ten, and from the age of thirteen he dedicated himself exclusively to the guitar. He continued his studies at the Royal College of Music in London where he was invited to teach immediately upon completing his studies there in 1972.

The first major breakthrough in Bonell's career came with his nomination as a 'Young Musician '73' by the Greater London Arts Association. This led to many concerts throughout the United Kingdom, including appearances at the Camden, City of London, Brighton and Harrogate festivals. After his first concert appearance with the Royal Philharmonic Orchestra in the Royal Festival Hall came invitations from many other great orchestras, including the London Symphony, the Hallé, the Amsterdam Chamber Orchestra and the Philharmonia. In 1975 came the first of many hundreds of concerts in Europe and America, including the New York 'Mostly Mozart', the Flanders and the Israel festivals.

Apart from his recital and concerto work, Carlos Bonell's enthusiasm for chamber music has led to many memorable performances with such artists as Pinchas Zukerman, John Williams, Teresa Berganza and Lynn Harrel.

His record releases include a recital disc for Decca (with the first recording of Tárrega's unpublished 'Traviata' fantasia) and the first digital recording of Rodrigo's 'Aranjuez' concerto.

The Carlos Bonell Ensemble, a group which includes flute, panpipes, charango and other ethnic instruments, has had considerable international success for the past few years.

SELECTED RECORDINGS

Guitar Music of Spain.	Enigma VAR1015 LP
Guitar Music of the Baroque.	Enigma VAR1050 LP
Guitar Showpieces.	Decca SXL6950 LP
Rodrigo's Aranjuez/Fantasia.	Collins 10322 CD

SELECTED READING

Interview.	Classical Guitar, May/June 1984

REMI BOUCHER

**Born - Rouyn-Noranda,
Quebec, Canada
23 March 1964**

Remi Boucher

Remi Boucher began to play the guitar as a child at home in Rouyn-Noranda, a mining centre in the Abitibi-Temiscamingue region of Quebec. By the age of 12 he was already competing in local music competitions. He studied classical guitar in the conservatory of Montreal, graduating with the highest honours, in 1989, at his Masters Degree concert. He also studied privately with Manuel Barrueco and David Russell. He went on to study in Spain with Josep Henriquez and Jose Luis Rodrigo. Boucher also studied with Vladimir Mikulka, and in Switzerland with Oscar Ghiglia. In 1991 he received a grant from the Canada Council to study with Victor Van Puijrnbroeck.

Boucher gained international recognition by winning five of the most important international competitions, Alessandria, Italy in 1989; the Segovia Competition, Palma de Mallorca, in 1989; Havana in 1990; Giuliani Competition, Turin in 1991; and the Sor Competition, Rome in 1991.

Remi Boucher is regarded as one of the best new young guitarists of the 1990s. He currently lives in Krems, Austria, where he has a teaching post. He also maintains a busy international concert and recording career.

SELECTED RECORDINGS
Torroba/Abril Guitar Concertos   Analekta AN 2 9502 CD
Collectici intim   Analekta AN 2 8775 CD

A Staufer guitar owned by Franz Schubert. Now in the Vienna museum.

LIONA BOYD

Born –

London, England

11 July, 1949

Liona Boyd

Liona Boyd's father, a psychologist/sculptor, first moved to Canada in 1958. He returned to England for a short while, but finally settled in Canada in 1962. Liona Boyd is now a Canadian citizen.

The young guitarist first took a serious interest in the instrument at the age of fourteen after hearing a concert given by Julian Bream. She then began to take lessons with the noted Toronto teacher Eli Kassner and soon showed remarkable progress. At the age of seventeen she was accepted into a masterclass given by Julian Bream in Stratford, Ontario.

In 1972 Liona Boyd graduated from the University of Toronto with a Bachelor's degree in music and performance. A little later she won the Canadian National Music Competition Award for the guitar. Following this achievement, she became a pupil of Alexandre Lagoya, both in Canada and later in Paris. She stayed in Europe for a year and a half, and on her return to Canada in 1974 signed a recording contract with Boot Records. Her first release for this label was highly successful. A concert tour of Canada followed, with the popular artist Gordon Lightfoot. It exposed Boyd's classical ability to a much wider audience, and since that time she has been one of the busiest guitarists in North America.

Her popularity with the general music public has resulted in total sales of her records in the USA and Canada alone in excess of 150,000, a phenomenal achievement for a classical guitarist, and one that makes her Canada's best-selling classical artist for CBS Records. She is also a popular radio and television performer in Canada, and had her own TV show in 1978.

In 1996 Boyd won her 5th Juno Award in Canada for 'Instrumental Artist of the Year'. She is the only guitarist who has ever received one of these awards. Boyd now lives in Los Angeles with her husband and devotes much of her time to composing. She played the guitar on the soundtrack of the film 'A Walk in the Clouds' which won the 1996 Golden Globe Award for best film score.

SELECTED MUSIC

First Lady of the Guitar.	Hansen House
Miniatures for Guitar.	Hal Leonard
A Guitar for Christmas.	Hal Leonard
Folksongs for Classical Guitar.	Hal Leonard
Meet Liona Boyd.	Mid-Continental Music
Favourite Solos for Classical Guitar.	Hal Leonard

SELECTED RECORDINGS

The Guitar – Liona Boyd.	Boot BMC3002 LP
Miniatures for Guitar.	Boot BOS7181 LP
Classical Guitar – Liona Boyd.	London CS7015 LP
Artistry of Liona Boyd.	London CS7068 LP
First Lady of the Guitar.	CBS MW M35137 LP
Liona Boyd with the English Chamber Orchestra.	CBS MW M35853 LP
First Nashville Quartet, with Chet Atkins.	RCA HL 1-3302 LP
Spanish Fantasy.	CBS MW M36675 LP
A Guitar for Christmas.	CBS MW FM37248 LP
The Best of Liona Boyd.	CBS MV FM37788 LP
Liona Boyd – Persona.	CBS FM2120 LP
Liona Boyd – Live in Tokyo.	CBS MW IM39031 LP
Virtuoso.	CBS IMT37829 LP
The Romantic Guitar.	CBS MR1005 LP
Christmas Dreams.	Moston/A&M CD 9513
Encore.	Moston/A&M CD 9509
Highlights.	Moston/A&M CD9510
Paddle to the Sea.	Oak Street/Sony POS CD 032
Dancing on the Edge.	Moston/A&M 70301957 2CD
Classically Yours.	Moston/A&M 2046795182 CD

SELECTED READING

Feature.	Hello Magazine, August 27, 1994
Interview.	Guitar Player, October 1978
Interview.	Frets, December 1980
Interview.	Guitarra, March 1980
'Jet-Guitarist'.	Chatelaine, March 1982
Interview.	Acoustic Musician, March 1995

FREDERICK BRAND

Born –
Regensburg, Germany, 1806
Died – Wùrzburg, Germany, 1874

Frederick Brand

Regarded by many as one of the great guitar virtuosos of the nineteenth century, Frederick Brand was known mainly in his native Germany. He was originally a teacher in Mannheim, but after his marriage he moved to Würzburg. Here he met the guitar virtuoso Adam Darr, and together these two great guitarists obtained very many engagements as a guitar duo and also as soloists. Both guitarists received high critical acclaim wherever they went.

As well as being a highly talented player, Frederick Brand was a most respected teacher of the instrument. He wrote many original compositions for the guitar, and these were published by Pacini of Paris and Schott of Mainz.

ARNE BRATTLAND

Born –
District of Meløy, Norway
6 May 1955

Arne Brattland

Arne Brattland began to play the guitar at the age of five and was self-taught until entering the Norwegian State Academy of Music in Oslo in 1975. He studied there with Erik Stenstadvold and Jan Danielsen.

He made his concert debut at the North Norwegian Festival in 1983. In 1985 he obtained a grant from Norwegian institutions and the British Council to study in London. During his three-year stay there, he studied with David Russell, Nigel North, Gilbert Biberian and John W. Duarte.

Arne Brattland returned to Norway in 1988 and has now established himself as one of the best young classical guitarists in Scandinavia with a busy career as a recitalist and teacher.

SELECTED RECORDINGS
Brattland plays Grieg, Duarte and Biberian.   VEPS 013-87 LP
Guitar Favourites.   VEPS CD 028-90 LP

SELECTED MUSIC
18 Lyric Pieces by Grieg transcribed Brattland Vols.1-3
VEPS Publishing

SELECTED READING
Profile.   Classical Guitar, March 1994

Julian Bream

JULIAN BREAM

Born – JULIAN ALEXANDER BREAM

Battersea, London, England

15 July 1933

Julian Bream is one of the greatest guitarists the world has known. By the time he was seventeen, although he had not played outside Great Britain, he was already known by reputation to guitarists all over the world.

Julian Bream was brought up in a musical environment. His father, a commercial artist and book illustrator, also ran a small dance band in which he played jazz guitar. The young Bream was very attracted to the jazz guitar style of Django Reinhardt, the legendary Gypsy guitarist. Bream's father encouraged his son to play the piano, but also taught him to play the plectrum guitar. On his eleventh birthday, Julian Bream was given a classical guitar by his father.

In 1945 Julian Bream won a junior exhibition award for his piano playing. This entitled him to study the piano and the cello at the Royal College of Music, London. In the same year his father took him to play at a meeting held by the London Philharmonic Society of Guitarists, where his obvious musical talent prompted Dr Boris Perott, the Society's president, to offer to teach him the classical guitar. This he did for one year. Dr Perott, and also Wilfrid Appleby, introduced Julian Bream to Andrés Segovia, who was so impressed by what he heard that he offered to give the thirteen-year old some lessons.

Julian Bream made his professional debut in Cheltenham in 1947. Encouraged by his father, he decided to make his career in music and the guitar, abandoning an almost equally strong ambition to become a professional cricketer. At the age of fifteen he was awarded a full scholarship at the Royal College of Music, and for three years studied piano, harmony and composition there – for it was a time when no guitar tuition could be offered by the College.

Great critical acclaim greeted his debut in the Wigmore Hall, London, in 1951. Despite three years in the British Army (1952-55), he continued to appear frequently on radio and television programmes as well as at public concerts. His first European tours took place in 1954 and 1955, and were followed by extensive touring in North America (beginning in 1958), the Far East, India, Australia, the Pacific Islands and other parts of the world. In addition to masterclasses given in Canada and the USA, Bream has also conducted an international summer school in Wiltshire, England.

Julian Bream's many recordings for RCA have made him well known to a large worldwide audience and have won for him some of the highest awards in the recording industry. They include the Award of the National Academy of Recording Arts and Sciences, two Grammy awards (1963 and 1966), and an Edison award (1968). In the Queen's Birthday Honours List of 1985 he was made a Commander of the Order of the British Empire (C.B.E.).

Since 1952, when he played part of a Wigmore Hall recital on the lute, Julian Bream has also been noted for his playing of this instrument, and is responsible for bringing to light much of its music which had lain dormant for over three hundred years. He has also done much to broaden the contemporary guitar repertoire by commissioning works from such famous composers as Benjamin Britten, William Walton, Hans Werner Henze, Peter Racine Fricker, Richard Rodney Bennett, Malcolm Arnold, Alan Rawsthorne, Lennox Berkeley and Michael Tippett. It is safe to say to that no guitarist has ever done more to enrich the repertoire in this way.

Bream's association with his fellow guitarist John Williams, which resulted in three recordings and a number of concerts, has been an enormous success. BBC Television have presented a special programme about Julian Bream's life as a concert guitarist, and also a series of four masterclasses presented by Bream for guitarists. Channel 4 Television produced a series of six half-hour programmes on the classical guitar by Bream, entitled ¡Guitarra!

SELECTED RECORDINGS

The Art of Julian Bream.	RCA RB 16239 LP
Popular Classics for Spanish Guitar.	RCA RB6593 LP
Guitar Music of Villa-Lobos & Torroba.	HMV CLP 1763 LP
Bach Recital for Guitar.	HMV CLP 1929 LP
Julian Bream plays Bach.	RCA RL 42378 LP
Rodrigo Concerto/Vivaldi Concerto/Britten Dances.	RCA SB 6635 LP
Baroque Guitar.	RCA SB 6673 LP
Twentieth Century Guitar.	RCA SB 6723 LP
Julian Bream & Friends. Boccherini Quintet/Haydn Quartet.	RCA SB 6772 LP
Classic Guitar. Giuliani/Diabelli/Mozart/Sor	RCA SB 6796 LP
Guitar Concertos Giuliani/Arnold.	RCA SB 6826 LP
Julian Bream plays Villa-Lobos.	RCA SB 6852 LP
Romantic Guitar.	RCA SB 6844 LP
Julian Bream 70s	RCA SB 6876 LP
Giuliani/Sor.	RCA ARL 1-0711 LP
Rodrigo/Berkeley Guitar Concertos.	RCA ARL 1-1181 LP
Julian Bream plays Villa-Lobos	RCA RL 12499 LP
Music of Spain. Sor/Aguado.	RCA RL 14033 LP
Live (2 LPs).	RCA SB 6862 LP
Granados & Albéniz.	RCA RS 9008 LP
Guitarra (2 LPs).	RCA RL 85417(2) LP
Brouwer/Rodrigo Concertos.	RCA RD 87718
Julian Bream – The Ultimate Guitar Collection (28 CD Set).	RCAV 09026-61583-2
A Segovia Celebration.	RCA 0902661 353-2 CD
A Bach Recital.	EMI Classics CDC7 7243-5
To the Edge of a Dream.	EMI Classics CDC7 54661-2
Nocturnal.	EMI Classics CDC7 54901-2
Sonata.	EMI Classics 55362-28 CD
Ultimate Guitar Collection (2 CDs).	RCAV 33705-2
Fretworks – Early Bream (2 CDs).	MCA 9830 CD
La Guitarra Romantica.	RCA RD60429 CD

Duo with John Williams:

Together.	RCA 61452-2 CD
Together Again.	RCA 61450-2 CD

Video recording:

¡GUITARRA! The Guitar in Spain.	RM Video 079-239-3

SELECTED READING

Interview.	Guitar, January 1973
Interview.	Classical Guitar, May/June 1983
Interview.	Classical Guitar, February & March 1986
Profile.	Guitar Review, Spring 1990
Interview.	BBC Music, July 1993
Interview.	Classic CD, August 1993
Special issue – Bream at 60.	Classical Guitar, August 1993
Interview.	Classical Guitar, September 1994
Profile.	Guitar Review, Winter 1994
Interview.	Classical Guitar, October 1996

Julian Bream
— playing music by Mudarra on the guitar —

Hundreds of eyes with eagerness impel
The Wizard-Medium towards his simple throne,
A crackle of applauding palms,
Welcoming, anticipating –
Then noiselessness.

From the tense silence the Six-voiced Oracle
Melodiously declaims, reincarnating
Alonso de Mudarra of Seville
Whose music was conceived
Four Spanish centuries ago.

Hundreds of ears miraculously
Hear, nay, SEE
Liquids sounds transformed into a stream
Dancing and sparkling –
And Spanish children singing.

The magic wanes, the sunlit music fades,
A silent mistiness pervades –
Or is it moistening of eyes
Brimming with wonder?

Wilfrid M. Appleby

ROBERT BRIGHTMORE

Born –

Leicester, England

25 January 1949

Robert Brightmore

From the age of five Robert Brightmore studied the piano with his father, but became fascinated with the guitar. By the time he had reached his early teens, he realized that his facility was greater for the guitar than for the piano, and the instrument became something of an obsession.

After completing his studies at the Nottingham College of Art and the London Film School, he studied classical guitar with George Zarb in London, and attended masterclasses with Julian Bream and Oscar Cáceres.

He made his Wigmore Hall debut in London in 1975 and since that time has established himself as a prominent recitalist, touring extensively and giving concerts, classes and courses.

Working with composers forms a strong element in Brightmore's career, and he has given first performances of many new works by foremost composers, among them Leo Brouwer, Reginald Smith Brindle, Oliver Hunt, Stépan Rak and Carlo Domeniconi. He has recently premiered two works by the South American composer Jaime Zenamon; the guitar concerto Iguaçu, dedicated to Brightmore, and Demian, a solo work based on the book by Herman Hesse. He also initiated the stage setting of Oliver Hunt's The Barber of Baghdad at the London Collegiate Theatre for a performance of the piece set to mime.

Robert Brightmore is active as an arranger, and has made several LPs. He is currently professor of guitar at the Guildhall School of Music and Drama in London.

SELECTED RECORDINGS
Robert Brightmore: Vista Records VPS 1077 LP
Profile.   Barry-Musik, EMI Electrola ASD BM 8401 LP
Robert Brightmore: Recital. Chorus Records CH 8601 LP

SELECTED READING
Interview.   Classical Guitar, July/August 1983
Article.   Classical Guitar, April 1990

Leo Brouwer

LEO BROUWER

Born – JUAN LEOVIGILDO BROUWER (MESQUIDA)

Havana, Cuba

1 March 1939

One of today's most outstanding guitarists and composers, Leo Brouwer first studied the guitar with Isaac Nicola, a pupil of Emilio Pujol. He specialized in composition, completing his studies at The Juilliard School and in Hartt College in Hartford.

In 1961 he was named Director of the Music Department of the Cinema Institute of Cuba, Professor of Composition in the Music Conservatory and musical adviser to the National Radio and Television Chain of Havana. He became Director of the experimental department of the Cuban Institute of Cinema Arts and Industry, where he continued his work as a composer.

Leo Brouwer was the first Cuban composer to use aleatory and 'open' forms, and his very many compositions include several works for guitar, percussion, prepared and non-prepared pianos, a cantata for two percussionists and piano, a contemporary ballet, a chorus of twelve members, three children and harp, and a series of orchestral works.

He has taken part as a guitarist and as a composer in the Festivals of Aldeburgh, Avignon, Edinburgh, Spoleto, Berlin (Festwochen), Toronto, Arles, Martinique and Rome, as well as in other important musical centres in Europe.

In addition to his outstanding contribution as a guitarist and composer, Leo Brouwer is also a talented conductor, and has worked with, among others, the BBC Concert Orchestra, the Langham Chamber Orchestra, the Philharmonic Orchestra of Berlin (FRG) and the National Orchestra of Scotland. He also conducted the Manson Ensemble in London and the Theatre Orchestra of Rome for the world premiere of his music for 'Julius Caesar' (1971). Brouwer was also guest composer of the Deustsche Akademische Austauschdienst in Berlin (1972) along with Morton Feldman, Earle Brown and St Bussot. He has conducted masterclasses for guitarists in France, Canada, Martinique, Cuba, Puerto Rico, Finland, Cuba and Greece, and has been a jury member in many international competitions, including those in Munich, Caracas, Esztergom, Paris and his native Havana. He founded the biennial Havana International Guitar Festival and Competition in the early 1980s, and has directed it ever since.

In recent years Leo Brouwer has concentrated more on composition than performance, producing a stream of works that reflect a moving away from his earlier experimental style towards music that contains strong elements of melody while employing certain minimalist techniques. He remains one of the most interesting figures on the contemporary guitar scene.

SELECTED MUSIC

Canticum.	GA 424
Danza Caracteristica.	GA 422
Elogio de la Danza.	GA 425
Fuga No.1.	ESC 7995
La Espiral Eterna.	GA 423
Parábola.	ESC 8198
Piece Without Title.	ESC 8000
Pieces Without Title Nos. 2 & 3.	ESC 8452
Preludio.	ESC 7996
Tarantos.	ESC 8293
Tres Apuntes (3 sketches).	GA 426
Two Popular Cuban Airs: Guajira Criolla, Zapateada.	ESC 7999
Two Popular Cuban Themes: Canción de Cuna, Ojos Brujos.	ESC 8182
Etudes Simples Nos.1-20 (4 vols.).	ESC 7997, 7998, 8494, 8495
Variations on a Theme of Django Reinhardt.	EMT 1743
El Decameron Negro.	EMT 1704
Cuban Landscape with Rain.	DO 92
Cuban Landscape with Bells.	DO
Concerto No.1 for Guitar and Orchestra.	ESC 8191
Concerto No.2 'Concierto de Lieja' for Guitar and Orchestra.	ESC
Concerto No.3 'Concierto Elegiaco' for Guitar and Orchestra.	ESC 8673
Concerto No.4 'Concierto de Toronto' for Guitar and Orchestra.	DO 100
Sonata.	Opera Tres

SELECTED RECORDINGS

Les Classiques de Cuba.	Erato STV 0669 LP
Scarlatti – Twelve Sonatas.	Erato STV 70870 LP
Leo Brouwer.	Deutsche Grammophon 2555 01 LP
Rara.	Deutsche Grammophon 2530 307 LP
Leo and Ichiro.	Camerata/Tokyo CMT-1065 LP
Guitarra.	Egrem LD 4189 LP
Leo Brouwer – Guitarrista.	Egrem LD 3876 LP
Contemporaneo 2.	Egrem LD 3653 LP
Brouwer – Twenty Studies – Leonardo de Angelis.	Quadrivium SCA 013 CD
Brouwer Concertos – Leonardo de Angelis.	Quadrivium SCA 020 CD
The Music of Leo Brouwer – Beer/Draper/Ljunestrom/Patterson.	Koch Swann 3-1174-2 CD
Alvaro Pierri plays Leo Brouwer.	Analekta AN2 875 2 CD
Flavio Cucchi plays Brouwer.	ARC EUCD 1192
Brouwer Guitar Concertos – Ricardo Cobo.	Essay CD 1040

SELECTED READING

Leo Brouwer.	Guitar, June 1976
Leo Brouwer.	Guitar, April 1977
Leo Brouwer.	Guitar & Lute, January 1982
Leo Brouwer.	Classical Guitar, September 1984
Leo Brouwer – works for guitar.	Guitar Review, Spring 1989
Interview.	Guitar Reviews, Summer 1990
Article.	Guitar Review, Summer 1994
Interview.	Sound Board, Spring 1995
Article.	Classical Guitar, December 1996

JULIAN BYZANTINE

Born –

London, England

11 June 1945

Julian Byzantine

Julian Byzantine began his advanced musical studies with John Williams at the Royal College of Music, where he was awarded the first ARCM for guitar. During this period he won scholarships to further his studies with Julian Bream in England and Andrés Segovia in Siena, where he was chosen by the maestro to give a solo recital. After finishing these studies he taught on the staff of the Royal Academy of Music, London, for two years.

Besides his recital work, Byzantine makes frequent concerto appearances and has performed with some of the leading orchestras in Britain, including the Royal Philharmonic, the City of Birmingham Symphony and the Scottish Chamber Orchestras, and with many national orchestras abroad.

In the field of contemporary music he has worked with Pierre Boulez and Peter Maxwell Davies, and on numerous occasions the Arts Council of Great Britain has had works commissioned for him.

Julian Byzantine's reputation as a soloist has been extended by his broadcasts for radio and television, and these have included a television documentary on the life and guitar music of Heitor Villa-Lobos. A particular interest in the manuscripts of the early guitarists and lutenists led him to become an exponent of the baroque guitar.

One of Britain's best established concert artists, Julian Byzantine has travelled widely, making extensive concert tours of Scandinavia, Latin America, the USA and, particularly, Australasia.

SELECTED RECORDINGS
Julian Byzantine Plays Villa-Lobos etc.
         Classics for Pleasure CFP 40209 LP
Masterpieces for Classical Guitar
         Classics for Pleasure CFP 40362 LP
Julian Byzantine plays Albeniz.
        Classics for Pleasure 0777 7 67750 2-9 CD

SELECTED READING
Julian Byzantine.   Guitar, December 1980

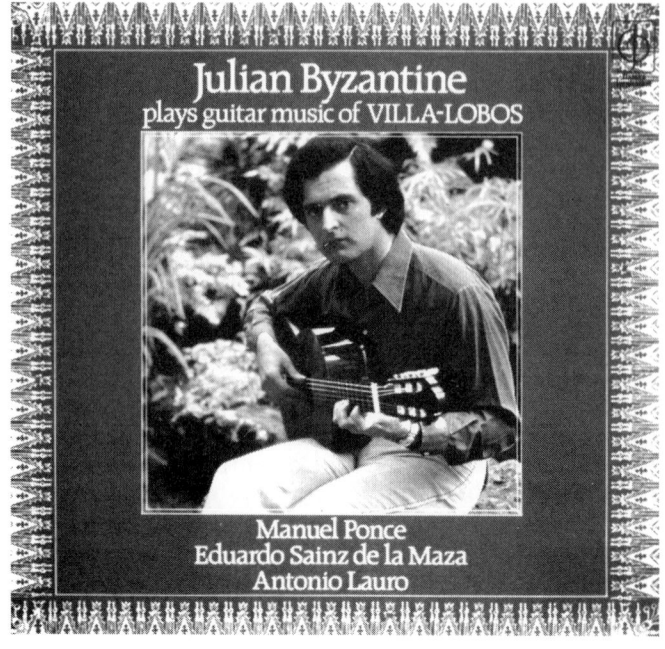

OSCAR CACERES

Born –

Montevideo, Uruguay

4 April 1928

SELECTED RECORDINGS

Les Grandes Etudes pour Guitare Vol.1.	Erato STV 70614 LP
Les Grandes Etudes pour Guitare Vol.2.	Erato ATV 70904 LP
Oscar Cáceres plays Leo Brouwer.	Erato STV 70734 LP
Musique pour Deux Guitares Vol.1 (with Turibio Santos).	Erato STV 70794 LP
Musique pour Deux Guitares Vol.2 (with Turibio Santos).	Erato STV 71092 LP
Trésors d'Amerique Latine.	Erato STV 70988 LP
Oscar Cáceres: Takemitsu/Brouwer.	Pavanne ADW7097 LP
Oscar Caleres Villa Lobos.	Pavanne ADW 7097 LP
Oscar Cáceres plays Bach/Weiss.	Pavanne ADW 7040 LP
Anthology of the Spanish Guitar (4 CD's)	ADDA 484/581214/17 LP

Oscar Cáceres

Oscar Cáceres began his serious study of the guitar under the guidance of the guitarists Ramon Ayestaran, Marin Sanchez and Atilio Rapat. As a child he made such good progress on the instrument that he was able to give his first public recital at the age of thirteen.

In 1957, when he was twenty-nine, Oscar Cáceres made his first European recital tour. He played with great success in Paris, Madrid, Valencia and Barcelona. On his return to South America he gave the first live performance on that continent of Rodrigo's Concierto de Aranjuez ..

Cáceres continued to make extensive concert tours of South America, at the same time devoting a large part of his work to musical research. He has a special love of Rensaissance music, but at the same time retains a keen interest in twentieth century music.

In 1967 Oscar Cáceres decided to settle in Paris. He has continued to give recitals and also to teach the guitar in most of the major cities of Europe.

An unusual 19th century guitar made by the Mauchant Brothers, Mirecourt, France. Now on display at the Gemeentemeseum – Gravenhage, The Hague, Netherlands.

BARTOLOME CALATAYUD

Born – Palma de Mallorca, Spain, 1882

Died – Palma de Mallorca, Spain, 1973

Bartolome Calatayud

Bartolome Calatayud's first teacher was Antonio Mestro, Professor and Director of the Instituto de Bachillerato and also a guitarist. To Mestro is owed the formation of an excellent group of guitarists that included Calatayud and the brothers Bernat.

Calatayud's progress with Mestro was such that he was soon giving guitar concerts in Mallorca. The eminent Catalan guitarist and composer Emilio Pujol was present at one of these concerts at the Circulo Mallorquín and invited Calatayud to give a concert in Barcelona. A great friendship between the two musicians developed after this meeting. Calatayud's first concert outside Spain was given in Toulouse, France, and soon concerts were taking place in other European countries.

Calatayud, who had had an inclination towards composition from his youth, had learned harmony from Mestro. He wrote many compositions for the guitar, including Una Lágrima, Danza Mora, Alegre Primavera, Gaviotas, and Suite Antigua. There are over fifty of his compositions listed in the catalogue of the Spanish publishers Unión Musical.

Calatayud did a great deal of work in the spreading and correct interpretation of Mallorquín folk music. In 1940 he was appointed director of Coros y Danzas of the Sección Femenina de Palma. With this organization he toured South American countries with great success and made several records which have carried Palma's folk music to all parts of the world.

Bartolome Calatayud had a special ability as a teacher, and as a result had many pupils. Such was his reputation that many guitarists came to study with him from countries other than Spain.

SELECTED RECORDINGS

Inolvidable Guitarra.	Impacto EL 225 LP
Gabriel Estarellas interprets Bartolome Calatayud.	Maller API 86 LP

SELECTED MUSIC

Alegre, Campina, Vals.	UME 2097
Alegre, Primavera.	UME 20434
Boceto Andaluz.	UME 20003
Cuatro Divertimientos.	UME 20557
Cuatro Juguetes.	UME 21719
Cuatro Piezas para Guitarra.	UME 19675
Cubanita, Habañera.	UME 21718
Danza Española.	UME 20212
Danza Mora.	UME 21780
Danza Popular de Campdevanol.	UME 21266
Dos Piezas para Guitarra.	UME 19674
Dos Piezas para Guitarra.	UME 20004
Estampa Gitana.	UME 20217
Estudio Melodico.	UME 21091
Galop.	UME 21781

MATTEO CARCASSI

Born –
Florence, Italy, 1792
Died – Paris, France, 16 January 1853

*Matteo Carcassi

Thousands of student guitarists throughout the world today know the name Carcassi as the author of their guitar method and the composer of many attractive compositions and studies. There is no doubt he is most well known for these works, but Carcassi was also one of the great guitarists of the nineteenth century.

Matteo Carcassi studied the guitar from an early age in his native Italy. Before he was twenty he already had a reputation in Italy as a virtuoso of the guitar. In 1815 he was established in Paris as a teacher of both guitar and piano. During a concert tour of Germany in 1819 he became friendly with the French guitarist Meissonier, who in 1812 had opened a publishing house in Paris. The two guitarists became firm friends, and Meissonier published most of Carcassi's works.

In 1822 Carcassi established himself in London, after only a few concerts, as an exceptional guitar soloist and teacher. He soon returned to Paris, but was able to make an annual trip to London, where his guitar talents were much in demand.

When he first arrived in Paris, Carcassi's talents had been somewhat overshadowed by the older Italian guitar virtuoso guitarist Ferdinando Carulli, but after a few years Carcassi attained very great success. He gave annual concerts in most of the major cities of Europe, including London, but, despite a brief return to Italy in 1836, Paris was to become his permanent residence. He died there in 1853.

SELECTED MUSIC

Andantino & Romanze, from op.60.	GA 305
Fifty-four Selected Pieces: Book I (Easy).	GA 4A
Book II (Medium).	GA 4B
Book III (Difficult).	GA 4C
My First Carcassi, ed. Skiera	Ricordi
Rondoletto op.41, ed. Danner (Fac. No.8).	Belwin
Selected Works (facsimiles), ed. Noad.	Hansen
Six Caprices op.26.	GA 72
Six Easy Caprices op.26, ed. Schwarz-Reiflingen.	Sik.
Six Easy Variations op.18.	Vieweg
Three Sonatinas op.1 & Six Caprices op.26.	GA 5
Twelve Easy Pieces op.10.	GA 73
Twenty Selected Waltzes.	GA 3
Twenty-four Little Pieces op.21.	GA 6
Two Waltzes from op.4.	GA 309
Variations on the Dream of Rousseau op.17.	Kalmus
Carcassi Op. 60 ed. Paul Henry. Hal Leonard Publishing	

SELECTED RECORDING
25 Etudes Carcassi – Minoru Inagaki. Super Nova – 0071 CD

Although this portrait has been attributed to be Carcassi for many years, some authorities now doubt its authenticity.

JORGE CARDOSO

Born – JORGE RUBEN CARDOSO KRIEGER

Posadas, Misiones Province, Argentina

26 January 1949

Jorge Cardoso

PHOTO: COLIN COOPER

Originally Jorge Cardoso studied the guitar with Lucas B. Arceo and Luis J. Cassinelli. On gaining a scholarship from the National Fund in Arts in Argentina, he was able to study with Maria Hermini A. de Gomez Crespo. Later he studied harmony with Mario Perini, and composition at the National University of Córdoba in Argentina. While studying compositon at this university he also studied medicine. He eventually qualified in both, which is probably a first for any leading classical guitarist.

Since the age of fourteen, Jorge Cardoso won first prizes in several important Argentinian competitions. In 1963 he won the solo instrumental class at the Festival of Music of the Littoral, at Posadas; in 1967 the National Folklore Composition Competition at Salta, and in 1973 the International Concourse of the Classical Guitar at Morón (Buenos Aires).

Cardoso has appeared in many recitals and concerts throughout Argentina, Spain, France, Japan and Poland, but as yet has received little or no exposure in other countries. He has several records to his name, and over 100 musical works published, including two concertos for guitar and orchestra.

Jorge Cardoso lives in Madrid, where he directs the Ibero American Guitar Orchestra of Madrid. He spends most of his year in Spain, and also some time in Japan, where he is very popular. He has established himself not only as a guitarist of outstanding ability, but also as a fine composer and teacher.

SELECTED RECORDINGS

Clásicos del Folklore SudAmericano.	DPM PM 2040 LP
Suite SudAmericana.	Dial Discos ND 5019 LP
Autores SudAmericanos.	Diapason Dial Discos 52-5038 LP
Lamento Caingua.	Diapason 52-5054 LP
Cardoso and the Niibori Guitar Orchestra.	APAC 8009 LP
Suite Litoralena.	Diapason 52-5067 LP
Jorge Cardoso.	Blue Angel BA 29005 LP
Cardoso Plays Cardoso.	OPUS 9311 2123 LP
Guitar Duets W. Francisco Ortiz.	Plectrum PL-MC-004
Misionerita.	Plectrum PL-CD-003

SELECTED MUSIC

Suite SudAmericana.	CASA 320
Twenty-Four Pieces – SudAmericana.	UME 22310, UME 22353
Gavota del Crepusculo.	UME
Mitosis. Guitar Music,	Tokyo UT 40
Suite Portena.	Guitar Music, Tokyo
Preludes by Bach.	UME

SELECTED READING

Ciencia y Método en la Tecnica Guitarristica	Capsa de los Americas (Cuba)
Interview.	Guitar International, December 1986
Interview.	Classical Guitar, June 1995

ABEL CARLEVARO

Born –
Montevideo, Uruguay
16 December 1918

Abel Carlevaro

Abel Carlevaro began his study of musical theory under Tomas Mujica and Pablo Kimlos. He was originally self-taught on the guitar, using the printed methods that were available in Uruguay at that time. He later studied harmony, instrumentation and orchestration, applying his knowledge of these subjects to his guitar studies. His original decision was to make his career in agriculture, but his love for the guitar eventually made him choose the field of music.

In 1937 Abel Carlevaro met Andrés Segovia. Following this meeting, he was able to study with the maestro for nine years. In 1942 Segovia presented him at the official music centre of the Republic of Uruguay. This recital established Carlevaro as a concert artist. In 1939, during the World Fair in New York, USA, Carlevaro broadcast several recitals for local radio stations. He received high critical praise for his playing, following which the Uruguayan Government gave him a special grant to enable him to travel.

Since the end of World War II Abel Carlevaro has given concerts in most countries of the world. He still appears regularly at major international guitar festivals, both in a playing and in a teaching capacity.

SELECTED RECORDINGS
Recital de Guitarra.   Antar Telefunken ALP 1002 LP
Carlevaro plays Carlevaro.   Chanterelle CR 1000 LP
Carlevaro's Art.   Formosa Melodiya TY 92901 CD

SELECTED MUSIC
Cronomias I – Sonata for Guitar.   B & C 4014
Preludios Americanos.   B & C 4010, 4011, 4005, 4023, 4018
Suite of Ancient Spanish Dances (on text & themes of Sanz).   B & C 4017
School of Guitar – An Exposition of Instrumental Theory.
                                        Dacisa Sa/Boosey & Hawkes, 1978
Guitar Masterclasses Vols.1-4.   Chanterelle ECH 711/714
Microe Studies Vols.1 and 2.   Chanterelle ECH 791/792

SELECTED READING
Interview.   Classical Guitar, February 1985
Profile.   Soundboard, Spring 1989

FERDINANDO CARULLI

Born – FERDINANDO MARIA MEINRADO
PASCALE ROSARIO CARULLI
Naples, Italy, 9 February 1770
Died – Paris, France, 17 February 1841

Ferdinando Carulli

Ferdinando Carulli was the son of a distinguished writer, who was secretary to the Neopolitan Jurisdiction Delegate. Carulli's first musical instrument was the cello, but he became attracted to the guitar at an early age. Although the guitar was extremely popular in Italy at that time, there were very few serious teachers of the instrument.

Carulli's musical genius became evident whilst he was still a young man. He developed a series of studies and exercises, revolutionary in their concept, to help his technique on the instrument. With these studies any dedicated guitarist could achieve excellent standards of musicianship on the guitar.

In 1797, already a highly respected teacher and player, Carulli moved to Leghorn. In 1808 he again moved, this time to Paris. Here he was to remain for the rest of his life.

In 1810 he wrote his comprehensive method for guitar (Op.27). Originally published by Carli of Paris, it became one of the standard instruction books for guitar. Its success was so great that four editions were printed in a relatively short period of time. Fifth, sixth and seventh editions (Op.241) followed; these were enlarged versions of the original, containing an appendix of forty-four progressive pieces and six studies. In 1825 Carulli wrote L'Harmonie appliqué à la guitare, a skilful work on the art of accompaniment, and the first of its kind. He published more than four hundred compositions for the guitar, including studies, concerti, several trios for guitar, flute and violin, trios for three guitars, and many compositions for two guitars and guitar and piano. All these compositions are characterized by their richness of harmony and elegance of form.

Carulli's original method is still widely used by teachers and students. Increasing interest in his music, particularly the ensemble pieces, is further evidence of his musical genius.

SELECTED MUSIC
Allegretto.	Bèrben EB 2112
Best of Carulli, ed. Castle (11 selections).	MB
Capriccio.	GA 310
Eighteen Little Pieces Op. 211, ed. Carfagna.	Bèrben EB 2180
Eighteen Very Easy Pieces Op.333.	GA 67
Nice und Fileno – Sonata Op.2.	ZM 1967
Overture Op.6 No.1.	N 3168
Preludes for Guitar Op.114, ed. Schwarz-Reiflingen.	N 3211
Six Andantes Op. 320, ed. Chiesa.	GA 313
Solo Op. 76 no.2.	Zerboni SZ 7732
Three Sonatas.	GA 40
Twenty-four Preludes Op.114, ed. Balestra.	Ricordi ER 2746
Two Minuets from Op. 270.	GA 311
Variations on a Theme of Beethoven.	Bèrben EB 2097
Variations on the Italian Aria 'Sul Margine d'un Rio' Op. 142.	Zerboni SZ 7727

SELECTED READING
Profilo biografico-critico e catalogo tematico della opere con numero. Vols.1 & 2 – Mario Torta (dissertation). Universita degli Studi di Roma 'La Sapienza', 1989.
Complete Works of Carulli – 4 part article.
    Ruggero Chiesa Classical Guitar April-July 1992
Catalogo Tematico dell Opere di Ferdinando Carulli.
Ed. Mario Torta (2 Vols.). Libreria Musicale Italiana 1996

SELECTED RECORDINGS
Carulli Guitar Works – Alfonso Baschiera.
    Nuova Era 710 2 CD
Carulli Sonatas – Richard Savino. Naxos 855 3301 CD
Carulli Piano/Guitar Works – Sonja Prunnbauer.
    DG MDG 603 0616 2 CD
Carulli Guitar Concerto – Pepe Romero.
    Philips 426 263 2 CD

LEIF CHRISTENSEN
Born –
Aarhus, Denmark, 1 March 1950
Died – Near Aarhus, 12 January 1988

Leif Christensen

Leif Christensen studied with Konrad Ragossnig in the Musikakademie der Stadt Basel, Switzerland. He graduated there in 1978, and from that time enjoyed an extensive and successful concert career throughout Europe and Scandinavia. From his early student days Leif Christensen was actively involved in researching original 18th and 19th century guitar music, which led to his performing the works on original instruments. He made several highly acclaimed recordings, both as a solo performer and as a guitar duo with his wife Maria Kämmerling.

At the time of his tragic and early death in a car accident, Leif Christensen was teaching as assistant professor at the Royal Danish Academy of Music in Aarhus.

SELECTED RECORDINGS
Guitar Works of Giulio Regondi.	Paula 10 LP
Fernando Sor – Duos with Maria Kämmerling	Paula 14 LP
Guitar Works of Miguel Llobet.	Paula 20 LP
Henze – Royal Winter Music.	Paula 25 LP
Mauro Giuliani – Guitar Duets with Maria Kämmerling.	Paula 34 LP
The Russian 7-String Guitar – W.S.Sarenko.	Paula 40 LP
Giuliani – Virtuoso Overtures for Two Guitars.	Paula 44 LP
Tárrega, Schumann & Thalberg.	Paula PACD 59

SELECTED READING
Leif Christensen: An Appreciation.
    Classical Guitar, June 1989
Interview. Classical Guitar, June 1996

GEORGE CLINTON

Born – Halifax, England, 6 May, 1931

Died – Bourton, Dorset, England

28 October, 1991

George Clinton was the editor of Guitar International, formerly Guitar magazine. This monthly magazine, which originally covered most styles of guitar playing, began publishing in 1972 and ceased publication in February 1992 a few months after his death.

Clinton's first instrument was the violin. His father was a professional violinist who started his son on the instrument at the age of ten. At the age of twelve, George Clinton changed to the clarinet, an instrument to which he devoted his musical studies until he finished his army service years later. It was then that he chose to study the classical guitar. He progressed on the instrument and in 1959 gave his first public performance, a lunchtime recital at Holborn Town Hall in London. Following this concert, he made several radio broadcasts for the then popular BBC programme 'Guitar Club'.

For many years George Clinton led a busy life as a guitar teacher and as a photographer for IPC. He was a regular contributor to the long-established BMG magazine. In August 1972 the first issue of Guitar magazine under his editorship was published by his company Musical New Services Ltd. Over the next

George Clinton

seventeen years this company also produced many guitar publications, some of which have been important additions to the growing library of guitar literature. In September 1989 his original company, Musical New Services Ltd, went into liquidation but he managed to continue the publication of his magazine under his editorship through another of his companies, Purestop Ltd. This business also went into liquidation a few months after his death in February 1992.

SELECTED READING
Guitar International Volume 1, Issue 1, August 1972, to the last issue, February 1992.
Obituary – Independent Newspaper.   9th November 1991

SELECTED MUSIC
Exercises and Development of Right and Left Hand.
Musical New Services
Anthology of Vihuela Music arranged for Guitar.
Musical New Services

RICARDO COBO
Born - Cali,
Colombia
12 April 1963

SELECTED RECORDINGS	
Tales for Guitar	ESSAY CD 1034
Brouwer Guitar Concertos	ESSAY CD 1040

SELECTED READING	
Interview	Soundboard, Spring 1995

Ricardo Cobo

Ricardo Cobo first studied the guitar with his father. He gave his first professional performance at the age of seventeen on a television broadcast with the Orquesta Filarmonica de Bogota, Colombia.

Cobo went on to study in the USA. There he studied at the Florida State University, the Peabody Conservatory in Baltimore, and the North Carolina School of Arts. He has also attended the Aspen Music Festival and studied at the Conservatorio Antonio Maria Valencia in Colombia. His primary teachers were Bruce Holzman and Aaron Shearer. Within a short period of time he earned consecutive prizes in six international competitions, including gold medals at the Fifth GFA International Competition held in Arizona, the M.T.N.A National Competition in New York, and the 8th International 'Alirio Diaz' Competition, Caracas, Venezuela. He is an honorary member of the Pi Kappa Lambda Fraternity, and a recipient of the 1988 Pi Kappa Phi Artist/Scholar Award.

Ricardo Cobo has established himself as a leading concert artist in the USA, Latin America and Europe. He is currently on the Artist Faculty of Temple University in Philadelphia.

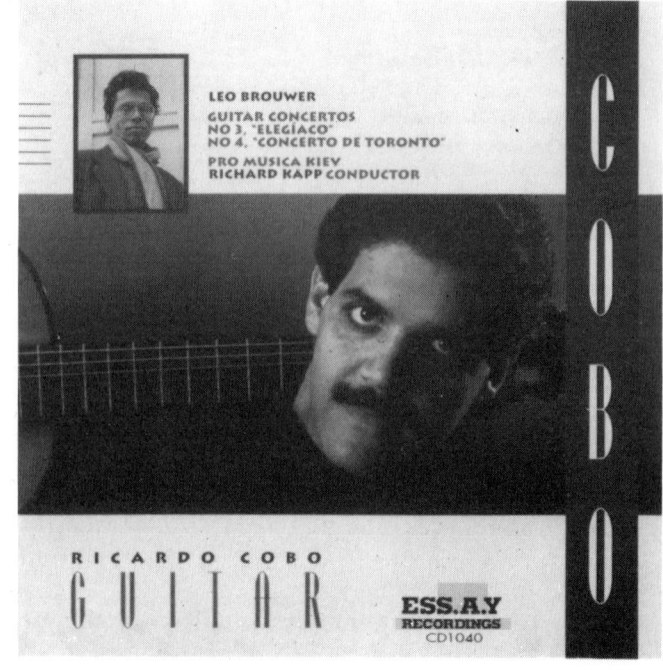

OLGA COELHO

Born –

Manaus, Amazonas, Brazil

1909

Olga Coelho

Olga Coelho is one of the finest singer/guitarists the world has known. Her musical instruction began at the age of six with piano studies, which she continued for more than ten years. She then studied harmony with O. Lorenzo Fernández, and received her diploma from the National Institute of Music in Rio de Janeiro, where her family made their home. One of Coelho's voice teachers was the noted Italian contralto Gabriella Besanzoni Lage.

Olga Coelho became intensely interested in Brazilian folklore at an early age. Through her love of this folklore she was attracted to the guitar. She has given concerts in South America, the United States, Canada, Europe, Australia, New Zealand and the Far East. She has recorded in the United States, London, Sweden, Brazil, Chile and Argentina, and has written many articles on music and folklore for magazines in South America and the United States. She speaks six languages (Portuguese, Spanish, French, Italian, German, English) and sings in several more, including Russian, Swedish, Polish, Maori and Malay. Songs have been composed for her by many outstanding composers, including Villa-Lobos, Castelnuovo-Tedesco, J. Rodriguez, Andrés Segovia, O. Lorenzo Fernandez, M. Carmargo Guarnieri, John W. Duarte and Hans Haug.

She has been honoured by many Brazilian cities; and in Rio de Janeiro there is a permanent exhibition at the Museu do Teatro Municipal of her programmes, photographs and other memorabilia. In Buenos Aires she has been honoured by membership of the Republica de la Boca. She also has the distinction of being one of the few artists honoured by the New York Society of the Classic Guitar with honorary membership.

For many years Olga Coelho was a close friend of Andrés Segovia, who transcribed much music for her. She was the first singer/guitarist for whom Segovia wrote accompaniments.

SELECTED RECORDINGS
Chants and Folk Ballads of Latin America. Decca DL 10018 LP

COLIN COOPER

Born –

Birkenhead, England

5 July 1926

Colin Cooper

Colin Cooper is recognized as one of the world's foremost writers on the classical guitar, yet he did not begin to play the guitar until the age of thirty-six. Tuition under various teachers culminated in his participation in Gilbert Biberian's advanced course at the Chiswick Music Centre.

Since 1982 he has been general and features editor of Classical Guitar magazine, widely regarded as the leading monthly publication devoted to the instrument. His perceptive interviews, thoughtful articles and sometimes provocative reviews display his wide knowledge of the guitar and music in general.

Colin Cooper is a unique figure in the music press. A professional writer since his early twenties, he is the author of five published novels, twelve performed plays (one of them a TV prizewinner) and innumerable general articles for publications great and small. He contributed a regular column to the Tokyo magazine Gendai Guitar for fifteen consecutive years, and was the first features editor of Guitar magazine, the first four issues of which were published from his house in London.

Although Colin Cooper has not performed as a solo guitarist, he has played in ensemble in public performance, has arranged music for the guitar and has had an original composition published.

He has served as a jury member in several international guitar competitions, in Hungary, Greece, Poland and Finland. He is also a keen photographer, and has contributed very many photographs of guitarists to Classical Guitar magazine, Gendai Guitar and other guitar journals.

SELECTED READING
Classical Guitar Magazine. Volume 1, Issue 1 to current issue

ERNESTO CORDERO

Born –

New York, USA

9 August 1946

Ernesto Cordero

Ernesto Cordero's parents were Puerto Rican. His family returned to Puerto Rico in 1953. He began to play the guitar at the age of fourteen, studying privately with Jorge Rubiano and Ramón Molinary. In 1963 he entered the Conservatory of Music of Puerto Rico to study music theory.

In 1967 Cordero was given a scholarship to study guitar in Spain with Regino Sainz de la Maza, Jorge Ariza and Renata Tarragó. In 1970 he graduated from the Real Conservatorio Superior in Madrid, earning the title Professor of Guitar. Following this success, Cordero went to Italy in 1972 to study with Alirio Diaz.

It was at this time that he recognized his growing ability as a composer. He studied composition with Boris Porena and Roberto Caggiaro in Italy, and with Julian Orbón in New York.

Ernesto Cordero is currently on the faculty of the Music Department at the University of Puerto Rico, and is recognized as both a fine guitarist and a composer of originality. He has appeared as a soloist with the Puerto Rico Symphony Orchestra and has performed in the USA and Europe. He has made several recordings in Puerto Rico, and in recognition of his contribution to guitar literature a concert of his work was organized in Cuba.

SELECTED MUSIC
Concierto Evocativo.	Eschig ME 8702
Concierto Antillano.	Zanibon
Descarga.	MB 94080
Tres Cantigas Negras.	Hubertus Nogatz
Album para La Juventud.	Zanibon ZA 6148
Proteus.	Bèrben EB 2946
Concerto de Bayoan.	Hubertus Nogatz
Modern Times (Vols.1,2,3).	Chanterelle
Due Canzoni Popolari Andaluzie.	Zanibon
Cinco Preludios.	Zanibon

SELECTED READING
Interview.	Guitar International, August 1989
Interview.	Guitar Review, Winter 1989
Interview.	Soundboard, Fall/Winter 1992

SELECTED RECORDINGS
Danzas y Musica Puertoriquena.	ICP C-11 CD
Musica de Ernesto Cordero.	ICP-C14 CD
Concerto Antilano – Costas Cotsiolis.	Musica Viva MV88-045

IRMA COSTANZO

Born –

Buenos Aires, Argentina

18 December 1937

Irma Costanzo

Highly regarded throughout the guitar world as one of Argentina's finest classical guitarists, Irma Costanzo studied the guitar with Abel Carlevaro in Montevideo. Later she studied with Narciso Yepes in Buenos Aires and Paris. For a time she also studied chamber music with Lyenko Spiller.

At the age of sixteen Irma Costanzo won the prize for the best performance in a competition held by the Association of Chamber Music. In 1961 she won first prize in the competition 'Juventudes Musicales de Argentina', and also, in 1962, the Grand Prix of the Fondo de las Artes. Since that time she has established herself as a leading guitar soloist, appearing in concert in most countries of the world including North and South America, Europe, Britain and Japan.

SELECTED RECORDINGS
La Maja de Goya.	EMI (Spain) J063-21010 LP
Villa-Lobos & Turina for Guitar.	EMI (VIC) 30215 LP
Plays Villa-Lobos & Carlevaro.	Qualiton Q1 4000 LP

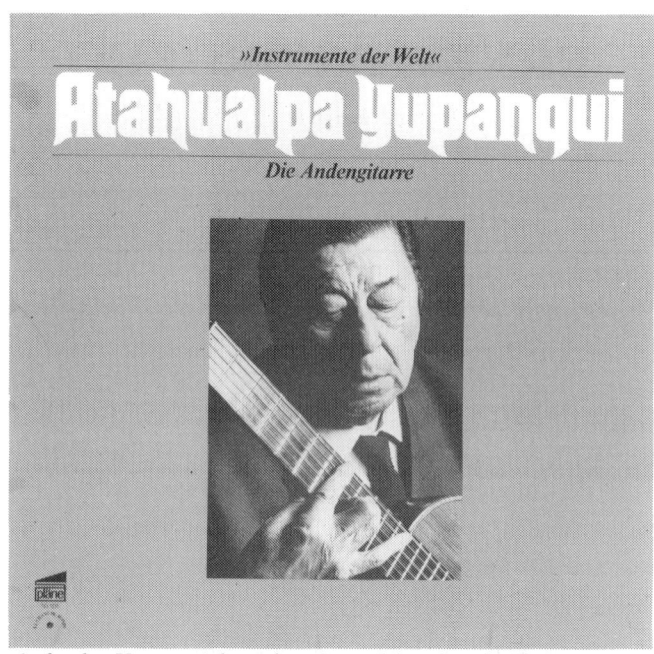

Atahualpa Yupanqui, legendary Argentinian singer/guitarist

A picture on December 31st, 1952 at the Conservatory of Pablo Escobar in Buenos Aires, Argentina. In the back row, fourth from the right, is Pablo Escobar. Jorge Morel is in the middle row, fifth from the right.

NAPOLÉON COSTE

Born – Doubs, France
27 June 1805
Died – Paris, 17 February 1883

Napoléon Coste

Napoléon Coste started to play the guitar at the age of six. By the time he was eighteen he was not only teaching the guitar but appearing regularly as a guitar soloist for the Philharmonic Society of Valencienne, France. For a period of four years, between 1824 and 1828, he took part in several concerts with the guitar virtuoso Luigi Sagrion.

Coste decided to move to Paris in 1830. Here he soon made a name for himself as a guitarist and teacher. His concert performances were attended by the élite of Parisian society, and he received high critical acclaim from the press.

Whilst living in Paris, Coste was able to meet other great masters of the guitar, and developed intimate friendships with Aguado, Carulli, Carcassi and Sor. So impressed was he by these great musicians that he decided to make an even more serious study of the guitar in music. Coste spent the next ten years studying harmony and counterpoint.

In 1840 he first published some of his original compositions for the guitar. He submitted four compositions to the international music contest in 1856 organized in Brussels by Nikolai Makarov, the Russian guitarist, officer and nobleman. His Sérénade won second prize, the first going to J.K.Mertz for his Concertino.

Following his success in the competition, Napoléon Coste was to have over sixty of his compositions published. He wrote a second guitar part, in substitution of the orchestra, to Giuliani's Concerto for Guitar op. 36 making it a guitar duet. He also revised the original edition of Fernando Sor's guitar method for the publisher Schonenberger. It was reprinted by Lemoine of Paris.

Around 1860 Coste fell after a concert and broke his right arm. After this accident he was never able to perform again in public. This was a great tragedy, for there is little doubt that he was one of the greatest guitar virtuosos and composers France has produced. His guitar was bequeathed to the Museum of the National Conservatoire in Paris. This instrument, of Coste's own design, was unique. It was of much larger dimensions than usual, and tuned a fifth lower than the ordinary guitar. It also had a fingerplate raised from the table of the guitar, not unlike those seen on twentieth century jazz guitars.

SELECTED MUSIC

Autumn Leaves – 12 Waltzes op.41.	GA 12
Barcarole, Rondoletto, Marsch.	GA 315
Rêverie.	Ricordi
Rondeau.	EMT 1406
Rondo op.51 no.11.	Bèrben EB 2184
Zur Erholung (The Guitarist's Recreation) op.41 (14 pieces).	GA 13
Complete works of Napoléon Coste.	Chanterelle

SELECTED RECORDINGS

Napoléon Coste Music for Guitar and Oboe (Simon Wynberg) Chandos ABR 1031 LP
Coste & Mertz: Guitar Duets (Simon Wynberg, David Hewitt) (Meridian KE 77095 LP
Raphaëlla Smits plays Napoléon Coste Academix DOR 1 LP
Abendlied-Reiner Stutz. FSM FCD 97789

SELECTED READING

Napoléon Coste's Duets for Guitar and Oboe. Simon Wynberg Classical Guitar, Sept/Oct 1983.

COSTAS COTSIOLIS

Born – CONSTANTINE COTSIOLIS

Athens, Greece

23 July 1957

Costas Cotsiolis

Now one of the foremost classical guitarists in Greece, Costas Cotsiolis began to play the guitar at the age of six, studying with Charalambos Ekmetsoglou at the Hellenic Conservatoire in Athens. He gave his first public recital in 1968 at the age of eleven in the Parnassos Room, Athens.

Between 1970 and 1973 he took part in several international competitions for guitar in France, Italy and Spain. He also studied at various international seminars with Andrés Segovia, Alirio Diaz and José Tomás. Cotsiolis eventually won a total of fifteen international prizes and diplomas for his guitar playing. In 1972 he completed his studies at the Hellenic Conservatoire. In November that year, at the age of fifteen, he performed the Concierto de Aranjuez by Joaquín Rodrigo in Athens with the State Symphony Orchestra.

Since 1972 Costas Cotsiolis has continued an active career as a classical guitarist, and has given concerts and recitals in the principal cities of Greece. He has appeared with the symphony orchestras of Athens and Thessaloniki, and has also broadcast many times on Greek radio and television. In 1976 he became head of the department for classical guitar in the Conservatoire of Athens. In the same year he was appointed the Artistic Director of the International Festival for the Classical Guitar in Volos, Greece.

Since 1978 Costas Cotsiolis has appeared all over Europe and in Russia and Cuba. He has been active in festivals in Esztergom in Hungary, Dubrovnik in Yugoslavia, and Donietsk in the USSR. His book Guitar Technique was published, in Greek, in 1978. Cotsiolis has also recorded for the record companies Electrecord in Romania, and Melodiya in the USSR.

In 1981 he was the featured soloist with the Pro Musica Orchestra of Oxford, England, at the Festival of Athens.

SELECTED RECORDINGS

Constantine Cotsiolis.	MelodiyaS 10-16481-2 LP
Giuliani/Tedesco Concertos.	Electrecord ST-ECE 01930 LP
Concierto de Lieja.	Auvidis, A5846 CD
Concierto Antilliano.	Musica Viva MV 88-045 CD

SELECTED READING

Interview.	Guitar, May 1976
Interview.	Classical Guitar, November 1987

BETHO DAVEZAC

Born –
Rocha, Uruguay
3 August 1938

Betho Davezac

Betho Davezac first learnt to play the guitar at the age of six. His first teacher was his father, a conservatory professor. Davezac soon showed great promise and studied harmony and counterpoint with the composer Guido Santórsola, who at the time was living in Montevideo.

Davezac later attended masterclasses by Andrés Segovia and Alirio Diaz, and led a very active musical life in Uruguay. He was one of the founders of 'Grupo Artemus', which won the Uruguayan Critics' Society prize for the best chamber ensemble in 1965. In 1966 he left Uruguay and went to live in Paris. He soon established himself as a teacher of the classical guitar. He was a prizewinner in the 8th Concours for Guitar held by Radio France in 1966, and later won first prize in both the 1967 Ville de Liège Competition and the 1969 Cittá di Alessandria Competition. His 1974 recording of Elizabethan music was awarded the Grand Prix International du Disque by the Charles Cros Academy. In 1984 he directed the audio-visual spectacle for narrator, synthesiser, guitar orchestra, 'Le Chant du Monde' by Reginald Smith Brindle.

Davezac, who has become a French citizen, performs and gives masterclasses throughout Europe, South America and Japan. He is a professor of guitar at the Conservatoire de Paris XV and also at the Ecole Nationale de Musique de Meudon. From 1981 to 1988 he was the Artistic Director of the Festival de Sablé. He is also the founder and director of the guitar ensemble 'Harmonique 12'.

SELECTED RECORDINGS
Musique Elizabethaine.	Erato STU 70830 LP
Variations sur la Guitare.	Erato STU 70926 LP
Guitare Française du XVIe Siècle.	Erato STU 71334 LP
Guitar Recital	Nippon Columbia 05 10-114N LP

ANIELLO DESIDERIO

Born - Naples,
Italy
13 June 1971

Aniello Desiderio

Aniello Desiderio comes from a musical family. His father is a percussionist, one of his two brothers plays the piano and the other the violin. He first studied the guitar with Bruno Battisti d'Amario and then with Stefano Aruta. He also studied with Leo Brouwer, Costas Cotsiolis and Ernesto Cordero. Desiderio gave his first concert recital at the age of eight, and was featured on several television programmes as a child prodigy.

Desiderio won the 1986 Maurizio Donia Prize in Messina, Italy, and the 1988 Havana International Guitar Competiton Prize. In 1988 he won the Neapolitan Musician of the Year Prize. In 1992 he graduated with honours from the conservatory of music in Alessandria. In the same year he won first prize at the Tárrega Competition held in Benicasim, Spain. In 1994 Desiderio won first prizes at the Cittá di San Remo Competition in Italy and the J.I. Guerrero Competiton in Spain. Since that time he has become regarded as one of Italy's best classical guitarists, and has performed all over the world both as a soloist and with many ensembles and orchestras.

SELECTED RECORDINGS
Aniello Desiderio - Tárrega/Paganini/Aguado/Llobet
　　　　　　　　　　　　　　　　　　Frame FR 9403-2 CD
Aniello Desiderio - José/Brouwer/Dyens/Ginastera
　　　　　　　　　　　　　　　　　　Frame FR 9509-2 CD

SELECTED READING
Profile　　　　　　　　　Classical Guitar, November 1992

ANTON DIABELLI

Born – Mattsee, near Salzburg, Austria

6 September 1781

Died – Vienna, Austria, 7 April 1858

Anton Diabelli

Anton Diabelli was not only one of the finest guitarists of the early part of the nineteenth century, but an excellent pianist and composer. He was also a highly respected publisher of music for both the piano and the guitar, as well as church music. He received his first musical education as a chorister in the Monastery of Michaelbearn, and then at the Cathedral of Salzburg. His parents originally had hoped he would enter the priesthood, and in 1800 he entered the Monastery of Reichenhaslach.

Before he was twenty years old, Diabelli's talents as a composer were already recognized through his many compositions for one or more voices. The guitar was already his main instrument, and most of his vocal arrangements had guitar accompaniment. In 1803 the young guitarist decided to make music his career, and abandoned his original idea to take holy orders. He left for Vienna, where his talents were immediately recognized by many of the musicians living there, including Joseph Haydn, whose brother Michael had supervised Diabelli's musical training.

In 1807 Diabelli struck up a friendship with the guitar virtuoso Mauro Giuliani. There is no doubt that Giuliani was technically the greater guitarist, but he found Diabelli's musicianship stimulating. The guitar had achieved enormous popularity at that time in most of Europe, especially in Vienna, and the two guitarists achieved much success.

As a notable teacher and recitalist of both the guitar and the piano, Diabelli earned a lot of money. He became a partner in the music publishing firm of Peter Cappi in 1818. Six years later, in 1824, he bought out his partner and changed the name of the company to Diabelli and Company. Diabelli became Schubert's main publisher (sometimes complaining that Schubert wrote too much), and the company prospered under his management. He also published the music of Czerny and Strauss, and became a close friend of Beethoven and Schubert. Beethoven used a Diabelli composition as the theme for his famous Variations for Piano op.120.

In 1853 Diabelli sold his copyrights (at that time he had printed over 25,000 works) and business to C. A. Spira. He died in Vienna in 1858 at the age of seventy-six. During his highly successful career as both a musician and a businessman, he had earned enormous respect from his many friends and admirers, and has gone down in history as one of the most important guitar personalities of the nineteenth century.

SELECTED MUSIC

Sonata for Guitar op.29/1 in C Major.	UE 14472
Five Easy Recital Pieces op.39.	GA 322
Little Pieces for Beginners op.39.	UE 14464
Präludium & Andante Cantabile from op.39, ed. Teuchert.	SY 2248
Due Fughe op.46, ed. Ablóniz.	Bèrben EB 2035
Two Fugues op.46: no.1 in Am, no.2 in A.	Ric. 132512
Five Viennese Dances.	UE14463
Four Little Rondos, ed. Schindler.	N 1516
Minuetto from Sonata in C.	Bèrben EB 2177
Präludium from op.103.	GA 321
Sonata in A Major, ed. Bream.	Faber
Sonatina in A Major, ed. Nagel arr. Meunier.	Breitkopf
Three Sonatas.	Kalmus
Twenty-Four Easy Old Viennese Ländler op.121.	GA 85

SELECTED RECORDINGS

Music for Guitar and Piano. Romulo Lazarde.
   Harmonia Mundi HM 435 CD
Diabelli – Complete Sonatas – Anthony Glise.
   Dorian DIS-80113 CD

ALIRIO DIAZ

Born –
Caserio la Candelaria, near Carora, Venezuela
12 November 1923

Alirio Díaz

Aliro Díaz's first guitar teacher was his uncle, who taught him to play by ear. By the age of ten he had already written several interpretations of popular Venezuelan airs. When he was fifteen years old, he was taken by Cecilio Zubbilaga to Trujilla to receive his first lessons in theory and solfeggio with Laudelino Mejias.

Díaz soon achieved great success in his musical studies, but earned his living as a proof-reader. He also wrote articles for a weekly music paper, The Crescent. In 1945 he went to Caracas and advanced his guitar studies, together with Raúl Borges, at the Higher School of Music under the tuition of Clement Pimentel. Díaz was able to pay for his music education with the money he earned playing in military bands and dance orchestras. After his graduation he gave his first recital at the National Library and received high critical acclaim. Subsequent recitals were so successful that in 1958 he was given a grant by the Mnistry of Education to help him travel to Europe to further his guitar and music studies.

After studying in Spain with Regino Sainz de la Maza for one year, Díaz was awarded the first prize at the Royal Conservatory of Music in Madrid. The young guitarist left Madrid for Siena, Italy, and for four years attended special courses given by Andrés Segovia at the Musical Academy of Chigiana. He earned the high distinction of being the assistant professor of guitar on two of these courses.

Alirio Díaz then embarked on a strenuous concert tour of most countries in Europe and the Americas, achieving enormous success. He has made a particularly strong impression amongst guitarists, not only with his superlative guitar technique but also through his many interpretations of the music of his fellow Venezuelans. His renderings of compositions by Antonio Lauro (and those of other South American composers) have established him as one of the most important guitarists of the twentieth century.

SELECTED RECORDINGS

Masters of the Guitar Volume Two.	RCA RB 6599 LP
400 Years of Classical Guitar.	Everest 3155 LP
Virtuoso Guitar.	Vanguard HM 32SD LP
Four Centuries of Classical Guitar.	Vanguard VSD 71135 LP
The Classical Spanish Guitar (2 LPs).	Vanguard VPD 20002 LP
Guitar Music of Spain and Latin America	EMI/HMV HQS 1175 LP
Díaz Plays Bach.	EMI/HMV HQS 1145 LP
Díaz Plays Tedesco Quintet/Ponce-Sonata.	EMI/HMV HQS 1250 LP
Masterpieces of Spanish Guitar.	Vanguard OVC 5004 CD
Four Centuries of Spanish Guitar.	Vanguard OVC 5006 CD
The Art of the Spanish Guitar.	Laserlight 14 129 CD

SELECTED READING

Interview.	Guitar, August 1974
Interview.	Guitar, November 1979
Interview.	Guitar International, May 1988
Article.	Classical Guitar, October 1993
Interview.	Classical Guitar, March 1994

SIMON DINNIGAN
Born - Sheffield,
UK
11 June 1968

Simon Dinnigan

Simon Dinnigan began to play the guitar at an early age. He gave his first public performance at the age of eleven, and his first solo recital at the age of twelve for the Sheffield Music Society. In 1982 he won a scholarship to study under Gordon Crosskey at the prestigious Chetham's School of Music in Manchester. He went on to study at the Royal College of Music in Manchester, and then at the Guildhall School of Music and Drama in London where he won the Principal's Guitar Prize. Whilst at the Guildhall Dinnigan was heard by Jose Tomas and subsequently invited by Tomas to study with him in Alicante, Spain.

In 1981 and 1982 Dinnigan won the Junior Young Musician of the Year Competition held in Sheffield. In 1982 he was overall winner at the Harrogate Music Festival, UK. In 1983, at the age of fourteen, he won second prize at the Domecq International Guitar Competition held in Surrey near London. In 1984 he reached the national string finals of the 1994 BBC Young Musician of the Year Competition.

Simon Dinnigan attended masterclasses given by Andres Segovia, John Williams, David Russell, and Roberto Aussel. He is currently Professor of Guitar at the Birmingham Conservatory of Music, a position he combines with a busy international performing career. In recent years he has played all over Europe, USA, Central and South America, and South-East Asia.

SELECTED RECORDING
Simon Dinnigan   BGS Records   BGCD 101

SELECTED READING
Interview   Classical Guitar, January 1995

MICHEL DINTRICH
Born –
Bar sur Aube, France
10 June 1933

Michel Dintrich

Michel Dintrich is one of the most influential and popular guitarists in France today. He first studied the guitar with Ida Presti at the Schola Cantorum in Paris, and later participated in Andrés Segovia's masterclasses at the Accademia Musicale Chigiana in Siena.

Dintrich has given concerts throughout Europe and North Africa. He has made many transcriptions for the guitar of baroque music. In recent years he has changed to a ten-string guitar, similar to the one developed and used by Narciso Yepes.

As well as playing and teaching the guitar, Michel Dintrich has made several recordings, and broadcasts regularly on French radio and television. He has written and played the soundtrack music of several French films, including Madagascar au Bout de Monde. He also owns a very fine collection of rare antique guitars.

SELECTED RECORDINGS
Recital de Guitarre (2 LPs).	Musidisc 16030
Les Immortels	Barclay 920 104
With Duo Patrice Fontanarosa.	Classic 991 025

CARLO DOMENICONI

Born –

Cesena, Italy

20 February 1947

Carlo Domeniconi began his studies on the guitar in 1960, with Carmen Lenzi Mozzani, granddaughter of Luigi Mozzani. In 1962 and 1964 he won first prize at the Ancona International Festival of Guitar. At the age of eighteen he completed his studies in Pesaro, earning a diploma. He then went to West Berlin, where he obtained a diploma from the Hochschule für Musik in 1966. Since that time Domeniconi has established himself as a concert artist in both the classical and the jazz idioms. He has played and taught throughout Europe, and in recent times has become known as a distinctive composer for the guitar. His compositions often have a Turkish flavour, as can be heard on his recording Koyunbaba, which reflects the time he spent in Turkey. He was a professor of guitar in Istanbul and also taught solfeggio.

SELECTED MUSIC
24 Präludien Vols I & II.	Gitarren-Studio GS 50, GS 51
Gli spiriti	Gitarren-Studio GS 59
Suite Sudamericana.	Gitarren-Studio (GS?) TPM 135
7 Compositions for Guitar.	Rüssl 066 32856
Moon Lights. Bote & Bock	B&B 22695
20 Turkish Folksongs.	Gitarren-Studio GS 65
Koyunbaba Suite	Edition Margaux EM1006
Variations on a Turkish Folk Song.	B&B 23010
Fantasia di luci e tenebre	
Suite in modo antico. Gitarre Aktuell	TPM 137
Orient Express. Gitarre Aktuell	TPM 36
Homage to A. de Saint-Exupéry.	Gitarren-Studio GS 66

Carlo Domeniconi

For two guitars:
Naturgeister.	Edition Margaux EM 2041

SELECTED RECORDINGS
Luci e Tenebre.	Podium Gitarre 8402.11 LP
Koyunbaba.	Bestell-Nr EULP 1044 LP
To Play or not to Play.	Classic Studio 315 2183 CD
Works for Two Guitars w/Silvia Ocougne.	
	Classic Studio 315 2322 CD

SELECTED READING
Interview.	Classical Guitar, April 1989

JOHN W. DUARTE

Born – JOHN WILLIAM DUARTE

Sheffield, England

2 October 1919

John W. Duarte

John Duarte is not only one of the foremost twentieth century composers for the guitar, but is also regarded as a world authority on matters relating to the guitar and its music.

He started playing the ukulele at the age of fourteen, and a year later he was introduced to the plectrum guitar by a local dance band guitarist. Soon afterwards he began to take lessons from Terry Usher in Manchester. Six years later, in 1940, he began to take an active interest in the classical guitar, an instrument on which he was self-taught.

Deciding that the concert platform was not his métier, John Duarte embarked upon an intensive study of the classical guitar as a musical instrument and its relationship to the world of music as a whole. His understanding and panoramic view of the guitar have been invaluably assisted by friendships with many of the world's greatest players, including Andrés Segovia and Ida Presti.

As a composer and arranger, John Duarte has had more than one hundred works published in six countries. Many of these have been recorded by the major guitarists of the age. In 1958 his composition, based on the American folk song 'The Colorado Trail', won first prize in a worldwide competition arranged by the Classical Guitar Society of New York. Duarte currently lives in London, and teaches in all aspects of guitar playing, at all levels. He is the author of several didactic works, including a comprehensive book written specifically for teaching the guitar to children. He has also published a book of technical studies endorsed by Segovia.

A prolific journalist, John Duarte has published hundreds of articles in guitar magazines all over the world. He reviews for 'The Gramophone', writes sleeve notes for guitar records for most of the major record companies, and regularly adjudicates in international guitar competitions. His special talents have made him into one of the most influential guitar personalities of the twentieth century.

SELECTED MUSIC

All in a Row, op.51	Bèrben EB 1971
Birds, op.66. Zanibon	ZA 5733
English Suite, op.31.	Novello NOV 12010108
Fantasia & Fugue on Torre Bermeja, op.30.	Bèrben EB 1717
A Flight of Fugues, op.44.	Broek BVP 1015
Meditation on a Ground Bass, op.5	Schott 11955
Miniature Suite, op.6.	Schott SCS 6
Mutations on the Dies Irae, op.58.	Bèrben EB2042
Night Music, op.65.	G 124
Partita, op.59.	CO 215
Petite Suite Française, op.60	ESC ME 8214
Simple Variations on Las Folias, op.10.	CO 152
Sonatina Lirica, op.48 – Homage to Mario Castelnuovo-Tedesco	Bèrben EB 1972
Sonatinette, op.35.	Novello NOV 19720
Sua Cosa, op.52.	Bèrben EB 2043
Suite Ancienne, op.47.	Bèrben EB 2203
Suite Piemontese, op.46.	Bèrben EB 1514
Three Modern Miniatures, op.9.	Schott SCS 12
Tout en Ronde, op.57 – Ritual Dance, Waltz, Spring Dance.	UE 29153
Variations on a Catalan Folk Song, op.25.	Novello NOV 12031108

SELECTED BOOKS

The Young Person's Way to the Guitar	Novello NOV 12030100
The Guitarist's Hands (with Luis Zea).	Universal UE 26926

SELECTED READING

John Duarte.	Guitar, February 1974
John Duarte	Guitar, March 1975
John Duarte – Complete list of works	Guitar & Lute, October 1979
Interview	Classical Guitar, October 1994

SELECTED RECORDINGS

English Suite Op.31: Segovia.	Decca DL 710140 LP
Neil Smith plays John W. Duarte.	Guitar Masters GMR 1006 LP
Prague Guitar Quartet.	Panton 81-1394-2131 CD

ARNAUD DUMOND

Born –

Paris, France

2 June 1950

Arnaud Dumond

Arnaud Dumond studied at the Ecole Normale de Musique de Paris, from which he earned a concert-level diploma. He studied with Alberto Ponce, Narciso Yepes and Emilio Pujol.

In 1971 Dumond won first prize at the 15th International Guitar Festival presented by Radio France. He was the first French guitarist to win this prestigious event. He also won the Third International Festival of Jeunesses Musicales, held in Belgrade in 1971.

Since that time Arnaud Dumond has performed as a concert guitarist throughout Europe, Scandinavia, Africa, USSR and the USA. He is also a composer of originality and daring, his compositions often reflecting an interest in the possibilities of sound in the context of electronics and prepared tape.

SELECTED RECORDINGS
La Guitare D'Amerique Latine	Cezame CEZ 1048 LP
20th Century Guitar & Recorder Duos	Arc en Ciel SM301261 LP
La Plus Belles Pages de la Guitarre	Pierre Vernay CA 803 LP
Totem	FLM GF001 CD

SELECTED READING
Interview.	Guitar International, September 1987
Interview.	Classical Guitar, August 1985

ROLAND DYENS

Born –

Tunisia, North Africa

19 October 1955

Roland Dyens

Roland Dyens began to study the guitar with Robert Maison at the age of nine. He later enrolled at the Ecole Normale de Musique in Paris, where he studied with Alberto Ponce. Within a short time he was awarded a diploma in concert performance, and in 1979 he was the prize winner at the Palestrina International Competition in Porto Alegre, Brazil. In the same year he won the Special Prize at the Alessandria Competition in Italy.

Roland Dyens has also proved to be an original composer; he studied with Raymond Weber and Désiré Dondeyne. He is currently Professor of Guitar at the Conservatoire de Chaville (Hauts-de-Seine).

SELECTED MUSIC
Eloge de Leo Brouwer.	Lemoine 24975
Hommage à Villa-Lobos.	Lemoine 24885
Libre Sonatine.	Lemoine 24794
Tango en Skaï.	Lemoine 24793
Valse en Skai.	Lemoine 26172
Hommage à Frank Zappa.	Lemoine 26186
French Songs Vol.1.	Lemoine 26112

SELECTED RECORDINGS

Villa-Lobos & Dyens.	Disques S-M 121872 CD
Hommage à Brassens with the Enesco Quartet.	Auvidis AV 4731 CD
Villa-Lobos Concerto.	Auvidis AV 6114 CD
Concerto En Si for Guitar Ensemble.	l'empreinte digitale ED 13030 CD
Ao Vivo.	Celluloid 34550-2 CD
French Songs Vol.1.	SM 122131/SM63 CD
French Songs Vol.2.	l'empreinte digitale ED 1305 3 CD

SELECTED READING

Interview.   Classical Guitar, March 1995

HERBERT J. ELLIS

Born – Dulwich, London, England

4 July 1865

Died – London, 13 October 1903

Herbert J. Ellis

Herbert Ellis's first instrument was the piano, but he became fascinated by the banjo. Although he had no true academic music education, his natural musical talent enabled him to write a highly successful tutor, 'Through School for the Banjo'.

In 1888, with the rising popularity of the guitar and the mandolin, Ellis decided to study and master these other fretted instruments. His 'Through School for Mandolin', which soon appeared, was also highly successful, and several editions had to be printed. He then completed his trio of best-selling fretted instrument tutors with the publication of 'Through School for Guitar'. With its unique and simple manner, this became the most popular guitar method of its type for many years. It is in fact still used today, in a revised edition by Bernard Sheaff.

Herbert J. Ellis proved to be one of the most important and lasting guitar personalities on the English scene. In all, over one thousand of his original compositions for guitar and mandolin were published. Although they were very popular in the latter part of the nineteenth century, they are seldom played today.

MARGARITA ESCARPA

Born - Madrid,

Spain

21 August 1964

Margarita Escarpa

Margarita Escarpa began to study the guitar at the age of nine. She received tuition at the Madrid Royal Music Conservatory from Valentin Bielsa and Demetrio Gallesteros. She received the highest honour possible, the 'Premio Extraordinario Fin de Carrera' from this conservatory in 1990. At the same time she graduated in Mathematical Sciences from the Autonomous University of Madrid. Escarpa went on to study the guitar with José Luis Rodrigo, Gerardo Arriaga, David Russell and Miguel Angel Girollet.

Escarpa was a prizewinner in several important international guitar competitions including the 1988 Young Performers Competition organised by the Spanish Musical Youth Associations, the 1990 Alhambra Competition in Alcoy, the 1991 Esztergom Competition in Hungary, the 1992 Radio France Competition in Paris and the 1993 Andrés Segovia Competition in Palma de Mallorca. In 1994 she was a prizewinner in the Andrés Segovia Competition held in Granada, and the GFA Competition held in Quebec, the latter an important 1st prize that led to an extensive concert tour of the USA.

Margarita Escarpa currently lives in Madrid from where she maintains a busy career as a teacher, international concert recitalist, and recording artist.

SELECTED RECORDINGS

Recital   Spanish National Radio   RNE   M3/05 CD
Moreno Torroba Guitar Works Vols 1 & 2   Opera Tres
                                          CDS 1013/14

GABRIEL ESTARELLAS

Born –

Palma de Mallorca, Spain

14 October 1952

Gabriel Estarellas

Gabriel Estarellas is one of the finest guitarists to emerge from Spain in recent years. He began his music and guitar studies at an early age, and by the time he was twelve he had given his first public recital. This performance was received with great enthusiasm. Estarellas crossed to the mainland of Spain to study with José Tomás, and later completed his musical studies with Gerardo Perez Busquier.

In 1970 Estarellas was awarded the first prize at the 'Ramírez' International Guitar Competition in Santiago de Compostela. In the same year he also won first prize at the Viotti International Guitar Competition.

An intensive concert tour of Europe was made in 1972, during which Gabriel Estarellas gave the first performance of Tansman's concerto for guitar and orchestra, Musique de Cour. Over the next few years the young guitarist was much in demand for concerts and radio and television broadcasts throughout

Europe. In 1975 he won the 'Francisco Tárrega' Competition in Benicasim, Spain. In the same year he gave the first performance of A. Blanquer's Concertino for Guitar and Orchestra. Many contemporary composers, including Richard Stoker, Angelo Gilardino and Bernardo Juliá, have dedicated works to him. In 1978 he was nominated to be the conductor of the Manacor Chamber Orchestra, and in the same year he gave the first performance of Bernardo Juliá's Concierto Juglar for guitar and orchestra.

Gabriel Estarellas currently spends much of his year in Spain, where he holds the post of Director and Professor of Guitar at the Academia de Auditorium, Palma de Mallorca, and also teaches in Madrid.

SELECTED RECORDINGS
Estarellas Interprets.	Fonal MM-S56 LP
Estarellas Interprets Calatayud.	Maller API-86 LP
Gabriel F. Alvez – Complete Guitar Works.	Opera Tres CD1012
Anton G. Abril – Complete Guitar Works.	Caskabel CD 113
Tomas Marco – Complete Guitar Works.	Caskabel CD 108
Angel Barrios – Complete Guitar Works.	Opera Tres CD 1019/20

SELECTED READING
Interview. Classical Guitar, November 1986

REINBERT EVERS

Born –

Dortmund, West Germany

23 August 1949

Although he had been playing the guitar from the age of ten, Reinbert Evers first studied the instrument seriously at twenty-two. His first teacher was Maritta Kersting in Düsseldorf. He went on to study with Karl Scheit in Vienna. From the age of fourteen he had also studied the double bass and had become an accomplished player on this instrument, but gave it up at the age of twenty-two when he made the decision to devote his full time to the guitar.

In 1976 Evers was appointed Professor of Guitar at the Music Academy of Westfalen-Lippe, Institut Münster. In 1980 he received a Young Artist's award from the city of Dortmund.

Over the past few years Reinbert Evers has established himself as one of Germany's finest classical guitarists. He has made many radio broadcasts, several recordings, and performed extensively widely throughout Germany and other parts of Europe. Prominent contemporary composers, including Gunther Becker, Edison Denisov, Tilo Medek, Luca Lombardi and Manfred Trohjahn, have written works especially for him.

SELECTED RECORDINGS
Classical Sonatas for Guitar.	FSM 53221 EB
Virtuoso Fantasias & Variations: F. Sor.	FSM 53213 EB

Reinbert Evers

Twentieth Century Guitar Music.	EMI Electrola CD MD G3292
Galante-Music for Flute and Guitar.	EMI Electrola CD MD G3061
New Guitar Music.	Pro Viva ISPV 118
Royal Winter Music 1 & 2: Henze.	EMI Electrola CD MD G1110
Bach Lute Suites etc.	EMI Electrola MD G1119
Bach Lute Suites etc.	Ambitus CD 97818
Edison Denisov Sonatas.	EMI Electrola MD G1269
Serenades for Flute & Guitar.	Pantheon CD D 14112
Klangsa E Iten.	Ambitus 97 841 CD

SELECTED READING
Interview. Classical Guitar, January 1989

EDUARDO FALU

Born –

El Galpon, Province of Salta, Argentina

7 July 1923

Eduardo Falú

Eduardo Falú is Argentina's best-known folk guitarist/composer and singer. Although not a classical guitarist, he has a brilliant technique on the instrument, and his music over the years has influenced, and become part of, the classical guitar repertoire.

Falú was given a guitar as a child, and soon was playing many of the traditional folk airs of the Argentine. During his teens he formed a duo with Cesar Perdiguero. The partnership was successful, and they soon had many radio broadcasts to their credit. When Perdiguero decided to devote his carer to literature, journalism and poetry, Falú continued his career as a solo artist.

Falú used the classical methods of Sor and Aguado to extend his technique on the instrument to a very high level. To improve his musical knowledge he studied harmony, theory and composition privately with the composer Carlos Guastavino. At the same time he co-operated with many leading Argentinian poets, in particular Jaime Davalos, to write what have now become some of his country's best-loved folk songs. Falú possesses a beautiful natural baritone voice, and as a singer and guitarist has become an international concert performer and prolific recording artist. In recent times he has appeared in duos with his son Juan José Falú, and with the flamenco guitarist Paco Peña. His evocative solos and folk song transcriptions for guitar are played on stage and record by many of today's leading classical guitarists.

SELECTED MUSIC
El Condor Pasa.	BA 13454
Preludio del Pasto.	G + L 111
La Cuartelera.	Ricordi BA 12059
Suite Argentina.	Ricordi BA 13267
Variaciones de Milonga	Ricordi BA 12058
Preludio y Danza	Ricordi BA 12103

SELECTED RECORDINGS
Lo Mejor de Falú.	Caravelle 70-02 7 LP
Señor del Folklore.	Caravelle 70-26 3 LP
Nocheando con Falú.	DM Series 70-159 LP
Eduardo Falú: Solos de Guitarra Vol.2	
	DM Series 50-4548-9 LP
Simplemente Falú.	Epic 60.327 LP
Tonada del Viejo Amor.	Music Hall M-504.031 LP
Falú: A Solas con mi Guitarra.	Music Hall S-32.559 LP
Suite Argentina: Falú & Guastavino Quartet.	
	Philips 812 287-4 CAS
Eduardo Falú: Recital	Philips 818 448-4 LP
Guitarra y Una Voz.	Philips 63 47 160 LP
Eduardo Falú: Vol.1	Aconcagua A-3539 LP
Eduardo Falú: Vol.2	Aconcagua A-3908 LP
Eduardo Falú: Vol.3.	Aconcagua A-4455 LP
Eduardo Falú: Vol.4.	Aconcagua LP
Resolana: Eduardo Falú	Nimbus NI 5281 CD
Encuentro Paco Pena	Nimbus NI 5196 CD
Tonada del Viego Amor	Music Hall MH 10-062 CD

SELECTED READING
Interview.	Guitar International, October 1984
Interview.	Classical Guitar, October 1986
Interview.	Classical Guitar, July 1996

DIMITRI FAMPAS

Born – Melina, near Volos, Greece

22 December 1921

Died – Athens, Greece, 3 May 1996

SELECTED MUSIC
Bolero.	CO 154
Greek Dance No.1.	Ric. 129953
Greek Suite No.4.	BR 3221

SELECTED RECORDINGS
Greek Music for Guitar.	Polydor Greece 45-96 LP
Dimitri Fampas Plays.	Odeon EMI Greece OMGC 67 LP
Eva Fampas plays Dimitri Fampas.	Motivo NP1022 LP

Dimitri Fampas

Dimitri Fampas was one of the most important guitar personalities in Greece. He showed musical talent from an early age. When he was twenty years old he studied the guitar under Niko Ioannou, at the same time studying theory and harmony at the Athens Conservatory. Fampas graduated in 1953, winning not only the first prize in his year but also a special award for his musical ability.

An active concert career followed for Fampas in the major recital halls of Greece. In 1955-56 he won scholarships to study with Andrés Segovia and Emilio Pujol at the Academy of Chigiana in Siena, Italy. In 1959 he again studied with Segovia, in Santiago de Compostela, Spain.

From that time Fampas continued a busy career as a concert artist and teacher. He played in nearly every major European city, and has made several radio broadcasts. He wrote several original compositions for the guitar, which he also recorded. Fampas was involved in teaching, not only in Athens, where he was the Professor of Guitar at the National Conservatory, but also abroad. His daughter Eva is a prominent guitarist and teacher in Athens.

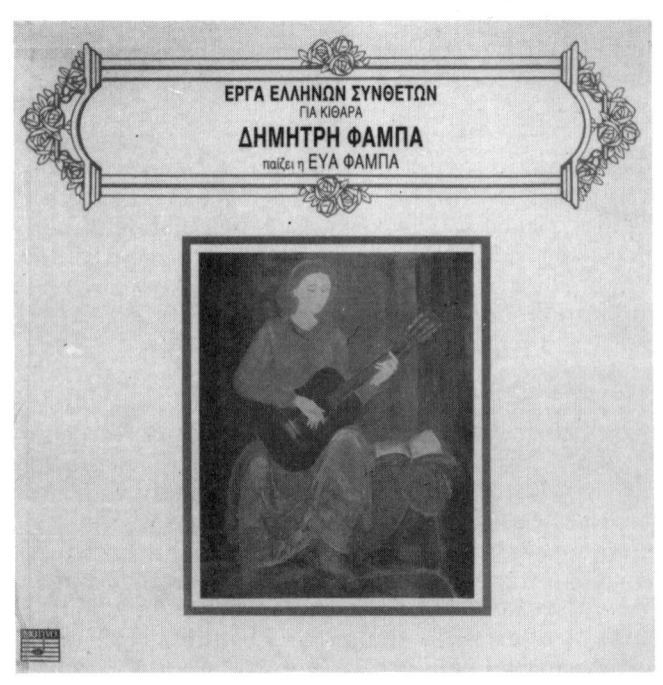

EDUARDO FERNANDEZ

Born –

Montevideo, Uruguay

28 July 1952

SELECTED RECORDINGS
Legnani, Giuliani, Sor, Diabelli, Paganini.	Decca 414 160-1 LP
Rodrigo, Falla, Granados Albéniz, Turina, Torroba.	Decca 414 161-1 LP
Rodrigo, Tedesco Concertos.	Decca 417 199-1 LP
Albéniz, Granados, Tárrega. Turina, Segovia, Llobet.	Decca 417 618-1 LP
Villa-Lobos Preludes/Etudes, Ginastera Sonata.	Decca 414 616-1 LP
Ponce, Brouwer, Savio etc.	Decca 421 816-2 CD
Arnold/Chappell/Brouwer Concertos.	Decca 430 233-2 CD
Previn Guitar Concerto.	Decca 425 107-2 CD
Avant-Garde Guitar.	Decca 433 076-2 CD
Fernando Sor.	Decca 425 821-2 CD
La Danza!	Decca 443 999-2 CD

SELECTED READING
Interview.	Guitar International, July 1984
Interview.	Classical Guitar, October 1985
Interview.	Classical Guitar, May 1993

Eduardo Fernández

Eduardo Fernández began his study of the guitar at the age of seven with Raúl Sanchez, a former pupil of Andrés Segovia. Further studies included work with the composer Guido Santórsola in interpretation, harmony, counterpoint and fugue. His study of the guitar continued with Abel Carlevaro, the famous Uruguayan guitarist.

Fernández began to give concerts in 1963 as part of a duo guitar team with his brother, but since 1971 he has pursued a career as a soloist. He won first prize in the Uruguayan Guitar Society Competition and in the International Competition of Porto Alegre, Brazil. In both competitions the judges were unanimous in their choice. In 1975 he was chosen as one of four finalists in the Radio France Competition in Paris, and in the same year he was a prizewinner in the 'Andrés Segovia' Competition in Palma de Mallorca, Spain.

In 1977 Eduardo Fernández gave a highly acclaimed performance at his United States debut in New York. Since that time he has maintained a very active concert career in both North and South America. He has also taught at several international guitar seminars, including those held in São Paulo and Buenos Aires.

ZANI DE FERRANTI

Born – MARCO AURELIO MARIA LUIGI
FELICE GIOVANNI
BATTISTA DE FERRANTI
Bologna, Italy, 23 December 1801
Died – Pisa, Italy, 28 November 1878

SELECTED MUSIC
Trois Mélodies Nocturnes et une Etude.   Leduc
Selected Works.   ECH 416
Complete Works of Zani de Ferranti (14 volumes).
Chanterelle ECH 900

SELECTED RECORDINGS
Zani de Ferranti and José Ferrer Simon Wynberg.   Chandos
CHAN 8512 CD

SELECTED READING
Zani de Ferranti: Biography (Simon Wynberg)
Chanterelle (1989)
Ferranti, Makaroff and the 1856 Competition: Simon Wynberg.
Classical Guitar, July 1989

Zani de Ferranti

At the age of twelve Zani de Ferranti was recognised as a child prodigy, not only as a violinist but also as a poet and linguist.

In 1818 he made a highly successful concert tour of Europe on the violin. Everywhere he played, his virtuoso performances were received with high acclaim. In 1820 he went to Russia and gained the position of librarian to Senator Miatleff in St Petersburg. A little later he was appointed secretary to Count Kyrille Alexandrovich Narischkin, a cousin of the Tsar. It was during his stay in Russia that Ferranti became attracted to the guitar, and within a relatively short period of time he became a virtuoso guitarist. He gave his first public recital as a guitarist in Hamburg, Germany, in 1824. He later played in Brussels (1821), Paris (1826) and London (1827).

Ferranti toured the United States of America in 1845 with the famous violinist Camillo Sivori. On his return to Europe in 1846 he was appointed Court Guitarist to King Leopold of Belgium. In 1854 he once again made a concert tour of France and Italy. At the end of this tour he decided to remain in Bologna, his native town. Ferranti continued to devote his life to the guitar, both playing and composing, until his death in Pisa, in 1878 at the age of seventy-six.

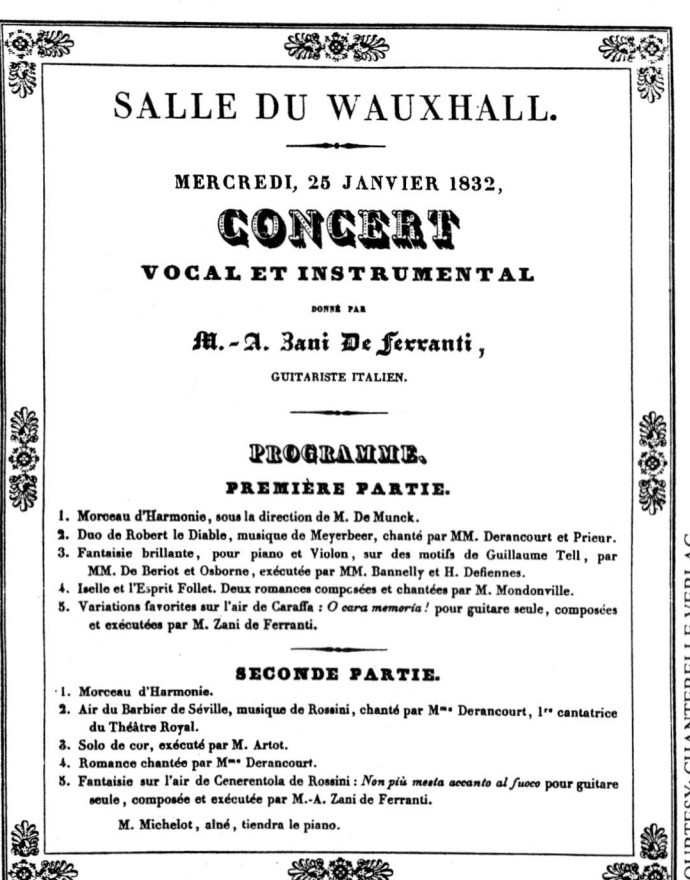

1932 Concert Programme

COURTESY: CHANTERELLE VERLAG

ELIOT FISK

Born –
Philadelphia, USA
10 August 1954

Eliot Fisk

Eliot Fisk began to study the guitar at the age of seven. His father was a professor of marketing at the Wharton School of the University of Pennsylvania. He studied first with William Viola in Philadelphia, and performed his first solo recital at the age of thirteen. In 1970 he won a full scholarship to the Aspen Music School, where he studied with Oscar Ghiglia before joining the Aspen faculty as Ghiglia's assistant at the age of eighteeen. In the same year he received a grant to study at the Banff School of Fine Arts with Alirio Diaz.

Eliot Fisk graduated summa cum laude from Yale College in 1976. His studies there with Ralph Kirkpatrick, the noted harpsichordist and Scarlatti scholar, inspired him to continue his interest in expanding the guitar repertoire through transcriptions of works by Scarlatti, Haydn, Mozart, Beethoven and Paganini, amongst others. In 1977 he received his MA degree from the Yale School of Music, and that autumn he founded the School's guitar department.

In addition to teaching at Yale, Eliot Fisk serves on the faculty of the Aspen School of Music and frequently gives masterclasses at universities throughout the USA. While keeping a demanding solo concert schedule, he has performed in duo recitals with the renowned soprano Victoria de los Angeles. He is also a co-founder of the Concerto Soloists of Philadelphia, with whom he has appeared as a soloist at the Wolf Trap and in the group's Carnegie Hall debut in 1979.

As his many concert performances and recordings have confirmed, Eliot Fisk is without doubt one of the world's finest classical guitarists. Since 1996 he has been on the guitar faculty of the New England Conservatory in Boston.

SELECTED RECORDINGS

Plays Scarlatti and Bach.	MLAR C45 000 006 LP
Latin American Guitar.	Music Masters MM 20008 LP
American Virtuoso.	Music Masters MM 20032 LP
Eliot Fisk Plays Scarlatti etc.	Gitarre & Laute G & L 8201 LP
Eliot Fisk Plays Villa-Lobos, Morel, Barrios etc.	EMI 14-6757-1 CD
Guitarra Española.	EMI 27-0216-1 CD
Guitar Fantasies.	Music Masters 67008-2 CD
Bell Italia.	Music Masters 67079-2 CD
Paganini 24 Caprices.	Music Masters 67092-2 CD
Vivaldi Concerti.	Music Masters 67097-2 CD
Latin American Guitar.	Music Masters 67127-2 CD
Scarlatti, Bach and Froberger.	Music Masters 67128-2 CD
Baroque Guitar.	Music Masters 67130-2 CD
Sequenza.	Music Masters 67150-2 CD
Fur Eliot.	GSP 1008 CD
Segovia – Canciones Populares.	Music Masters 67174-2 CD

SELECTED READING

Eliot Fisk.	Guitar Player, June 1980
Eliot Fisk.	Guitar & Lute, July 1981
Interview.	Classical Guitar, May 1985
Interview.	Guitar International, December 1989
Interview.	Classical Guitar, March 1991

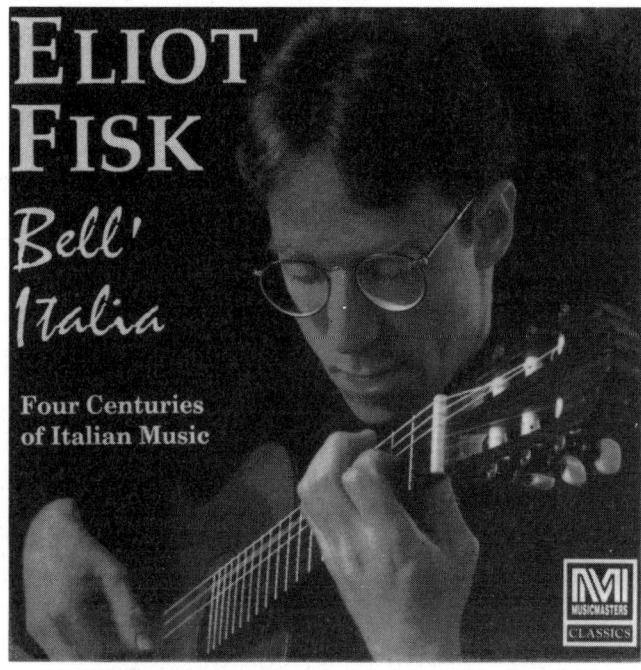

ABEL FLEURY

Born - Dolores, Argentina 5 April 1903
Died - Buenos Aires, Argentina
9 August 1958

Abel Fleury

Abel Fleury first studied the guitar and composition with Pascual Galeano, Froilan Rojas and Honorio Sicardi. He later studied in 1928-29 with Domingo Prat. As a young man he was a championship standard chess player.

Fleury appeared in a duo with Remo Ricco at the Fiesta de la Guitarra held in the Teatro Colon, Mar del Plata on 9 September 1927. In 1933 he moved to Buenos Aires. Here his association with the poet Capitan Sarmiento brought him wide public recognition. His guitar ensembles, consisting of ten to fifteen guitarists, also caused a lot of public interest, with frequent national tours and radio broadcasts. He transcribed and arranged for the guitar many works of the great classical composers. In the 1940s and 1950s he toured Uruguay, Chile, Brazil and parts of Europe as a solo concert recitalist.

Fleury maintained a busy career as a teacher and recitalist throughout his relatively short life, but he made a major impact on the guitar in Argentina as a prolific composer who closely followed the folkloric forms of the Argentine Pampas tradition.

SELECTED RECORDINGS
The Guitar of the Pampas - Roberto Lara
Lyrichord LLST 7253 LP

SELECTED MUSIC
El Cuando	Antigua Casa Nunez
Estilo Pampeano	Antigua Casa Nunez
Milonga del Ayer	Antigua Casa Nunez
Relato	Antigua Casa Nunez
Ausencia	Antigua Casa Nunez

SELECTED READING
Abel Fleury - El Poeta de la Guitarra
Hector Garcia Martinez BA (1988)

WILLIAM FODEN

Born – St Louis, USA

23 March 1860

Died – St Louis, 9 April 1947

William Foden

William Foden was of English ancestry. His father was the owner of a music store in St Louis. Foden's instrument was the violin, and he began his musical studies at the age of seven. By the time he was sixteen he had already become the leader of a local orchestra. At the same age, he became attached to the guitar, an instrument played by one of his school friends.

In 1887 he became a member of a professional trio comprising violin, flute and guitar. In the same year he organized the Beethoven Mandolin and Guitar Orchestra, later known as the Foden Mandolin and Guitar Orchestra.

Foden's first concert as a guitar soloist was on 29 January 1904, when he appeared at the Carnegie Hall, New York. By that time he was accepted as a virtuoso of the guitar, and his frequent public performances were highly acclaimed by critics and audiences alike.

In 1921 William Foden published in two volumes his Guitar School (William J. Smith & Company, New York). The work proved very practical in its development of technique through easy pieces to more difficult pieces. He also published a graded series of guitar lessons as a correspondence course, as well as two books of guitar chords and chord progressions. His most important work, begun in 1904 and completed in 1941, was his Grand Sonata for Guitar.

William Foden spent many years as a leading teacher and recitalist in New York. In his later years he returned to St Louis, continuing to devote his life to teaching and playing the guitar. An outstanding musician, William Foden was one of the foremost guitar personalities and players the United States has produced.

SELECTED MUSIC
Six Short Preludes.   CO 159
American Guitar Pioneers.   Mel Bay Publications

SELECTED READING
William Foden's Guitar Idiom – John F. Green.
                                    Soundboard, Spring 1991.
Special Issue.   Guitar Review, Summer 1995
Article.   Soundboard, Spring 1996

SELECTED RECORDING
American Guitar Pioneers – Douglas Back.
                              Mento Music SMM 3023 CD

DANIEL FORTEA

Born - DANIEL FORTEA GUIRMERA
Bennloch, Castellón de la Plana, Spain
28 April 1878
Died – Castellón, 5 March 1953

Daniel Fortea

Daniel Fortea is regarded by many as one of the most important guitarists and teachers that Spain has produced. He began to study the guitar at an early age, using the methods of Aguado and Tárrega. At the age of twenty he began to take lessons with Francisco Tárrega in Castellón. He made such good progress that on several occasions Tárrega devoted part of his concert programmes to guitar duos with him.

In 1909, after Tárrega's death, Daniel Fortea moved to Madrid, where he became a popular and successful concert artist. It was in Madrid that he founded the Academia de Guitarra and also the Biblioteca Fortea, which eventually became a world-famous publisher of guitar music.

Fortea also edited and published a regular news sheet, Boletin Revista de la Biblioteca Fortea, which first appeared in 1935 and which, apart from its news items, contained a regular music supplement.

Daniel Fortea was a prolific composer for the guitar. He also made hundreds of transcriptions from classical and modern composers, as well as a Method for Guitar (based on the studies of Sor and Aguado), which was published in 1921. A second edition, in two volumes, was published in 1930.

Daniel Fortea continued to devote his life to the guitar right up to his death, following a heart attack at the age of 75, in 1953.

FRANÇOIS DE FOSSA

Born – Perpignan, France
31 August 1775
Died – Paris, 33 June 1849

François de Fossa

It was only after the publication of Matanya Ophee's book 'Luigi Boccherini's Guitar Quintets – New Evidence' (Editions Orphée, 1981) that François de Fossa's ability as a guitarist, composer and arranger became widely recognized.

François de Paule Jacques Raymond de Fossa joined an army regiment in 1793 at the age of seventeen. This unit, the Legion de Pyrenees, was one of many French emigré groups that joined the Spanish coalition, fighting the new revolutionary government in France. From this time, and for most of his life, de Fossa was to lead a long and distinguished career as a military officer in various regiments of the French army. Parallel to this career, it has now been revealed that de Fossa was active as a fine musician and guitarist.

De Fossa was a friend of Dionisio Aguado (1784-1849). He collaborated with Aguado on that famous guitarist's method, which was first published in 1825. He was also the copyist of Boccherini's well-known guitar quintets. Around 1826, Richault of Paris published his own three guitar quartets Opus 19. De Fossa also made many arrangements for classical guitar of popular opera overtures of the day by Piccinni, Boieldieu, Spontini and others. These arrangements and de Fossa's original works reveal the influence of some of the leading contemporary composers, including Beethoven, Haydn and Boccherini. The technical demands of the guitar parts in de Fossa's quintets, which give full status to the instrument in the ensemble, prove the high calibre of his ability on the instrument.

SELECTED READING
Luigi Boccherini's Guitar Quintets New Evidence.
Matanya Ophee (Editions Orphée 1981)
François de Fossa's Three Quartets op.19
Classical Guitar, April 1985

SELECTED MUSIC
Three Guitar Trios, op.18.	Chanterelle ECH 506
Three Guitar Quartets, op.19	Chanterelle ECH 524

SELECTED RECORDINGS
François de Fossa: Three Guitar Quartets Op.19
Simon Wynberg and the Gabrieli String Quartet.
Chandos ABRD 1109
K. Yamashita – François de Fossa RCA BVCC-719 CD
Simon Wynberg – Trio Concertante Naxos 8-550760 CD

ALEXANDER FRAUCHI
Born –
Rostov, Yaroslavski, USSR
4 January, 1954

Alexander Frauchi

Alexander Kamilovich Frauchi first learnt to play the violin, receiving lessons from his father. At the age of ten he changed to the guitar, and in 1969 entered the guitar class at the Tchaikovsky Conservatory in Moscow. His teacher was Natalia Ivanova-Kramskaya. He graduated in 1973 with honours, and in 1974 went on to study with Professor Dezun at the Sverdlovsk Conservatory.

In 1979 Alexander Frauchi completed the course at the Mussorgsky Conservatory and went on to win the first prize in a national music competition held in Leningrad. Then, in 1986, he won first prize in the Havana International Guitar Competition, Cuba. Since then he has led a busy career as a concert artist and teacher, and is now recognized as one of the best classical guitarists to appear in the Soviet Union in recent years.

Alexander Frauchi is professor of guitar at the Gosudarstvenny Musicalno-Pedagichesky Institut imeni Gnesinykh in Moscow.

SELECTED RECORDINGS
Alexander Frauchi.   Melodiya C10-17193-4 LP

SELECTED READING
Interview.   Guitar International, November 1986
Interview.   Classical Guitar, December 1986

JOAQUIM FREIRE
Born -
Recife, Brazil
6 August 1956

![Joaquim Freire]
Joaquim Freire

Joaquim Freire spent his childhood in Chile, and it was there that he started to play the guitar. He moved to Switzerland with his family when he was thirteen years old. Freire went on to study music and the guitar at the conservatories in Geneva and Lausanne.

Joaquim Freire has established himself as an international concert and recording artist, and is currently active in a duo with guitarist Susanne Mebes. He also teaches guitar at the Conservatoire de Fribourg.

SELECTED RECORDINGS
Ponce/Villa-Lobos/Ginastera Leman Classics LC 42601 CD
Nobre/Villa-Lobos   Leman Classics LC 44601 CD
Freire/Mebes Guitar Duo   Leman Classics LC 44401 CD

Italian Chitarra Battente (17th century)

SHIN-ICHI FUKUDA

Born -

Osaka, Japan

25 December 1955

Shin-ichi Fukuda

Shin-ichi Fukuda began to study the guitar at the age of 12 with Tatsuya Saito. He was a prizewinner at the 3rd and 4th Japan Guitar Competitons held in Osaka 1976 and 1977 respectively. Fukuda went on to study in France. In 1978 he graduated from the Ecole Normale de Musique in Paris with the highest score in his grade. In the same year he won first prize at the 4th Gargnano International Guitar Competition in Italy.

In 1981 Fukuda won 1st prize at the 23rd International Guitar Competiton in Paris. Earlier that year he had won 2nd Prize in the guitar section of the 27th Maria Canals International Competiton in Barcelona, Spain. Fukuda also studied privately with Alexandre Lagoya, Alberto Ponce, Oscar Ghiglia, John Williams and Manuel Barrueco. In 1985 he won the Osaka Art Festival Award with his 'Guitar Cycles '85' recital. In 1987 Fukuda was selected as the 'Best Performer of the Year' for the Muramatsu's Newcomer Award.

In recent years Shin- ichi Fukuda has established himself as one of the world's finest classical guitarists. He concertises on a regular basis throughout Japan and many other countries of the world, and is also a major recording artist for the JVC and Denon companies.

SELECTED RECORDINGS

Guitar Recital	JVC VDC-1213
Invocation et Dance	JVC VDC-1100
Tango	JVC VDC-1210
The Music of Spain	JVC VDC-1237
Platero & I	JVC VDC-1336
Villa-Lobos Complete Guitar Solo Works	JVC VDC-1405
All In Twilight	JVC VICC-78
19th Century Guitar	Denon COCO-78950
Aquarelle	JVC VICC-173
Schubertiana	Denon COCO-78978
Jongo	JVC VICP-228
Golden Duo w/ Shingeri Kudou Vol 1	JVC VDC-1278
Golden Duo w/ Shingeri Kudou Vol 2	JVC VDCC-35
Golden Duo w/ Shingeri Kudou Vol 3	JVC VICC-93

PAUL GALBRAITH

Born –
PAUL MICHAEL GALBRAITH
Edinburgh, Scotland, 18 March 1964

Paul Galbraith with his Rubio 'Brahms' guitar

PHOTO: MAURICE J. SUMMERFIELD

Paul Galbraith studied the piano at first, but changed to the guitar when his parents bought him one for his ninth birthday. After playing folk and popular music for a year he was advised to begin classical guitar. His first classical teacher was Graham Wade, who at that time, like the Galbraith family, was living in London. After a few months the Galbraiths moved to Cornwall, where the young guitarist continued his studies with Ian Jackson. In 1975 Paul returned to Edinburgh with his family, where he attended St Mary's Specialist Music School. There he studied piano with Francesca Uhlenbruek and guitar with Barry Shaw.

Encouraged by the distinguished Venezuelan guitarist Alirio Díaz, Galbraith studied with Gordon Crosskey in Manchester. From 1975 to 1978 he studied at Chetham's School of Music in Manchester, and from 1978 to 1981 he completed his studies at the Royal Northern College of Music. During this period he studied guitar with Gordon Crosskey and took part in many school concerts and recitals for guitar societies.

In 1980 he gained third prize in the string section of BBC TV's prestigious Young Musician of the Year Competition, going on in 1982 to win first prize in the same competition. This success, and his second prize in the 1981 Segovia International Competition held at Leeds Castle, Kent, led to many television, radio and concert appearances throughout Great Britain and Europe. Later study was done with the pianist and composer George Georgiadis.

Paul Galbraith is a guitarist of great talent, and has established himself as one of Britain's foremost classical guitarists.

In 1994 Galbraith developed, with luthier David Rubio, 'The Brahms Guitar'. This instrument, based on the 16th century orphareon, has two extra strings. One fitted to each side of the usual six strings. The top string is an A, the bottom a low C or A. Paul Galbraith now plays this guitar for all his concerts. The extra strings extend the guitar's range, and also simplify fingering in Bach and other music where voicing is of paramount importance.

SELECTED RECORDING
Music of Ponce.   Watercourse Records WCR CD-01
Introducing the Brahms Guitar.
                                   Watercourse Records WCR CD-02

SELECTED READING
Interview.   Guitar, September 1982
Article.   Classical Guitar, October 1984

JOSÉ MARIA GALLARDO DEL REY

Born Seville, Spain

18 May 1961

José Maria Gallardo del Rey

PHOTO: O. GOMEZ SEBLECHERO

José Maria Gallardo del Rey was born into a musical and artistic family. His grandfather had been a composer and conductor. Gallardo del Rey began to play the guitar at the age of nine. As a youth he studied at with America Martinez at the junior department at the conservatory in Seville. He continued with his studies at the conservatory for nine years, attending classes in harmony, counterpoint, choral singing and the history of music. In 1979 he was awarded his degree in Performance with highest honours. He also studied composition and conducting, and received additional honours in theory, guitar, chamber music and pedagogy.

Gallardo del Rey moved to Granada to study for four years under José Tomás. During this time he attended a masterclass given by Segovia in Granada. He also attended summer courses given by Regino Sainz de la Maza and Rodrigo de Zayas. He went on to win first prizes in several international competitions including the 1979 and 1981 international competitions held in Santiago de Compostela, and the Medal of Honour in the 1981 Maria Canals International Competiton of Musical Execution held in Barcelona.

In recent years Gallardo del Rey has held important teaching positions at the Conservatory of Seville, and the Conservatory of San Lorenzo de El Escorial. At the same time he maintains a full schedule as a concert guitarist performing throughout Europe and in the Americas.

SELECTED RECORDINGS

In Memoriam - Andrés Segovia
    Junta de Andalucia DS 0112
Suite Sevilla w/ Rafael Riqueni   JMS 065-2 CD
Concierto Romantico   SoSoSol Records 001CD
Concierto en Varsovia   Elbo 1142 CD
Carta Abierta   CDM 167 M14359

SELECTED READING

Interview   Guitar International, April 1990

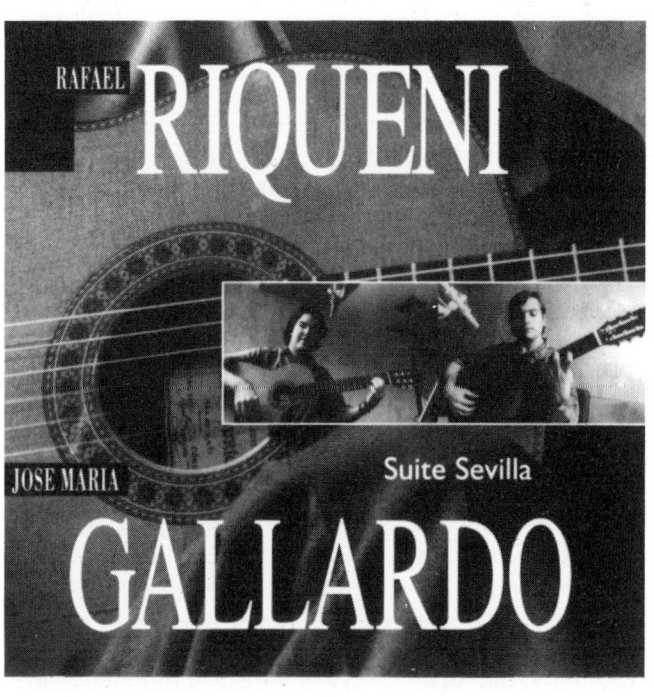

GERALD GARCIA

Born –

Hong Kong

11 August 1949

Gerald Garcia

Gerald Garcia studied chemistry at New College, Oxford, graduating in 1971. At the same time he showed great talent, mainly self-taught, as a classical guitarist. Encouraged by John Williams, Garcia developed his natural talents on the guitar and made his Wigmore Hall debut in 1979.

Since that time Gerald Garcia has made several tours of Europe and the Far East. He has played with many leading ensembles and musicians including the London Sinfonietta, Paco Peña and the cellist Rohan de Saram. With his own group 'Attacca' he has written and performed many of his own arrangements. As a teacher and lecturer he has been involved in workshops with the English National Opera and Kent Opera.

Gerald Garcia has broadcast in numerous countries on both radio and television and is much in demand as a concert artist offering a wide repertoire, both as a soloist and an ensemble artist.

SELECTED RECORDINGS
Garcia/Conway – Flute & Guitar Duo
                              Psyche Records PSY 1LP
Chinese Popular Music for Violin & Guitar. HK Records LP
Concierto de Aranjuez/Granados/Albéniz.
                              Naxos CD 8-550220
Brazilian Portrait.   Naxos CD 8-550226
Latin American Guitar Festival.   Naxos CD 8-550273
Romantic Favourites.   Naxos CD 8-550296
Baroque Guitar Concert.   Naxos CD 8-550274
Romantic French Music.   Naxos CD 8-550480

SELECTED READING
Interview.   Guitar, September 1980
Gerald Garcia & New Music.   Classical Guitar, July 1986
Interview.   Classical Guitar, December 1987

SELECTED MUSIC
25 Etudes Esquisses.   Mel Bay Publications

HECTOR GARCIA

Born –

Havana, Cuba

19 November 1930

Hector García

Hector García's first guitar teachers were Eduardo Saborit and Fela Gonzáles Ruberia. He completed his education, receiving Master of Guitar and Master of Music degrees from Peyrellade Conservatory. On graduation in 1954, he joined the faculty at Peyrellade as an instructor of classical guitar, and remained there until 1960. During this period he also performed as a concert guitarist and as a soloist with various orchestras. He then decided to further his education by studying with Emilio Pujol in Barcelona, Spain.

In 1960 Hector García left Cuba, but was taken prisoner after the 'Bay of Pigs' invasion of that country. Although he had no musical instrument in prison, he did continue to compose a lot of music for the guitar. He was released on 24 December 1962 and went to the United States of America. He moved to Albuquerque, New Mexico, in 1963 and resumed his career as a concert guitarist. He gave concerts on the West Coast and also performed as soloist with the Los Angeles Symphonette. He also performed in New York's famed Town Hall, the Smithsonian Institute in Washington D.C. and other principal cities in the east. An extensive concert tour of major European cities included Madrid, Barcelona, Bilbao, Paris, London, Stockholm, The Hague, Amsterdam, Brussels and the Canary Islands.

He was honoured by the outstanding contemporary composer Mario Castelnuovo-Tedesco, who wrote a guitar composition on the name of Hector García. In 1967 García was appointed to the faculty of the University of New Mexico when the chair in classical guitar was established. He has generated a high degree of interest there in the classical guitar, drawing students from throughout the United States. The programme includes intensive study and research in the history of the guitar and its literature.

In 1969 García was appointed assistant to Emilio Pujol in the masterclasses held for guitarisrts in Cervera (Lerida), Spain.

SELECTED READING
Hector García.   Guitar Player, June 1975

OSCAR GHIGLIA

Born –

Livorno, Italy

13 August 1938

Oscar Ghiglia

Oscar Ghiglia grew up in an artistic atmosphere: his mother was a pianist, his father a painter. Initially it was thought he would become a painter. His father wanted to paint a family portrait one day, and to entice his son to remain still during the long sittings put a guitar into his hands, each session teaching him a bit more of the rudiments of playing. By the time the painting was done, Oscar Ghiglia had decided to become a professional guitarist and not a painter.

Ghiglia enrolled in Rome's Santa Cecilia Conservatory. His teacher was Benedetto di Ponio. After graduating with honours in 1961, he was admitted to Andrés Segovia's masterclasses in Siena, and made his professional debut at the Festival of Two Worlds in Spoleto the following year. In 1963 he was the judges' unanimous choice for the first prize at the International Guitar Competition in Paris, and he then won first prize at the Guitar Competition in Santiago de Compostela, Spain. Then came an invitation from Segovia to be his assistant for two years at the University of California, at Berkeley. With this rare honour, Oscar Ghiglia's career took on great momentum, and many international recitals and concerts soon followed. In addition to appearing extensively in all parts of North and South America and Europe, Oscar Ghiglia is a frequent performer in the Far East, Israel, Australia, New Zealand and the South Pacific.

Oscar Ghiglia is very much in demand as a teacher all over the world. In North America he has given masterclasses in, among others, Chicago, Detroit, Los Angeles, Salt Lake City and Toronto. He has also taught at the University of Missouri, Southern Methodist University, Florida State University, the San Francisco and Cincinnati Conservatories, and the Juilliard School and Mannes College. Since 1969 he has been Artist-in-Residence at the Aspen Festival, and from 1976 he taught annually in Siena.

SELECTED RECORDINGS
Schubert & Carulli for Guitar.	World Record Club ST 1040 LP
Paganini for Guitar and Violin	EMI/HMV CSD 3511 LP
Guitar Music of Four Centuries	Angel S 36282 LP
The Guitar in Spain.	Angel S 36508 LP
Spanish Guitar.	Angel S 36849 LP
Ghiglia Plays Baroque Masters	Angel S 39715 LP

SELECTED READING
Interview.	Guitar Player, March 1972
Interview.	Guitar, August 1974
Interview.	Guitar International, July 1989

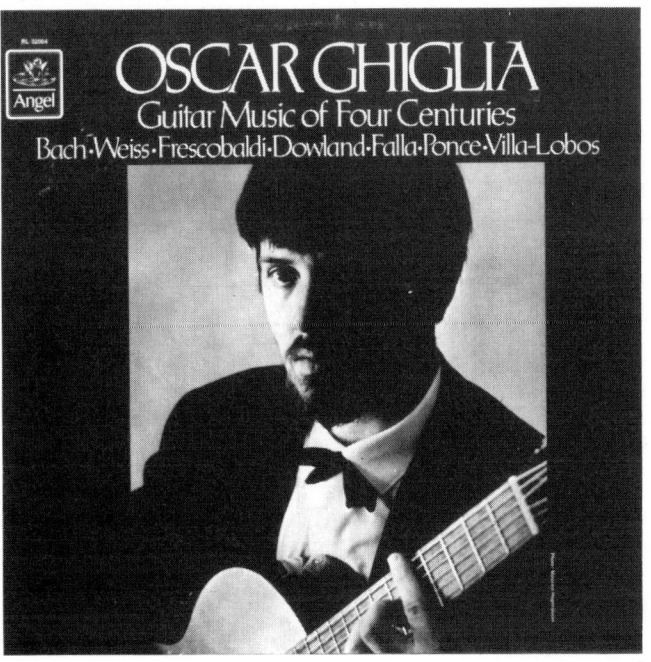

ANTHEA GIFFORD

Born -
Bristol, UK
17 February 1949

Anthea Gifford

Anthea Gifford first studied the guitar at school in Bristol. Her tutor was Michael Watson. She made quick progress and at the age of fifteen went to Siena to study with Alirio Diaz. In 1965 she was awarded a place at the Royal College of Music in London to study under John Williams.

After graduating from the Royal College of Music Gifford has led a very active performing career, both as a soloist and in ensemble. She broadcasts regularly for the BBC. She has performed with the Amici String Quartet, the Cummings String Trio, the Chilingirian String Quartet, the tenors Neil Jenkins and Alexander Young and the pianist Keith Swallow. In 1982 she formed a duo with the violinist Jean-Jaques Kantorow, and this long standing musical partnership continues to enjoy great success.

Gifford has commissioned several new works for the guitar, including Stephen Dodgson's Duo Concertante for violin, guitar and strings. This work was given its first performance in the 1991 City of London Festival by the City of London Sinfonia with Anthea Gifford as the guitar soloist.

SELECTED RECORDINGS
Kantorow/Gifford Duo	BBC Records BBC CD 845
Anthea Gifford at Coughton Court	National Trust CD 001
Kantorow/ Gifford Duo	National Trust CD 003

SELECTED READING
Interview	Guitar, January 1973
Interview	Guitar International, March 1984
Interview	Classical Guitar, February 1994

MIGUEL ANGEL GIROLLET

Born - Buenos Aires, Argentina 1947
Died - Madrid, Spain 24 April 1996

Miguel Angel Girollet

Miguel Angel Girollet studied with Graciela Pomponio and Jorge Martinez Zarate in the Juan José Castro Conservatory in Buenos Aires. He went on to study with Abel Carlevaro and Ljerko Spiller.

Girollet was a prizewinner at several international guitar competitions. After this he established himself as a successful recitalist on the world concert circuit, and for a considerable time was a member of the Zarate-Pomponio Guitar Quartet. He was also a professor at several music conservatories in Argentina, and taught for ten years at the international seminar in Porto Alegre, Brazil. In his last few years he lived in Madrid, Spain.

SELECTED RECORDING
Musica Barroca – Recital	Opera Tres CD 1006

An interesting nineteenth century music cover

Mauro Giuliani

MAURO GIULIANI

Born – Bisceglie, near Bari, Italy
27 July 1781
Died – Naples, Italy, 8 May 1829

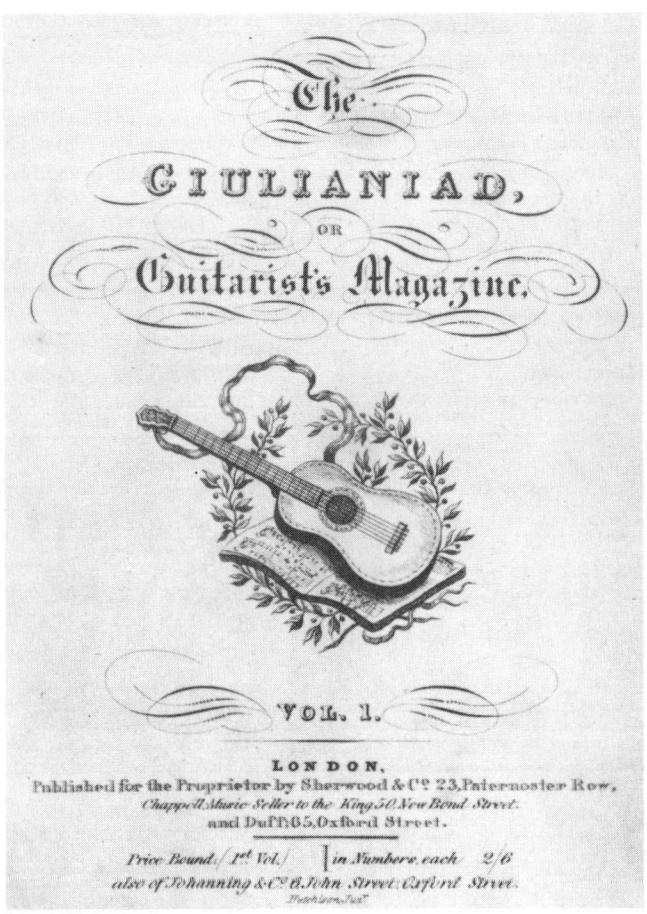

The 'Giulianiad' magazine

Mauro Giuliani was one of the most famous nineteenth century guitarists and probably one of the most brilliant guitar virtuosos ever.

As a young boy, Giuliani could play the violin, flute and guitar well, but by his teens the young musician had decided to devote his life to the guitar. A self-taught player, Giuliani not only was a great guitarist, but also became one of the instrument's supreme composers.

By the time he was twenty years old, Giuliani was already regarded as a virtuoso in his native Italy. A European concert tour in 1800 established his reputation throughout the continent. For the next seven years he continued to give recitals in the major cities of Europe.

In 1806 Giuliani settled in Vienna, one of the great musical centres of Europe. There he led a highly successful career as a teacher and recitalist. His musicianship and artistry are said to have inspired Beethoven to say that 'The guitar is a miniature orchestra', a comment used by Berlioz years later. He was appointed Chamber Musician and Teacher to the Arch-Duchess Marie Louise. Many members of the Austrian royal family and nobility studied the guitar with him. He developed close friendships with Moscheles, Hummel and Diabelli, who was himself a fine guitarist.

Giuliani was a prolific composer for the guitar. Over three hundred of his compositions were published, ranging from very simple exercises and studies to works demanding virtuoso ability. Among these are several concertos with orchestral accompaniment, duets for violin, and duets for flute and guitar. The first guitar magazine ever published, the 'Giulianiad', was named in his honour. It was first published in London in 1833.

Mauro Giuliani died in Naples at the age of forty-eight. One hundred and sixty years later his reputation is undiminished, and his outstanding contribution is celebrated daily in performances of his remarkable music throughout the world.

SELECTED MUSIC
Complete Works. Tecla Editions
Various Works. Suvini
Complete Giuliani Guitar Studies. Mel Bay Publications

SELECTED RECORDINGS
Handel Variations/Grand Sonata (Pepe Romero).
Philips 9500 513 LP
Guitar Concertos op.36 & op.70 (Pepe Romero).
Philips 9500 320 LP
Guitar Concertos op.30 & op.70 (Angel Romero).
EMI CDC 7 479862 LP
Guitar Concertos (with Julian Bream) RCA SB 6826 LP
Le Rossiniane: (Angel Romero). Angel SZ 37326 LP
Le Rossiniane: (Julian Bream). RCA ARLI 0711 LP
Guitar Duets composed and arranged by Mauro Giuliani:
Kämmerling & Christensen. Paula 34 LP
Gran Duetto Concertante op.52: Nigel North (guitar),
Beznosiuk (flute). Amon Ra CD-SAR 33
Deux Rondeaux op.68: Prunnbauer (guitar), Heller (hammerklavier). Christophorus SCGLX 74044
Rossiniane – Bruno Giuffredi. Arkadia CD AK128-1
Le Rossiniane – Frederic Zigante Pilz 447146-2 447147-2 CD
Chamber Works – Eros Rosellie Ensemble. Nuova Era 7194 CD
Guitar Works – Carlo Barone. Rugginenti 55203-2 CD
Guitar & Forte Piano Works – Francesco Roman.
Nuova Era (2 CDs) 7227/8
Giuliani Guitar Quintet op. 65
Music Minus One MMOCD 3602

SELECTED READING
The Birth of the Classic Guitar – Thomas F. Heck.
Dissertation, Yale University (1970).
Guitar Concertos of Giuliani. Guitar, November 1976
Mauro Giuliani. Guitar Review No.18, 1955
Mauro Giuliani. Guitar Review No.37, 1972.
The Guitar Concertos of Mauro Giuliani: Magula.
Soundboard, May 1976
The Genius of Mauro Giuliani.
Classical Guitar, August 1986
Mauro Giuliani – Virtuoso Guitarist and Composer –
Thomas F. Heck Editions Orphee (1995)

VICENTE GOMEZ

Born –

Madrid, Spain

8 July 1911

Vicente Gomez

Vicente Gomez began to play the guitar when he was seven years old. His father owned a tavern, and by the time he was eight years old the young Gomez was already entertaining customers with flamenco music on his guitar. His obvious talents were quickly recognised, and he was encouraged by his schoolteacher to take private lessons in solfeggio.

Gomez turned to the classical guitar after he became a pupil of Don Quintin Esquembre, a former pupil of Tárrega. He made rapid progress, and furthered his classical training when he entered the Madrid Conservatory.

Vicente Gomez made his first public appearance at the age of thirteen in the Teatro Español. A highly successful concert tour of Spain soon followed, and in 1932-33 he toured France and North Africa. An extensive tour of Russia and Poland was made in 1936, and later in the same year he gave recitals in Cuba, Mexico and the United States of America.

For the next twenty years Vicente Gomez enjoyed enormous success both in Spain and in the United States. He gave numerous public recitals and radio broadcasts, and his guitar playing and original music were featured in several Spanish and Hollywood films. In 1948 he opened a night-club, 'La Zambra', in New York, and late in 1953 he established a school in Los Angeles, with the title 'The Academy of Spanish Arts'.

Since 1959 Vicente Gomez has dedicated most of his time to teaching and the writing of music.

SELECTED MUSIC
Vicente Gomez Guitar Album.	Belwin

SELECTED RECORDINGS
Guitar Recital.	Decca DL 8018 LP
Guitar Extraordinary.	Decca DL 4312 LP
Concerto Flamenco.	Decca DL 74088 LP
Toros – Suite for Two Guitars.	Decca DL 4873 LP
Romantic Guitar.	Brunswick LAT 8602 LP
Blood Wedding Suite.	Decca DL 78918 LP
Artistry of Vicente Gomez.	Decca DL 78965 LP

SELECTED READING
Interview.	Guitar Player, December 1977
Interview.	Guitar & Lute, July 1979
Interview.	Guitar International, June 1987

JOSÉ LUIS GONZALEZ

Born –

JOSÉ LUIS GONZALEZ JULIA

Alcoy, Spain, 2 July 1932

José Luis González

José Luis González gave his first public guitar recital at the age of sixteen in Madrid's Realto Theatre. In 1957 he graduated from the Valencia Conservatory. His talents were recognised very early in his career, and the young guitarist became a scholarship pupil of Regino Sainz de la Maza in Madrid. Later he studied several times with Andrés Segovia at Santiago de Compostela.

In 1961 he won the Margarita Pastor prize in a competition organised by the Orense Conservatory which was being held in conjunction with the Santiago de Compostela Festival. José Luis González has given many highly successful concerts in Europe and North Africa, emerging as one of the most important classical guitarists since the end of World War II.

In 1962 González decided to move to Australia. There he settled in Sydney and soon established himself as a busy recitalist and teacher. He continues to give many guitar concerts throughout the world, achieving particular success in Japan. He has now once again settled in Alcoy, Spain.

SELECTED RECORDINGS

El Arte de la Guitarra Española.	CBS S 73656 LP
Portrait of the Guitar.	CBS 61654 LP
Art of José Luis González: Vol.1.	CBS/Sony 28AC 1184 LP
Art of José Luis González: Vol.2.	CBS/Sony 28AC 1239 LP

PAUL GREGORY

Born –

Beirut, Lebanon

26 January 1956

Paul Gregory

The British guitarist Paul Gregory's first teacher was Robert Sutton in Brighton. Subsequently he studied with Carlos Bonell, Baltazar Benitez and Oliver Hunt.

Gregory gave his first public concert in 1972. Many concerts throughout Great Britain followed. In 1973 he was nominated one of 'Tomorrow's Musicians' by the Croydon Music Council, which led to a major concert at the Fairfield Halls. In 1978 he won the prestigious Andrés Segovia Competition in Mallorca, Spain. Since that time he has been much in demand as a concert artist throughout Europe. As well as being a fine solo artist, Paul Gregory has shown a keen interest in integrating his instrument into general music making. This has been aided by studies on the cello and the composition of numerous chamber works. He has performed with the Lontano ensemble, the De Fossa Trio, the violinist Andrew Sherwood and the harpsichordist Sharon Gould among many others. He broadcasts frequently for the BBC.

SELECTED RECORDINGS

Encore.	Airship AP 128 LP
Bach/Scarlatti/Alberti Recital.	Opus 1 821 Cassette
20 Studies: Fernando So.	Opus 1 841 Cassette
Romantic Guitar Music.	Meridian E 77092 CD
Guitar Music of Four Centuries.	Meridian CD E 84146
Tango!	Claudio CC4319-2 CD

SELECTED VIDEO

Guitar Music of Villa-Lobos.	Stentor Music Co.

SELECTED READING

Interview.	Classical Guitar, September 1984

SLAVA GRIGORYAN

Born - Alma Ata,
Khazakstan
31 October 1976

Slava Grigoryan

Slava Grigoryan began to play the guitar at the age of five while his Russian family were living in Italy for a year waiting for their Australian residency. His parents are both professional violinists. His first guitar teacher was a tutor hired through the local library.

Grigoryan's first concert exposure came as a soloist with the award-winning Melbourne Mandolin Orchestra. He toured Japan, Spain, France, Belgium, Germany and the UK with this ensemble. He was a finalist in the 1992 Tokyo International Guitar Competition, in which he was its youngest ever competitor. His musical talents gained a special bursary from the Australian Music Foundation, which helped him study in Spain with Jose Tomas. A special scholarship from the Monash University in Melbourne provided the costs for three years of international concerts forming the performance component of his Bachelor of Music degree.

At the age of sixteen Slava Grigoryan recorded his first CD for the SONY company. This became a best seller in Australia. He has now contracted to make several more recordings for this major international company.

SELECTED RECORDING
Spirit of Spain - Slava Grigoryan   SONY   SMK 68351 CD

DAVID GRIMES

Born - Centralia,
Illinois, USA
28 November 1940

David Grimes

David Grimes first became interested in the classical guitar after hearing a Segovia recording. At the time he was a junior mathematics major at the California Institute of Technology. He completed his degree in mathematics and went on to work as a scientist at Caltech's Jet Propulsion Laboratory. At the same time he studied the guitar, initially with Guy Horn and later with Oscar Ghiglia.

From 1971 until 1990 Grimes toured extensively in the USA, Canada and Mexico as a soloist. He also appeared with orchestras and gave masterclasses. His performing career was interupted by a hand injury in 1990, but he recovered and began giving concerts again in 1996. Grimes has inspired a number of composers to write new works for him.

In recent years Grimes's strong interest in the music written for related and earlier instruments has led to the publication of his series `Treasures of the Baroque` with the Mel Bay Publishing Company. These highly acclaimed books are collections of Grimes`s arrangements from the tablatures for Baroque lute and guitar.

David Grimes is an important figure in the Guitar Foundation of America. He served as their president in 1996, and is the Music Reviews Editor for their quarterly journal, Soundboard. He also directs the comprehensive programme of guitar studies at the California State University at Fullerton.

SELECTED MUSIC

Treasures of the Baroque Vols. 1-3	Mel Bay Publications
The Complete Sor Studies	Mel Bay Publications
The Complete Giuliani Studies	Mel Bay Publications
Favourite Sonatinas	Mel Bay Publications

busy international concert career, appeared on television and radio broadcasts, and given many master classes in Europe and the USA.

SELECTED RECORDINGS

Stefano Grondona Plays Bach, Giuliani, Turina, Ponce
 CLS 91042
Grondona Plays Bach, Henze, Petrassi   Dynamic CDS 59
Novecento-Stefano Grondona   Sonar CRR 9602 CD

STEFANO GRONDONA

Born -

Genoa Italy

21 July 1958

Stefano Grondona

Stefano Grondona studied in Rome with Sergio Notaro and Oscar Ghiglia. He received the Diploma of Merit from the Accademia Musicale Chigiana in Siena. He also attended masterclasses given by Andres Segovia and Julian Bream.

Grondona won first prizes at the 1975 Castelnuovo-Tedesco Competition in Parma, the 1976 Gargnano Competition, and the 1978 Città di Alessandria Competition. He won prizes in several inter-national competitions including the 1979 Segovia Competition in Palma de Mallorca, Spain, and the 1981 Leeds Castle Segovia Competition, UK.

Since 1974 Stefano Grondona has maintained a

MARIA ESTHER GUZMAN

Born - Seville, Spain
22 September 1967

Maria Esther Guzman

Maria Esther Guzman began to play the guitar at the age of eight. She studied with America Martinez at the Conservatorio Superior de Musica de Sevilla, and graduated in 1985 with high honours. She also studied privately with Abel Carlevaro, Betho Davezac, Narciso Yepes, David Russell, Leo Brouwer and Alirio Diaz.

Since the age of fourteen Guzman has won numerous prizes in international guitar competitions, including first prize in the 1987 Segovia Competition in Almunecar, the 1987 Seville 13th Year Anniversary of Spanish Classical Guitar Competition, the 1988 Regino Sainz de la Maza Competition held in Okayama, Japan. Since that time Maria Esther Guzman has maintained a busy career as a teacher, recitalist and recording artist.

SELECTED RECORDINGS
Segovia Competition 1988.	Pasarela AMC-136LP
In Memoriam – Andrés Segovia.	Junta de Andalucia DS 0112
The Music of Julian Arcas.	Junta de Andalucia DS 0103
Sevilla.	Selva SE-01CD
Cantas de España.	Fun House FHCE-2001CD
Homentage a Tárrega.	Fun House FHCE-2006CD
El Remodino Latino.	Fun House FHCE-2009CD
Emocion.	Fun House FHCE-2011CD
Fantasia Española.	Fun House FHCE-2024CD
Fantasia El Paño.	Almaviva DSO103CD
Recital.	Video Selva SE001

FRANZ HALÁSZ

Born -
Chicago, USA
15 May 1964

Franz Halász

Franz Halász began to play the guitar and the violin at the age of eight. In his early twenties he studied with Eliot Fisk at the Musikhochschule in Cologne, Germany. He received scholarships from the DAAD (German Academic Exchange Scheme), and the European Chamber Association led by Boris Pergamenschikow. He graduated in 1991 with the distinction 'Summa cum Laude'.

In 1993 Halász became the first German guitarist to win the Andrés Segovia Competition in La Herradura, Spain. In the same year he was a prizewinner in the Guerrero Competition, Madrid, and also won first prize in the Seto-Ohashi International Competition in Okayama, Japan.

Halász is currently (1996) professor of guitar at the Leopold Mozart Conservatory in Augsburg, Germany. He was also appointed to develop the guitar department at the Staatliche Hochschule für Musik in Detmold. His wife is the concert pianist Debora Halász

SELECTED RECORDINGS
Piano & Guitar Ginastera/Brouwer w/ Debora Halász (piano)	BIS CD-671
Piano & Guitar Santorsola/Haug w/ Debora Halász (piano)	BIS CD-717
Halász Plays Gerhard, Turina, Falla, Jose	BIS CD-736
Halász Plays Berio, Petrassi, D'Angelo	BIS CD-823

OLE HALÉN

Born –

Hameenlinna, Finland

3 April 1944

Ole Halén

Ole Anders Halén started to play the guitar at the age of thirteen. He studied electric guitar with the well-known Finnish studio guitarist Ingmar Englund. At the age of fifteen he joined a touring pop/rock music band which made several hit records.

At the age of seventeen, Halén became fascinated with the guitar style of Chet Atkins, and began to study the classical guitar a year later to improve his fingerstyle technique. He studied with Ivan Putilin who, impressed by the young guitarist's ability, encouraged him to study classical music at the Sibelius Academy in Helsinki. In 1979 he received a degree in music as a guitar teacher at the Academy, and is now on the teaching staff there.

Ole Halén retains an intense love of all styles of music, and his endeavours have helped to make Finland one of the most active guitar centres in the world. He owns the Helsinki-based Chorus publishing company, which features several important names in its catalogue including Stepán Rak and Jorge Morel. His Chorus recording company has made several important recordings by various artists including Robert Brightmore and Seppo Siirala. Halén has also been involved in guitar string production, and has personally built several classical guitars. He is a director of the Scandinavian International Guitar Festival and is the organizer of the annual Midnight Sun Guitar Festival held in Ikaalinen.

NICOLA HALL

Born –

Ipswich, England

3 March 1969

Nicola Hall

Nicola Hall began to play the guitar at the age of eight. At ten, sponsored by the City of Derby, she studied with Robin Pearson at the Spanish Guitar Centre in Nottingham. She continued to show exceptional talent on the guitar, and in 1982 she was awarded a place at Chetham's School of Music in Manchester. There she studied with Gordon Crosskey, Professor of Guitar at the Royal Northern College of Music. In her final year at Chetham's she was awarded the Midwood Prize, the highest honour the school awards to string players. In 1987 she continued her studies at the Royal Northern College of Music with John Williams and the violist Roger Bigley. In 1989 she was awarded the Professional Performer's Diploma (PPRNCM), two years early and with distinction.

Nicola Hall made her London recital debut at the age of fifteen, at which age she also performed her first public concerto (Rodrigo's Aranjuez) with a professional orchestra. Since then she has given many concerts as a solo player and in ensemble throughout the United Kingdom. She has also played in Hungary, Poland, Holland, Yugoslavia, Denmark, Finland and Canada. In 1986 she won first prize in the first Polish International Guitar Competition, and in 1987 she won second prize in the Toronto International Guitar Competition. In May 1989 she was the winner of the Eagle Star Award for strings in the Royal Over-Seas

League Music Competition in London. She went on to win the gold medal and Champagne Pommery award in the grand finale of the same competition. In February 1990 she won the Malcolm Sargent Music Award. A recording contract with Decca International was signed during the same year. Her virtuoso technique and mature musicianship continue to dazzle audiences in her many performances in the concert hall and on radio and television.

SELECTED READING
Interview.	Classical Guitar, January 1987
Interview.	Classical Guitar, July 1992

SELECTED RECORDING
Virtuoso Guitar Transcriptions.	Decca 430 839-2CD
Guitar Concertos.	Decca 440 293-2CD
Art of the Guitar.	Decca 440 678-2CD

FREDERICK HAND

Born –

Brooklyn, New York, USA

15 September 1947

Frederick Hand

Frederic Hand attended the High School of Music and Art in New York, and is a graduate of the Mannes College of Music, where he is now a member of the faculty. He has taught several of the new generation of American guitarists including Stephen Funk Pearson and Benjamin Verdery. Hand began to play the guitar at the age of nine, inspired by some recordings of Andrés Segovia. He made good progress during the next few years and in 1972 he received a Fulbright Scholarship to study with Julian Bream in England.

As a guitar soloist he has performed in North and South America and in Europe. He has been an affiliate artist with the state art councils of Arizona, Alabama, California, Colorada, New York and Washington. He has been a guest artist with the Marlboro and Newport Music Festivals.

In addition to his concert performances, Frederic Hand has composed and arranged numerous scores for the cinema and television. His arrangement and performance of Vivaldi's Mandolin Concerto in C for the film Kramer v Kramer earned him special recognition for his treatment of Renaissance and Baroque music.

SELECTED MUSIC
Trilogy.	Theodore Presser PRE 41441152
Late One Night.	Theodore Presser PRE 11440393
Five Studies.	G.Schirmer S 47945

SELECTED RECORDINGS
Trilogy: The Guitar Music of Frederick Hand.	
	Music Masters MM 20065 LP
Baroque and On The Street.	Columbia FM-36687 LP
Jazzantiqua.	RCA AMLI 7126 LP

SELECTED READING
Interview.	Guitar Player, November 1986
Interview.	Acoustic Guitar, July/August 1991

JOSEP HENRIQUEZ

Born –

Barcelona, Spain

22 December 1951

Josep Henríquez

Josep Henríquez was a pupil of Graciano Tarragó and Eduardo Sainz de la Maza. In 1971 he began his professional career as a founder member of the Tarragó Guitar Quartet. He left the ensemble in 1977, his place being taken by Jaume Torrent.

In 1976 Josep Henríquez obtained his Ph.D degree in music at the Conservatorio Municipal de Música de Barcelona. In 1982 he was appointed professor at the San Francisco Music and Arts Institute. He is currently head of the Guitar Department at the Music Conservatory of Granollers, Barcelona.

Josep Henríquez has a busy performing career. In recent years he has played throughout Europe, the USSR, the USA, Canada, Central and South America, Africa and Israel.

SELECTED RECORDING
Recital.   BCD 1069 CD

SELECTED READING
Interview.   Classical Guitar, November 1984
Interview.   Guitar International, August 1987
Profile.   Classical Guitar, November 1990

JOSEF HOLECEK

Born –

Prague, Czechoslovakia

28 October 1939

Josef Holecek

Josef Holecek showed obvious talent on the guitar at an early age. After examinations he entered the guitar class of Prague Conservatory, finishing his studies there under Professor Sádlik and receiving his diploma in 1966.

In the same year he was one of the five finalists in the ORTF (French radio and television) International Guitar Competition in Paris. He was awarded a scholarship to study under Professor Karl Scheit at the Academy of Music in Vienna, where he completed his studies, receiving an honours diploma in 1967 after only one year.

From 1961 to 1967 Josef Holecek was engaged as a guitarist in the National Theatre of Prague. As well as teaching the guitar at the State School of Drama in Prague from 1961 to 1966, he also led a guitar class at the Conservatory of Pilsen during his last year in Prague.

After finishing his studies with Karl Scheit in Vienna, Holecek went to Sweden and was engaged as a teacher of the guitar at the Framnas Folkhogskola. He also directed several international summer guitar courses in Sweden and Finland. Since 1970 he has been a guitar teacher at Gothenburg Conservatory. He has given concerts throughout Czechoslovakia, and also in the major cities of Austria, Sweden and Finland.

Among those who have written works for Josef Holecek is the prominent Finnish composer Einojuhani Rautavaara, whose Serenades of the Unicorn was premiered by Holecek in Gothenburg.

SELECTED MUSIC

Six Aquarelles.	Schirmer S 3497
Swedish Romance.	Schirmer
Nevergreens.	Schirmer S 3496
Guitar Jokes. Parodies and Transcriptions.	CG 5946
Guitar Moods.	CG 5915
Ministudies.	CG 5914

SELECTED RECORDINGS

With Marta Schele.	BIS LP-31
Romantic Guitar Music from Sweden.	BIS LP-203

JUSTIN HOLLAND

Born - Norfolk County, Virginia, USA 29 July 1819

Died - New Orleans, Louisiana, USA

24 March 1887

Justin Holland

Justin Holland became interested in the guitar at the age of fourteen after hearing a concert by the Spanish guitarist Mariano Perez. By that time Holland was living in Boston, and he began to study with a local guitarist, William Schubert. Holland left Boston when he was 22 to study at Oberlin College.

Holland qualified from Oberlin and moved to Cleveland, Ohio where he established himself as a guitar and mandolin teacher. He also taught the piano and flute. He had the distinction of being Cleveland's first black professional.

Justin Holland became known to guitarists throughout the USA for his guitar works and methods. He did not give many public concerts, but there is no doubt his music and methods were a major force on the USA classical guitar scene of the 19th century. He was fluent in Spanish, Italian, French and German. He was also an important figure in organisations working for African-American rights. He was able to put his linguistic ability to great use in these organisations, and as a leader of the black Free Masons (Prince Hall).

Holland died in March 1887 at the home of his son Justin Minor Holland, who was also a respected guitar teacher.

SELECTED RECORDINGS

American Pioneers of the Classic Guitar   Douglas Back
Mel Bay Publications

The Music of Justin Holland   Ernie Jackson
Cherry Lane Music

SELECTED READING
Article   Soundboard, Fall 1994

SELECTED MUSIC
American Pioneers of the Classic Guitar   Douglas Back
Mel Bay Publications
The Music of Justin Holland   Ernie Jackson
Cherry Lane Music

JOHN HOLMQUIST

Born –

Wyoming, USA

7 February 1955

John Holmquist

John Holmquist began his guitar studies at the age of seventeen with Jeffrey Van. He later attended the University of Minnesota, where he received a Bachelor of Fine Arts degree in guitar performance. He also studied with Alirio Díaz, first in Banff, Canada, and later in Castres, France. In 1978 he was awarded the first prize in the Toronto International Guitar Competition. From 1978 to 1980 he lived in London, where in addition to teaching and performing he studied with the guitarist-composer Gilbert Biberian.

In 1985 John Holmquist was the recipient of a National Endowment for the Arts Solo Recitalist Fellowship. In addition to performing, John Holmquist is in great demand as a teacher and lecturer. He is currently Head of the Guitar Department at the Cleveland Institute of Music. He has also served on the faculties of the Wisconsin Conservatory of Music and Northwestern University.

SELECTED RECORDINGS
Las Folias de España.   Cavata CV 5001 LP
Music of Edvard Grieg, for Two Guitars (with Daniel Estrem).   Cavata CV 5002 LP
Gershwin by Guitar.   Pro-Arte/Pro-Jazz CDJ 226
In The Still of the Night.   Pro-Arte/Pro-Jazz CDJ 606
Love You Madly: Duke Ellingt   Pro-Arte/Pro-Jazz CDJ 628

SELECTED READING
Interview.   Classical Guitar, July/August 1983
Interview   Classical Guitar, May 1990

HARVEY HOPE

Born –

Stratford-upon-Avon, England

27 May 1943

Harvey Hope and Voboam guitars

PHOTO: COLIN COOPER

Harvey Hope began to play the guitar at the age of fourteen. He became interested in the music of the Baroque period early in his professional career and, during the 1960s, embarked upon an intensive study of the performing styles and repertoire of the five-course guitar. His research into what was then a neglected field led him abroad to the conservatories of Paris, Rome and Barcelona to study surviving source material at first hand. During the course of his studies he formed what is now regarded as one of the finest private collections in the world of rare 17th and 18th century guitars. His unique playing collection includes magnificent instruments by some of the greatest 17th century luthiers: Tielke, Fleischer and the Voboams.

Harvey Hope has lectured and given recitals in most of the universities in Great Britain and also in many similar establishments abroad. He has performed at leading European early music festivals, and has established an international reputation through his concerts, recordings and broadcasts of early guitar music played on original 17th century instruments. In addition to solo recitals, Hope regularly performs with the London Concert Orchestra, the Bournemouth Symphony Orchestra and BBC orchestras. He has provided music for the Royal Ballet and the Royal Shakespeare Company. He has contributed articles to a number of music journals and is currently the history editor of Classical Guitar magazine.

SELECTED RECORDINGS

Baroque Guitar.	Pye/Response RE 800 LP
Italian Baroque Guitar.	Pye/Response RE 804 LP
Gitarrenmusik des Barock.	Bellaphon 68 07 001 LP
Harvey Hope: French Baroque Guitar.	Lyric LYR 303 LP

SELECTED READING

Harvey Hope.	Article. Observer, January 1979
Harvey Hope.	Article. Music Week, April 1979
Harvey Hope.	Article. Soundboard, January 1982
Interview.	Classical Guitar, October 1989

TILMAN HOPPSTOCK

Born -
Darmstadt, Germany
13 February 1961

Fernando Sor Guitar Works	Signum X 14-00 CD
Villa-Lobos, Ponce, Brouwer, Paganini	Signum X 41-00 CD
El Ultimo Tremolo	Christophorous 0055-2 CD
Keyboard Works transcribed for Guitar	Signum X 42-00 CD
Bach for Baroque Cello & Guitar	Signum X 55-00 CD
Bach - Transcriptions for Guitar	Christophorous 0072-2 CD
Tilman Hoppstock & Friends	Signum X 71-00 CD
Klassiche Werke Sor, Marschner	Signum X 79-00 CD

Tilman Hoppstock

Tilman Hoppstock began to play the cello at the age of eight, and then the guitar at the age of ten. He studied both instruments in Darmstadt (1977-81), and then in Cologne (1983-84). He studied guitar with Wilfried Senger, Olaf Van Gonnissen and Eliot Fisk.

Hoppstock soon established himself as a virtuoso performer, and in 1978 he began an intensive concert and recording career. In the two-year period 1983-85 he gave over 200 concerts in Europe, North America, Japan, Israel, Morocco, Singapore and Mexico. He has also appeared extensively on television and radio. In 1987 he appeared on television in Germany as a solo artist, and in a duo with pianist Alexis Weissenberg in a major music production.

Since 1985 Hoppstock has been a lecturer at the diploma department of music at the Johannes-Gutenberg University in Mainz, Germany. Since 1988 he has been a lecturer in solo and chamber music at the Academy for Tonal Art in Darmstadt. He has also given masterclasses in Germany, England, Italy and Greece. Since 1983 he has been on the jury of several international guitar competitions. A specialist in the music of the 17th and 18th century, Hoppstock is the editor of a series guitar music based on the original editions of Bach's lute works and related compositions. He also continues to play the cello in a string quartet at the Darmstadt Music Academy.

SELECTED RECORDINGS

Tilman Hoppstock	Da Camera SM 93 610 LP
Tilman Hoppstock Plays	PMA 130261 LP
Bach Lute Suites	PMA 130366 LP

DON A. F. HUERTA

Born – Orihuela, Valencia, Spain

6 June 1804

Died – Paris, France, 1875

Don Huerta

Don A. F. Huerta was one of the great guitar virtuosos of the nineteenth century. As a child he showed a strong inclination for music, and from the age of fourteen studied music at the San Pablo College in Salamanca. His special subjects were singing and guitar playing, and he achieved distinction in both. His most important guitar teacher was the renowned Manuel García.

During the unsettled period following the Peninsular War in Spain, Huerta enlisted in the army in the cause of General Riego, but had to flee to France when Riego was defeated. In Paris he devoted himself entirely to music, in particular the guitar and singing.

Very impulsive by nature, Huerta suddenly decided to cross the Atlantic to go the United States of America. There he was to make his living singing and playing the guitar. After a visit to Martinique, he lost his voice and was forced to devote himself exclusively to the guitar. He began an intense study of the instrument and was soon giving solo recitals throughout the United States. He became generally regarded as one of the greatest guitarists of the period on the North American continent.

Huerta returned to Europe in 1826 and settled in London, where he became associated with many distinguished musicians including La Pasta, Moscheles, Donizetti and La Blanche. He married one of the daughters of the guitar maker Louis Panormo, and enjoyed enormous success as a guitarist in London.

In 1830 Huerta returned to France and once again decided to live in Paris. As in England, he enjoyed great popularity and success in France and Europe as a whole. Over the next few years he toured throughout Europe and the Middle East, dazzling audiences with his guitar virtuosity. He was made a Knight of the Order of Gregory the Great, an honour of which he was particularly proud. While in Spain, he declined an offer from Queen Isabella II to become her permanent court guitarist. He preferred to continue living in Paris, and it was there that he died in 1875 at the age of seventy-one.

Dr Walter James Leckie – patron, friend and confidant of the great Spanish guitarist, Francisco Tàrrega

MINORU INAGAKI

Born - Akashi city,
Hyogo, Japan
11 August 1958

Minoru Inagaki

Minoru Inagaki studied guitar with Hiroshi Samoto and Toshiaki Kondo. In 1975 he won first prize at the Japan Guitar Competition. After this success he moved to France to study with Alexandre Lagoya at the Conservatoire Musique Supérieure de Paris. Inagaki graduated with first prize from this prestigious conservatory in 1980. In the same year he won first prize at the U.F.A.M International Guitar Competition held in Paris, and also at the Segovia International Competition, Spain. In 1984 Inagaki was awarded a scholarship to further his music studies from the CZIFFRA Foundation. In 1987 he won first prize at the Sablé International Guitar Competition.

Since that time Minoru Inagaki has established himself as one of Japan's best classical guitarists. A world-class recitalist, he is a frequent performer on radio and television.

SELECTED RECORDINGS

Sonatine	Sound Matrix CD SNCD-0001
Fantasia	Sound Matrix CD SNCD-0002
Reverie	Sound Matrix CD SNCD-0003
Carcassi Studies	Sound Matrix CD SNCD-0071

EDUARDO ISAAC

Born - Entre Rios,
Argentina
16 March 1956

Eduardo Isaac

Eduardo Isaac has won many international competitions, including Porte Alegre, Rio de Janeiro, Vina del Mar, Caracas, and 'Le printemps de la Guitare' in Belgium. He won the first prize at the 1978 Concurso Nacional de Guitarra "Fundacion Gillette" in Argentina, and later first prizes at the Infanta Cristina Competition in Madrid, and the Andrés Segovia Competition in Palma de Mallorca. These wins set him on to an international career as a concert recitalist and recording artist.

Isaac currently teaches at the Entre Rios Conservatory in Argentina, and concertises throughout Europe and South America. In recent times he has specialised in twentieth century music.

SELECTED RECORDINGS

20th Century Guitar Music Vol 1	GHA 126-008 CD
20th Century Guitar Music Vol 2	GHA 129-019 CD
20th Century Guitar Music Vol 3	GHA 126-030 CD

SELECTED READING

Interview	Gitarre & Laute	3/1995

SHARON ISBIN

Born –

Minneapolis, Minnesota, USA

7 August 1956

Sharon Isbin

Sharon Isbin began to play the guitar at the age of nine. Her first serious study of the instrument was with Aldo Minella in Italy. Her father, a professor at the University of Minnesota, had taken the family with him to Italy for a year's sabbatical.

On her return to Minneapolis, Sharon Isbin continued her studies with Jeffrey Van, and later with Sopohocles Papas. She made rapid progress, and attended masterclasses given by Oscar Ghiglia and Alirio Diaz.

In 1979 Isbin received her master's degree in music from Yale University, where she had conducted weekly masterclasses for three years. She also studied with the renowned Bach interpreter and scholar, Rosalyn Tureck, in Oxford, England.

Since 1974, when she gave her first European tour at the age of seventeen, Sharon Isbin has been acclaimed by guitar enthusiasts and critics alike all over the world. In 1975 she was awarded the first prize in the international competition 'Guitar '75' held in Toronto, Canada. The following year she won the top prize in the guitar division of the Munich International Competition. Her performances for this event were televised and broadcast throughout the world. As a winner of the Queen Sofia 1979 International Competition in Madrid, she performed Rodrigo's Concierto de Aranjuez in a nationwide broadcast with the Spanish National Radio Orchestra.

In May 1977 Sharon Isbin made a highly acclaimed debut at the Wigmore Hall, London, followed by the first of several BBC broadcasts. Her New York debut, at Alice Tully Hall, Lincoln Centre, in March 1979 was again well received. The previous year she performed as a guest soloist with the Minnesota Orchestra, premiering Concerto for Guitar, a work written for her by the Israeli composer Ami Maayani. In June 1978 she made her first solo tour of Japan, and later that summer gave masterclasses and performances for the Rubin Academy Summer Festival in Jerusalem. She has also appeared as a guest artist at the Grand Teton Music Festival in Wyoming, the Festival les Arcs in Bourg Saint Maurice, and the Strasbourg International Music Festival.

Sharon Isbin is today one of the world's foremost guitarists. She lives in New York City, and as well as leading a busy life as recitalist is a member of the guitar department at the Manhattan School of Music. In 1989 she was appointed the first professor of guitar at the Juilliard School of Music, a position she still holds.

SELECTED RECORDINGS

Bach, Britten, Brouwer.	Sound Environment TR 1013 LP
Concierto de Aranjuez.	Denon/PCM OX 7210 ND LP
Guitar Recital.	Denon/PCM OX 7224 ND LP
Spanish Works for Guitar.	Denon/PCM OF 7012 LP
Road to the Sun : Latin Romances.	EMI/Virgin 59591 CD
Bach Lute Suites.	EMI/Virgin 59503 CD
Rodrigo/Vivaldi Concertos.	EMI/Virgin 59024 CD
Love Songs and Lullabies.	EMI/Virgin 59226 CD
Brazil with Love.	Concord CCD-235
Nightshade Rounds.	EMI/Virgin 72345/45024 CD
Black Topaz.	New World 80470-2 CD
American Landscapes.	EMI/Virgin 55083 CD

SELECTED READING

Sharon Isbin.	Guitar, September 1977
Sharon Isbin & Rosalyn Tureck.	Guitar, September 1980
Sharon Isbin.	Guitar & Lute, April 1981
Sharon Isbin.	Guitarra, September 1980
Sharon Isbin.	Guitar Player, May 1980
Interview.	Classical Guitar, December 1985
Interview.	Frets, October 1988
Interview.	Classical Guitar, October 1990
Article.	Classical Guitar, July 1992
Profile.	Guitar Player, July 1995
Article.	Guitar Review, Spring 1995
Interview.	Acoustic Guitar, March 1996
Interview.	Classical Guitar, July 1996

ALEXANDER IVANOV-KRAMSKOY

Born – Moscow, Russia, 1912

Died – Minsk, Russia

11 April 1973

SELECTED RECORDINGS
Concert for Guitar and Strings. Monitor MG 2024 LP
A. Ivanov-Kramskoy. Melodiya CM 03111-12 LP
A. Ivanov-Kramskoy. Melodiya CM 02579-80 LP
Paganini: Violin & Guitar Duets (with Leonid Kogan).
  Melodiya M10 44933 005 LP

Alexander Ivanov-Kramskoy

Alexander Ivanov-Kramskoy was one of the best-known contemporary Russian guitarists. He devoted himself to the classical guitar rather than to the seven-string instrument which from the time of Andrei Sychra (1773-1850) dominated the Russian guitar world until fairly recently.

Ivanov-Kramskoy published a method for the six-string guitar which, although specially adapted for self-study, is still widely used in schools of the Soviet Union. He gave many concerts and radio performances of his own compositions and those of other Russian composers, as well as music from the standard concert repertoire.,

Ivanov-Kramskoy was a very capable musician, and wrote a large number of original pieces for the guitar. He transcribed for the guitar all kinds of interesting music by Soviet and other composers, and was also a talented and respected chamber music player. He made a recording of his own variations on Russian themes for guitar and orchestra, now out of print, on the Monitor label. This record confirms the fine technical ability of Alexander Ivanov-Kramskoy.

RICARDO IZNAOLA

Born – RICARDO FERNANDEZ IZNAOLA

Havana, Cuba

21 February 1949

Ricardo Iznaola

Ricardo Iznaola was born in Cuba, but his parents moved shortly after the revolution, first settling in Colombia, where he began to play the guitar. The family later moved to Caracas, Venezuela, where the young guitarist continued to teach himself for four years, using the available written methods and listening to records. He then entered the Escuela Superior de Música in Caracas and studied under Professor Manuel Perez Díaz. Iznaola soon made remarkable progress, and in 1968 won third prize in the Manuel Leonicio Porras Competition in Caracas. In the same year he went to Madrid, Spain, to study with Regino Sainz de la Maza, eventually becoming his assistant in 1973 and working closely with him until his death in 1981.

In 1968 he won the first prize at the Franciso Tárrega Competition in Benicasim, Spain. In 1969 and 1971 he also won prizes in competitions held in Munich, Granada, Madrid and Caracas.

Ricardo Iznazola has been a naturalized Venezuelan since 1970. He returned to the United States in 1980, and is now the chairman of the Guitar Department at the University of Denver's Lamont School of Music.

He also directs the University's annual International Guitar Week Festival.

Ricardo Iznaola has composed a variety of works for the guitar, his Monologue II winning a prize at the Stroud Festival International Composers' Competition in 1983. His Monologue I for double bass was acclaimed by the famous double bass player Gary Karr.

SELECTED RECORDINGS
Original Guitar Music.	Belter 70912 LP
Venezuelan Music for Guitar, Vol.1.	Promus LPP 2048 LP
Venezuelan Music for Guitar Vol.2.	Promus LPPS 20154 LP
South American Music for Guitar.	Columbia CS 8566 LP
The Guitar in Latin America.	Promus LPPS 20238 LP
Iznaola – Valses Venezolanos.	Alcasa No.8 LP
Vibraciones con Iznaola.	Toison de Oro LP
Iznaola interprets Ponce.	Promus LPPS 20294 LP
Originales para Guitarra: Lauro/Sonata.	America LPA 20 LP
The Icarus Collection (2 CDs).	IGW 22874-5

SELECTED READING
Article.	Guitar, December 1975
Interview.	Guitar, April 1980
Interview.	Guitar & Lute, March 1977
Interview.	Guitar International, February 1986
Interview.	Classical Guitar, August 1991

SELECTED MUSIC
'Kitharologus' – The Path to Virtuosity. Chanterelle ECH 730
On Practising. Chanterelle ECH 738

PER-OLOF JOHNSON

Born –

Västra Vingåker, Sweden

8 October 1928

Per-Olof Johnson began playing the guitar at the age of fourteen but only became seriously interested in the instrument after completing his military service. After studying with David Berg and Sven Hammarberg-Kritschevsky in Stockholm, he went to Vienna in 1955 to study with Karl Scheit for two years. He continued his studies for several more years, completing them in 1960-61 at the Schola Cantorun Basiliensis in Basle, Switzerland. In 1962 he came second in the Concours International de la Guitare in Paris.

Per-Olof Johnson returned to Sweden and held a variety of positions in Malmö and Arvika as a guitar teacher. In 1966 he received an offer to work in Copenhagen, and two years later he was given the lectureship in classical guitar at the Royal Danish Conservatory. As Johnson still retained a part-time

Per-Olof Johnson

position at the Malmö State College of Music, there began a sixteen-year period of commuting between Sweden and Denmark.

In 1980 Per-Olof Johnson was knighted as 'Ridder af Dannebrogen' by Queen Margarethe of Denmark. In July 1982 the Swedish authorities created a personal professorship for him at the University of Lund/Malmö State College of Music, the first of its kind in Sweden, and a position he has held since.

For many years Per-Olof Johnson has performed widely throughout Europe and Scandinavia. At the same time he has established himself as Sweden's foremost classical guitar teacher and it is for this he is most widely known. Göran Söllscher is one of his many pupils. In 1989 he was invited to Yale University School of Music as a research affiliate in notation, performance technique and transcriptions for lute and vihuela.

SELECTED RECORDINGS
Per-Olof Johnson.	EMI SCLP 1037 LP
Per-Olof Johnson.	EMI LP 34395 LP
Swedish Guitar Music.	Caprice CAP 1236 CD

JEAN-PIERRE JUMEZ

Born –

Hesdin, Pas de Calais, France

9 February 1943

Jean-Pierre Jumez

Jean-Pierre Jumez came from a family of pianists and organists. He first studied the guitar with Jean Lafon in Paris, from 1959 to 1961. From 1962 to 1963 he studied under José Sierra at the Music Conservatory of Saint Germain en Laye, near Paris. The following year he studied the art of flamenco with Pedro Soler, and in 1966 he went to the USA to study jazz with Charlie Byrd in Washington.

Returning to Europe, Jumez completed his music studies at the Santa Cecilia Academy in Rome, with the conductor Gianluigi Gelmetti and with Professor Nataletti, a specialist in the study of popular music around the world.

In 1972 Jean-Pierre Jumez made his United States debut at the Carnegie Recital Hall, New York. He has since become one of the most travelled of contemporary classical guitarists, appearing in over one hundred countries, including concert tours of the Soviet Union. In 1977 he became the first classical guitarist to, perform in Peking, China.

Many works have been dedicated to Jumez, among them the Petite Suite Française by John Duarte, and Pictures at an Exhibition by the Soviet composer Piotr Panin. Jumez has given the first performances of a large number of compositions, particularly in the French repertoire. They include Concerto for Guitar and Symphony Orchestra (Jacques Casterede, 1978), Swing No.2 (Jacques Bondon), Deux Etudes de Concert (André Jolivet), Soliloque en Souvenir de Manuel de Falla (Henri Sauguet), and Hommage à Alonso Mudarra (Georges Auric).

Jean-Pierre Jumez is the founder of the Martinique International Guitar Festival, and a permanent member of the Yehudi Menuhin Foundation jury (France). He is also President of the International Guitar Information and Documentation Centre ('Guitarothèque') in Saint Germain en Laye. He has conducted various masterclasses around the world.

Aside from the classical field, Jumez has constructed a unique repertoire of works inspired by folk music discovered through his many travels. These include pieces from Africa, Asia, Russia and South America, as well as Eskimo and Arab music.

SELECTED RECORDINGS

Les Couleurs de la Guitar No.1.	Festival FLD LP
Les Couleurs de la Guitar No.2.	Festival FLD 700 LP
Les Couleurs de la Guitar No.4.	Festival FLD 709 LP
Nimble Fingers of Jean-Pierre Jumez.	
	Westminster WGS 8240 LP

SELECTED READING

Jean-Pierre Jumez.	Guitar, May 1977
Jean-Pierre Jumez.	Guitar Player, November 1974
Jean-Pierre Jumez.	Guitar & Lute, March 1982
Interview.	Classical Guitar, Nov/Dec 1982

DEAN KAMEI

Born –

Honolulu, USA

20 November 1950

Dean Kamei

Dean Kamei began to play the guitar at the age of thirteen. For a period of about seven years his interest lay in the field of popular music and rock and roll. After completing his studies in engineering, Kamei at the age of twenty-one began his involvement with other styles of music and the guitar. It was then that his love for the classical guitar began, and in 1974 he opened his first guitar shop and teaching studio in San Francisco.

Under Kamei's enthusiastic and expert management, his establishment became the most important of its type in California. The introduction of an extensive mail-order catalogue, concentrating on classical guitar products, spread his business throughout the USA, and indeed internationally. In 1985 he began his Guitar Solo Publications (GSP) business with the publication of two works by Antonio Lauro. In a relatively short period of time the GSP catalogue has blossomed, and with the benefit of Kamei's exceptional energies is now one of the most important publishing houses for classical guitar music. Kamei has on his current roster of composers and arrangers for GSP many prominent names including Carlos Barbosa-Lima, Eliot Fisk, David Tanenbaum, William Kanengiser, Luis Bonfá and Stephen Funk Pearson. 1989 saw Kamei extending his interests into manufacturing with the introduction of his GSP classical guitar string line.

MARIA KÄMMERLING

Born –

Leverkusen, West Germany

20 February 1946

Maria Kämmerling

Maria Kämmerling studied with Karl Scheit at the Hochschule für Musik und Darstellende Kunst in Vienna, where she received her degree with honours in 1971.

Since her debut as a concert guitarist, she has performed widely as a soloist and chamber musician. In addition to numerous concerts in Denmark and other European countries, she has performed at international music festivals such as Guitar Québec, the Copenhagen Summer Festival and the Volos Guitar Festival. She has also appeared at many contemporary music festivals including ISCM World Music Days and The Nordic Music Days.

In Scandinavia Maria Kämmerling has established herself as an important interpreter of contemporary music, and a number of distinguished Danish composers have written guitar works especially for her. She has given the first Danish performances of guitar works by Apostel, Henze, Halffter, Maderna, Takemitsu and others.

Over the past few years, she has been active in working with historical original instruments as well as with the modern guitar. She has given concerts on the baroque guitar regularly since 1977 with the Danish recorder player Leif Ramlov Svendsen, and in 1981 she began performing with the Danish guitarist, the late Leif Christensen, who was also her husband, as a duo specializing in the performance of classical and romantic guitar duets on original 19th century instruments.

Maria Kämmerling has lived in Denmark since 1971, where she holds the post of assistant professor of guitar at the Royal Danish Academy of Music in Aarhus.

SELECTED RECORDINGS
Maria Kämmerling: Recital. Paula 3 LP
Recorder/Baroque Guitar Duos.
Kämmerling/Svendsen. Paula 7 LP
Maria Kämmerling plays Gunnar Berg Guitar Works.
Paula 9 LP
Fernando Sor Guitar Duos: Kämmerling/Christensen.
Paula 14 LP
Maria Kämmerling plays Vagn Holmboe. Paula 30 LP
Giuliani Guitar Duos: Kämmerling/Christensen. Paula 34 LP
Giuliani Virtuoso Overtures:
Kämmerling/Christensen. Paula 44 LP
Baroque Works for Guitar/Recorder:Kämmerling/Svendsen.
Horizon 8601 LP

SELECTED READING
Interview. Classical Guitar, June 1996

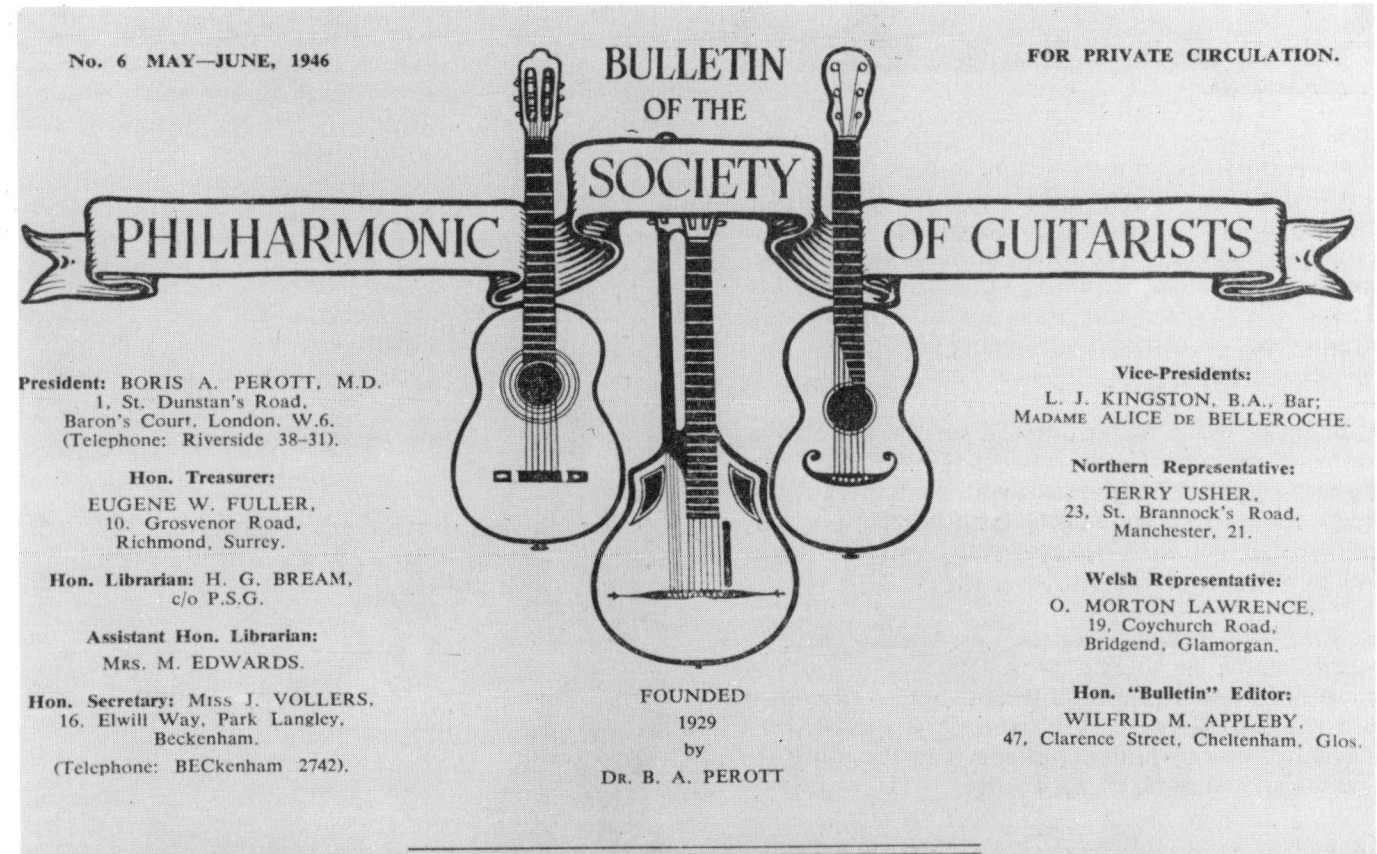

1946 Bulletin of the Philharmonic Society of Guitarists

WILLIAM KANENGISER

**Born - Orange,
New Jersey, USA
22 July 1959**

William Kanengiser

William Kanengiser first studied guitar at Mannes Conservatory Preparatory School in New York, and received his music diploma there in 1977. He went on to study at the University of Southern California. His principal teachers were Malcolm Hamilton, Pepe Romero and James F. Smith. On receiving both his Bachelor's (1981) and Master's (1983) degrees Kanengiser was named 'Outstanding Graduate of the School of Music'.

Kanengiser was a prizewinner in several important competitions, including first prize in the 1981 Toronto Guitar Competition, the first silver medal in the 1983 Radio-France International Guitar Competition, and first prize in the 1987 Concert Artists Guild New York Competition.

He is a founder member of the Los Angeles Quartet with whom he has toured all over the world. He has transcribed and arranged music for both solo guitar and the Los Angeles Quartet. He was Ralph Macchio's guitar double and coach in the popular Columbia Pictures film 'Crossroads'.

Kanengiser is currently a professor at the University of Southern California, a position he has held since 1987. He was also Artist-in-Residence at Whittier College (1990-94). Kanengiser is also an editor and arranger for Guitar Solo Publications of San Francisco.

SELECTED RECORDINGS

Rondo Alla Turca		GSP 1004 CD
Echoes of the Old World		GSP 1006 CD
El Amor Brujo	LA Guitar Quartet	GHA CD 126.001
Recital	LA Guitar Quartet	GHA CD 126.016
Dances	LA Guitar Quartet	Delos DE 3132 CD
Evening in Granada	LA Guitar Quartet	Delos DE 3144 CD
Labyrinth	LA Guitar Quartet	Delos DE 3163 CD
Effortless Classical Guitar 1	Instructional Video	Hot Licks Videos
Effortless Classical Guitar 2	Instructional Video	Hot Licks Videos

SELECTED READING

Interview	Soundboard, Winter 1983-84
Interview	Soundboard, Fall 1993

HUBERT KÄPPEL

Born –

Bensberg, West Germany

3 July 1951

Hubert Käppel

Hubert Käppel first studied classical guitar at the Musikhochschule, Cologne. He went on to complete his studies under Konrad Ragossnig at the Musikakademie in Basel. He also attended masterclasses given by Narciso Yepes. In 1978 Hubert Käppel won first prize at the Concorso Internazionale di Interpretazione in Gargnano, Italy. This success established him as one of Europe's finest young guitarists and led to a busy concert and teaching career. His version for the solo guitar of Bach's 6th keyboard Partita BWSV830 set new standards in the transcription of Bach's music.

SELECTED RECORDINGS
Bach (BWV1006a), Granados, Rodrigo, Brouwer.	Exaudio 2982/S LP
Bach (BWV830), Kellner.	GSP 1003 CD
Romantische Gitarren Musik.	FSM FCD97 760

SELECTED READING
Interview.	Classical Guitar, April 1985
Interview.	Guitar International, October 1988

ELI KASSNER

Born –

Vienna, Austria

27 May 1924

Eli Kassner

As a boy of fifteen Eli Kassner escaped the Nazi Holocaust in Europe, leaving Austria to work on a kibbutz in Palestine. In 1951 he emigrated to Canada to join his elder brother. Within two years he had established himself as a classical guitar teacher in Toronto.

In 1958 Andrés Segovia heard Kassner play and invited him to study with him in Spain at Santiago de Compostela. On his return to Canada he was invited to join the faculties of both the University of Toronto and the Toronto Conservatory of Music as their first teacher of classical guitar. In 1967 he founded his own Guitar Academy in Toronto, and it has become the most important institution of its type in Canada. His many pupils have included Liona Boyd and Norbert Kraft.

Eli Kassner is also a founder of the Guitar Society of Toronto, which sponsored in 1975 its first international guitar festival. This event is now held every three years and has become one of the largest and most important guitar festivals in the world. In 1978 he formed the University of Toronto Guitar Ensemble and has been its artistic director since. Kassner has also been instrumental in persuading prominent Canadian composers, including Milton Barnes, Lothar Klein, Harry Somers, Kenin Talivaldis, John Weinzeig and others, to compose for the guitar.

Kassner's daughter Danielle is a talented classical guitarist and has made several duo recordings (since 1987) with guitarist Guillem Pérez-Quer.

SELECTED READING
Eli Kassner: A Biography.	Guitar Canada, Spring 1989

MARCELO KAYATH

Born –

Belem-State, Brazil

15 January 1964

SELECTED RECORDINGS

The Twentieth Century Guitar.	Hyperion A 66203 LP
Latin Guitar.	MCA Classics MCAD 25963 LP
Guitar Classics from Latin-America.	IMP Classics PCD853
Guitar Classics from Spain	IMP Classics PCD 876
Marcelo Kayath.	3M/RCA (Brazil) 7M5/0003
Guitar Favourites.	Pickwick PCD1036

SELECTED READING

Interview.	Guitar International, February 1985
Interview.	Classical Guitar, June 1986

Marcelo Kayath

Marcelo Kayath first studied with Leo Soares, Jodacil Damacino and Turibio Santos in Brazil.

In 1980 he won the Andrés Segovia Prize at the International Villa-Lobos Competition, and in 1982 he won the coveted Young Concert Artists of Brazil Award. He then went on to win, in 1984, two major international competitions – the Paris Concours International de Guitare and the Fourth Toronto International Guitar Competition.

Although still only twenty-five years old, Marcelo Kayath has already established himself as one of the most talented guitarists of the eighties. He also holds a degree in electrical engineering from the University of Rio de Janeiro. He has given many concerts to wide critical acclaim throughout Europe and the USA, and has made several recordings on the Hyperion and IMP labels.

CHRIS KILVINGTON

Born –
18 June 1944
York, England

Chris Kilvington

Chris Kilvington first played the guitar at the age of thirteen. After receiving his degree from Hull University, he spent several years in the Bahamas, where he won first prize in the National Music Festival in 1972. Upon returning to England he established himself as a soloist with a series of recitals in 1977, eventually moving to Cambridge in 1979.

He has since given many concerts throughout the UK and also in Austria, Germany, Spain, Italy and Venezuela. With his duo partner Lorraine Eastwood he has also performed in the Czech Republic, Germany, Russia and Ireland. He has recorded albums of both solo and duo music.

Chris Kilvington is widely recognised as one of Britain's foremost teachers of the instrument. His permanent post is that of Lecturer in Guitar and Instrumental Teaching at Anglia Polytechnic University, Cambridge. He has given masterclasses in most of the countries in which he has performed, and also in the USA for the Guitar Foundation of America International Festival; additionally, he has adjudicated at several international competitions. Kilvington's wide experience has included the posts of Director of the Scottish International Guitar Festival (1985-1994), Director of the Cambridge Guitar Summer School (1980-1990), Co-Director of the Cambridge International Guitar Festival (1991-1992) and Deputy Director of Cannington International Guitar Summer School (1977-1990). The Eastwood-Kilvington Duo co-direct the internationally renowned Cambridge Guitar Project courses held at Cambridge University, which they established in 1993, and for five years they lead the Cambridge Guitar Orchestra (1991-1996). From 1997 he has been appointed Festival Manager for the Classical Guitar Festival of Great Britain held at West Dean.

Chris Kilvington is a composer with his own publishing house, *Cambridge Music Works*. He is also published internationally in a variety of other editions. His pieces include music for one, two and four guitars, two guitars and string quartet, guitar and flute, plus various anthologies, albums of arrangements, and didactic works. Some of these have been used by the examining bodies of both the Associated Board and the Guildhall School of Music. His works include commissions both at home and abroad.

Since 1983 Chris Kilvington has been the Reviews Editor of Classical Guitar magazine, heading a staff of some 25 writers. In addition to his editorial duties he has contributed many articles concerned with the development of the guitar, and also interviews with the major players.

SELECTED MUSIC
Progressive Guitar Technique.	Hampton Music Publishers
Rain Suite.	Hampton Music Publishers
Dowland's Dozen – Arrangements.	Ricordi
Dowland's Half Dozen.	Ricordi
Dream of Black Isle.	Ricordi
Chanson du Soir.	Editions Musicales Transatlantique
Paintbox Music.	Cambridge Music Works
Colours in a Cage.	Ricordi
Edinburgh Quartet.	Corda Music
From Starlight to the Ice of Dawn.	Edition Daminus
Farewell to Inverness.	Verlag Hubertus Nogatz
The Guitarist's Collection.	Kevin Mayhew Publishers

SELECTED RECORDING
Images. (Cassette).	Gemini
Here and Now.	Daminus DAM936 CD

SELECTED READING
Nervousness.	Classical Guitar, October 1984
The Performance of Ensemble Music.	Classical Guitar, February 1988
Start at the Top, parts 1/2/3.	Classical Guitar, March, June, July 1989
Step by Step Analysis.	Classical Guitar, August 1989
Scales for Guitarists – Series.	Classical Guitar, 1990/1991
Bar by Bar – Series.	Classical Guitar, 1996

HORST KLEE

Born –

Bad Kreuznach, West Germany

1 April 1952

Horst Klee

Horst Klee first started to play the guitar at the age of twelve. His first interest was in popular music, and he gave many concerts in semi-professional groups. From 1973 to 1977 he studied classical guitar with Gunter Alenburg at the Conservatory of Wiesbaden. He also studied with Robert Brojer, a professor at the Vienna Conservatory. From 1977 to 1981 he studied with Michael Teuchert in Frankfurt.

Since 1977 Horst Klee has taught in the Wiesbaden Conservatory and given many recitals throughout Germany.

SELECTED RECORDINGS
Meisterwerke der Gitarre.	Sonata 96080 LP
Die Spanisch Gitarre.	Sonata 96082 LP
Gitarrenmusik des Barock.	Sonata 86000 LP
Gitarrenmusik des 18 und 19 Jahrhunderts.	Sonata 96088 LP
Gitarrenmusik von Manuel Ponce.	Koch Swann 310177 CD
Recital.	Koch Swann 31227 2 CD

FRANCIS KLEYNJANS

Born –

Paris, France

15 April 1951

Francis Kleynjans

Francis Kleynjans began his serious guitar studies at the Conservatoire National Supérieur de Musique in Paris with Alexandre Lagoya. He went on to study with Alirio Díaz. His ability as a concert performer soon showed, and won him a first prize from the Yehudi Menuhin Foundation. Since that time he has given concerts throughout Europe and has made several broadcasts on French radio stations.

Kleynjans is also an important composer, having written over 300 pieces for the guitar including pedagogical and concert works, pieces for two, three and four guitars, and film scores. He was awarded the prize for composition at the 22nd International Guitar Competition organized by Radio France with his work, A l'Aube du Dernier Jour, which has been recorded by Roberto Aussel.

In April 1984 Francis Kleynjans wrote his first concerto for guitar and string orchestra, Op.62. He performed the work with the Philharmonic Chamber Orchestra of Nice at the 2nd Nice International Guitar Festival.

SELECTED MUSIC

A L'Aube du Dernier Jour.	LEM 25017
Arabesque en Forme de Caprice, Op.99.	LEM 25062
Cinq Nocturnes.	LED 25866
Cinq Nouvelles Estudines.	LED 25945
Impromptu et Berceuse Op.65.	LEMOINE
Passacaille en A, Op.87.	LEM 24944
Suite Brésilienne, Op.51.	LEM 25001
24 Preludes Vol.1.	LEM 24748
24 Preludes Vol.II.	LEM 247482
Concerto No.1 (guitar part).	LED 27166

SELECTED RECORDINGS

14 Etudes de Concert pour Guitare.	EL Classique SEL 300 247 LP
Music of Satie and Kleynjans.	Context GX 311105 LP
Ouevres de Kleynjans.	Daminus DR 885CD
Les Preludes – Ralk Winkelman.	Daminus DR901 CD
Oceano Nox.	Daminus DR931 CD
Los Cuatro Elementos.	Opera Tres CD1018

SELECTED READING
Francis Kleynjans.　　　　Classical Guitar, May 1980

Timo Korhonen

TIMO KORHONEN

Born -

Rautalami, Finland

6 November 1964

Tino Korhonen's parents sang in a church choir, and he developed an early interest in music. He began to play the guitar at the age of ten after seeing John Williams play in the television programme 'Masters of the Guitar'.

His first teacher was Esko Hartikainen, a jazz guitarist in his home town. Then in 1979 he travelled to Helsinki to study with Pekka Vesanen. He then went to live in Helsinki to continue his studies with Vesanen, and later Seppo Siirala, at the Sibelius Academy. In 1982, at the age of seventeen, Korhonen won the Munich Competition in Germany. In 1985 he went to Basle to study with Oscar Ghiglia. At the 1986 Havana Competition he was the first European to win the prize for best interpretation of a Latin-American composition.

Timo Korhonen has in recent years established himself as one of Finland's finest classical guitarists. He teaches at the Sibelius Academy in Helsinki and at the conservatory in Turku, and is a member of the Finnish contemporary music ensemble 'Toimii'.

SELECTED RECORDINGS

Folk Songs for soprano & guitar	Ondine ODE 730-2 CD
Tárrega/Torroba/Albéniz	Ondine ODE 752-2 CD
Manuel Ponce	Ondine ODE 770-2 CD
Fernando Sor	Ondine ODE 816-2 CD
Villa-Lobos for Guitar Vol 1	Ondine ODE 837-2 CD
Villa-Lobos for Guitar Vol 2	Ondine ODE 838-2 CD

SELECTED READING
Interview　　　　Classical Guitar　February 1996

NIKITA KOSHKIN

Born –

Moscow, USSR

28 February 1956

SELECTED MUSIC
The Prince's Toys.	LEM 25214
Suite 'Les Elfes'.	LEM 25069
Maskarades Vols. I & II.	LEM 24886/ LEM 24887
Russian Collection Vol.5.	Editions Orphée
Prelude and Waltz.	LEM 25390
Suite 'Six Cordes'.	LEM 24888
Usher Waltz.	EM 1026
Three Stops on the Road.	Chorus 033

SELECTED READING
The Guitar in Russia.	Guitar International, October 1985
Interview.	Guitar International, September 1986
Interview.	Classical Guitar, September 1993

SELECTED RECORDINGS
Vladimir Mikulka plays Koshkin & Rak.	BIS LP-240
Tschechow plays Koshkin.	Classic 315 2103 CD

Nikita Koshkin

Nikita Koshkin enjoyed music from a very early age. At the age of four, two of his favourite composers were Shostakovich and Stravinsky, yet he did not start to study music and the guitar until he was fourteen. He received his first guitar as a present from his grandfather, together with a record by Andrés Segovia. Koshkin was so impressed by the recording that he made a decision to make music his career. His first guitar teachers were Vladimir Kapayev (at primary school) and George Emanov (at secondary school). He later studied at the Gnessin Conservatory in Moscow with Alexander Frauchi. He also studied composition with Victor Egorov.

Although his chosen instrument is the guitar, Koshkin regards himself now as mainly a composer. He believes that guitarists should interest themselves in music of all kinds, and this is reflected in his own highly original music for the guitar and other instruments. His musical style contains elements of the post-Stravinsky Russian composers, notably Shostakovich and Prokofiev.

Nikita Koshkin lives in Moscow, where he divides his time between composing and teaching.

ELEFTHERIA KOTZIA

Born –

Alexandroupolis, Greece

24 January 1957

SELECTED RECORDING	
The Blue Guitar.	Pearl/Pavilion SHE CD 9609
Mediterraneo.	Pearl/Pavilion SHE CD 9634

SELECTED READING	
Interview.	Guitar International June 1986
Interview.	Classical Guitar, September 1989

Eleftheria Kotzia

Eleftheria Kotzia studied at the National Conservatory in Athens with Dimitri Fampas and A. Paleoglogos. She later studied at the Conservatoire National Supérieure in Paris with Alexandre Lagoya, having earned a scholarship from the French Government. Kotzia then gained a scholarship to take part in a masterclass given by Julian Bream in Lichtenstein in 1977. In the same year she was awarded the first prize of the Athens Conservatory and also the first prize of the Sixth International Guitar Competition in Milan. In 1982 she won first prize in guitar at the Ville de Juvisy competition in France.

In 1984, under the auspices of the British Council and the Hellenic Foundation, Eleftheria Kotzia came to London to study at the Guildhall School of Music. Since that time she has maintained a busy career as a solo recitalist throughout Europe and Scandinavia. She made her first visit to the United States in 1990. Her debut recording includes the first recorded version of Sir Michael Tippett's The Blue Guitar.

NORBERT KRAFT

Born –

Linz, Austria

21 August 1950

Norbert Kraft

Norbert Kraft emigrated to Canada with his family in 1954. He first studied the guitar seriously at the Royal Conservatory of Music in Toronto with Carl van Feggelen. He later studied with John Mills and Aaron Shearer.

In 1979 Kraft was the Grand Prize Winner of the CBC (Canadian Broadcasting Corporation) Young Artist Competition. In 1985 he won the first prize in the Andrés Segovia Competition held in Mallorca, Spain. Since that time he has become an international concert artist. He has appeared with every major orchestra in Canada and with the Boston Pops and the Baltimore Symphony in the USA. He is a regular performer on both Canadian radio and television. He has been featured in his own series on CBC television featuring the guitar and the guitar in chamber music, called 'The Art of Guitar'. He also often appears with his ensemble 'Kraft & Company' in concerts to the smaller communities throughout Canada. Kraft was a representative for Canada in 'The Year of Canadian Music' held in Washington DC in 1987.

Norbert Kraft has commissioned and premiered several new works for guitar, including a new guitar concerto by R. Murray Schafer. He is currently Professor of Guitar and Chamber Music at the faculty of Music, University of Toronto. He is also on the faculty at the Royal Conservatory of Music of Toronto. He is responsible for introducing their graded guitar repertoire series. Kraft was also Artistic Director at the first Toronto GuitarFest held in the summer of 1990.

SELECTED RECORDINGS

Duets for Cello and Guitar (with Ofra Harnoy).	Moss MMG CMG 1144 LP
Music for Guitar & Harpsichord (with Bonnie Silver)	Chandos CHAN 8937 CD
Villa-Lobos & Rodrigo Concertos.	CBC SM5000 LP
Tippett, Schafer & Britten.	Chandos 8784 CD
Romantic Works for Guitar.	Chandos 9033 CD
Guitar Concertos.	Naxos 8 550729 CD
19th Century Guitar Favourites.	Naxos 8 553007 CD
Norbert Kraft plays Granados.	Naxos 8 553037 CD
Paganini Guitar/Violin Sonatas Vol.1. W/Moshe Hammer (Violin).	Naxos 8 553141 CD

SELECTED READING

Interview.   Classical Guitar, June 1993

ALEXANDRE LAGOYA

Born –

Alexandria, Egypt

21 June 1929

Alexandre Lagoya

Alexandre Lagoya is without doubt one of the foremost guitarists of the twentieth century. Born in Alexandria, Egypt, the son of an Italian mother and a Greek father, Lagoya began to play the guitar at the age of eight.

He gave his first concert at the age of thirteen and, despite some objections from his parents, decided to make the guitar his career – although at one time he found professional boxing almost equally attractive. He gave many recitals in the villages of Egypt and toured other parts of the Middle East and Europe. At the age of eighteen he moved to Paris, France, and furthered his musical education at the Ecole Normale de Musique. By the time he was nineteen he had given more than five hundred concerts, and his career as a professional guitarist was assured. It was in Paris that he was able to perfect his technique, at the same time studying harmony and counterpoint with Saudry and meeting such famed musicians as Milhaud, Poulenc, Dutilleux, Messiaen, Rodrigo and Villa-Lobos.

In 1950 Lagoya went to Siena to study with Andrés Segovia. In the same year he met Ida Presti, a guitarist he much admired. They met in the home of André Verdier and a mutual love for the instrument developed into a love for each other. They married in 1952 and not only joined lives but musical forces as well to become the legendary concert duo Presti-Lagoya. Though they had made formidable reputations as solo performers, their work together brought them even more fame. They founded a guitar class at the Schola Cantorum in Paris and also made regular world tours. In fifteen years they played 2,000 concerts and also worked out many brilliant new techniques for the guitar.

In 1967 the Presti-Lagoya duo was at the height of its fame when Ida Presti, whilst preparing for a concert in New York City, suddenly fell ill and died. Lagoya, grief-stricken, continued teaching but did not perform in concert. Emotionally he had been devastated, and it took him a year and a half to re-study his repertoire. After a break of five years he began a new career as a solo guitar recitalist.

Alexandre Lagoya is now one of the world's busiest guitarists. He is also Professor at the Paris National Conservatoire, a position he has held since 1969, when he created a guitar class for the institution. In the summer, he teaches at the International Academy of Music in Nice, a position he has held since 1960, as well as in other parts of the world.

SELECTED RECORDINGS

L'Extraordinaire Alexandre Lagoya.	Philips 6521 013 LP
La Guitare est mon Maître.	Philips 6504 041 LP
Lagoya.	Philips 6504 120 LP
Lagoya Plays Sor and Villa-Lobos.	Philips 6504 131 LP
Concerto for Classical Guitar and Jazz Piano (Bolling).	RCA CY 3007 LP
Rampal and Lagoya in Concert (2 LPs).	RA ARL 2-2631 LP
The Spanish Guitar	CBS M35857 LP
Duo with Simion Stanciu (Pan Flute).	ERATO 45161-2 CD
Lagoya plays Bach.	ERATO 45692-2 CD
Carmen Suite.	Philips 446-002-02 CD

With Ida Presti

Music for the Classical Guitar.	Nonesuch H 71161 LP
Musique Baroque pour deux Guitares	Philips 6504 003 LP
Concertos pour deux Guitares.	Philips 6504 018 LP
Musique Espagnole pour deux Guitares.	Philips 6504 020 LP
Presti-Lagoya: Oeuvres pour deux Guitares.	Philips 6504049 LP
Masters of the Guitar: Volume One.	RCA RTB 6589 LP
Presti-Lagoya Duo (3 CD set).	Philips 446 213-2

SELECTED READING

Interview.	Guitarra, May 1980
Interview.	Guitar Player, February 1982
Interview.	Classical Guitar, December 1989, January 1990
Article.	Classical Guitar, May 1992

SELECTED MUSIC

Caprice.	Ric. R1608
Rêverie.	Ric. R1607

ROBERTO LARA

Born – Tres Arroyos, Argentina

23 May 1927

Died – Buenos Aires, Argentina, 1988

Roberto Lara

Roberto Lara completed his musical studies at the Music Conservatory in Buenos Aires, subsequently making several concert tours of South America and Europe. A noted teacher, he also recorded Qualiton record company. Several of his recordings were released by Lyrichord Disc Incorporated in the United States of America. Lara also made many transcriptions for the guitar, including a large amount of traditional Argentine melodies.

SELECTED RECORDINGS

The Guitar of the Pampas.	Lyrichord LLST7253 LP
The Classic Guitar.	Lyrichord LLST7299 LP

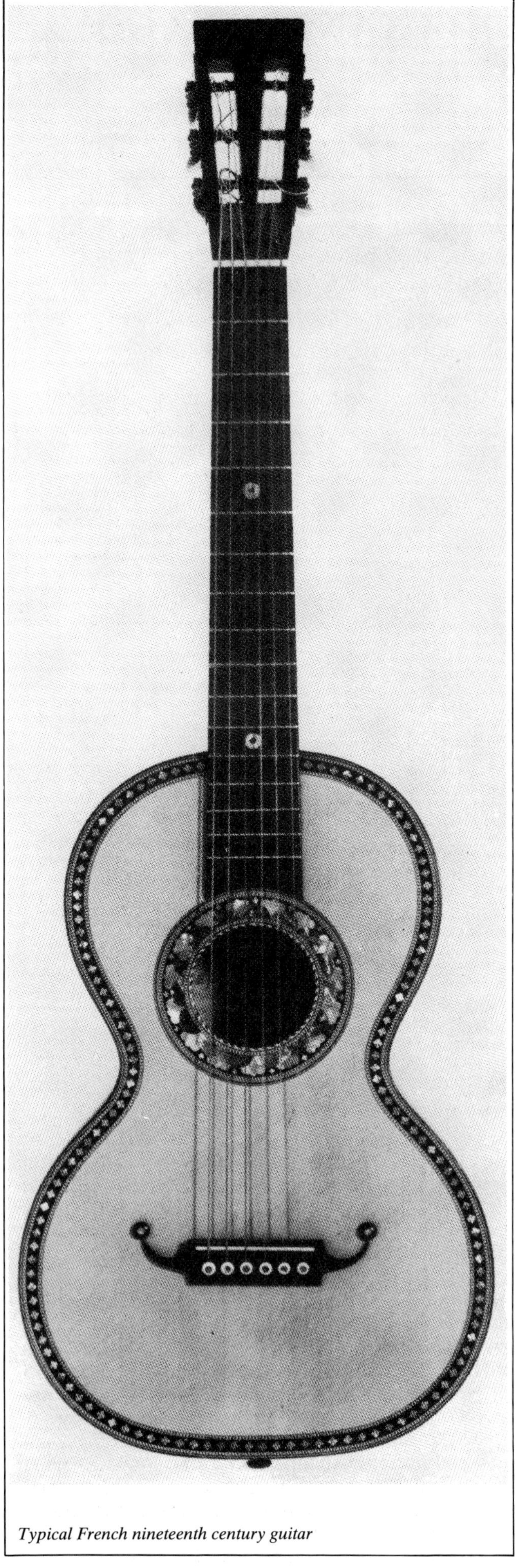

Typical French nineteenth century guitar

ANTONIO LAURO

Born – Ciudad Bolívar, Venezuela

3 August 1917

Died – Caracas, Venezuela, 18 April 1986

Antonio Lauro

The popularity of Antonio Lauro's music has grown enormously in recent years. He has made a great contribution to the library of contemporary classical guitar music, not only through his own compositions but also through his many arrangements for the guitar of the music of fellow Venezuelan composers such as Sojo, Borges, Cisneros, Ramón y Rivera, and Landaeta.

Lauro had an academic musical background. He studied at the Academy of Music in Caracas under Vicente Emilio Sojo and Juan Bautista Plasis. His original instrument was the piano, but on hearing the Paraguayan guitar virtuoso Agustín Barrios Mangoré in concert, he decided to devote his musical study to the guitar.

Lauro wrote and arranged many works, the bulk of which are as yet unpublished. Most of them are for the guitar, but he also composed works for a cappella choral group, orchestra, orchestra and choir, piano, piano and voice, organ and voice, string quartet, wind quartet and other instrumental combinations. More often than not, the inspiration for his compositions was derived from the folkore, instruments and regional dance rhythms of Venezuela.

It was the Venezuelan virtuoso guitarist Alirio Díaz who really first drew the guitar world's attention to the genius of his fellow countryman. Lauro and Díaz enrolled as students of Raúl Borges around the same time, and became close friends. Díaz revised and fingered many of Lauro's original compositions and arrangements for the guitar, and has often included a selection of them in in his concert tours around the world. As a result, the music of Antonio Lauro has featured prominently in the concert repertoires of many other leading guitarists. Lauro is now regarded as one of the great 20th century composers for the guitar.

SELECTED MUSIC
Angostura: Valse Venezolano, ed. Díaz.	B 901
Carora: Valse Venezolano, ed. Díaz.	B 903
El Marabino: Valse Venezolano, ed. Díaz.	B 904
Four Venezuelan Waltzes, ed. Díaz.	B 794
María Luisa: Valse Venezolano, ed. Díaz.	B 905
Sonata.	ZA 5539
Suite Venezolano, ed Díaz.	B 793
Two Venezuelan Pieces: Valse Criollo & Pavana, ed. Papas.	CO 166A
Variations on a Venezuelan Children's Song, ed. Díaz.	B 940
Aire de Joropo: Canonico arr. Lauro.	B 902

SELECTED RECORDINGS
Guitar Music of Spain and Latin America: Alirio Díaz.
    EMI/HMV HQS 1175 LP
Concerto for Guitar: Miloslav Matousek.   Panton 8111 0318 LP
Jesus Castro Balbi plays Antonio Lauro.
    Etcetera KTC 1110 CD
David Russell plays Antonio Lauro.
    Guitar Masters GMR 101-93 CD
La Danza! Eduardo Fernandez.   Decca 443 999-2 CD

SELECTED READING
Antonio Lauro.   Guitar & Lute, January 1980
Antonio Lauro.   Guitar, October 1980
Antonio Lauro: complete list of works.
    Guitar & Lute, January 1980
Antonio Lauro: special tribute issue.
    Guitar International, August 1986
Article.   Classical Guitar, November 1986
Lauro Solo Guitar Works – Series by Luis Zea.
    Classical Guitar, 1994/96
Antonio Lauro, un Músico total – Alejandro Bruzual.
    CVG Siderurgica del Orinoco, 1995

JONATHAN LEATHWOOD

Born - Warrington, Lancashire, UK

20 January 1970

Jonathan Leathwood

Jonathan Leathwood completed his studies for a Bachelor of Music degree in 1991 at King's College, London. He graduated with first-class honours and won the Purcell Prize for academic achievement. His principal guitar teachers were Gordon Crosskey, Paul Galbraith and Richard Wright. Following his graduation, Leathwood received awards from the Countess of Munster Trust, the Myra Hess Trust, the Ian Fleming Trust, the Holst Foundation and the Eric Falk Trust. These awards helped him continue his studies in interpretation with the Greek pianist and conductor George Hadjinikos, and in conducting with Peter Gellhorn.

In 1988 Leathwood won third prize in the String Final of the prestigious BBC Young Musician of the Year Competition. Later that year he made his London concerto debut at the Queen Elizabeth Hall. In 1993 he took part in the Park Lane Group's Young Artists Series at the Purcell Room in London. Since that time Jonathan Leathwood has maintained a busy career as a concert recitalist and lecturer in the UK, the USA, and in several European countries.

He currently holds the post of assistant lecturer in Techniques of Composition at King's College, London.

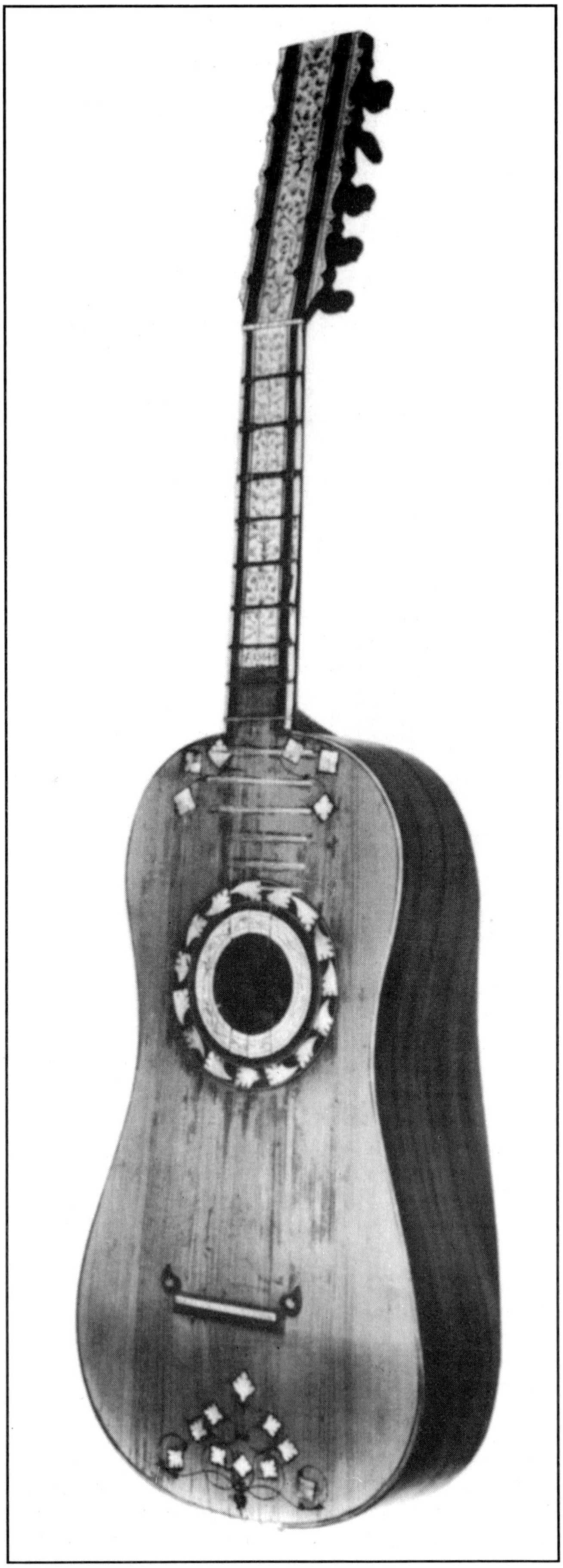

Italian Chitarra Battente c.1564

SELECTED READING
Interview   Classical Guitar, March 1996

LUIGI LEGNANI

Born – Ferrara, Italy

7 November 1790

Died – Ravenna, Italy, 5 August 1877

Luigi Legnani

Luigi Rinaldo Legnani began his musical education at the age of eight when his parents moved to Ravenna. As a singer and guitarist he soon showed immense talent, and by the time he was seventeen he was taking a prominent part in the opera at the Ravenna Theatre.

Legnani's first public recital as a guitar virtuoso was in Milan in 1819. From that time he was regarded as one of the foremost guitarists in Europe. He toured Europe extensively from 1822, appearing in Austria, Italy, Switzerland and Russia, where he played before the Grand Duke Nicolas. In 1836 a close friendship developed between Legnani and the violinist and guitarist Nicoló Paganini.

Legnani became very interested in the construction of the guitar, and when he visited the leading guitar makers in Vienna – Staufer and Ries – he left with them designs of several new models, including a terz guitar (a guitar tuned a minor third higher than the standard instrument). Both these makers produced guitars bearing Legnani's name. In 1850 Legnani decided to give up his career as a concert recitalist, and returned to Ravenna to devote his life to the construction of guitars.

Legnani was not only a talented luthier and a virtuoso guitarist, but also a prolific composer for the guitar. He wrote over two hundred and fifty compositions for the instrument, including a Method for the Guitar, op.250, which was published by Ricordi of Milan. The bulk of his compositions was published in Vienna by the publishing house of Leidesdorf.

Luigi Legnani, an honorary member of the Philharmonic Societies of Rome, Florence, Ferrara and Munich, and one of the greatest classical guitarists of the nineteenth century, died in Ravenna in 1877 at the age of eighty-seven.

SELECTED MUSIC

Caprices in all Major and Minor Keys op.20. Nos.1-18 & 19-36.	Kalmus
Caprices in all Keys op.20, Books 1 & 2.	GA 35/GA 36
36 Caprices, op.20, ed. Wynberg.	ECH 440
Introduction, Theme, Variations & Finale, op.64.	SZ 7765
Introduction, Theme & Variations, op.224.	GA 74
Introduction & Theme, op.237.	Kalmus
Six Little Caprices, op.250, ed. Pomilio.	BA 11240
Six Caprices, op.250.	Bèrben 2240
Ten Selected Caprices, ed. Storti.	Bèrben 1383
Twelve Selected Caprices, ed. Savio.	BA 11363
Variations on the duet 'Nel cor píu' from La Molinara, op.16, ed. Chiesa.	SZ 8359

SELECTED RECORDING

36 Capriccia – Léopoldo Saracino.	Nuova Era 7239 CD

DAVID LEISNER

Born –

Los Angeles, California, USA

22 December 1953

David Leisner

Since his success as a prizewinner in the 1975 International Guitar Competition in Toronto, Canada, David Leisner has come to be regarded as one of the best classical guitarists in the United States of America, an opinion that is confirmed by his recent concert performances and his record release on the Titanic label. He also won the Silver Medal at the 1981 International Guitar Competition held in Geneva, Switzerland.

Although born in California, Leisner is a graduate of Wesleyan University in Connecticut, and is now a resident of New York. Over the years he has studied the guitar and music with several important teachers, both in the USA and in Europe. He has studied the guitar with John Duarte, Angelo Gilardino, Theodore Norman and David Starobin; interpretation with Karen Tuttle and John Kirkpatrick; and composition with Richard K. Winslow.

Leisner is also a talented singer and composer, and in the latter capacity had two works commissioned by a London choral group and a New York theatre company. He has appeared several times on national radio in the USA, and also in concert with the famous harmonica player Larry Adler.

David Leisner holds an appointment in the faculty of the New England Conservatory of Music in Boston, and is also on the roster of Affiliate Artists Incorporated.

SELECTED MUSIC
Suite Op.1.	Bèrben
'Billy Boy' Variations.	Merion Music
Passacaglia and Toccata.	Merion Music
The Cat that Walked by Himself.	Merion Music
Three Moons (cello & guitar).	Merion Music
Outdoor Shadows (voice & guitar).	Merion Music

SELECTED RECORDING
The Viennese Guitar.	Titanic TI-46 LP

SELECTED READING
Interview.	Soundboard, Winter 1992
Interview.	Guitar Review, Summer 1994

PHILIPPE LEMAIGRE

Born –

Vise, Belgium

16 February 1950

Philippe Lemaigre

Philippe Lemaigre first studied the piano, but at the age of thirteen he changed to the guitar. His first guitar teacher was Gonzalez Mohino in Liège, although earlier he had studied harmony, counterpoint and musical analysis with Félix Mahieu. He entered the Liège Conservatory when he was seventeen and graduated in 1971. He won first prize for guitar and chamber music on his graduation. Later he studied with Leo Brouwer and Alberto Ponce.

Philippe Lemaigre also plays the lute, and has given concerts throughout Europe on both this instrument and the guitar. In recent years he has established himself as one of Belgium's leading guitarists, often appearing with his fellow Belgian Guy Lukowski, and also as a composer of note. Some of his recordings have featured the works of contemporary Belgian composers including P.Boesmans, H.Pousseur, J. Absil and J. L. Robert.

SELECTED MUSIC
Douze Etudes.	Mourat
Esquisses.	Mourat
Miniatures.	Mourat
Six Preludes en Hommage à Debussy.	Mourat

SELECTED RECORDINGS
The Guitar works of Leo Brouwer.	Ricercare RIC 028 LP
Carulli Guitar Duos (with Guy Lukowski).	EMI C 069-19069 LP
Sor Guitar Duos (with Guy Lukowski).	Pavane ADW 7016 LP
Virtuoso: Giuliani, Tárrega, Sor, Coste, Albert.	EMI 1 A 065 1654671 LP
Compositions by Lemaigre.	Pavane ADW 7148 LP
Recital de Guitare: Sor & Villa-Lobos.	Alpha DB 208 LP
La Guitare à Versailles.	Alpha DB 234 LP
La Guitare Romantique.	Music Magna Mag 20004 LP
Fernando Sor.	Music Magna Mag 50018 LP
Philippe Boesmans: Intrusion.	Music Magna Mag 50024 LP
Lemaigre: Improvisations.	Music Magna Mag 20008 LP
Jean Absil Guitar Works.	Ricercar RIC 124113 CD

WOLFGANG LENDLE

Born –

Ludwigsburg, Germany

5 January 1948

Wolfgang Lendle began his guitar studies in Trier with H.J.Volkholz, continuing with Jiri Jirmal at the Musikhochschule in Saarbrücken. There was further study with Andrés Segovia, Alirio Diaz, José Tomás, Alvaro Company and Regino Sainz de la Maza. He built up a considerable part of his repertoire with the German pianist Martin Galling.

Lendle won the 15th competition of the German Music Council as well as the international Competition 'Maria Canals' in Barcelona in 1969 and the 'Francisco Tárrega' in Benicasim in 1974. He has given concerts in nearly all European countries, the USSR, North and South America, and has appeared in international festivals such as Esztergom, Volos, Krakow, Istanbul, Jerusalem, Paris and Havana. Since 1985 he has been teaching at the Music Academy of Kassel. In addition to his career as a solo concert guitarist, he performs in a duo with his wife, the mezzo-soprano Bertha Casares. He is also a talented composer, whose works are published by Editions Orphée.

SELECTED MUSIC
Variations Capricieuses d'aprés Paganini.	Editions Orphée

SELECTED RECORDINGS
Saudade (with Françoise Reuter, voice)	Luxembourg Sound SA 76 23691 LP

Wolfgang Lendle

Scarlatti/Rodrigo Sonatas.	Leico Records 8155 LP
Songs by Ginastera, Guastavino, Villa-Lobos, Almeida, Lendle/Bertha Casares, mezzo-soprano, with Wolfgang Lendle.	TGF Records 20-8504 LP
Recuerdos de la Alhambra – Spanish Guitar Music.	Teldec 243 717-2 CD
Villa-Lobos:Complete Solo Works for Guitar.	Teldec 8.44143 ZK, 244 2197-2 CD
Music of Barrios.	Opus 91 2405-2 CD
Favourites for Guitar.	Opus 91 2422-2 CD

SELECTED READING
Interview.	Classical Guitar, August 1985
Wolfgang Lendle.	Classical Guitar, August 1989

WULFIN LIESKE

Born –

Linz an der Donau, West Germany

6 March 1956

SELECTED RECORDINGS

Bach/Schubert for Guitar	Intercord CD INT 830-804
La Catedral: Barrios.	Intercord CD INT 830-846
Preludio Latino	Saphir INT 830.877 CD
Guitarra Española.	Intercord CD 830-886
Adios Nonino.	EMI Classics 5 44007 2 CD
Albeniz.	EMI Classics 5 44073 2 CD

SELECTED READING

Interview.   Classical Guitar, July 1990

Wulfin Lieske

Wulfin Lieske began to study the guitar at the age of twelve. In 1973 he studied the classical guitar with Karl-Heinz Bottner and Hubert Käppel at the Musiktheorie am Konservatorium der Stadt Köln. At the same time he studied jazz with Manfred Schoof at the Musikhochschule Köln. His first recording, Bitternis, was with a jazz quartet and was released in 1979.

Since that time Wulfin Lieske has concentrated on the classical guitar, winning several important international competitions including Alicante, Spain, in 1981, Gargagno, Italy, in 1982, and the Andrés Segovia Competition in Almuñecar, Spain, in 1985. Following these successes, Lieske has performed throughout Europe, establishing himself as one of Europe's finest young classical guitarists.

Wulfin Lieske lives in Cologne where he teaches at the Hamburg State School of Music.

DAGOBERTO LINHARES

Born –

São Paulo, Brazil

9 September 1953

Dagoberto Linhares

Dagoberto Linhares started his guitar studies with Manuel São Marcos at the age of nine, continuing with his daughter Maria Livia São Marcos at Geneva Conservatoire. At fourteen he won first prize at the City of São Paulo City Competition as well as the Young Instrumentalists' award. In 1971 he played the solo guitar part in the South American première of Castelnuovo-Tedesco's Romancero Gitano (based on García Lorca) for chorus and guitar.

Linhares moved to Europe in 1972 and was appointed professor at the Fribourg Conservatoire, Switzerland. Currently he holds diploma and virtuosity classes at Lausanne Conservatory.

He attended masterclasses given by Turibio Santos and Julian Bream, and continued his success in international competitions when he won first prize in the Geneva Conservatory 'Virtuosité' examination in 1973. He was also granted the Swiss Musician Association Award. The following year he was laureate at the Maria Canals Competition in Barcelona and, in 1975, at the International Competition of Musical Performance in Geneva.

Since his debut at the Wigmore Hall, London, in 1974, Dagoberto Linhares has given numerous concerts throughout Europe, the United States (where he performed at the Lincoln Centre, New York) and Latin America, and has made several broadcasts for continental radio stations. He also appears frequently at music festivals, including the Esztergom International Guitar Festival, the Bratislava Festival (where he played Rodrigo's Concierto de Aranjuez), the Tibor Varga Festival (Villa-Lobos Concerto), the Festival Estival in Paris, and Lisbon's First International Festival. He has performed with orchestras such as the Suisse Romande, Birmingham, Sofia, Detmold and Gulbenkian Foundation, and is also the founder of his own chamber group, the Linhares Guitar Quartet.

Dagoberto Linhares currently lives in Geneva, Switzerland.

SELECTED RECORDINGS

Villa-Lobos: Cinq Preludes, Suite Populaire Brésilienne.
　　　　　　　　　　　　　　　　　　　Alvarez 817 LP
Dagoberto Linhares: Musique espagnole pour guitare.
　　　　　　　　　　　　　　　　　　　Gallo 30507 LP
Ouevres pour choeur et guitare. Tedesco, Nobre, Prado.
　　　　　　　　　　　　　　　　　　　Arion 36641 LP
Trios: Paganini.　　　　　　　　　　SMS 2843 LP
Yanomamy: Nobre.　　　　　　EMI 063422921 LP
Musique pour quatre guitares:
Piazzolla, Joplin, Granados, Falla, Dowland. Gallo CD 517
Villa-Lobos. 12 Etudes/5 Preludes.　　Gallo CD 572
Guitar Concertos.　　　　　　　Naxos 8 550483 CD

147

MIGUEL LLOBET

Born – Barcelona, Spain
17 October 1878
Died – Barcelona, 22 February 1938

Miguel Llobet

Miguel Llobet's father was a noted wood carver of religious images. Many distinguished artists and musicians used his studio as a meeting place, and as a result Llobet was brought up in an artistic atmosphere. His father had hoped that he would follow in his footsteps and also become an artist. In fact Llobet was a skilful artist, as can be seen by the excellent sketches he made throughout his life.

Llobet's uncle gave him his first guitar when he was eleven years old. He began to study the instrument with Macan Alegre at the Municipal School of Barcelona. Alegre immediately recognised his special musical talent and introduced him to the leading guitarist in Spain at that time, Francisco Tárrega. Llobet soon made great progress under Tárrega's tutelage, and in 1900 he made his recital debut in Málaga. The concert was a resounding success, and as a result he was invited to play for the Spanish royal family in Madrid. True international fame came to Llobet after his first concert in Paris at the Salon Washington-Palace on 26 January 1905. A series of highly acclaimed concerts followed.

Llobet's reputation was established in Paris with the help of his friend, the pianist Ricardo Viñes, whose influence often resulted in the presence of musicians such as Debussy, Ravel, Fauré, Dukas and Stravinsky at Llobet's concerts.

Continuing his highly successful career as a recitalist, Llobet toured throughout Europe, South America and the United States of America. There is no doubt that he was one of the most influential guitarists of the era. He was probably the first guitarist to make a recording with a microphone. These first records were made by Parlophon Electra in Barcelona in 1926. He also made several duo recordings with the Argentinian guitarist Maria Luisa Anido.

Llobet was not only a great guitar virtuoso, but also a fine transcriber and arranger for the instrument. It was as a result of his repeated requests that Manuel de Falla wrote his only guitar work, Homenaje pour le Tombeau de Claude Debussy in 1920.

Miguel Llobet died in Barcelona at the age of 59 during the Spanish Civil War. Despite rumours that he was the victim of a bombing raid, there is positive proof that he died of natural causes after a bout of pleurisy.

SELECTED MUSIC
Le Mestre: Catalan Folk Song.	BA 12124
Estilo Popular Argentino No.1.	UME 21317
Estilo Popular Argentino No.2.	UME 21318
Five Catalan Folk Melodies, ed. Papas.	CO 232
La Filla del Marxant.	BA 12123
Leonesa.	UME 21939
Respuesta.	UME 20370
Romanza (in C minor).	UME 21695
Scherzo: Waltz.	UME 20371
Ten Popular Catalan Songs.	UME 20372
Complete Guitar Works (5 Vols).	Chanterelle ECH 890

SELECTED RECORDINGS
The Recordings of Miguel Llobet
(2 LPs). El Maestro EM 8003 LP
Miguel Llobet: The Guitar Recordings c.1925.
Chanterelle CHR 001 CD
Leif Christensen plays Llobet and Tarrega. Paula 20 CD
Michael Troster plays Miguel Llobet. Super Nova SNCD-0031

SELECTED READING
Miguel Llobet,Chitarrista dell Impressionismo –
Bruno Tonazzi. Bèrben, Milan, 1966

MICHAEL LORIMER

Born –

Chicago, USA

13 January 1946

Michael Lorimer

Born in Chicago, Michael Lorimer was raised in Los Angeles, California. He became interested in the classical guitar at the age of ten when he heard one of his father's records of Andrés Segovia. Lorimer's first teacher was the Los Angeles guitarist Guy Horn, and he studied with him until he was fourteen years old.

Dorothy de Goede, a former pupil of Segovia, introduced Lorimer to Segovia in 1962. The master guitarist was impressed by the young player and suggested a visit to Siena, Italy, in order to study with him. This Lorimer did after graduating from high school at the age of seventeen. He continued his studies with Segovia at Santiago de Compostela, Spain.

After returning to the United States, Michael Lorimer began a busy career, giving a minimum of thirty recitals a year and teaching on a regular basis at Berkeley, California, and at the San Francisco Conservatory of Music.

In 1980 he was the visiting professor of guitar at the University of Carolina, at Wilmington, USA. For several years he wrote a column on the classical guitar for the magazine Guitar Player.

Michael Lorimer has also made a study of the baroque guitar, and has included it in many of his concert recitals.

One of the leading recitalists and teachers in the United States today, Michael Lorimer has also achieved prominence as a transcriber of several excellent books of guitar music, for Charles Hansen Music, USA, and for the Mel Bay Publishing Company.

SELECTED READING

Michael Lorimer.	Guitar Player, October 1973
Michael Lorimer.	Guitar Player, December 1975
Michael Lorimer.	Frets, September 1980
Michael Lorimer.	Guitar & Lute, July 1980

GUY LUKOWSKI

Born –

Brussels, Belgium

7 March 1942

Guy Lukowski

The son of a Polish father and a French mother, Guy Lukowski began his studies on the guitar at the age of thirteen. After leaving university he attended the Conservatory of Liège, where he was a pupil of Gonzalez Mohino.

149

In 1972 Lukowski was chosen by Alexandre Lagoya to join the Ensemble Français de Musique de Chambre Pupitre XIV, performing throughout France. Since then he has led a busy concert career in Europe, North and South America and the Middle East. He has made over twenty recordings.

Guy Lukowski teaches classical guitar at the Academie de Musique César Franck in Belgium. He is the founder and artistic manager of the Festival International de la Guitare in Liège, and is regarded by many as Belgium's most important guitarist and guitar personality.

SELECTED RECORDINGS

Ma première guitare.	Decca 146Y LP
Guitar Romance.	WEA 58071 LP
Guitare.	RKM 805 LP
Spanish Guitar.	IBC 97212 LP
Romance.	Barclay 93021 LP
Guitar Music of Barrios.	EMI Angel S-37844 LP
Vivaldi, Boccherini, Rossini Paganini, Mozart.	EMI 1A 067-2702521 LP
Carulli Guitar Duets (with Philippe Lemaigre)	EMI PM C 069-19069 LP
Fernando Sor Duets (with Philippe Lemaigre).	Pavane ADW 7016 LP
Sor-Carulli.	EMI 37845 LP
Piazzolla: Histoire du Tango (with M. Grauwels, flute).	Carrere CA 681 66.325 LP
Alternances for guitar & flute.	EMI 99544 LP
Guy Lukowski.	Vogue DIA 336 LP
Patchwork.	EMI 2401261 LP
South American Music.	Pavane ADW 7310 CD
Italian Music.	Pavane ADW 7311 CD

VINCENZO MACALUSO

Born –

Milwaukee, Wisconsin, USA

9 January 1941

Vincenzo Macaluso

Vincenzo Macaluso began his studies on the guitar at the age of ten with his father. His first interest was jazz, and he eventually studied with the jazz guitarist Barney Kessel. Macaluso made great progress and soon established himself as a prominent jazz/studio guitarist in the Los Angeles area.

It was during his late teens that Macaluso began a serious study of classical music. Within a few years he developed a fine technique on the classical instrument and became generally accepted as one of the leading classical guitarists on the West Coast of America.

Macaluso was one of the few American guitarists to change over to the ten-string guitar originally designed by Narciso Yepes. He played this instrument exclusively for several years, recording four albums for the Klavier label. More recently, he returned to playing the six-string guitar exclusively, feeling that the sonority of this instrument could not be duplicated on the ten-string guitar.

Vincenzo Macaluso is currently Artist-in-Residence and Professor of Guitar at Whittier College, California.

SELECTED RECORDINGS

10-String Guitar Interprets the Classics.	Klavier KS 508 LP
10-String Guitar Interprets theFrench Classics.	Klavier KS 523 LP
10-String Guitar Interpretsthe Spanish Classics.	Klavier KS 552 LP

Heitor Berlioz featured on French postage stamps, 1983

Francisco Tarrega – honoured as one of Spain's foremost personalities on Spanish postage stamps 1977

Fernando Sor featured on Spanish postage stamps, 1985

Mario Maccaferri in 1926

MARIO MACCAFERRI

Born Cento, Bologna, Italy

20 May 1900

Died – New York, USA, 16 April 1993

Mario Maccaferri in 1989

Mario Maccaferri gained his diploma and left school at the age of nine. He began to work as a dish washer and then later as an apprentice carpenter. After a while he heard of a vacancy in the workshops of the famous Italian luthier Luigi Mozzani, which he was to fill in 1911.

It was during his apprenticeship with Mozzani that Maccaferri took an interest in the playing of the classical guitar. By the age of sixteen he had gained a high reputation as a concert guitarist. He studied music seriously at the Academy in Siena from 1916, and during the period 1920-1923 he gave many guitar recitals. Throughout this period he maintained his interest, as a technical adviser in the Mozzani workshops, in the technical side of guitar making and engineering as a whole. In 1926 he received the highest possible diploma for music and guitar playing from the Academy in Siena, and in the same year became that institution's first professor of guitar.

In 1923 Maccaferri left Mozzani and embarked on a European concert tour that included Italy, Switzerland, France and Germany. In the eyes of some press reviewers he was an artist of the highest calibre, equal in both artistry and interpretation to the then young Andrés Segovia. During this period he advertized as a maker of all fretted instruments, violins, violas and cellos, and in 1926-1927 he won top prizes in the violin and cello making contests held in Rome, Fiume and Montecatini. In 1926 Maccaferri visited London, appearing in concert at the Wigmore Hall. He decided to stay for a while to try and earn a living as a guitar teacher, and it was in London that he developed the prototypes of the distinctive and famous Maccaferri guitars that were to be built later in Paris and used by Django Reinhardt and other top European jazz guitarists. Those revolutionary guitars had closed, lubricated and geared tuning machines, predating those on today's instruments.

In 1933 Maccaferri continued his career as a concert artist, playing in Berlin, Hamburg, Cologne, Brussels and Antwerp. This suddenly came to a halt when he broke his hand in a swimming pool accident. Having studied the manufacture of saxophone reeds in Paris, he founded the French American Reed Mfg Company, moving it from Cento to the United States in 1938. Within a short period of time his company became the leading supplier in the United States of clarinet and saxophone reeds.,

Maccaferri then went into plastics, and his company, Mastro Industries, developed a line of best-selling plastic guitars and ukuleles. His engineering genius undoubtedly helped millions of children throughout the world to buy a playable guitar at an affordable price.

In 1981 Mario Maccaferri finally closed Mastro Industries. In his eighties, he designed some new guitars for the Saga company in Japan. In 1990, within a few weeks of his ninetieth birthdayt, he heard one of his plastic violins played in a recital at Carnegie Hall, New York.

Maccaferri had a strong friendship with artists such as Andrés Segovia and, among his earlier pupils, Ida Presti and Len Williams, the father of John Williams. Mario Maccaferri was a guitarist, luthier and innovator of unusual ability.

SELECTED READING
The Rebirth of Django's Guitar. M.J. Summerfield.
CSL Booklet, 1974

Article.	Guitar Player, April 1974
Article.	Guitar, May 1975
Article.	Guitar Player, November 1976
Interview.	Guitar, January 1976
Interview.	Guitar, August 1977
Interview.	Classical Guitar, September 1984
Interview.	Guitar Player, February 1986
Article.	Acoustic Guitar, March/April 1992
Article.	Vintage Guitar Magazine, March and April 1995

IVOR MAIRANTS

Born –

Rypin, Poland

18 July 1908

Ivor Mairants

Ivor Mairants is well known throughout the world to guitarists of all styles. In recent years he has devoted more of his time to the classical guitar, and has composed several original works for the instrument, made many transcriptions of classical melodies, and written a best-selling flamenco guitar method.

He became a professional guitarist at the age of twenty. Over the past sixty years he has come to be regarded throughout the world as one of the leading authorities on the guitar in all its forms. Although not strictly a classical guitarist, his contribution to the promotion of the classical guitar in Britain over the years has been enormous.

He was a featured member of many of Britain's leading dance bands in the nineteen-thirties and forties, including those of Ambrose, Roy Fox, Lew Stone, Geraldo and Ted Heath. In later years he was often heard with the popular Mantovani orchestra, and more recently with Manuel and his Music of the Mountains.

Of particular importance to guitarists is the fact that Ivor Mairants has devoted so much of his time to writing music and methods for the guitar. He established a school of music in London (1950-60), and among his many pupils were several players who today are some of Britain's top guitarists. For many years he devoted a lot of his energies to developing his music store in the West End of London, with his wife Lily, offering one of the world's finest selection of classical guitars.

Ivor Mairants still spends every spare moment writing for the guitar – jazz, classical and flamenco. Many of his methods and solos, old and new, are used by thousands of guitarists throughout the world. He is a regular contributor to Classical Guitar magazine.

In 1995 Ivor Mairants saw the publication of his marvellous work 'The Great Jazz Guitarists'. This unique book of note-for-note transcriptions of many outstanding jazz guitar solos took several years to compile.

SELECTED MUSIC

6 Solos for Classic Guitar.	EMI
6 Bagatelles.	EMI
A Bundle of Blues.	Chappells/Hansen
6 Progressive Pieces for Solo Guitar.	EMI
6 Easy Pieces.	EMI
6 Lute Pieces.	EMI
6 Part Suites.	Breitkopf & Härtel
Sonata (to a Sonic Age).	Brons/Hansen
Sonata No.2.	AP
Meditation.	Chappells/Hansen
The Spirit of New Orleans.	Chappells/Hansen
Travel Suite.	EMI
3 Rhythmic Dances.	EMI
Four Biblical Sketches	Fentone
Triptych.	Fentone

SELECTED READING

My Fifty Fretting Years: An Autobiography: Ivor Mairants.	Ashley Mark, 1980
Interview.	Classical Guitar, February 1986
The Great Jazz Guitarists.	Music Maker Publications, 1995

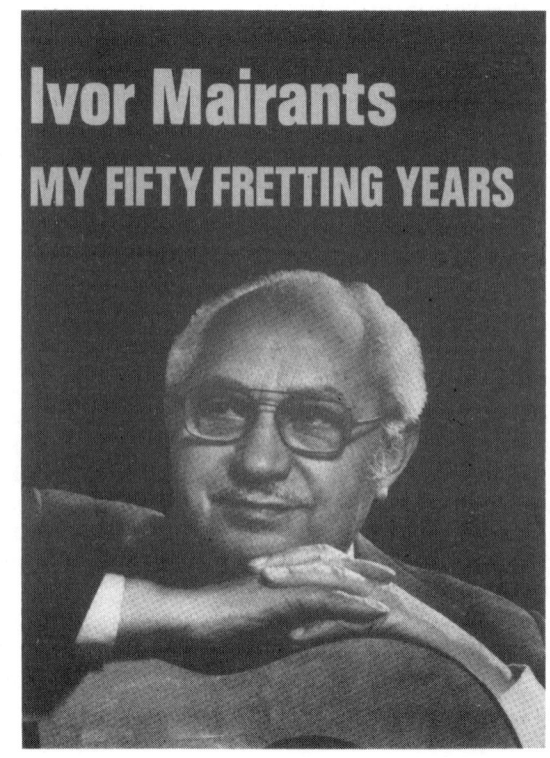

DEBORAH MARIOTTI

Born –

Zürich, Switzerland

26 September 1959

SELECTED RECORDINGS
Deborah Mariotti, Gitarre.	Ex Libris PAN 130 053 LP
Rodrigo: Concierto Madrigal.	EMI Digital ASD 1651411 LP
Deborah Mariotti spielt.	Jecklin 240 LP
Musik aus Spanien und Sudamerika.	Jecklin JS 263-2 CD
Romantic Guitar Music.	Jecklin JS 293-2 CD

SELECTED READING
Interview.	Classical Guitar, September 1986
Interview.	Guitar International, March 1987
Interview.	Guitar International, May 1989

Deborah Mariotti

Deborah Mariotti began to play the guitar at the age of four under the instruction of her father Luigi Mariotti, a guitarist and luthier. Through him the young guitarist benefited from personal contact with many prominent guitarists, including Manuel López Ramos, Ernesto Bitetti and Alfonso Moreno, who were regular visitors to the Mariotti home.

In 1978 Deborah Mariotti won first prize in the Concours des Jeunesses Musicales Suisses and was awarded the Villa-Lobos interpretation medal in Milan, Italy. In 1979 she continued her studies at the Academy Estudio de Arte Guitarristico in Mexico City with Manuel López Ramos, and in the same year was awarded the soloist diploma. In 1982 she was a prizewinner at Guitar '81 in Toronto, Canada, and she also made a highly acclaimed debut recital at the Wigmore Hall, London.

Since 1980 Deborah Mariotti has maintained a very active concert schedule, performing throughout Europe, Scandinavia, North America, Mexico and the Far East. She has also appeared on radio and television and recorded with major orchestras including the London Symphony Orchestra.

BARRY MASON

Born –

Cottingham, Yorkshire, England

6 September 1947

Barry Mason

SELECTED RECORDINGS

Popular Music of Elizabeth I.	Saga 5447 LP
16th Century Music.	Saga 5454 LP
The Queen's Men.	CRD 1055 LP
Music in Pictures.	NGS 100 LP
Portraits in Music.	NGS 101 LP
The Music of Thomas Campion.	Meridian E 77009 LP
Music of Kings & Courtiers.	Saga 5467 LP
English Social Music (with James Tyler).	Saga 5479 LP
English Ayres & Duets.	Hyperion A 66003 LP
Italian Bel Canto Arias (with James Tyler).	Hyperion A 66153 LP
Masters of the Baroque Guitar.	Amon Ra SAR45 CD
Now what is love? (with Glenda Simpson).	Amon Ra CD-SAR 50
Shakespeare's Musicke.	Meridian CDE 84198

SELECTED READING

Interview.	Guitar International, December 1985
Interview.	Classical Guitar, 1990

Barry Mason was educated at Hull College of Technology. He studied classical guitar at the Royal Academy of Music in London, where he studied with Anthony Rooley and David Munrow, specializing in early guitar and the lute. He made his concert debut at the Purcell Room in 1973.

Mason left the Academy in 1974 and went on to study with Diana Poulton at the Royal College of Music for a year. By this time he was recognized as a leading performer on the lute, vihuela and other early fretted instruments. He became director of the early music group Camerata of London in 1974, and in 1977 he was director of the First Early Music Centre Festival in London. Since that time Mason has been a leading international concert recitalist of early music and a prolific recording artist.

In 1991 Mason founded, and now directs, the annual Classical Guitar Festival of Great Britain. This week long festival is held in the historic West Dean College, formerly an English stately home which is situated near to Chichester in southern England. This festival is now regarded as one of the most important annual international classical guitar events.

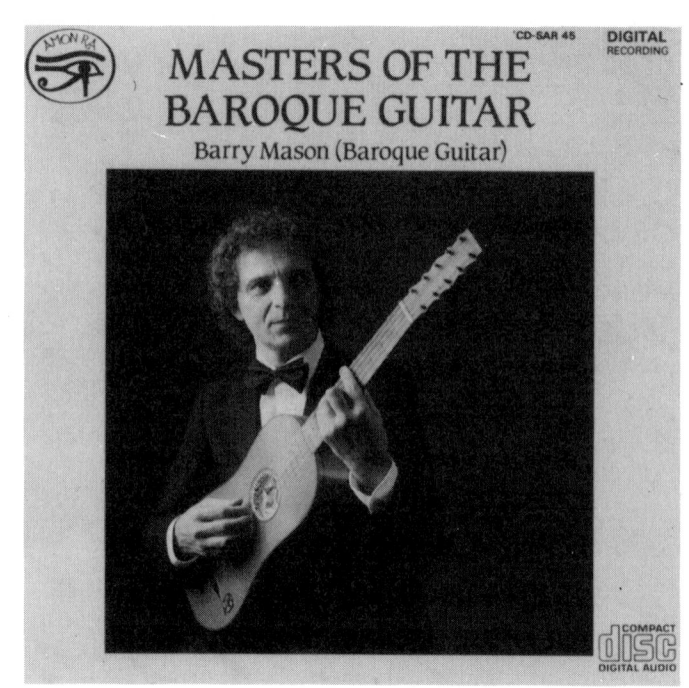

AKINOBU MATSUDA

Born – AKINOBU JIRO MATSUDA

Himeji, Japan

28 June 1933

Akinobu Matsuda

Akinobu Matsuda graduated at Kobe University in 1957, where he read Economics. He had begun to play the guitar at the age of fourteen and had immediately shown great promise.

His first public recital, in Kobe, Japan, 1958, was a great success. In 1959 his playing was commended by Andrés Segovia, who was principal artist at the Osaka International Festival in Japan that year. In 1969 Matsuda travelled to Europe, where for two years he studied with Segovia and Alirio Díaz. During this time he also studied with John Williams at the Royal College of Music in London.

In 1962 Akinobu Matsuda made the first of three concert tours in the United States, going on to make his debut in Singapore and Hong Kong in 1964. His debut at Carnegie Hall, New York, took place in 1969. In the same year he also appeared for the first time at the Wigmore Hall, London. In 1973 he undertook a successful concert tour of Great Britain, and made radio broadcasts in Dublin and Paris. He also gave a recital in Bergen, Norway. The following year he performed at the Hong Kong Arts Festival as a soloist.

Akinobu Matsuda has been awarded many prizes, including the Papas-Puyana Prize at the International Guitar Competition under the auspices of Andrés Segovia and sponsored by the Conservatory of Music at Orense, Spain. In 1963 he received the Japan Critics Club Prize of the Year, and in 1979 he became an honorary member of the Board of Directors of the International Castelnuovo-Tedesco Society. In the same year he was given the award of the Cultural Services from Himeji City. He performs widely in addition to recording and teaching. In 1982 he appeared on the Japan National TV series 'Let's Play Guitar'.

SELECTED RECORDINGS

Romance de Amor.	Columbia (Japan) WS-3063 LP
Maisuda plays Bach Columbia (Japan).	JX-19 LP
Platero y Yo Columbia (Japan).	JX-20 LP
Japanese Melodies Columbia (Japan).	OS-10126 LP
Home Concert Delux.	Victor JV 2045-46-S LP
The Classic Sound of the Guitar.	Argo ZDA 205 LP
Sound of the Guitar (Vol.1).	ARM 30011 LP
Sound of the Guitar (Vol.2).	ARM 3002 CD

SELECTED READING

Interview.	Guitar, March 1973
Interview.	Guitar International, April 1989

SELECTED MUSIC

Up-to-date Guitar Method, 1 and 2.   Ongaku No Tomo Sla

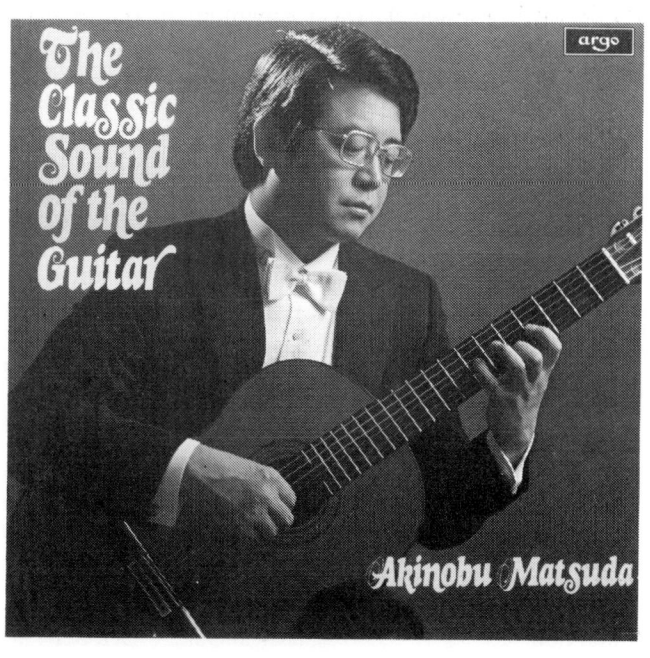

SUSANNE MEBES
Born -
Essen, Germany
12 May 1960

Susanne Mebes

Susanne Mebes won first prize in the German National Music 'Jugend Musiziert' competition at the age of fourteen. She went on to study with the Uruguayan guitarist Antonio Pereira Arias, and the Japanese lutenist Toyohiko Satoh, at the Royal Conservatory of Den Haag in the Netherlands. She also attended master classes given by Julian Bream and other important classical guitarists.

Susanne Mebes graduated with her recital diploma in 1980. In 1981 she was a prizewinner in the Segovia International Competition, Spain, and in 1983 won the Concertgebouw Prize in Amsterdam. Since that time Mebes has led a busy career as a concert, broadcasting and recording artist, and is now active in a duo with the Brazilian guitarist Joaquim Freire. Several new works have been written for and dedicated to her including, *Rememorias* by Marlos Nobre, *Sensations* by Nobert Moret, and *Concertino* for guitar and cello by Jost Meier.

SELECTED RECORDINGS
Susanne Mebes - Guitar Recital	Saturn YA 8202
Castelnuovo-Tedesco Guitar Works	Leman Classics LC 42501 CD
Manuel M. Ponce Guitar Works	Leman Classics LC 42701 CD
Recital Catalan	Leman Classics LC 44201 CD
Freire/Mebes Guitar Duo	Leman Classics LC 44401 CD

SELECTED READING
Interview	Guitar International, June 1985
Interview	Classical Guitar, October 1985

DOMINGO MERCADO
Born - Arroyito, Neuquen Province, Argentina
1 January 1919
Died - La Plata, Buenos Aires Province, Argentina
1 August 1994

Domingo Mercado

Domingo Mercado was for many years a leading figure in the classical guitar world of Argentina, both as a recitalist and as a teacher. He also had many of his transcriptions for guitar of famous classical works published by Ricordi in Argentina.

Mercado first began to play the guitar with the encouragement of his father. By the time he was seventeen he was a serious student of the instrument. In 1939 he gave the first of what were to be many radio broadcasts on local and national radio stations.

In 1961, already an established concert guitarist in Argentina, Mercado made a concert tour of Italy, where his performances received critical acclaim. On his return to Argentina he held several teaching posts including a professorship at the Academy of Belle Artes at the University de la Plata. For many years Mercado was regarded as an authority on the music of Abel Fleury. He was associated with many leading Argentinian musicians including Alberto Ginastera and Abel Fleury. His sons Andres and Adrian continue the Mercado contribution to the guitar in Argentina. Andres is the producer of a weekly classical guitar radio programme, and Adrian is a prominent teacher and recitalist.

SELECTED RECORDINGS
Domingo Mercado - Solo de Guitarra	London LLS-14501 LP
Domingo Mercado - Estudio	Estudio Gismonti K300-029 CAS

SELECTED READING
Tribute Articles	Mundo Guitarristico, August 1995

JOHANN KASPAR MERTZ

Born – Poszony, Hungary

17 August 1806

Died – Vienna, Austria, 14 October 1856

Johann Kaspar Mertz

Johann Kaspar Mertz began his study of music, on both the guitar and the flute, at an early age. A child prodigy, he was able at the age of twelve to support his parents from the income he earned as a teacher.

In 1840 he left Poszony (later known as Pressburg, and now the Czechoslovakian city of Bratislava) for Vienna, less than forty miles distant. There, on 29 November 1840, he made his concert debut in front of the Empress Carolina Augusta at the Court Theatre. The recital was a great success, and Mertz embarked on a concert tour of several European countries.

Whilst living in Vienna, Mertz met and marrfied Josephine Plantin. She was a pianist, and they often appeared together in concert. They enjoyed great success and popularity, and as a result were much in demand as teachers, especially to the society élite of Vienna.

Johann Kaspar Mertz was not only a virtuoso guitarist, but also a prolific composer. He composed, arranged and transcribed over one hundred works for the guitar. His composition Concertino won the first prize at the Brussels Competition in 1856, but his untimely death at fifty from a heart complaint of long standing meant that the award had to be made posthumously.

SELECTED MUSIC

Capriccio, op.13 no.3.	Bèrben 2138
Kindermärchen (Children's Fairytale), ed. Leisner.	Presser 11440262
Polacca, ed. Leisner.	Presser 11440259
Romanze.	Presser 11440261
Tarantelle.	Presser 11440260
Three Nocturnes, op.4 .	N 3326
Selected Works: 10 volumes.	ECH 416

SELECTED READING

Mertz's Last Compositions.   Soundboard, Spring 1982
Caspar Joseph Mertz: Leben und Werk des Ietzten Gitarristen Im Östereichischen Biedermeir
    Astrid Stempnik Verlag Peter Lang, 1990

SELECTED RECORDINGS

Guitar Music of Mertz: Szendrey-Karper.	Hungaroton SLPD 12894 LP
Abendlied-Reiner Stutz.	FSM FLD97789
Richard Savino plays Mertz.	Harmonia Mundi HMU907115 CD
Mertz Guitar Duos – Duo Favori. tacet	42 CD

VLADIMIR MIKULKA

Born –

Prague, Czechoslovakia

11 December 1950

Vladimir Mikulka

Vladimir Mikulka started playing the classical guitar at the age of thirteen. Within two years he was a student of the foremost Czech guitarist Jiri Jirmal at the State Conservatory in Prague. At the age of nineteen, he proved to the world his outstanding ability on his chosen instrument by winning the international guitar competition in Paris, organized by the French radio and television organization ORTF.

Mikulka's success in this competition led to many concert bookings throughout the world. He played to enthusiastic audiences in most countries in Europe, Scandinavia, the Soviet Union, Cuba and Australia.

One of the finest guitarists to have emerged in recent years, Mikulka is not only a great player but also a talented teacher, and as a result he has been called upon to conduct many international masterclasses for guitarists.

Since 1980, Vladimir Mikulka has established himself among the élite of today's classical guitarists. He has participated in many international music festivals, including those held in Helsinki, Paris, Rome and Amsterdam. His several recordings are outstanding. He currently lives in Paris, where he is Professor in the conservatoires of the XIIIth and XXth arrondissements. He is also an editor for the publishers Henri Lemoine of Paris for their guitar series 'Vladimir Mikulka Presents...'

SELECTED RECORDINGS

Vladimir Mikulka Plays Bach.	Supraphon 1-11-15 LP
Guitar Recital.	Denon (Japan) OX-7164 ND LP
Rodrigo/Tedesco Concertos.	Panton 11-0608 G LP
Haydn Quartet/Giuliani Op.3.	Supraphon 1100-2700 LP
The Music of Stepán Rak.	GHA 126-003 CD
Koshkin, Rak, East European Music.	BIS LP 240
Ibero-American Guitar.	BIS CD 340
European Guitar Premieres.	Supraphon 111418 CD
Classics from Bohemia.	GHA 126-032 CD
Live in Prague (Video).	CTV

SELECTED READING

Interview.	Classical Guitar Jan/Feb 1983
Interview.	Classical Guitar, October 1984
Interview.	Guitar International, July 1986
Interview.	Classical Guitar, July 1989

JOHN MILLS

Born –

Kingston-upon-Thames, England

13 September 1947

John Mills

John Mills was initially a self-taught player from the age of nine. After making exceptional progress as a pupil at the Spanish Guitar Centre in London, he studied from 1966 to 1969 at the Royal College of Music, London, with John Williams. In 1968 he went to Spain to take part in masterclasses given by Andrés Segovia at Santiago de Compostela.

John Mills has been giving recitals regularly throughout the British Isles for many years. He has performed a number of times at the Wigmore Hall, the Purcell Room and the Queen Elizabeth Hall in London. In 1972 he made his international debut with a concert tour of Eastern Canada, and has since returned many times to perform throughout Canada and the United States. In the summer of 1975 he was chosen to play one of the major evening recitals at the Guitar '75 Festival in Toronto. He has also made concert tours of Australia, Sweden and Japan. In one period of ten years, John Mills gave over two thousand recitals.

John Mills is recognized world-wide not only as one of Britain's finest guitarists but also for his excellent teaching. His guitar method, The John Mills Guitar Tutor, was published by Musical New Services of Britain. He has also given many masterclasses, both at home and abroad, and has several records to his credit. Mills appeared several times on the BBC Radio programme The Classical Guitar, and has also been featured on television and local radio stations in Great Britain. He spent some time in New Zealand, but has now settled once again in England.

He is married to the classical guitarist Cobie Smits.

SELECTED RECORDINGS
Five Centuries of Classical Guitar.	Discourses ABK 10 LP
Student Repertoire: Volume One.	Guitar G 101 LP
Student Repertoire: Volume Two.	Guitar G 102 LP
20th Century Guitar Music.	Guitar G 105 LP

SELECTED READING
Interview.	Guitar, December 1973
Interview.	Guitar, June 1978
Interview.	Guitar International, December 1988

SELECTED MUSIC
John Mills Guitar Method.	Music Sales
Student Repertoire 1 and 2.	Music Sales

SIMON MOLITOR

Born Neckarsulm, Wurtemburg, Austria

3 November 1766

Died Vienna, Austria, 21 February 1848

Simon Molitor

Simon Molitor originally studied the guitar with his father, Johann Michael Molitor. He continued his studies with the Abbe Vogler and was soon regarded as one of the best guitarists in Vienna at the end of the eighteenth century. After a short period as a orchestral conductor (1796-97) in Venice Molitor returned to Vienna in 1798 to take up a position in the War Office. He was to become a superintendent of the Italian and Dalmatian borders. During his period as a clerk and official Molitor composed many works for the guitar and also collaborated on a guitar method in his spare time, but his work as a guitarist was obviously limited. Molitor retired from the War Office in 1831 and was then able to devote the rest of his years entirely to music.

SELECTED READING
Simon Molitor, Viennese Guitarist & Composer – Josef Zuth
Anton Goll, Vienna 1919

Jorge Morel

JORGE MOREL

Born – JORGE SCIBONA

Buenos Aires, Argentina

9 May 1931

Jorge Morel showed a musical aptitude at a very early age. His father, an actor and an accomplished guitarist, began teaching his talented son the rudiments of the instrument when he was only eleven years of age. It soon became apparent that the youngster was destined for a career in music. He entered the University of Musical Studies in Buenos Aires, where he learned all the basic music subjects and majored in guitar under the guidance and inspiration of the renowned South American guitarist and composer Pablo Escobar. It was Escobar who gave Morel his professional debut at the age of sixteen, in a radio programme featuring both teacher and pupil. The young guitarist was immediately recognized as a major talent, and began his concert career at that time, while still a student at university.

Not until he received his degree at the age of eighteen did Jorge Morel begin to experiment and develop the unique style and brilliant technique that today are so much a part of his artistic identity. As is the case with all great virtuosos, his own arrangements and compositions are the most tangible examples of his aims, standards and ideals as a creative and performing musician. Jorge Morel's prime calling is based in contemporary modes of expression. His compositions abound in bracingly modern rhythms and harmonies, leading naturally towards the melodies and idioms of South America. A fine interpreter of the standard classical repertoire, Morel has also dazzled audiences throughout the world with his exciting transcriptions for guitar of the music of Gershwin, Bernstein, Lennon & McCartney and other modern composers.

Jorge Morel first went to the United States in 1961, making a highly successful debut at Carnegie Hall. Since that time he has toured throughout North America and in Hawaii and Puerto Rico, but remained virtually unknown to European audiences until his London debut at the Wigmore Hall in October 1979. That was a great success, and Jorge Morel has since made frequent visits to Great Britain and Europe, in addition to the very many concerts he gives in North America. He holds the post of Professor of Guitar at the Lehman College in New York.

SELECTED MUSIC

Virtuoso South American Guitar Vol.1.	Ashley Mark
Virtuoso South American Guitar Vol.2.	Ashley Mark
West Side Story/Porgy and Bess.	Ashley Mark
Virtuoso South American Guitar Vol.4.	Ashley Mark
Virtuoso South American Guitar Vol.5.	Ashley Mark
Virtuoso South American Guitar Vol.6.	Ashley Mark
Virtuoso South American Guitar Vol.7.	Ashley Mark
Virtuoso South American Guitar Vol.8.	Ashley Mark
Virtuoso South American Guitar Vol.9.	Ashley Mark
Sonatina.	Chorus
Allegro in Re.	Chorus
Four Pieces.	Chorus
Latin Impressions.	Chorus
Variations on a Gershwin Theme.	Chorus
Danzas para Emiko.	Chorus
Prelude.	Chorus
Little Rhapsody.	Chorus
Preludio y Giga.	Chanterelle ECH 705
Guitareando.	Chorus

SELECTED RECORDINGS

The Warm Guitar.	Decca DL 4167 LP
Artistry of Jorge Morel.	RCA LSP 3953 LP
Guitar Moods.	SMC 1110-2 LP
Magnificent Guitar.	Decca DL 4966 LP
The Fabulous Jorge Morel.	Village Gate VGLP 2001 LP
Virtuoso South American Guitar.	Guitar Masters GMR 1002 LP
Jorge Morel Plays Broadway.	Guitar Masters GMR 1004 LP
Latin Impressions	Guitar Masters GMR 1005 LP
Morel y su Guitarra	Panart LP-3068 LP
Meet Morel	Sesac S-601/602 LP
Encore	Sesac S-603/604 LP
Art of Jorge Morel	Luthier CD 61411-2
Latin Impressions	Luthier CD 61413-2
Pelech plays Morel	Guitar Masters GMR 102-94 CD
Very Best of Jorge Morel	Guitar Masters GMR 103-95 CD
Pelech plays Morel Concertos	Luthier CD 2881-61413

SELECTED READING

Interview.	Guitar Player, March 1970
Interview.	Frets, September 1979
Interview.	Guitar, December 1979
Article.	Classical Guitar, Nov/Dec 1982
Article.	Classical Guitar, March/April 1983
Interview.	Guitar Player, June 1987
Interview.	Classical Guitar, November & December 1985
Interview.	Classical Guitar, August 1996

ALFONSO MORENO

Born –

Mexico,

1950

Alfonso Moreno

Alfonso Moreno began his musical training at the age of eight, studying violin and composition. In 1964 he took up the guitar and studied with Manuel López Ramos in Mexico City. In 1968 he won first prize at the Radio France International Classical Guitar Competition in Paris. Since that time he has led a busy concert career playing throughout Mexico, the USA, Europe and the Soviet Union. He has also recorded for the EMI company.

Alfonso Moreno is regarded as one of Mexico's leading classical guitarists.

SELECTED RECORDINGS
Fantasia para un Gentilhombre: Rodrigo. EMI ESD 7145 LP
Alfonso Moreno.   GAMMA CG-351 LP
Ponce: Concierto del Sur.   EMI ESD 1651051 LP
Rodrigo: Concierto de Aranjuez.   EMI ASD 4159 LP
Rodrigo: Concierto Madrigal (with Deborah Mariotti).
                                   EMI ASD 1651411 LP
3 Guitar Concertos.   ASV CD DCA887

LUIGI MOZZANI

Born –

Faenza, Italy, 9 March 1869

Died – Rovereto, Italy, 12 August 1943

Luigi Mozzani

COURTESY: MARIO MACCAFERRI

Luigi Mozzani showed a great interest in music at an early age, and dedicated every free moment he had to the study of the guitar. He later studied the oboe and composition at the Conservatory of Music in Bologna under Professor Castelli, earning his diploma at the age of eighteen. For two years he was first oboist at the San Carlo Theatre, Naples, after which he travelled throughout Europe and Asia. At the age of twenty he went to North America with a symphony orchestra, but the tour proved a financial disaster and Mozzani decided to make the guitar his career rather than the oboe.

His first public recitals on the guitar met with great success, and he was regarded as a virtuoso. He returned to Europe and lived in Paris, where at the age of twenty-five he became one of the most sought-after teachers of the guitar by Parisian high society. He continued to give many highly acclaimed recitals in France, Austria and Germany. A distinctive feature of his guitar technique was the use of a metal thumb pick on the right hand, a technique also used by Mario Maccaferri throughout his concert career in the 1920s.

During these years as a recitalist, Mozzani became frustrated with some of the limitations of the guitar as it was then constructed, and decided to return to Italy to study guitar construction in depth. He eventually founded important schools for luthiers in Cento, Bologna and Rovereto. One of his most famous pupils was Mario Maccaferri. Mozzani continued to study the construction of the guitar right up to his death, and his workshops produced a large number of instruments. Among his many patents was the well-known guitar-lyre, an instrument with an adjustable neck.

Although latterly much of his time was devoted to instrument construction, Mozzani was also a talented composer and transcriber of guitar music. Quite a lot of his works were published, but many of his compositions remain unedited and unpublished.

SELECTED MUSIC
Esercizi Di Tecnica Superiore.   Bèrben
Mozzani Opere per Chitarra – edited Angel Gilardino.
        Bèrben 3800

SELECTED READING
Mozzani – Un liutaio e la sua arte.
        Cento Arts and Crafts 1990

THOMAS MÜLLER-PERING
Born - Cologne, Germany
22 April 1958

Thomas Müller-Pering

PHOTO: KLAUS ERICH HAUN

Thomas Müller-Pering began to play the piano at the age of six. He changed to the guitar at the age of thirteen. His first teachers were Heiner Viertmann and Volker Glaser. Within a year or so he began to give some short guitar recitals. He then began to study, over a period of seven years, with Tadashi Sasaki. He also attended masterclasses with Oscar Ghiglia, Hubert Käppel, José Tomás and John Williams.

Muller-Pering won prizes in several international guitar competitions, including first prize in the 1983 Vinar del Mar Competition in Chile. In 1980 he gained his soloist's Diploma and began to teach in Aachen. He is now established as a leading international concert recitalist and recording artist.

SELECTED RECORDINGS
Torre Bermeja   King Records   K33 Y 143-CD
Guitar Music of Villa Lobos   King Record   K32 Y 248 CD
Colleccion Caracteristica   Aurea Vox   CDC 9519-011
Les Deux Amis   Teldec   624406-LP
Granados/Falla Duo w/ Manuel Barrueco
    EMI   CDC 7 54456 2
Famous Modern Duos w/Burkhard Wolk
    FONO FSM 97702 CD
Tango en Skai - Video   Chimoto CCV 1008

SELECTED READING
Interview   Classical Guitar, November 1996

MARTIN MYSLIVECEK

Born –
Prague, Czechoslovakia
12 June 1950

Martin Myslivecek

Martin Myslivecek studied classical guitar at the Brno Conservatory under Prof. A. Sadlik from 1966 to 1972 and with Prof. Roland Zimmer at the Franz Liszt University of Music at Weimar from 1972 to 1978.

He began his concert career while still a student at the Brno Conservatory. While he was at the Liszt University, he entered and won prizes at several important guitar competitions including Markneukirchen (1975), Paris (1976) and Caracas (1977). These successes led to many concert engagements throughout Europe, the USSR, Cuba and Venezuela.

Martin Myslivecek, who is also a fine lute player, is regarded as one of Czechoslovakia's finest classical guitarists. He currently holds a teaching appointment in Graz, Austria.

SELECTED RECORDINGS
Martin Myslivecek Plays. Panton 8111 0174 LP
Martin Myslivecek plays Bach Sanz, Weiss.
Supraphon 1111 3425 LP

SELECTED READING
Interview. Guitar International, December 1983
Interview. Classical Guitar, March/April 1984
Article. Classical Guitar, July 1993

Gerard Deleplangue 10-string guitar, Lille 1782

SANTIAGO NAVASCUES

Born –

Madrid, Spain

23 July 1933

Santiago Navascues

Santiago Navascues is a graduate of the Real Conservatorio in Madrid, and also of the Music Academy in Munich, Germany.

Navascues is highly regarded as one of Europe's finest teachers. Although he gives frequent recitals and has made several recordings for the German company Arcola Eurodisc, it is as a teacher that he spends most of his year. He is currently professor of the guitar at the Richard Strauss Conservatory in Munich, where he has been teaching since 1972. He conducts the International Guitar Seminar annually in Reisbach, and is the editor of guitar works for the publishing house Biblioteca de la Guitarra.

SELECTED RECORDINGS
Music for the Spanish Guitar.	Vanguard 10137 LP
Santiago Navascues.	Eurodisc 86852 LP
Santiago Navascues.	Eurodisc 86853 LP
Santiago Navascues.	Eurodisc 88597 LP
Santiago Navascues.	Eurodisc 89247 LP
Santiago Navascues.	Eurodisc 28902 LP

MICHAEL NEWMAN

Born –

New York, USA

21 December 1957

Michael Newman

Since his Carnegie Hall debut in March 1974, Michael Newman has established himself as one of the United States' most accomplished classical guitarists.

He was brought up in a musical environment. His father, who worked for the Guild Guitar Company in New York, was a lover of music and had a large record collection in which were many classical guitar recordings. They were to influence the young musician.

At the age of seven, however, Newman began to study the piano. Losing interest in this instrument, he took up the guitar and studied with a local teacher, Thomas Anthony, for three years. He made such good progress that, in 1971, he began studying with Albert Valdes Blain at Mannes College of Music, New York. On the advice of Blain, he enrolled full time at Mannes College, where he eventually earned his Bachelor of Music degree. He also studied with Oscar Ghiglia at the Aspen Music Festival and the Accademia Musicale Chigiana in Siena, Italy.

Michael Newman has been a guest soloist with the Hartford and Rochester Chamber Orchestras, the Omaha Symphony, the Cleveland and Fort Wayne

Philharmonics, and the renowned Atlanta Symphony. He has given solo guitar recitals throughout the United States, and was a recipient of the Concert Masters' 'Young Artist Award' in 1973. He was a prizewinner at the International Guitar Competition at the Guitar '78 Festival held in Toronto, Canada.

Michael Newman is also highly regarded as a teacher, and is currently on the faculty of both Mannes College of Music and Rutgers University as instructor in guitar. In addition he has conducted many workshops and masterclasses.

Since 1986 Newman has performed in a guitar duo with Laura Oltman. They have recorded for the Music Masters label, and are currently the Ensemble-in-Residence at Mannes College.

SELECTED RECORDINGS
Michael Newman.	Sheffield Lab SL 10 LP
Italian Pleasures.	Sheffield Lab SL 16 LP
Tango Suite (Duo with Laura Oltman).	Music Masters 7071-2-6 CD
Laments and Dances (Duo with Laura Oltman).	Music Masters 67145-2 CD

SELECTED READING
Michael Newman.	Guitar & Lute, October 1981

Douglas Niedt

SELECTED RECORDINGS
Classic Guitar Artistry.	Antigua S-1000 LP
Virtuoso Visions.	Antigua S-2000 LP
After Hours.	Antigua S-3000 LP

SELECTED MUSIC
Classic Guitar Artistry.	Sherry-Brener
Virtuoso Visions.	Sherry-Brener

DOUGLAS NIEDT

Born –

St Louis, Missouri, USA

8 October 1952

It was hearing Andrés Segovia on a record that first inspired Douglas Niedt. His father, also a guitarist, gave him his first lessons at the age of seven. By the time he was fourteen he had received first-prize awards in competitions sponsored by the American Guild of Music in Pittsburgh, Louisville and Kentucky. The young player continued his studies at the Juilliard School, Segovia masterclasses in Spain and privately with Narciso Yepes, Christopher Parkening, Jorge Morel and Oscar Ghiglia.

At the age of twenty-one, Niedt made his debut recital at the Carnegie Recital Hall in New York, since when he has given many concerts throughout the USA. In 1987 he was awarded a Solo Recitalist Fellowship by the National Endowment for the Arts.

Douglas Niedt has made several recordings, and is Chairman of the Guitar Department of the Conservatory of Music, University of Missouri at Kansas City.

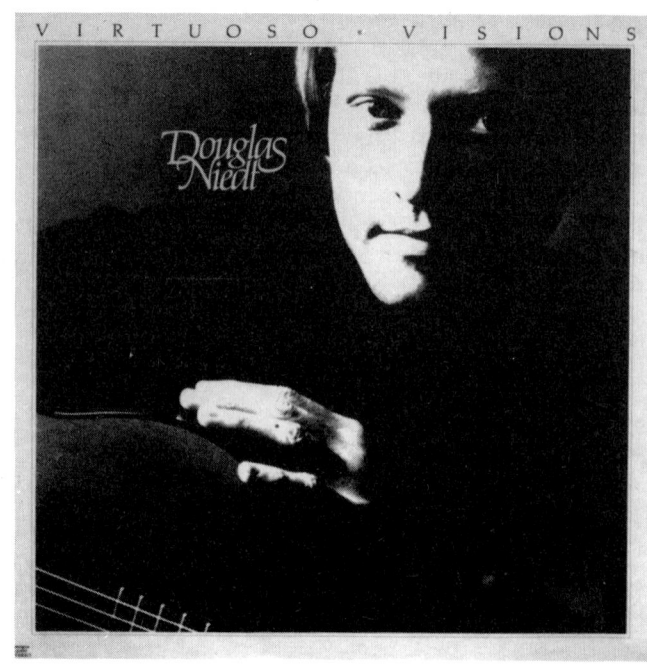

KAARE NORGE
Born -
Brorup, Jutland, Denmark
12 July 1963

Kaare Norge

Kaare Norge began to play the guitar at the age of twelve. He made remarkable progress on the guitar and gave his first Danish television broadcast at the age of fourteen. At the age of seventeen he was admitted to the Royal Academy of Music in Aarhus, where he studied under Leif Christensen. By 1988 Norge had already established himself as a concert performer. He was invited to study privately with Manuel Barrueco in New York. Whilst studying with Barrueco, he gave several well received recitals in New York and New Jersey. He also attended masterclasses with David Russell, Oscar Ghiglia, Hubert Käppel, Nicolas Goluses and Costas Cotsiolis.

In recent years Kaare Norge has established himself as Denmark's foremost classical guitarist. He has given over 500 concerts all over the world since 1985, and has also appeared on many television and radio broadcasts. Norge won Danish Radio's Bolero Prize in 1991, and the State Award of Art in 1992.

SELECTED RECORDINGS
Bach/Rodrigo/Paganini	BMG GEN CD 199
Tango	BMG GEN CD 179
Con Amore	BMG GEN CD 186
La Guitarra	BMG GEN CD 205
Guitarplayer	Interrecord BMG IR CD 017
Movements	BMG 88712 CD

NIGEL NORTH
Born –
London, England
5 June 1954

Nigel North

Nigel North began to study the violin from the age of seven, and won scholarships to study at the junior department of the Guildhall School of Music from 1964 to1970. In 1964 he began to teach himself the classical guitar. In 1969 he began to teach himself to play the lute.

From 1971 to 1974 North studied classical guitar with John Williams and Carlos Bonell at the Royal College of Music in London. He also studied viols with Francis Baines. In 1974 he gained an ARCM Diploma with distinction, for lute performance. He returned in 1974 to the Guildhall, where he joined the new postgraduate course in Early Music. In 1975 he became a member of staff as lute teacher, and since 1976 he has been Professor of Lute there.

His knowledge and experience in the art of continuo playing led him to write the first modern practical continuo method for the lute and theorbo, published by Faber in 1987.

Nigel North has given many workshops and masterclasses for lutenists and guitarists throughout Europe and North America. He is recognized as one of the world's foremost lutenists, yet he also remains a great exponent of the early classical guitar. A soloist on both lute and guitar, he gives many concerts all over the world. His recordings range in style from the mid-sixteenth century to the mid-nineteenth. As an ensemble player he has made many more recordings and concert appearances with leading Early Music groups of the day, including the English Concert, the London Baroque, Romanesca, and the Taverner Players. He has also made several broadcasts on both radio and television for the BBC.

SELECTED MUSIC
Continuo Playing on the Lute, Archlute and Theorbo.
Faber 1987

SELECTED RECORDINGS
De Visée. Decca 'Florilegium' L'Oiseau-Lyre DSLO 542 LP
Dowland Lute Works.
Decca 'Florilegium' L'Oiseau-Lyre D187 D5 LP
Pieces de Luth.   UEA 81704 LP
Guitar Collection.   Amon Ra RA SAR 18 LP
Bach Lute Music.   Amon Ra RA SAR 23 LP
Concord of Sweet Sounds (with Lisa Beznosiuk).
Amon Ra SAR 33 CD
Weiss/Vivaldi.   Linn CKD 006 CD
Bach on the Lute (Vol.1).   Linn CKD 013 CD
Bach on the Lute (Vol.2).   Linn CKD 029 CD
Bach on the Lute (Vol.3).   Linn CKD 049 CD
Bach on the Lute (Vol.4).   Linn CKD 055 CD

SELECTED READING
Interview.   Classical Guitar, September 1987

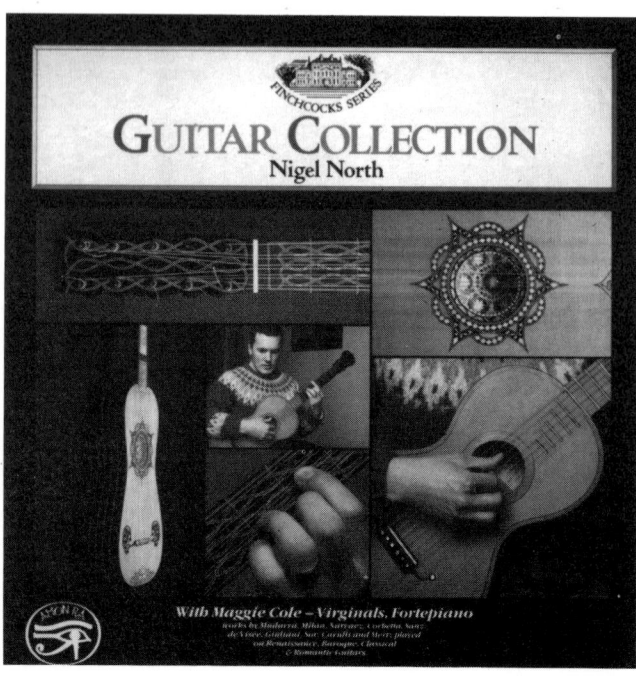

CRAIG OGDEN
Born -
Perth, Australia
11 July 1967

Craig Ogden

Craig Ogden studied the guitar from the age of seven and percussion from the age of thirteen. After gaining a music degree with honours from the University of Western Australia he moved to the UK in 1990. Here he undertook two years of performance study at the Royal Northern College of Music. In 1992 he graduated with the Professional Performance Diploma with Distinction.

Craig Ogden is the winner of several important guitar competitions, including the Shell Darwin International Guitar Competition and the AT & T ISTEL Young Musicians Award Strings Competition. He also won first prize in the 1995 inaugural Unisa Transnet International Guitar Competition in South Africa.

In the last few years Ogden has performed as a soloist in Australia, the USA and in the UK, in recital and on radio and television broadcasts. He has performed with the Halle Orchestra and the BBC Philharmonic Orchestra. He made his London debut at the Purcell Room in December 1994, and appeared in a tribute to Sir Michael Tippett at the Wigmore Hall in January 1995. Craig Ogden is also active as a teacher, and holds positions as tutor in guitar at Chetham's School of Music and at the Royal Northern College of Music in Manchester, UK.

SELECTED RECORDINGS
20th Century Guitar Classics   Nimbus NI 5390
Britten - Folksong Arrangements   Hyperion CDA 66941/2
Yoshimatsu Concertos   Chandos   CHAN 9438 CD

STEIN-ERIK OLSEN

Born –

Bergen, Norway

8 September 1953

Stein-Erik Olsen

Stein-Erik Olsen was educated at the Bergen Conservatory of Music and the Norwegian State Academy of Music. He then studied with Alexandre Lagoya for two years at the Paris Conservatoire National Supérieur de Musique. He has also studied with Per-Olof Olson and Manuel Barrueco.

Stein-Erik Olsen has played at international festivals throughout Norway, and has made several television and radio broadcasts there. He has also given concerts throughout the rest of Scandinavia and Europe. In 1986 he made his concert debut at the Wigmore Hall in London. Several eminent contemporary composers, including Ketil Hvoslev and John W. Duarte, have written works especially for him.

SELECTED RECORDINGS
Guitar.	Simax PS 1008
Stein-Erik Olsen Guitar plays – Kucera, Duarte, Castérède, Brouwer.	Samt 184
Panorama.	FXLP 60
Double Delight: Flute/Guitar Duo.	BD 7004
Blue Sonata.	Simax PSC1029
Mosaic.	For-X FXCD 81
Hommage!	Simax PSC 1008 CD
Songs and Dances.	Simax PSC 1084 CD
Balleto.	Alba 1001 CD

SELECTED READING
Interview.	Guitar International, January 1986
Interview.	Classical Guitar, July 1987

JORGE ORAISON

Born –

Montevideo, Uruguay

26 June 1946

Jorge Oraison

Jorge Oraison's first guitar teacher was Lola Gonella de Ayestaran, in Montevideo. He also studied music theory at the Conservatorio Municipal, then musicology at the University of Montevideo.

In 1969 Oraison was granted a scholarship from the Instituto de Cultura Hispanica to study in Spain with José Tomás at Santiago de Compostela. In 1971 he won the silver medal at the XIII Radio-France Concours International de Guitarre in Paris. Shortly after that, he moved to the Netherlands, where he has lived since.

Jorge Oraison performs widely throughout Europe, and is professor of guitar at the Rotterdam and Twents Conservatories of Music in the Netherlands.

SELECTED RECORDINGS
South American Guitar Music.	EMI 037-26 019 LP
Castelnuevo-Tedesco Guitar Works.	Etcetera ETC 1001 LP
Astor Piazzolla Guitar Works.	Etcetera ETC 1023 LP
Leo Brouwer Guitar Works.	Etcetera ETC 1034 LP

JESÚS ORTEGA

Born –

Havana, Cuba

1935

Jesús Ortega

Jesús Ortega's introduction to the guitar and music came through listening, as a child, to his grandfather's record collection of flamenco music. It was not until he was seventeen that, with the encouragement of his friend Leo Brouwer, he began to study the guitar. He studied with Isaac Nicola at the Conservatorio Musical de Havana. Here he developed a love for chamber music, and decided also to study the cello.

After finishing his studies, Ortega performed professionally as a soloist, in a duo with Leo Brouwer and also as an ensemble player. He has given concerts throughout Latin America and Europe. His repertoire has always emphasized Cuban, Latin American and contemporary works. He has toured the USA as an accompanist for a Cuban dance company.

Ortega was director of the Conservatorio Amadeu Roldán (1966-68), National Co-ordinator of Music in the Consejo Nacional de Cultura (1961-65), and is currently professor of guitar at the Instituto Superior de Arte in Havana. He also heads a state publishing concern for guitar music, and plays a prominent part in the organization of the biennial Havana International Guitar Competition.

An enthusiastic musicologist, Jesús Ortega divides his time between playing, teaching, composing and writing about the guitar. He has had many works for guitar dedicated to him by leading contemporary Cuban composers.

SELECTED RECORDING
Solistas Cubanos – Jesús Ortega. Egrem LD-3553 LP

SELECTED READING
Interview. Guitar Review, Summer 1988

JULIO MARTINEZ OYANGUREN

Born – Uruguay, 3 July 1905

Died – Montevideo, Uruguay

15 September 1973

Julio Martínez Oyanguren

Julio Martínez Oyanguren established himself as a concert performer when he was a teenager, giving his first concert in Montevideo. He had studied music and the guitar with Alfredo Hargain. After some years in the Uruguayan and Italian navies, Oyanguren settled in the USA in the 1930s and established himself as a leading performer on the classical guitar.

Although much of his repertoire was devoted to South American music, he did include classical works in his concert programmes. In the 1930s and 1940s he made many recordings for the American Decca company, establishing himself as one of the foremost players of the period. A high spot of his career was his appearance with the New York Philharmonic Orchestra. He was also a regular broadcaster on the NBC radio network in the USA.

Oyanguren resettled in Uruguay in the 1960s and was not involved in music from that time.

SELECTED RECORDING
Latin American Folk Music. Decca DL 8018 LP
Un Retrata de Espana. Decca LTC 9558 LP

IVAN PADOVEC

Born - Varazdin, Croatia 17 July 1800
Died - Varazdin, Croatia
4 November 1873

Ivan Padovec

Ivan Padovec's parents were Czech immigrants. His first interest in music was in 1817, when he began to study the violin. In 1818, whilst visiting an uncle in Vienna, Padovec attended a concert given by Mauro Giuliani. He was so impressed by the great guitarist's performance that he decided to play the guitar. On returning home he taught himself, using the Bartoluzzi Guitar Method. He made quick progress and was soon taking pupils for the instrument. In 1819 he also began to study piano, theory and harmony with Juraj K. Morgenstern (1783-1855). After five years study he had gained a reputation as a virtuoso guitarist and composer for the instrument.

In 1827 Padovec gave concerts in the larger cities of Croatia. In 1829 he settled in Vienna, where he succesfully established himself as a teacher and concert performer of the guitar. Some of his original music was published by Anton Diabelli. Padovec lived in Vienna until 1837, during which time he made concert tours of Germany, Czech Republic, Poland, Russia, and England.

In 1836 Padovec had problems with his eyesight. He decided to return home to Varazdin. By 1840 his eyesight had improved and he gave concerts in and around his home town. During this period he continued to write many new compositions, and a guitar method. This method, published in 1842 by the Viennese publisher Werner, received first prize in a Russian guitar competition.

Padovec designed a 10-string guitar at this time and had one made by Stauffer, the famous Viennese guitar maker.

By 1849 Padovec's health had declined and he was now totally blind. Unable to compose or teach, he suffered great poverty in his last years. He did eventually get a pension from the Croatian parliament, plus an annual sum from a foundation for blind artists. Padovec managed, despite his disability, to give some concerts. His last was on 2 April 1873 in Varazdin, a few months before his death in November of that year.

SELECTED READING
Article   Soundboard, Winter 1995
Article   Classical Guitar, April 1995

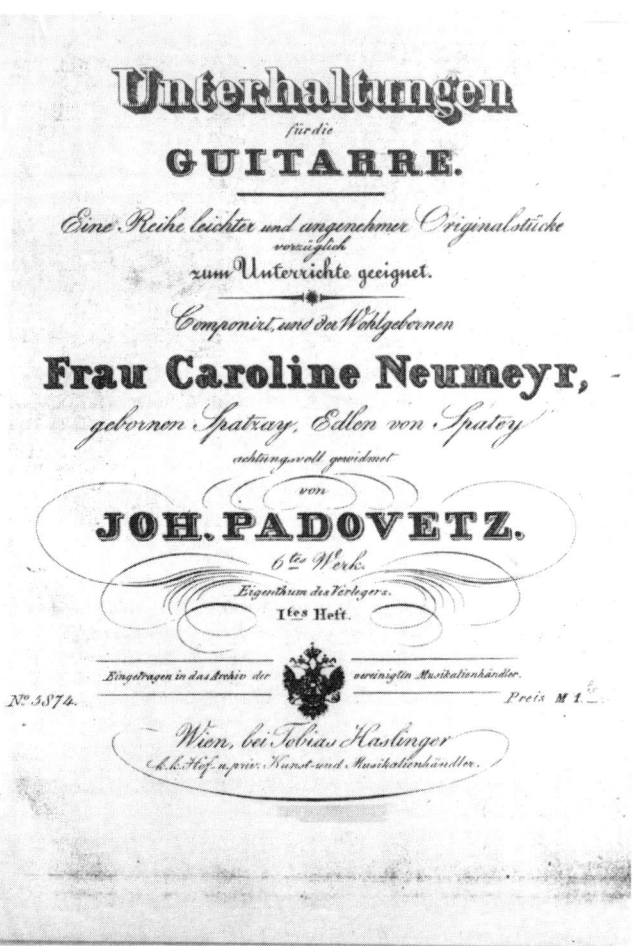

NICOLO PAGANINI

Born – Genoa, Italy
27 October 1782
Died – Nice, France, 27 May 1840

Nicoló Paganini

Until comparatively recently only a few music lovers realized that the nineteenth century virtuoso violinist Nicoló Paganini was also a virtuoso guitarist. Ferdinand Carulli, a contemporary of Paganini, wrote in his guitar tutor 'The fact may not be generally known that Paganini was a fine performer on the guitar, and that he composed most of his airs on this instrument, arranging and amplifying them on the violin according to his fancy.'

Nicoló Paganini's first instrument was the mandolin. His father had a great love of music, and from the day his son was able to hold the mandolin he ensured that every spare moment was spent in practising. Paganini's musical talent was soon very obvious, and he began to study the violin with the noted teachers Casta and Servetto.

It was in 1795, at the age of thirteen, that Paganini began to study the violin with Alessandro Rolli. Rolli was not only a violin virtuoso but also a talented guitarist. It seems likely that Paganini also studied the guitar with him. Nevertheless, for the next few years Paganini devoted his talents entirely to the violin, his virtuoso performances exciting audiences throughout Italy.

In 1801 Paganini became attached to an aristocratic lady whose favourite instrument was the guitar. During the three years he lived in this lady's château, he devoted himself to the guitar. His first composition for the instrument was written in 1801. In 1805 he returned to touring the continent, his concerts once again devoted to his violin playing. Among his close friends was the guitar virtuoso Luigi Legnani.

In Turin, on 9 June 1837, Paganini gave what was to be his last public concert. His health began to deteriorate in 1838-39, and in 1840 he moved to Nice in the South of France in order to miss the winter and try to recuperate. Unfortunately, his health deteriorated very rapidly, and he died in Nice on 27 May 1840 at the age of fifty-seven.

Nicoló Paganini, the legendary violinist, was not only a virtuoso guitarist but also a prolific composer for the instrument. He composed at least one hundred and forty solos for the guitar, many duets for violin and guitar, and several trios and quartets which included a guitar part. His most outstanding composition for the guitar is probably the Grand Sonata in A.

SELECTED MUSIC

Caprice No.24, arr. John Williams.	B & H
Five Compositions for Solo Guitar, ed. Pila.	RIC 132432
Five Pieces for Guitar, ed. Behrend.	EMT 1420
Grand Sonata, arr. Meyerriecks.	CO 214
La Campanella, ed. Casuscelli.	BA 8442
Minuet & Sonatina op.25, tr. Prat.	BA 9548
Perpetual Motion, for 1 or 2 guitars, tr. Fleury.	BA 11585
Pièce Intime.	ZM 1863
Romanze, ed. Scheit.	UE 13068
Six Original Compositions, ed. Scheit.	UE 14465
Sonatina, ed. Scheit.	UE 14455
Twenty-six Original Compositions for Guitar.	Z 11250
Complete Guitar Works of Paganini.	Chanterelle ECH 096

SELECTED RECORDINGS

John Williams plays Paganini.	CBS 73745 LP
Quartets with guitar, Op.4 Nos. 1, 2, 3: Prunnbauer & strings.	EMI 067 169600 1 LP
Quartet Op.4 Nos.3, 7, 14 : Quartteto Paganini.	Dynamic CDS 46
Sonatas Op.2, Op.3 etc. for violin & guitar: Mezzena/Sebastiani.	Dynamic CDS 62
Paganini Ensemble / Anthea Gifford.	Biddulph WT CD002
Anthea Gifford / Jan Kantara.	BBC Records CD 845
Paganini Guitar Quartet.	Dynamic CDS 17/1-2
Quarteto Paganini.	Dynamic CDS 98
Variations on Carmagnola-Adriani Sebastiani.	Dynamic 03 CD
24 Caprices – Eliot Fisk.	Music Masters 67092-2 CD
Paganini for Two – Goran Sollscher / Gil Shaham.	Deutsche Grammophon 437 837-2 CD
Paganini Guitar/Violin Duos (2 CDs) Simon Wynberg / Scott St John.	8550 690 and 8550759 CD
Paganini Sonatas for Violin and Guitar – Norbert Kraft / Moshe Hammer (Violin).	Naxos 8-553141 CD
Guitar/Violin Sonatas – Giovanni Grano / Vadim Brodsky (Violin).	Zero Point CVD 003 Z 94 CD

SELECTED READING

Nicoló Paganini.	Guitarra, March 1979
New Light on Paganini.	Guitar Review, Nos. 2,3,5
Paganini. Sheppard/Axe/Rod.	Paganini Publications, 1979
Paganini: Ruggero Chiesa.	Classical Guitar, July, August, September, 1988.

SOPHOCLES PAPAS

Born – Sopiki, Epirus, Greece, 18 December 1893

Died – Alexandria, Virginia, USA
26 February 1986

Sophocles Papas

Sophocles Thomas Papas was born in a small town in Greece, and received his first musical instruction from his father, an amateur violinist. Later, whilst living in Cairo, Egypt, he took lessons on the mandolin, but soon changed to the guitar.

Papas went to the United States in 1914 to study agriculture in Massachusetts. In World War I, he joined the American Army, in which he served as a gunsmith. He took his guitar with him, having taught himself to play with the aid of Carcassi's Classical Guitar Method, and his playing was much admired by other soldiers. It was during his army service that he formed the idea of becoming a guitar teacher.

Papas in fact played and taught almost every kind of plucked instrument, but it was as a guitar teacher that he established himself in Washington D.C. after the War. In 1922 he founded his Columbia School of Music. Papas's talents as a solo guitarist and teacher were quickly recognized. His school of music, offering instruction in nearly all instruments but specializing in the guitar, was a great success. The school became the only such establishment in the United States where a student could work for a bachelor's degree in music with the guitar as the principal instrument.

Sophocles Papas became a close friend of Andrés Segovia, and many of his teaching methods were based on the technique and musical approach of Segovia. His pupils have included Burl Ives, Peter Ustinov, the poet Carl Sandburg, the Hollywood actors Gregory Peck and Bette Davis, and the famous jazz guitarist Charlie Byrd.

Papas wrote a guitar method for the classical guitar which has proved over the years to be a worldwide best seller. He was a founder of the prestigious Washington Guitar Society, and also involved himself as a prominent publisher of guitar music.

SELECTED MUSIC
Five Solos for Guitar.   CO 102

SELECTED READING
Sophocles Papas.   Guitar Player, February 1975

CHRISTOPHER PARKENING

Born –

Brentwood, California, USA

14 December 1947

Christopher Parkening

Christopher Parkening began to play the guitar at the age of eleven after hearing his cousin Jack Marshall, who was a leading Californian studio guitarist.

Parkening's first teachers were Celedonio and Pepe Romero. They soon noticed the young guitarist's exceptional talent, and within one year Parkening gave his first public recital. At the age of fourteen he entered the annual state-wide auditions of the Young Musicians Foundation. Among the judges were Jascha Heifetz, Gregor Piatigorsky and Mario Castelnuovo-Tedesco. The Foundation at that time offered no category in which guitarists could compete; but so impressed were the judges with Parkening's virtuosity that he was scheduled as a special 'out-of-competition' performer.

After this competition Parkening developed a friendship with Castelnuovo-Tedesco, and a little later made his formal concert debut playing his Concerto in D for Guitar and Orchestra under the auspices of the Young Musicians Foundation of Los Angeles on 10 March 1963. This highly acclaimed performance led to further engagements with the Los Angeles Philharmonic Orchestra, the Pasadena Symphony Orchestra and numerous other orchestras in Southern California.

With letters of recommendation from Castelnuovo-Tedesco and the cellist Joseph Schuster, Parkening was accepted as a scholarship student by Andrés Segovia in a masterclass at the University of California at Berkeley. Segovia chose him from three hundred students present to perform daily before the class, later selecting him as a soloist when the masterclass was televised nationally.

In January 1966 Parkening gave the first performance of the Second Concerto in C for Guitar and Orchestra by Castelnovo-Tedesco. In the same year he took up academic and musical studies at the University of Southern California; and he again attended on full scholarship a Segovia masterclass held at the North Carolina School of Arts. In July 1968 he was named one of the outstanding young artists of the year by High Fidelity magazine. The following September he made his first concert tour of the United States and Canada. In the same year he began to make the first of several recordings for Angel Records, several of which have been best sellers. His recording of the music of Bach reputedly sold over one hundred thousand copies.

In the autumn of 1968 Parkening was invited by Segovia to serve with him on the panel of judges for the International Guitar Competition in Santiago de Compostela, Spain. Parkening then became one of the United States' busiest recitalists, making his New York debut at the Alice Tulley Hall in November 1972. In August and September of that year he completed his first tour of Japan. While there, he was chosen to be the principal soloist at the country's first Rodrigo Festival.

Christopher Parkening is the author of The Guitar Method and a number of books of classical transcriptions for the guitar. For several years he was head of the guitar department of the University of Southern California School of Music. He now lives in Montana, where he holds a series of annual masterclasses for the guitar at Montana State University.

SELECTED RECORDINGS

In the Classic Style.	EMI Angel S.36019 LP
In the Spanish Style.	EMI Angel S.36020 LP
Romanza.	EMI Angel S.36021 LP
Parkening Plays Bach.	EMI Angel 47191 CD
Parkening and the Guitar.	EMI Angel S.36053 LP
Christopher Parkening Album.	EMI Angel S.36069 LP
Christopher Parkening and Kathleen Battle (Soprano).	EMI CDC 7 47196/2
Virtuoso Guitar Duos with David Brandon.	EMI CDC 7494062
A Tribute to Segovia.	EMI CDC 7 49404/2
Rodrigo and Walton.	EMI CDC 7 64665 2
Parkening – The Great Recordings (2 CDs).	EMI ZDCB 7 54905 27

SELECTED READING

Christopher Parkening.	Guitar Player, June 1970
Christopher Parkening.	Guitar Player, June 1972
Christopher Parkening.	Frets, June 1980
Interview.	Classical Guitar, February 1987
Interview.	Fingerstyle Guitar, September/October 1995

MARIO PARODI

Born – Istanbul, Turkey, 5 March 1917

Died – Buenos Aires, Argentina, 27 October 1970

SELECTED MUSIC
Seis Instantaneas.	BA 12564
Poema.	BA 12565
Prelude No.1.	BA 10270
Three Preludes, Nos. 3, 4, 8.	BA 11823

SELECTED RECORDINGS
The Classical Guitar.	Music for Pleasure MFP 2094 LP
Transcriptions for Classical Guitar.	MFP 2140 LP
Guitarra Romantica.	Angel/EMI LPA-11205 LP
Magia en la Guitarra.	Angel/EMI LPA-11207 LP
Instantaneas.	Angel/EMI LPA-11208 LP
Facetas – Mario Parodi.	Angel/EMI SLPA-11211 LP
Concierto sobre Seis Cuerdas.	TK LD 80.003 LP

Mario Parodi

COURTESY: JAQUES CHAÎNE

Mario Parodi was born in Istanbul of Italian parents. From an early age he was drawn to music, his first instrument being the piano. On hearing a concert given by an Argentinian orchestra that included a number of guitarists, Parodi decided that the guitar was to be his instrument. As there were virtually no guitar teachers in Turkey at that time, Parodi was self-taught.

As a concert artist, Parodi toured throughout Turkey, Greece, Italy, Switzerland, Germany and Argentina, performing in a style that was very individual and probably unique. He recorded in both Italy and Argentina and published numerous transcriptions and compositions of his own. He dedicated most of his concert programmes to his own transcriptions of the romantic composers, including Liszt, Schumann, Chopin, Debussy, Beethoven and Brahms. One of his records sold 30,000 copies in Britain alone.

CARLOS PAYES

Born - Carlos Rodriguez Payet
Zacatecoluca, El Salvador
21 March 1944

Carlos Payes

Carlos Payes, a doctor by profession, is a talented classical guitarist and a leading personality in the guitar world of El Salvador. He started to play the guitar at an early age, completing his first studies at the age of twelve with Dolores Rodriguez in Zacatecoluca. After his family moved to San Salvador, He continued his studies with Candido Morales, a former pupil of Agustin Barrios. In 1969 he went to Santiago de Compostela, Spain to study with José Tomás. On his return to El Salvador in 1970 he studied harmony and composition with Esteban Servellon. As well as studying music Payes had concurrently studied medicine and in 1972 Payes received his degree in medicine from the University of El Salvador, his specialist subject being psychiatry. In the same year Payes studied the guitar with Sila Godboy.

Since that time Carlos Payes has written many solo and ensemble works for the guitar. He has performed in, and been associated with, many music festivals in Spain and El Svador. His 'Concierto a la Italiana' for guitar and orchestra was premiered by the Spanish guitarist Renata Tarrago at the 1973 Tercer Festival de Musica in San Salvador. A member of the Sociedad de Autores de Espana, Payes received in 1975 a gold medal and diploma of honour from the Union General de Autores y Artistas Salvadorenos.

In 1974 he was elected President of the Agustin Barrios Mangore Association in El Salvador, an institution dedicated to the promotion and development of the guitar.

Carlos Payes continues to promote the classical guitar in El Salvador, and was the organiser of the 1994 Agustin Barrios Mangore Festival held there in August of that year.

SELECTED MUSIC
Dos Canciones Salvadoreñas	UME 21808
El Adios – Serenata	UME 21810
Lejania	Mid Continental Music

Carlos Payes with Jorge Morel at the grave of Agustin Barrios Mangore

STEPHEN FUNK PEARSON

Born –
Poughkeepsie, New York, USA
22 January 1950

Stephen Funk Pearson

Both Stephen Funk Pearson's parents are musicians. His father, an organist and harpsichordist, was a professor at Vassar College. His mother is a pianist, organist and choir director. His first instrument was the piano, which he studied with his mother and later with a member of the Vassar faculty. Despite good progress, he lost interest in the piano and turned to a steel-strung guitar belonging to his brother. For some time the young musician developed his guitar technique on this instrument in the styles of folk and bluegrass. He also experimented with other instruments, including the cello, saxophone, string bass, banjo and mandolin.

Stephen Funk Pearson soon realized that he wanted to devote his life to the guitar and music, and decided to study classical guitar technique with Alexander Bellow. Having qualified in philosophy and studied ecology at Vassar, he returned there to study music and composition. He also studied guitar with Luis Garcia-Renart at Vassar, and then went to study in New York with Frederic Hand and later with Alice Artzt. In 1980 he won first prize in the Bunyan Webb National Guitar Competition in Memphis, Tennessee, and was placed second in the International Guitar Competition in Puerto Rico. In 1981-82 he was awarded the Maguire Fellowship for study in Europe, where he worked with John Mills and David Russell in England, José Tomás in Spain, and Oscar Ghiglia at the Accademia Musicale Chigiana in Siena, Italy. On his return to the USA he won the national Mohonk Music Fund competition for instrumentalists.

With this unique musical background, Pearson has developed into a highly individual composer/guitarist. He has composed for several instruments including the bassoon, flute, oboe, harpsichord and organ, but now performs his own music exclusively on the classical guitar. Some of his compositions have been premiered by Paul Gregory, the Buffalo Guitar Quartet, the Newman/Oltman Duo and Neil Anderson amongst others.

Stephen Funk Pearson is at present Visiting Artist in the programme of the North Carolina Arts Council, serving Alamance County as a performer and composer.

SELECTED MUSIC
Four Skaals.	Theodore Presser
Thusslegarth.	Theodore Presser
Tsamaloon.	Theodore Presser
Brunella the Dancing Bear.	Theodore Presser
Six Mixtures.	Guitar Solo
Mummychogs (Le Monde).	Doberman-Yppan
Not Just Classical Guitar (6 teaching cassettes).	
	Homespun Tapes
Six Mixtures.	GSP
Tusitala.	GSP
5 Bilbarns.	GSP

SELECTED RECORDINGS
Hudson River Debut.   GSP 1001 CD

SELECTED READING
Interview.	Classical Guitar, November 1984
Composer/Performer Capsule Series.	Classical Guitar, December 1988 to April 1989
Interview.	Guitar Review, Fall 1990
Interview.	Classical Guitar, February 1991
Interview.	Soundboard, Spring 1994

KRZYSZTOF PELECH

Born -
Wroclaw, Poland
21 May 1970

Krzyzstof Pelech

Krzysztof Pelech began to play the guitar at the age of twelve. He completed his studies at Wroclaw's Secondary School of Music. He went on to study under Piotr Zalewski. In 1984 he won the first of many competition prizes, the first prize in the Strzelce Opolskie Nationwide Competition. He won the Costas Cotsiolis Prize at the 1985 Esztergom International Festival, and went on to win first prizes in the 1986 Kraków Nationwide Competition, the 1990 Rene Bartoli Contest in France, the 1991 Villa de Laredo Competition in Spain, and the 1992 Alexandre Tansman Competiton in Carpentras, France. Pelech has participated in masterclasses given by Costas Cotsiolis, Jorge Morel, Roberto Aussel, Jorge Cardoso and Joseph Urshalmi.

In 1992 Krzysztof Pelech moved to England to study with Gordon Crosskey at the Royal Northern College of Music in Manchester. Around this time he began to study privately with Jorge Morel. Within a short time Pelech was playing professionally in a duo with Morel, and is now regarded as one of the finest interpreters of his music.

In 1994 Pelech was awarded second prize at the Great Lakes Classical Guitar Festival and Gold Competition in Oberlin, USA. Considered one of Europe's finest guitarists, he performs frequently on Polish Television and Radio, and at many international guitar festivals.

SELECTED RECORDINGS
Krzysztof Pelech - Recital	KOS Records KOS CD 11
Pelech Plays Morel	Guitar Masters GMR 102-94 CD
Vivaldi Guitar Concertos	D-DUR RV 93
Morel Guitar Concertos	Luthier 2881-61413
Pelech - Live in Prague	Melantrich MCD 017

SELECTED READING
Interview   Classical Guitar, November 1994

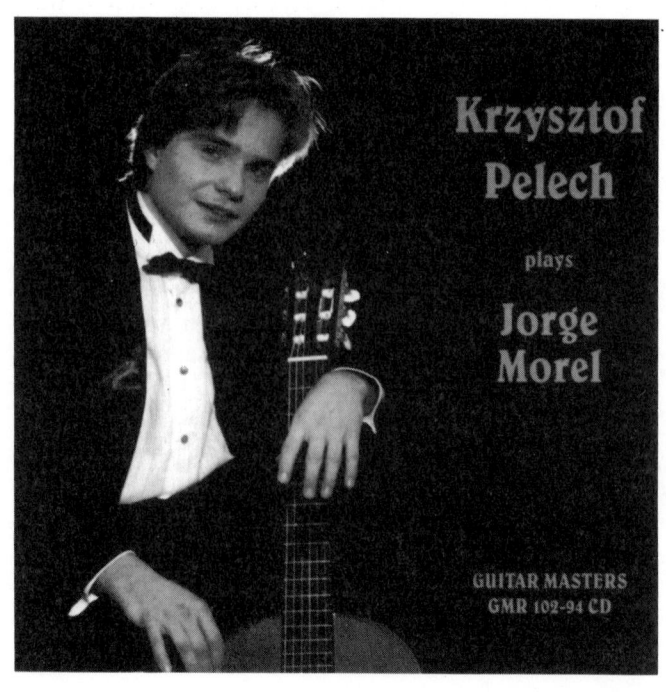

BORIS A. PEROTT

Born –
St Petersburg, Russia, 1882
Died – London, England, 12 March 1958

Boris A. Perott

For many years Boris Perott was one of the most important guitar personalities in Great Britain. Born in Russia, he became a naturalized British subject. By profession a doctor of medicine, he had studied the piano at an early age, later turning his attention to the balalaika and the mandolin.

Perott's introduction to the guitar took place at the age of eight. His first lessons (on the seven-string guitar) were with the famous guitar virtuoso J.Decker-Schenk. It was not long before he took up the six-string guitar under the guidance of V.P.Lebedev, making his first public appearance as a soloist in St Petersburg in 1903, a performance that was warmly acclaimed by the press.

The following year he toured Siberia, Germany and France with Lebedev and V.Ivanov. Perott made an appearance before the Imperial Court, for which he was presented with a gold watch by the Emperor of Russia, Nicholas II.

Boris Perott continued his career in medicine, but gave many public and private performances on the guitar for a period of twelve years. After the death of Lebedev, his widow chose Perott to be her teacher and to guide her with her studies of the guitar, together with several of her husband's pupils.

Following the revolution in Russia, Boris Perott came to Britain and set up in practice as a doctor in London, where for many years he was a noted teacher of the classical guitar. His most outstanding pupil was Julian Bream. It was Perott who introduced Bream to Segovia, who quickly recognized the young guitarist's enormous talent. Help in promoting the early career of the young prodigy came from the Philharmonic Society of Guitarists, which Perott had founded in London in 1929.

In 1930 Boris Perott began to contribute a regular series to B.M.G. magazine in London, proving himself to be an expert historian of the guitar.

Although Boris Perott's professional career was in medicine – he became an eminent heart specialist – his first love throughout his life was always the guitar.

SELECTED READING
Article.   Classical Guitar, December 1991

RICHARD PICK

Born –

St Paul, Minnesota, USA

20 October 1915

Richard Pick

Richard Pick's first encounter with music was through his father, who taught him the piano and the violin at the age of five. On the death of his parents, Pick became the foster son of Max Pick, who was the concert master of Minneapolis, Minnesota, and a professor of musicology, violin and piano.

Living in such a musical environment, it was natural that Pick developed a great love for music. The piano was his first instrument, although he did play the guitar to accompany his singing. Pick then met Frank Lannom, a well-known Chicago guitar teacher. For the next six or seven years he took guitar lessons from Lannom, then went to Urbana to enter the University of Illinois. Needing money to finance his studies, Pick worked in local dance bands, playing the plectrum guitar. A few opportunities arose for him to play the classical guitar on radio, and Pick suddenly realized that the classical guitar was the instrument through which he was able to express his musical talent. He entered DePaul University of Chicago, and earned his B.Sc. degree. Soon afterwards, on 2 March 1941, he gave his first public guitar recital, sponsored by the University of Chicago Music Department.

Today, Richard Pick is known throughout the United States as a fine classical guitarist and a composer of many pieces for the guitar. Over the years he has lectured on music and the guitar at many American universities, including the Chicago School of Music. He retired from teaching in 1986.

SELECTED MUSIC
Favourite Classic Guitar Solos.   MB 93613
Richard Pick School of Guitar.   Mel Bay Publications

SELECTED RECORDINGS
Above & Beyond.   International IRC 3324
Guitar.   Music Library MLR 7066

ALVARO PIERRI

Born –

Montevideo, Uruguay

18 January 1953

Alvaro Pierri

Alvaro Pierri was born into a musical family. José Pierri Sapere, his grandfather, was a composer; Ada Estades, his mother, a pianist; and Olga Pierri, his aunt, a well-known Uruguayan guitarist.

Pierri began his studies at the age of eleven. His talent soon showed, and he began to win prizes in competitions for young guitarists in Uruguay. He went on to win first prizes at the Concurso Internacional de Guitarra in Buenos Aires, Argentina, and the

International Guitar Competition in Porto Alegre, Brazil. Moving to Europe, Alvaro Pierri won the 18th Radio France International Concours in Paris, which established him as a guitar soloist of world class. He made his USA debut at the Kaufmann Concert Hall, New York, in 1978.

Since 1981 Alvaro Pierri has taught at the University of Santa Maria in Brazil. He is also professor of guitar at the University of Québec in Montréal, Canada.

SELECTED RECORDINGS
Alvaro Pierri plays Bach, Sor, Albeniz.
    Metropole 2599 019 LP
Alvaro Pierri.   Blue Angel BA29002
Alvaro Pierri plays Berkley, Walton.
    Blue Angel BA 29003 LP
Alvaro Pierri plays Brouwer, Torroba.
    Amplitude CLCD-2010
Piazzola/Falla/Paganini – Guitar/Violin Duets.
    Analekto AN 2 8706 CD
Pierri plays Brouwer.   Analekta AN 2 8752 CD
Pierri plays Villa-Lobos.   Analekta AN 2 8751 CD
Guitare Québec '94.   Doberman DO 179 CD

SELECTED READING
Article.   Guitar International, March 1985
Interview.   Classical Guitar, May/June 1983

BARBARA POLASEK
Born –
Reichenberg, Germany
8 March 1939

Barbara Polasek

Barbara Polasek was born into a family of Bohemian musicians in Reichenberg, Germany (now Liberec, Czechoslovakia). Her exceptional musical talents were obvious at an early age and, encouraged by her family, she made great progress on the guitar.

At the age of twelve Barbara Polasek gave her first public recital. She continued her music studies at the Weimar Academy and the Prague Music Conservatory. She then went to Spain and studied with Andrés Segovia. In 1959 she won the First International Prize of Vienna, and in 1964 she won the First Prize for Interpretation at the Concours de Guitare in Paris, organized by the ORTF (French Radio and Television Service).

Since that time Barbara Polasek has continued an active career as a guitar recitalist and teacher. Her highly successful British debut took place at the Wigmore Hall, London, on 26 October 1966. She also appeared at the Festival Malais in Paris, and the Flanders Festival in Louvain in 1969. She is married to the prominent cellist Jan Polasek.

SELECTED MUSIC
Gitarre im Gruppenunterricht.   SY 2221

SELECTED RECORDINGS
Anthology of the Guitar: Volume One. RCA VICS 1038 LP
Barbara Polasek Plays Bach.   Erato STU 70573 LP

ALBERTO PONCE

Born –

Madrid, Spain

13 March 1935

Alberto Ponce

Alberto Ponce's first guitar tutor was his father. He later went to the Barcelona Municipal Conservatory for seven years, where he completed his course with honours.

The young guitarist was introduced to Emilio Pujol, who invited him to study with him at the Lisbon Conservatory of Music. Ponce became very taken with Pujol's approach to music and the guitar, studying with him in Lisbon for three years and later in Siena.

While he was in Siena, Alberto Ponce specialized in the music of Spain's golden age, in particular the vihuela and its music. He studied the vihuela in addition to the guitar, and in 1961 was awarded the first prize for the vihuela by the Accademia Musicale Chigiana in Siena.

In 1962 Ponce won the First Prize for Interpretation at the Concours de Guitare in Paris, organized by ORTF (French Radio and Television). In the same year he began teaching at the Ecole Normale de Musique, Paris, under the directorship of Alfred Cortot.

Alberto Ponce has remained in this important teaching position, at the same maintaining a busy concert schedule throughout Europe and Canada. He has also made several recordings for the French company Arion.

SELECTED RECORDINGS

Ohana: Oeuvres de Guitare.	Arion ARN 38240 LP
La Guitare au 20ème Siècle.	Arion ARN 30S150 LP
Sourire de la Guitare.	Arion ARN 36341 LP
Masterpieces of 20th Century Guitar Music.	Musical Heritage Society MHS 3603 LP
Charmes de la Guitare.	Arion ARN 68185 CD

DOMINGO PRAT

Born – MARSAL DOMINGO PRAT

Barcelona, Spain, 17 March 1886

Died – Buenos Aires Argentina, December 1944

Domingo Prat

Domingo Prat originally studied the guitar at the Municipal Music School of Barcelona. Later he was a pupil of the outstanding guitarist Miguel Llobet.

Prat established himself in Buenos Aires, where he became highly regarded as an authority and teacher of the classical guitar. He was the first exponent of the Tárrega method in South America, and was a prolific writer of guitar methods, studies and transcriptions. His most lasting achievement is the 'Dictionary of

Guitarists', published in Spanish in 1934 by Romero and Fernandez of Buenos Aires.

SELECTED MUSIC
Bajo el Sauce: Milonga Criolla.	BA 11675
Danza Española No.1.	BA 9579
El Escondido: Danza Argentina.	BA 8989
El Palito: Danza Argentina.	BA 8991
Gran Jota, Con Variaciones.	BA 11549
Gueya (1 or 3 guitars).	BA 9501
La Firmeza: Danza Argentina.	BA 8990
Pasionaras: Vidalitas.	BA 11676
Recuerdos de Saldungaray: Triste Argentino.	BA 9561
Recuerdos de Santiago del Estero: Triste.	BA 9562

SELECTED READING
Diccionario de Guitarras, Guitarristas y Guitarreros: Prat. Romero & Fernandez, Buenos Aires 1934 (reprinted Editions Orphée, 1986).

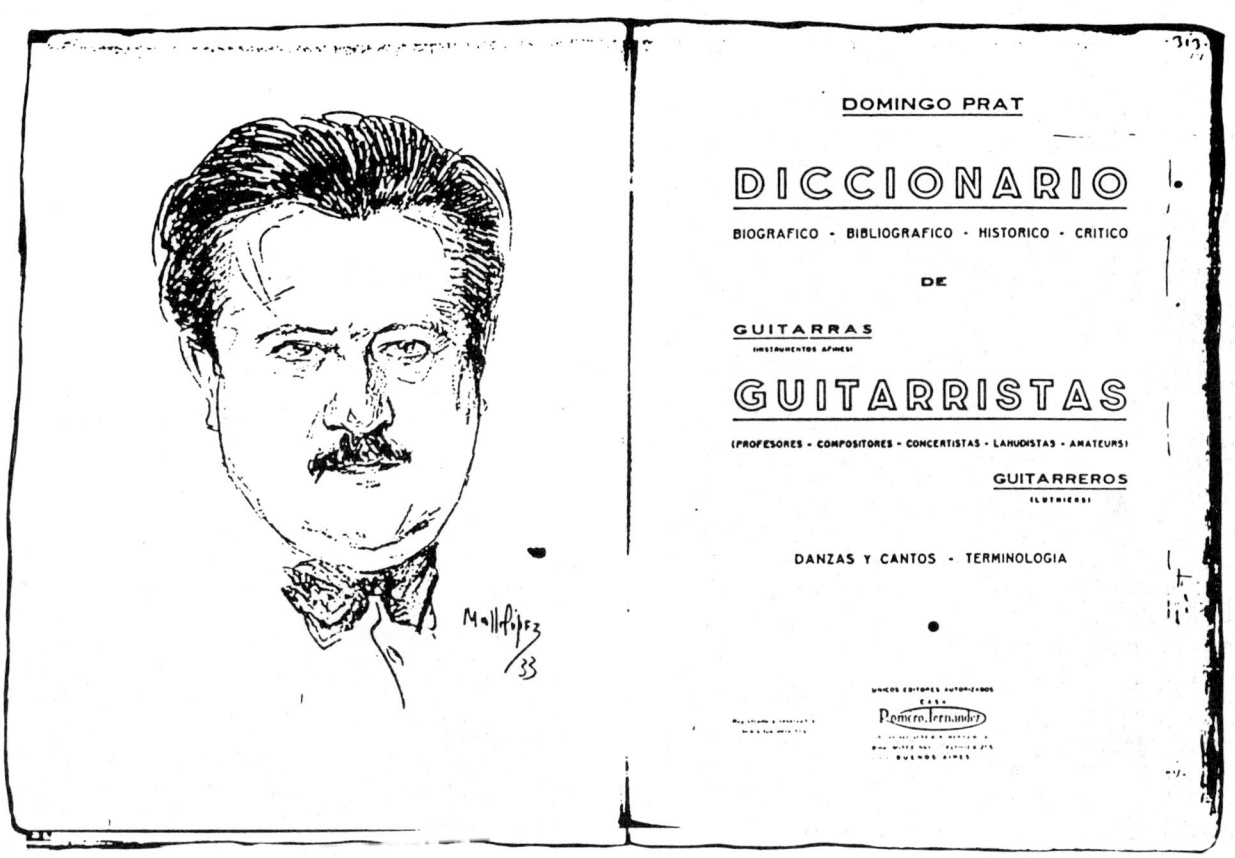

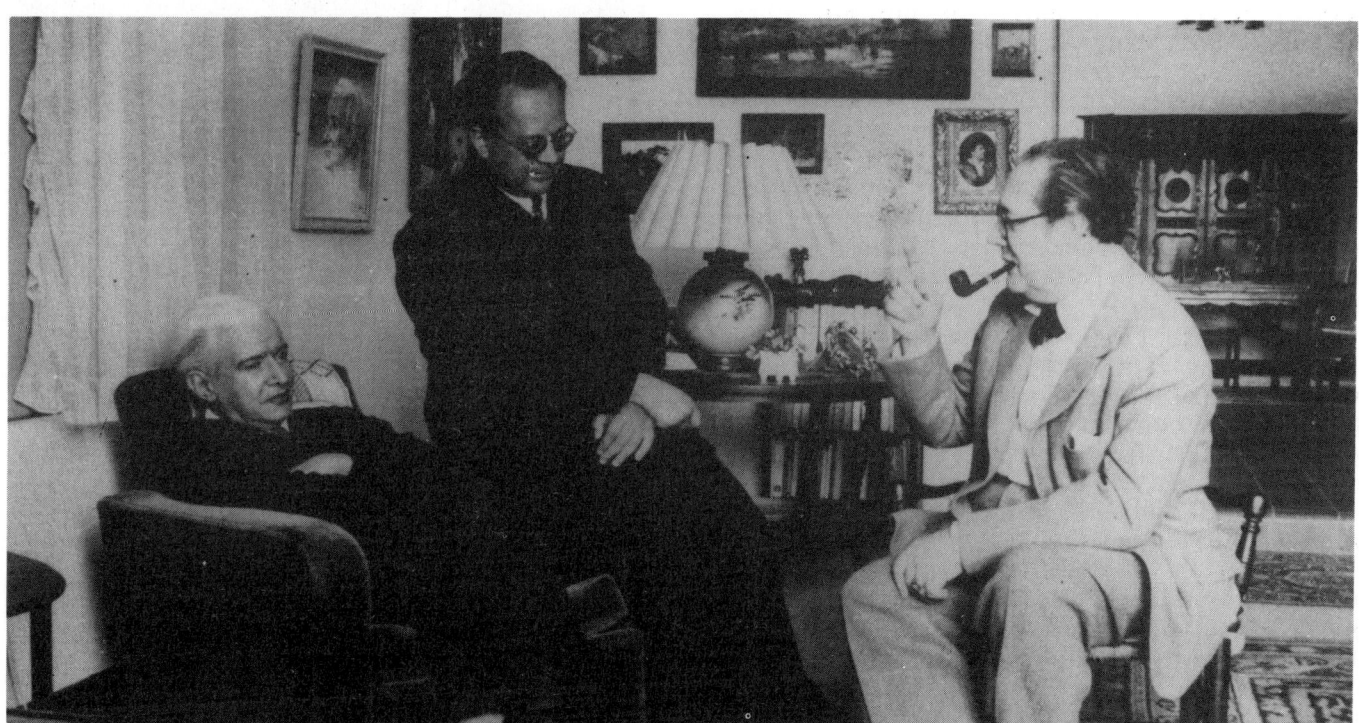

Historic photograph of Manuel Ponce with Andrés Segovia at Ponce's home in Mexico City. Padre Brambila is in the centre.

MADAME SIDNEY PRATTEN

Born – CATHERINE JOSEPHA PELZER

Mulheim, Germany, 1821

Died – London, England, 10 October 1895

Madame Sidney Pratten

Madame Sidney Pratten was one of the most important classical guitarists of the nineteenth century. Her first guitar teacher was her father, Ferdinand Pelzer. By the time she was seven years old, she was already regarded as a highly accomplished guitarist.

In 1829 the Pelzer family moved to London. Here Catherine Pelzer dazzled British audiences with her appearances with the opera singer Madame Gringi, and also with another young guitar prodigy, Giulio Regondi.

After establishing herself as a teacher in Exeter. she was persuaded to return to London by one of her pupils, Lady John Somerset, in order to teach the guitar to members of the nobility. This she agreed to do, and it was in London that she met the distinguished flautist Robert Sidney Pratten. They married in 1854.

In 1868 Robert Pratten died, and his distressed widow gave up her public performances for three years. In 1871 she returned to the concert stage to perform Giuliani's third Concerto, a work she had played (using her terz guitar) in her tour of Europe in 1837. Giuliani's niece played the piano part for this concert.

Madame Sidney Pratten gave her last public performance at the age of 72 in 1893. There is no doubt that she was one of the outstanding figures of the nineteenth century guitar. She also wrote several popular guitar methods, and the prominent guitar makers, Panormo and Lacôte, labelled hundreds of guitars with her name in order to promote sales of their instruments.

SELECTED READING

Article.	Guitar News, July/August 1962
Article.	Classical Guitar, December 1994

Madame Pratten with a Portuguese machette

IDA PRESTI

Born – YVETTE IDA MONTAGNON

Suresnes, France, 31 May 1924

Died – Rochester, NY State, USA, 24 April 1967

Ida Presti

Ida Presti's father, Claude Montagnon, was a French piano teacher. Her mother, Olga Lo-Presti, was of Italian birth. Ida Presti received her first music lessons on the piano at the age of five from her father. At the age of six she changed to the guitar and soon showed that this was the instrument on which her extensive musical talents would be exposed. For two years from 1932 she studied the guitar with Mario Maccaferri, who was living in Paris at the time. Her father continued to teach her harmony and musical theory.

Ida Presti gave her first public recital in 1932, at the age of eight. She made her concert debut in Paris two years later. On 13 February 1938 she was invited to play at the Société des Concerts du Conservatoire de Paris, the first time a guitarist had performed there since Napoléon Coste claimed to have played his Op.15 (dedicated to Berlioz). In 1940, on the occasion of the centenary of Paganini's death, Ida Presti played his guitar in a commemorative concert. Her performances were outstanding, and over the next twenty years she was to make extensive concert tours both in France and abroad. She also appeared in a French film entitled La Petite Chose.

In 1952 she met the classical guitarist Alexandre Lagoya at the home of a mutual friend, André Verdier. A year later, on 23 May 1953, they were married; and two years later the Lagoya-Presti guitar duo made its appearance. Widely regarded as the finest classical guitar duo ever, Presti and Lagoya were to perform two thousand concerts all over the world. Together they founded a prestigious guitar class at the Schola Cantorum in Paris, and made several magnificent recordings for the Philips Record Company, which bear testimony to their greatness.

Tragically, while preparing for a concert in New York in 1967, Ida Presti, one of the finest classical guitarists of the twentieth century, suddenly fell ill and died shortly afterwards from an internal haemorrhage resulting from an aneurysm.

SELECTED RECORDINGS
With Alexandre Lagoya:
Music for the Classical Guitar.	Nonesuch H 71161 LP
Musique Baroque pour deux Guitares.	Philips 6504 003 LP
Concertos pour deux Guitares.	Philips 6505 018 LP
Musique Espagnole pour deux Guitares.	Philips 6504 020 LP
Oeuvres pour deux Guitares.	Philips 6504 049 LP
Masters of the Guitar: Volume One.	RCA RB 6589 LP
Presti/Lagoya Duo (3 CD set).	Philips 446 213-2
Ida Presti (Solo Recital) and Luise Walker.	Pavilion Gemm CD 9133

SELECTED READING
Ida Presti.	Guitar Review No.31, Memorial Issue, 1969
Ida Presti.	Les Cahiers de la Guitare Winter, 1984
Ida Presti.	Classical Guitar, May 1992

Presti-Lagoya Duo

SONJA PRUNNBAUER

Born –

Hamburg, West Germany

28 August 1948

Sonja Prunnbauer

Sonja Prunnbauer started playing the guitar at the age of thirteen and had her first professional lessons from Eike Funck in Hamburg. After receiving her high school diploma, she studied with Karl Scheit in Vienna for four years.

In 1972 she earned her soloist's diploma with distinction and returned to Hamburg, where she was offered a teaching position at the Hochschule für Musik und Kunst. In the same year she won first prize in the West German National Competition for Young Artists. Since then she has performed extensively throughout Europe, Africa, North America and Asia.

Sonja Prunnbauer has made many recordings, both solo and ensemble. She has appeared on all major German radio and television stations, and in 1982 she made the first videotape lessons for classical guitar beginners. In addition to her many concert performances, she teaches at guitar seminars in Germany and abroad.

SELECTED RECORDINGS

Klassisch-Romantische Gitarrenmusik.	Harmonia Mundi HM 805-2 CD
Modern Solo Guitar Works.	Aurophon AU-11057 LP
Gitarrenmusik.	Da Camera Magna SM 93609 LP
Musik für Gitarre und Hammerklavier.	Christophorus DMM 74044 LP
Paganini: Tre Gran Quartetti Op.4.	Harmonia Mundi 067EL169600 1 LP
Musik des Besonderen Klanges Vol.1.	Schwann Musica VMS 1050-1 LP
Musik des Besonderen Klanges Vol.2.	Schwann Musica VMS 1051-2 LP
Virtuose Gitarrenkonzerte.	Schwann Musica VMS 2062 E LP
Giuliani Violin/Guitar Duos.	Marco Polo 6.220151 LP
Paganini Violin/Guitar Duos.	Telefunken 6.35574
Eine Kleine Nachtmusik.	Telefunken 6.42171 AW
Carulli – Piano/Guitar Works.	DG MDG 603 0616-2 CD
Virtuoso Clarinet and Guitar.	DG MDG L 3319 CD

SELECTED READING

Interview.	Classical Guitar, March 1989

EMILIO PUJOL

Born – EMILIO VILLARUBI PUJOL

Granadella, Spain, 7 April 1886

Died – Barcelona, Spain, 15 November 1980

Emilio Pujol

Emilio Pujol's introduction to music was through singing and the bandurría, on which he became a soloist with a mandolin and guitar orchestra. The orchestra appeared with enormous success at the Paris Exhibition of 1900. It was in 1900 that Pujol changed to the guitar and became a pupil of Francisco Tárrega in Barcelona. In 1907 Pujol, who had already made a name for himself throughout Spain as a guitar virtuoso, left for a concert tour of Argentina, Uruguay and the United States.

Pujol married the talented flamenco guitarist Mathilde Cuervas. They appeared in concert together in many countries, including a successful tour of Great Britain in 1923. In 1924 Pujol discovered in a Paris museum an ancient vihuela. The instrument interested him very much, and over the years he became one of the leading personalities behind its revival.

In 1947 Pujol was appointed professor of guitar at the National Conservatory of Music in Lisbon, Portugal. He retained this position until his death in 1980.

Emilio Pujol was not only a fine guitarist and teacher, but also one of the foremost musicologists of the twentieth century. He wrote several important books about the guitar, including 'Rational Method for the Guitar', 'The Dilemma of Timbre on the Guitar' and a biography of his teacher Francisco Tárrega.

SELECTED MUSIC

Atardecer: Crepuscule.	ESC
Bagatella.	BA 11006
Becquerian (Endecha-Complainte).	ESC
Canción de Cuna: Berceuse.	ESC
Canto de Otoño.	ESC
Caprice Varié sur un thème d'Aguado.	ESC
Cubana.	Celesta
Deuxième Triquilandia: 5 selections.	ESC
El Abejorro.	BA 11109
Els Tres Tambors (The Three Drums).	BA 11111
Endecha a la amada ausente.	ESC
Fantasía Breve.	BA 11110
Festival: Danza Catalana.	BA 12046
Four Short Pieces.	Kalmus
Homenaje a Tárrega.	GA 150
Manola del Avapies.	BA 11448
Pequeña Romanza.	ESC
Preludio Romantico.	BA 11007
Rapsodia Valenciana.	ESC
Salve.	BA 1112
Seguidilla.	BA 1113
Sevilla: Evocación.	ESC
Tonadilla.	ESC
Troisième Triquilandia: 3 selections.	ESC
Two Preludes.	ESC
Variations sur un thème Obsedant.	ESC
Veneciana.	ESC
Villanesca: Country Dances.	BA 12342
Guitar School	Editions Orphee RTFT-1

SELECTED READING

Emilio Pujol.	Guitar Review No.5, 1948
Tárrega: Ensayo Biográfico: Emilio Pujol.	Ramos & Alfonso, 1960
El Dilema del Sonido en la Guitarra: Emilio Pujol.	Ricordi, 1960
Emilio Pujol: Juan Riera.	Instituto de Estudios Llerdenses, Lerida, 1974
Emilio Pujol: Juan Riera.	Lerida, 1974
The Pujol XI Curso Internacional: Ickes.	Soundboard No.3, 1976
Emilio Pujol.	Guitar, July 1977
Emilio Pujol.	Guitar Player, April 1977
Guitar Travels: J. D. Roberts.	Valencia, 1977
Emilio Pujol. Complete list of works.	Guitar & Lute, May 1978
Interview.	Guitar & Lute No.9, 1979
Emilio Pujol In Memoriam: Purcell.	Soundboard, May 1981
Emilio Pujol: Purcell (short biography)	The Orphée Catalogue, 1986
Article.	Soundboard, Summer 1994

IVAN PUTILIN

Born –
St Petersburg, Russia
18 September 1909

Ivan Putilin

Ivan Feodorovitch Putilin's family settled in Finland in 1918. Putilin studied the double bass at the Sibelius Academy in Helsinki under Lauri Nissinen (1934-1938), under Ludvig Juht in the United States and privately under Alfred Burg-Schwendtner at the Mozarteum in Salzburg. He played double bass in the Helsinki City Orchestra and in the Radio Finland Symphony Orchestra (1947-1972). As a guitarist, he is practically self-taught. He also plays most other fretted instruments, including the balalaika and the mandolin. Playing all these instruments, he made many broadcasts on Radio Finland from 1927 until his retirement. The broadcasts included chamber music with guitar.

Putilin's contribution to the development of the classical guitar in Finland is quite extraordinary. He began teaching the guitar professionally in 1930, and was the first guitar teacher to be appointed at the Sibelius Academy (1967-1978). Most of the current teaching staff in the guitar department are his former pupils. He was the main driving force in the formation (on 5 November 1950) of the Helsinki Guitar Society, which has been instrumental in extending knowledge and appreciation of the guitar in Finland as a whole right up to the present day.

Ivan Putilin published a guitar tutor in 1960, and has also published several arrangements of Finnish music for guitar. Although now retired from professional performing, he continues to teach privately from his studio in central Helsinki.

RAFAEL RABELLO

Born –
Petropolis, Rio de Janeiro, Brazil, 31 October 1962
Died – Rio de Janeiro, Brazil, 27 April 1995

Rafael Rabello

Rafael Baptista Rabello began to study the guitar at the age of twelve with the well-known guitarist/teacher Jaime Florence. A talented classical guitarist, he also developed a great interest in the popular music of Brazil. In 1981 he received the 'Best Guitarist' award from the music reviewers of the magazine Playboy. In the same year he was awarded the title 'Best Instrumentalist' by the Associado Brasileira de Produtores de Discos.

Rabello enjoyed an association with the prominent Brazilian composer Rádames Gnattali during the last few years of Gnattali's life. He made several recordings and was regarded as one of Brazil's most important young guitarists before his early death at the age of 32.

SELECTED RECORDINGS
Rafael: Sete Cordas. Fontana 6488 174 LP
Tributo a Garoto (with Rádames Gnattali, piano).
Funarte PA 82001 LP
Rafael Rabello interpreta Rádames Gnattali.
Visom LPVO-006 LP
Relendo Dilermando Reis. RGE 344 6078 CD
Rafael Rabello and Deo Rean Duo. RCA M10-150 CD

KONRAD RAGOSSNIG

Born –

Klagenfurt, Austria

6 May 1932

Konrad Ragnossnig

Konrad Ragossnig received his first guitar lessons at the age of nine. In order to widen his musical studies, he also took lessons on the piano and cello at the Klagenfurt Conservatory of Music. He went on to complete his musical studies as a pupil of Karl Scheit, professor of guitar at the Academy of Music and Performing Arts in Vienna.

In 1960 Konrad Ragossnig was appointed a professor of guitar at the same Academy, a position he held until 1964. In 1960 he studied with Andrés Segovia in Spain. He won first prize at the Cheltenham Festival in England in the same year. A year later, in 1961, he won first prize for interpretation at the Concours International for Guitar in Paris. Following this, he made extensive concert tours of Europe as well as many appearances on radio and television.,

About this time, Ragossnig began to take an intense interest in the lute. He mastered the Renaissance instrument, and now often includes it with the guitar in his concert recitals. Numerous composers have written works especially for him, including H.E.Apostel, J.Bondon, Mario Castelnuovo-Tedesco, H.Haug, J.Rodrigo and A.Schibler.

An outstanding classical guitarist, Konrad Ragossnig has lived in Switzerland since 1964, where he is professor of guitar at the Basel Music Academy. He also continues an active career as a recitalist and recording artist on both the guitar and the lute.

SELECTED RECORDINGS

Master of the Guitar: Volume Three.	RCA RTB 6599 LP
Dances and Songs for Two Guitars (with Walter Feybli).	Turnabout TV 34605RS LP
Anthology of the Guitar: Volume Two (with Werner Tripp, flute).	RCA VICS 1504 LP
Bondon: 'Concerto de Mars'.	RCA VICS 1367 LP
The Spanish Guitar.	Turnabout TV 34494S LP
Guitar Recital.	Supraphon 1-11-1040 LP
Concertos pour Guitare 18me Siècle.	VOX Musicalis 35050 LP
Duo with Hans-Martin Linde (flute).	EMI 065-45-386 LP
Serenade Espagnole (guitar & cello duo).	Harmonia Mundi HM 686D LP
Tipico Brasilero.	Wergo 60150-50 CD
Spanish Guitar Music.	Claves CD 50-806

SELECTED READING

Handbuch der Gitarreund Laute: Konrad Ragossnig.	B. Schott, 1978
Interview.	Classical Guitar, September 1990

STEPAN RAK

Born –

Ukraine, USSR

8 August 1945

SELECTED MUSIC
Temptation of the Renaissance.	Chorus
Farewell to Finland.	Chorus
Romance.	Chorus
Decem.	Chorus
Remembering Prague.	Chorus
Cry of the Guitar.	Chorus
Five Preludes.	Chorus

SELECTED RECORDINGS
Remembering Prague.	Chandos CHAN 8622 CD
The Guitar of Stepán Rak.	Nimbus NI 5177 CD
Prague Marimba Trio.	Supraphon 104118-1 LP
Stepán Rak played by Vladimir Mikulka.	GHA 126.003 CD
Dedications.	Nimbus NI 5239 CD
The Melancholy Roar of Niagara.	Multisonic 31 0261-2 CD
Terra Australis Vol.1.	EMI Monitor 660352-CD

SELECTED READING
Interview.	Guitar International, January 1985
Article.	Classical Guitar, October 1986
Interview.	Classical Guitar, February 1988
Interview.	Classical Guitar, July 1994
Interview.	Classical Guitar, January 1996

Stepán Rak

Stepán Rak was born in a village in the Ukraine during the closing stages of World War Two, but the precise date is obscure. Advancing Soviet troops took him to Czechoslovakia, where he was adopted by the Rak family. He studied at the Fine Arts School in Prague, after which he went on to study guitar at the Prague Conservatory from 1965 to 1970. He also studied composition at the Prague Academy of Arts in 1975.

It was during his student period that Stepán Rak began to establish himself as a talented performer and an individual composer. In 1973 his symphonic composition Hiroshima won second place in the Czechoslovakian National Competition for Young Composers. In the following year his song Until, based on the lyrics of the poet V.Nezval, was placed among the winning compositions. In 1975 he was invited to teach in Finland at the Jyväskylä Conservatory. He maintained this position until 1980.

Rak's many innovative compositions for the guitar have been admired by guitarists everywhere. He has appeared at many international guitar events and made several recordings in Czechoslovakia with the Prague Marimba Trio band as a soloist on the UK record labels Chandos and Nimbus.

ALEXANDER-SERGEI RAMIREZ

Born - Lima, Peru

3 January 1962

Alexander-Sergei Ramirez

Alexander-Sergei Ramirez is the son of German-Peruvian artists. His father is the painter Antonio Maro, his mother is a pianist. Ramirez's first instrument was the cello, which he studied from the age of six. He took up the guitar at the age of seventeen after hearing a recording by Andrés Segovia. From 1981 he studied guitar with Professor Maritta Kersting at the Robert Schumann Musikhochschule in Düsseldorf. He qualified with the highest degree from this conservatory in 1991. Ramirez also studied for one year with José-Luis Gonzalez at the music conservatory in Alcoy, Spain, and with Pepe Romero in the USA (1987-94).

Alexander-Sergei Ramirez went on to win first prize at the 1984 Düsseldorf University Competition, and first prize at the 1987 Alhambra Guitar Competiton in Spain. In 1993 he was awarded the Mozarteum Prize in Salzburg, Austria, and in 1994 the Schmolz & Bickenbach Prize in Düsseldorf. Since that time Ramirez has established himself as a leading concert recitalist and recording artist, both as a soloist and as a chamber musician. He has played with the Amati String Quartet, violinist Isabelle Faust, and several leading orchestras. Ramirez also devotes some of his time to teaching, and has given masterclasses on both sides of the Atlantic.

SELECTED RECORDINGS
Canciones y Danzas Espanãolas	Denon CO-75357 CD
Recuerdos de la Alhambra	Denon CO-75715 CD
Villa-Lobos & Ginastera	Denon CO-78931 CD
Fernando Sor	Denon CO-78975 CD

SELECTED READING
Interview	Staccato, July/August 1996

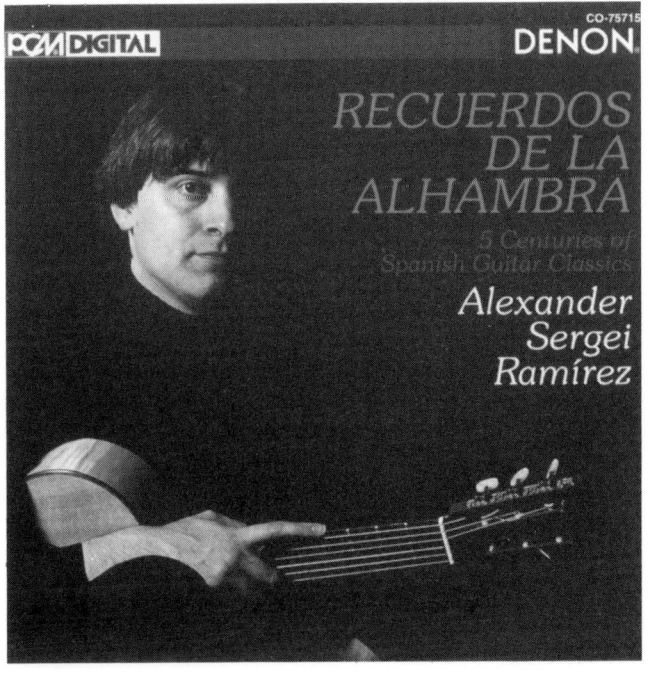

MANUEL LOPEZ RAMOS
Born –
Buenos Aires, Argentina
1929

Manuel López Ramos

Manuel López Ramos studied the guitar from an early age. His teacher was Miguel Michelone. At the age of nineteen Ramos was already regarded as one of Argentina's finest guitarists.

In 1948 he won the Argentine Chamber Music Associates first prize. In 1952 he embarked upon a highly successful international concert tour, appearing as a solo artist and with several leading symphony orchestras. He appeared in Mexico City in the same year, and soon afterwards accepted the position of professor of guitar at the Music School of the University of Mexico. In 1963 he toured the USSR, playing fourteen recitals.

Manuel López Ramos continues to lead a busy life as a recitalist and teacher. He has appeared at several international guitar festivals, and has also directed special courses for guitarists at the University of Arizona, the National School of Music of the UNAM, and the Conservatoire of Guatemala.

SELECTED RECORDS
Masters of the Guitar: Volume Two.	RCA RB 6599 LP
Anthology of the Guitar. Volume Three.	RCA VICS 1541 LP
Castelnuovo-Tedesco. Quintet for Guitar and String Quartet.	RCA VICS 1367 LP
La Guitarra Clásica.	Boston B-216 LP

SELECTED READING
Article.	Guitarra, September 1979
Interview.	Guitar International, October 1986
Interview.	Classical Guitar, April 1987

GIULIO REGONDI
*Born – Lyons, France, 1822
Died – London, England
6 May 1872

Giulio Regondi

One of the greatest guitar virtuosos of the nineteenth century, Giulio Regondi was originally taught the guitar by his father. By the time he was seven he had already made his first public recital in Paris. He amazed his audience with his immense talents, and was dubbed 'The Infant Paganini' by the critics. His father took advantage of his son's unique gifts by presenting him in concert in most of the principal cities of Europe.

In 1831 Giulio Regondi, who was also a virtuoso performer on the concertina, gave concerts in several British provincial cities. At the end of his concert tour his family settled in London, where Regondi lived until his death in 1872.

Giulio Regondi continued an active career as a virtuoso of both the guitar and the concertina. He was also a prolific composer. Much of his music has been out of print for most of the twentieth century, but there has been a revival of interest, and several of his republished works have found their way into public performances.

SELECTED MUSIC
Rêverie (Notturno) per Chitarra, op.19, ed. Chiesa.
　　　　　　　　　　　　　　　　　　Zerboni
Complete Guitar Works of Giulio Regondi.
　　　　　　　　　　　　　Chanterelle ECH 414
Ten Etudes – Giulio Regondi.　　Edition Orphee PWYS-17

SELECTED RECORDINGS
The Guitar Works of Regondi: Leif Christensen.　Paula 10 LP
The Great Regondi Vol.1. David Starobin.　Bridge BCD 9039
The Great Regondi Vol.2. David Starobin.　Bridge BCD 9055

SELECTED READING
Giulio Regondi.	Guitar & Lute, January 1982
Article.	Classical Guitar, August 1991
Article.	Guitar Review, Fall 1992
Article.	Guitar Review, Winter 1992
Article.	Soundboard, Spring 1993
Article.	Guitar Review, Winter 1993

*There is no positive proof of the date and place of Regondi's birth. Some scholars now favour Geneva as his place of birth.

Superb classical guitar made c.1834 by Christian Frederick Martin (1796-1873)

Giulio Regondi as a child prodigy

IGNACIO RODES

Born - Juan Ignacio Rodes Biosca

Alicante, Spain

24 August 1961

Ignacio Rodes

Ignacio Rodes began to study the guitar with his mother at the age of nine.

He went on to study under José Tomás at the Conservatoria Superior "Oscar Espla" de Alicante. He also attended masterclasses given by David Russell, Manuel Barrueco, and John Williams.

Rodes won first prize in several classical guitar competitions including, the 1983 Segovia Competiton in Palma de Mallorca, the 1985 Tárrega Competition in Benicasim, and the 1981 Ramirez Competiton

In 1983-86 Rodes received a grant from the British Council and the Spanish Ministry of Culture to study early music and the music of J.S. Bach with Nigel North in London. Since that time he has established himself an an international concert recitalist. He frequently performs at international guitar festivals, and has broadcast on European and USA television and radio.

SELECTED RECORDINGS
Sonatas para Guitarra   Opera Tres CD 1010 OPE
Guitar Concertos - Guinjoan/Villa-Lobos/Halffter
                Fundacio Musica Contemporania 4 CD

ISTVAN RÖMER

Born –

Zagreb, Yugoslavia

27 August 1962

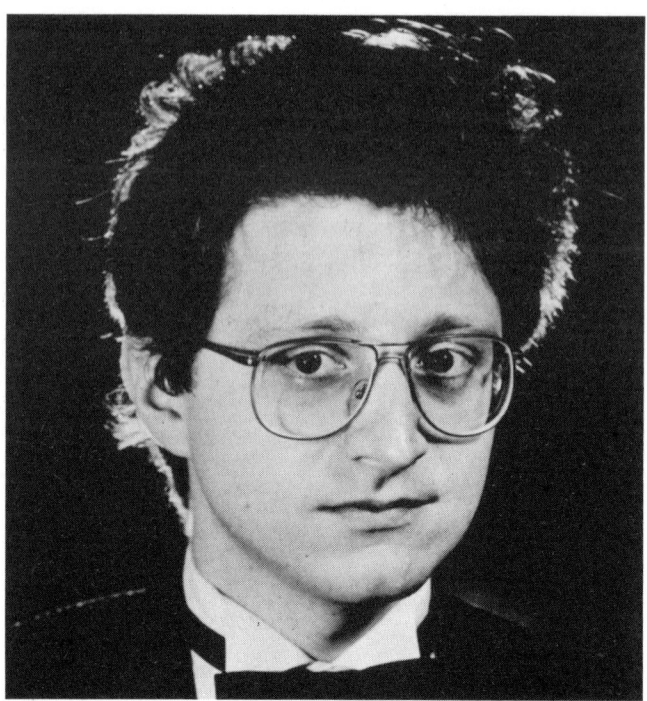

István Römer

István Römer studied guitar with Darko Petrinjak at the Zagreb Music Academy. He graduated in 1983, going on to study at the Hochschule für Musik und darstellende Kunst in Graz, Austria, with Marga Bäuml-Klasinc, graduating in 1984. He also took part in masterclasses with John Williams and Julian Byzantine.

István Römer won first prize at the Mettmann International Guitar Competition, West Germany, in 1983. He went on to win three major prizes at international guitar competitions in the following year: third prize in Gargnano, Italy, second prize at the Maria Callas Competition in Athens, Greece, and first prize at the Andrés Segovia Competition in Palma, Spain. He also won the Milka Trnina Annual Award given by the Association of Croatian Composers in 1984.

Since 1980, he has taught guitar at the Zagreb Music Educational Centre, and since 1984 he has been assistant professor at the Zagreb Music Academy. A member of the Zagreb Guitar Trio, István Römer is a fine solo artist in his own right, and has given concerts throughout Europe and the former USSR.

SELECTED RECORDING
Music by Bach, Papandopulo, Granados, Bogdanovic.
                        Yugoton LSY 66275 LP

ANGEL ROMERO

Born –

Málaga, Spain

17 August 1946

SELECTED RECORDINGS

Virtuoso Works for Guitar.	Angel S 37312 LP
Rodrigo Concerto and Fantasia.	Angel S 37440 LP
Classical Virtuoso.	Angel S 36094 LP
Music of Celedonio Romero.	Angel S 37311 LP
Angel Romero: Rodrigo and Torroba.	Angel S 37312 LP
The Divine Giuliani.	Angel SZ 37326 LP
Rodrigo: Concerto for Four Guitars: The Romeros.	Philips 3677 LP
Guitar Concertos for Two Guitars (with Pepe Romero).	Philips 6500-918 LP
Classical Music for Four Guitars: The Romeros.	Philips 9500-296 LP
A Touch of Class.	Telarc CD-80134
Granados 12 Danzas (with Celedonio Romero).	Telarc CD-80216
A Touch of Romance.	Telarc CD-80213
Angel Romero plays Bach.	Telarc CD-80288
Artistry of Angel Romero Video.	Kay J 065

SELECTED READING

Interview.   Classical Guitar, March/April 1983

Angel Romero

Angel Romero, the youngest son of the guitarist Celedonio Romero, made his debut as a guitar soloist with the family quartet at the age of six. A year later, he gave his first solo recital in Valencia, Spain.

In 1958 the Romero family emigrated to the United States and settled in the Los Angeles area. Celedonio founded a guitar school there, at the same time maintaining a concert career for himself and his three talented sons.

In 1964 Angel Romero became the first guitarist to appear at the famous Hollywood Bowl, where he performed Rodrigo's Concierto de Aranjuez with the Los Angeles Philharmonic Orchestra.

In 1970, together with his brother Pepe, Angel performed the world première of Rodrigo's Concierto Madrigal for two guitars and orchestra.

Angel Romero has developed into one of the world's most outstanding classical guitarists. He maintains a busy concert schedule throughout the United States and abroad. He currently has an exclusive recording contract with Telarc Records in America as well as appearing on Philips and Mercury recordings by the Romero Guitar Quartet.

CELEDONIO ROMERO

Born – Cienfuegos, Cuba, 2 March 1913

Died – La Jolla, California, USA

8 May 1996

Celedonio Romero

Celedonio Romero was the youngest son of the Spanish architectural engineer who designed the harbour of Gibraltar. Introduced to the guitar when he was five years old, Romero's talent convinced his family that he should follow a career in music. As a result he was enrolled at and later graduated from the Conservatory of Madrid. He was a student of Daniel Fortea, who had been a pupil of Tárrega.

Celedonio Romero's first public recital was in Madrid when he was twenty years old. His performance was well received by the audience and critics alike. Soon after his Madrid debut, he married a young actress from Málaga's Teatro Cervantes. During the Spanish Civil War he played the guitar many times for his fellow loyalists. When Málaga surrendered to General Franco's forces, Romero was imprisoned but later released. He then earned his living by entertaining the troops.

Celedonio Romero's reputation as a fine classical guitarist continued to grow, but because he refused to commit himself to the opposition, the Franco regime denied him the right to give concerts outside Spain. In 1957, after considerable pressure and governmental red tape, Romero and his family were granted a passport to visit Portugal. The following year, with the help of sympathetic American friends, they were able to emigrate to the United States. Celedonio Romero lived at first in the Los Angeles area of California.

A fine classical guitarist in his own right, Celedonio Romero made a unique contribution to the classical guitar in that, under his tuition, all his three sons developed into highly talented guitarists. In particular, Angel and Pepe have become two of the great guitar virtuosos of the twentieth century. For many years, Celedonio Romero appeared with great success in concert all over the world with his three sons as a guitar quartet, 'Los Romeros'.

SELECTED RECORDINGS
European Court Music.	Philips (Universo) 6582-001 LP
Compositions for Two Guitars.	Philips 9500-352 LP
Classical Music for Two Guitars.	Philips 9500-296 LP
Rodrigo Concertos Andaluz/Aranjuez.	Mercury 75021 LP
An Evening with the Romeros.	Mercury 75022 LP
Royal Family of the Guitar.	Mercury 75027 LP
Vivaldi Concertos.	Mercury 75054 LP
Evening of Guitar Music.	Delos D/CD 1004
Bach/Sanz Guitar Music.	Delos D/CD 1005
Granados 12 Danzas (with Angel Romero).	Telarc CD-80216

SELECTED READING
The Romeros.	Guitar Player, April 1972
The Romeros.	Guitar & Lute, September 1978
Los Romeros.	Classical Guitar, September/October 1982

SELECTED MUSIC
Classic Guitar Method.	Orozco, New York 1990

PEPE ROMERO

Born –

Málaga, Spain

8 March 1944

Pepe Romero

COURTESY: COLUMBIA ARTISTS; PHOTO: CHRISTIAN STEINER

Pepe Romero began his studies on the guitar at the age of three with his father, Celedonio Romero. He gave his first public performance with his father at the Teatro Lope de Vega in Seville, Spain, when he was only ten years old.

The Romero family moved to California in 1958. A year later, when he was fifteen, Pepe – by this time regarded as a highly talented flamenco guitarist – made his first recording, for the Contemporary record label.

Pepe Romero's only guitar teacher was his father, but he studied music both in Spain and in New York with the Basque pianist-composer Francisco de Medina. For well over twenty years he has appeared as a member of the family quartet, 'Los Romeros'. He has also appeared in duos with Celin or Angel, his older and younger brothers respectively. More recently, he has appeared more often as a soloist or in a duo with Angel. Together they gave the first performance of Rodrigo's Concierto Madrigal for two guitars and orchestra, in 1970.

Seven of Boccherini's Quintets have been recorded by Pepe Romero for Philips. Together with his concert performances and many other recordings, they established him as one of the great virtuosos of the day.

When he is not giving concerts, Pepe Romero teaches at the University of Southern California. He has written a guitar method entitled Guitar Style and Technique, which was published by Bradleys of New York.

SELECTED RECORDINGS
Compositions for Two Guitars.	Philips 9500-352 LP
Guitar Concertos for Two Guitars (with Angel Romero).	
	Philips 6500-918 LP
Rodrigo (Fantasia) and Giuliani.	Philips 9500-042 LP
Carulli Concertos / Moreno Concertos.	Philips 426 263-2 LP
Famous Guitar Music.	Philips 9500-295 LP
Classical Music for Four Guitars.	Philips 9500-296 LP
Boccherini Guitar Quintets Nos.4 & 5.	Philips 9500-621 LP
Boccherini Guitar Quintets Nos.1, 2 & 7.	Philips 9500-985 LP
Boccherini Guitar Quintets Nos.3 & 9.	Philips 9500-789 LP
Sor's Guitar Sonatas, Op.22 & Op.25.	Philips 9500-586 LP
Rodrigo for Solo Guitar.	Philips 9500-915 LP
Carulli/Moreno Concertos.	Philips 426 263-2 LP
Rodrigo Concertos and Solos.	Philips 438 016-2 CD
Noches de Espana.	Philips 442 150-2 CD

SELECTED READING
Article.	Guitar, April 1979
Article.	Guitar Player, 1981
Article.	Guitar International, October 1983
Interview.	Classical Guitar, Nov/Dec 1983
Article.	Classical Guitar, March 1987

SELECTED MUSIC
Guitar Method.	Bradleys

David Russell

DAVID RUSSELL

Born –

Glasgow, Scotland

1 June 1953

Regarded as one of the greatest guitar virtuosos to have emerged in recent years, David Russell was born in Scotland, and spent most of his childhood on the Spanish island of Menorca, where his parents had decided to live.

He was attracted to the guitar at an early age by the records of Andrés Segovia. His father, a professional artist, was also a keen guitarist and was his son's first teacher. At sixteen David Russell, already recognized as a highly talented guitarist, moved to London to study at the Royal Academy of Music, where he twice won the Julian Bream Guitar Prize. Over the years he studied with several teachers, but his two main influences were Hector Quine in London, and José Tomás in Spain.

Russell's career developed rapidly after he won several of the major guitar competitions in Spain, amongst them the 'Ramírez' Competition, the 'Franciso Tárrega' Competition and the Concurso 'Andrés Segovia'.

Since the late 1980s David Russell has lived in Vigo, Spain, with his wife Maria. He spends much of his working year touring North America, most countries of Western Europe, and the United Kingdom, giving recitals and masterclasses. He has appeared many times on BBC television and radio. He has also taken part in many major international music festivals, including the Edinburgh Festival, the Esztergom International Guitar Festival, the Concours of Radio France, the Toronto Guitar Festival, the Classical Guitar Festival of Great Britain, the Scandinavian Guitar Festival, and the International Guitar Festival of Havana.

SELECTED RECORDINGS
Musique pour Basse et Guitare.   Festival FC 501 LP
Something Unique.   Overture OR 1001 LP
David Russell plays Antonio Lauro.
  Guitar Masters GMR 101-93 CD
Bach, Handel & Scarlatti.   Guitar Masters GMR 1007 LP
David Russell (with Raphaëlla Smits &
Jos van Immerseel): Castelnuovo-Tedesco solos and duets.
  Academix AX 850218
Sor & Kaufman: duets with Raphaëlla Smits.
  Pocketino PL 0008 LP
David Russell plays Mertz, Regondi, Coste.   GHA 126-003 CD
Rodrigo/Concierto de Aranjuez; Giuliani/Concerto in A Op.30.   Polskie Nagrania SX 2611 LP
Bach, Handel & Scarlatti.   GHA 126-006 CD
Francisco Tarrega, Integral de Guitarra (2 CD set).
  Opera Tres CDS 100314
David Russell plays Barrios.   Telarc CD-80373
Guitare Quebec '94.   Doberman DO179 CD

SELECTED READING
David Russell.   Guitar, November 1978
David Russell.   Guitar Player, October 1981
Interview.   Classical Guitar, November/December 1982
Interview.   Classical Guitar, July, 1985
Interview.   Classical Guitar, July 1989
Interview.   Soundboard, Fall 1994
Article.   Soundboard, Spring 1995

MICHEL SADANOWSKY

Born –

Maulde, Lille, France

11 January 1950

Michel Sadanowsky

Of Russian and French parentage, Michel Sadanowsky began to play the violin at the age of seven. He continued studying for ten years, and played in a symphony orchestra. During this time he discovered the guitar, and at the age of eighteen decided to devote himself entirely to this instrument.

Sadanowsky settled in Paris in 1969, where he studied with Turibio Santos and later with Oscar Cáceres. Subsequently he was greatly influenced by Abel Carlevaro's approach to playing the guitar. In 1976 he obtained the Maîtrise of the Music University of Paris.

In 1979 he won the first prize at the Concours International de Guitare de Paris, organized by Radio France. Since that time he has given concerts and taught throughout Europe, Africa, Asia, Australia, South and North America. In 1984 he formed the Paris Guitar Trio, consisting of Yves Godeau, Jean-Françcois Ruzel and himself.

Sadanowsky has taught the guitar at the International Music University of Paris, and gives a regular masterclass at the Royal Conservatory of Ghent, Belgium. He is the editor of a collection of guitar transcriptions, including the complete works for cello and lute by J.S.Bach, published by Billaudot.

SELECTED RECORDINGS
The Guitar of Michel Sadanowsky.	Verseau M 10.034 LP
Michel Sadanowsky Plays.	Podium 8004.17 LP
The Art of Michel Sadanowsky.	Istria DI 3533 LP

EDUARDO SAINZ DE LA MAZA

Born- Burgos, Spain 5 January 1903

Died-Barcelona, Spain 1982

Eduardo Sainz de la Maza

Eduardo Sainz de la Maza, with his brother guitarist, Regino, came from a musical and artistic family. He began to study music at the age of six, but only took up the guitar at the age of eight when the family moved to Madrid. Sainz de la Maza studied there with Daniel Fortea. A few years later his family moved to Barcelona, where the young guitarist continued his studies with Miguel Llobet. Sainz de la Maza gave his concert debut at the age of fourteen in the Sala Mozart in Barcelona. Around this time he also studied cello and toured Spain in various string ensembles. In 1923 he decided to devote his life to the guitar.

Eduardo Sainz de la Maza never achieved the international fame of his brother Regino as a recitalist, yet he made his impact as a respected teacher and a gifted composer. His compositions have not yet earned the full recognition they deserve.

SELECTED READING
Article	Guitar International, October 1987

SELECTED MUSIC
Habanera	CASA
Campanas del Alba	UME
Sonando Caminos	UME
Bolero	UME
Evocacion Criolla	UME

REGINO SAINZ DE LA MAZA

Born – Burgos, Spain,
7 September 1896
Died – Madrid, Spain, 26 November 1981

Regino Sainz de la Maza

Regino Sainz de la Maza began his musical studies on the piano in his native town of Burgos. He then attended the Academia de Bellas Artes de San Sebastián, studying harmony with Beltrán Pagola and piano with Germán Cendoya. His studies took him later to both Barcelona and Madrid, where he continued to study the piano.

Madrid turned out to be an important turning point in Sainz de la Maza's career, for it was there that he began formal studies of the guitar with Daniel Fortea. It was at that time that he realized that the guitar was the instrument through which he could best display his musical talent. At the age of eighteen, he gave his first public recital at the Círculo de Belles Artes in Madrid. His performance was well received by audience and critics alike. On the recommendation of important musicians, including Tomás Breton and Emilio Serrano, he earned a grant to further his musical studies from the municipality of Burgos.

Regino Sainz de la Maza moved to Barcelona to study composition with Enrique Morera and Jaime Pahissa. He then completed a highly successful concert tour of Spain, and this led to further tours of South America and Europe.

When he returned to Spain, he worked with Manuel de Falla in the National Music Society, and was appointed to the newly established professorship of guitar at the Conservatory of Madrid in 1935. In 1937 he went to the United States to perform, returning after the Spanish Civil War to become a music critic for the Spanish daily journal ABC. He also became very involved in transcribing early Spanish works, and in doing so found himself in close contact with many of Spain's foremost musicians. In 1938 he met Joaquín Rodrigo and the Marquís de Bolarque. The latter was a famous music patron and an enthusiast for the guitar. The result of their meeting was Rodrigo's Concierto de Aranjuez, which he completed in the autumn of 1939. Sainz de la Maza was given the double honour of having the work dedicated to him and of giving the first performance in Barcelona on 9 November 1940. The work has since won world-wide acclaim, and is probably the most popular concerto ever written. Regino Sainz de la Maza was to perform it a further sixty times in Europe and the Americas.

Regino Sainz de la Maza was a very active teacher, not only in the Madrid Conservatory but also in private study and in masterclasses. He was an avid researcher on many aspects of the guitar and early Spanish music, and made numerous transcriptions as well as producing several original compositions. In 1955 he wrote a brief history of the guitar, La Guitarra y Su Historia. His erudition won him election to the Spanish Academy in 1958, making him the first guitarist to be elected since its foundation in 1752.

SELECTED MUSIC

Alegrías.	UME 16943
Canciones Castellanas.	UME 22146
Cantilena.	UME 15645
Cuatro Fantasías del Siglo XVI.	UME 18827
El Vito: New Version.	UME 19768
Frontera de Dios.	UME 20207
Petenera	UME 20347
Rondeña.	UME 19900
Seguidilla; Sevillanas.	UME 16944
Soléa.	UME 22145
Zapateado.	UME 19901

SELECTED RECORDINGS

Rodrigo – Concierto de Aranjuez and Fantasia.	RCA VICS 1322 LP
Regino Sainz de la Maza.	Barclay 920-230 LP
Recital.	RCA (Spain) 3L-16.118 LP
La Guitarra de Regino Sainz de la Maza.	RCA (Spain) NP 71736 CD
Encuentro con la Guitarra de Regino.	RCA (Spain) VictoLM-16.330 LP

SELECTED READING

Regino Sainz de la Maza.	Guitar & Lute, April 1980

GEORGE SAKELLARIOU

Born –

Athens, Greece

2 May 1944

George Sakellariou

George Sakellariou was the youngest of eight children. He was introduced to the guitar at an early age by one of his brothers.

Sakellariou studied at the Hellenikon Odeion (conservatory) in Athens with Professor Charalambos Ekmetsoglou. At the age of fifteen he gave his first recital, at the Parnassus Hall in Athens, and at eighteen he graduated, receiving first prize for an outstanding musical performance.

He emigrated to the United States in 1963, originally to study medicine at the University of California. He soon decided that music should be his career, and established himself as one of the finest guitarists and teachers on the West Coast of America. In 1964 he studied privately with Andrés Segovia, and attended some of his international masterclasses. Sakellariou has performed throughout the United States, Canada and South America. He has appeared in concert in many universities, and at the Carmel Bach Festival and Universidad de los Andes, Bogota, Colombia. He has been a soloist with several symphony orchestras and chamber groups in the United States. Over the years he has made numerous appearances on the CBC Television network in Canada and the NET network in the USA.

George Sakellariou now lives in San Rafael, California, giving many concerts and also teaching at the San Francisco Conservatory of Music.

SELECTED RECORDING
Music from South America.   Amat AGS 181 LP
Sakura.   Amat 385 CAS

SELECTED READING
George Sakellariou.   Guitar & Lute, May 1978
Interview.   Guitar International, May 1986

MARCO DE SANTI

Born –

Brescia, Italy

3 November 1957

Marco de Santi

Marco de Santi began studying the guitar at an early age with Fausto Bettelli. From 1972 to 1978 he studied with Angelo Gilardino at the Liceo Musicale G.B.Viotti in Vercelli and then graduated with distinction at the Conservatoire C.Pollini in Padua.

Santi won four national competitions and in 1974 was awarded the Mario Castelnuovo-Tedesco prize for the best Italian guitar student. In 1981 he won second prize at the International Competition for Musical

Performers in Geneva, and in 1982 won the 'Andrés Segovia' Competition in Palma de Mallorca.

Marco de Santi made his debut as a concert soloist in 1974, and since then has performed extensively both as a soloist and with orchestras or chamber groups throughout Europe. In 1987, together with the chamber group Carme and Astor Piazzolla, he gave the first Italian performance of Piazzolla's Double Concerto for guitar, bandonéon and strings. He has also made many radio and television broadcasts.

SELECTED RECORDING
Giuliani, Regondi, Legnani.   Lira 0028 CD
Piazzolla, Santórsola, Ginastera.   Lira 0022 CD

TURIBIO SANTOS

Born – TURIBIO SOARES SANTOS

São Luis, Maranhao, North Brazil

7 March 1940

Turibio Santos

Turibio Santos was attracted to the classical guitar at the age of ten. His first teachers were Antonio Rebello and, later, Oscar Cáceres. His first recital took place in 1962, in Rio de Janeiro, and was followed by a series of concerts all over Brazil. In the following year the Villa-Lobos Museum invited him to play the Brazilian composer's complete Twelve Studies for Guitar (1929) and to take part in the first public hearing of the Mystic Sextet (1917).

In 1964 Santos formed a duo with Oscar Cáceres and made several tours of South America. In 1965 he decided to establish himself in Europe, and attended masterclasses given by Andrés Segovia in Italy and Julian Bream in England. In the same year he won the first prize in the ORTF's International Guitar Competition in Paris. His subsequent appearances on both ORTF and BBC programmes, as well as his recording on disc of Villa-Lobos's Twelve Studies, made him well known to European audiences. From 1965 to 1969 he was professor of guitar at the Conservatoire Municipal in Paris.

Turibio Santos has performed with many orchestras as a soloist. They include the Monte Carlo Orchestra, the Philharmonic Orchestra of the ORTF, the English Chamber Orchestra, and the Royal Philharmonic Orchestra. Santos has also taken part in numerous festivals in Europe, including the fifth Croisière Méditerranée de Musique. In 1974 he joined Yehudi Menuhin and Mstislav Rostropovich in the opening concert for the Creation of International Funds for Musical Collaboration organised by UNESCO.

Santos established himself in North America with appearances in New York, Boston, Houston, Dallas, Minneapolis, Cincinnati and Washington DC. He was also featured at the Guitar '78 and Guitar '81 Festivals in Toronto, Canada. He was appointed General Director of the Sala Cecilia Meireles in Brazil.

SELECTED RECORDINGS
Concierto de Aranjuez: Rodrigo.   Musidisc 30 RC 894 LP
Villa-Lobos: Twelve Studies for Guitar. Erato STV 70496 LP
Villa-Lobos: Prelude, Concerto, Sextour Mystique.
                                       Erato STV 70566 LP
Classiques d'Amerique Latine.   Erato STV 70658 LP
Musique Française pour Guitare.   Erato STV 70767 LP
Musique pour deux Guitares: Vol.1 (with Oscar Cáceres).
                                       Erato STV 70794 LP
Danses Espagnoles: Volume One.   Erato STV 70844 LP
J. S. Bach.   Erato STV 70885 LP
Musique Brésilienne.   Erato STV 70913 LP
Danses Espagnoles: Volume Two.   Erato STV 71076 LP
Musique pour deux Guitares: Vol.2 (with Oscar Cáceres).
                                       Erato STV 71092 LP
Fernando Sor.   Erato STV 71268 LP
Chôros do Brasil.   Erato ERA 9155 LP
Valsas et Chôros.   Erato ERA 9231 LP
Duo for Flute and Guitar (with Christian Lardé, flute).
                                       Erato ERA 71127 LP
O Viola Brasileiro.   Columbia 2-464331 CD
Villa-Lobos – Complete Guitar Works.   KUARUP KCD-028

SELECTED READING
Interview.   Classical Guitar, December 1984

MARIA LIVIA SÃO MARCOS

Born –

São Paulo, Brazil

8 April 1942

SELECTED RECORDINGS

Classical Guitar and Strings.	Everest 34209 LP
A Internacional.	Fermata 303-1009 LP
Saudades do Brasil.	Fermata 303-1013 LP
Villa-Lobos: 12 Etudes.	Fermata 305-1039 LP
Maria Livia São Marcos plays Baroque Music.	Classic Pick Music 70-124 LP

SELECTED READING

Article. Guitar Player, January 1976

Maria Livia São Marcos

Maria Livia São Marcos began to study the guitar at the age of five. Her first teacher was her father, Professor Manuel São Marcos. It was soon obvious that she had enormous musical talent, and at the age of thirteen she gave her first public recital.

At the age of seventeen she was awarded a diploma with honours at the Conservatorio Dramático e Musical in São Paulo. Her first recording followed soon afterwards.

Maria Livia São Marcos went to Portugal, where she gave the first public performance of the guitar concerto Domingos Brandao.. Following this highly acclaimed concert, she went to Paris, where she gave several successful solo guitar recitals. In 1964 she went to Santiago de Compostela, Spain, to study with Andrés Segovia, and then to Lisbon for further study with Emilio Pujol.

After a highly successful career as a classical guitarist in Brazil, Maria Livia São Marcos accepted in 1970 a teaching post as professor of guitar at the Conservatory of Music in Geneva, a position she has held since. A highly respected teacher, she continues to give recitals in the principal cities of Europe and North and South America.

Manuel Sao Marcos

TADASHI SASAKI
Born -
Tokyo, Japan
3 March 1943

Tadashi Sasaki

Tadashi Sasaki began to play the guitar at an early age. His first teacher was his father. At the age of thirteen he gave a recital on the Japanese National Radio. In 1965 he gave his first public solo recital.

Sasaki went to Germany in 1966 to work as a guitar teacher at the Saarbrucken Music Academy. He also worked there at the local radio station. Over the next few years he studied privately with Siegfried Behrend, Narciso Yepes and José Tomás. In 1968 he became the first Japanese guitarist to win a prize at the Radio France International Guitar Competition in Paris.

In 1969 Sasaki moved to Cologne, where he took up the post of guitar teacher at the local music academy. In 1973 he obtained his Master's degree in lute playing from Cologne Music Academy. From 1979 he taught at the Aachen Music Academy, and since 1979 has been Professor of Guitar there.

As well as teaching, Tadashi Sasaki has maintained a busy concert career, and has edited several guitar editions for the Zen-on and Edition Moek companies.

SELECTED RECORDINGS
Gitarre Solo	APM F 666554 LP
Kammermusik von Pan Trio	PRE 68544 LP
Confrontation	APM 5189/K CD

JUKKA SAVIJOKI
Born –
Helsinki, Finland
8 June 1952

Jukka Savijoki

Jukka Savijoki began to play the guitar at the age of thirteen but only took up the classical guitar seriously at the age of eighteen. He studied the guitar in Finland with Ivor Putilin at the Sibelius Academy in Helsinki. He then studied in London with John W. Duarte (1975-76) and then with Oscar Ghiglia in Italy, in 1976 at a Siena masterclass.

Jukka Savijoki has given concerts throughout Scandinavia, Europe and also in Japan. Several important composers, including Paavo Heininen, Erik Bergman, Magnus Linberg, Jouni Kaipainen, Kalevi Aho, Usko Merilainen and Atli Heimir Sveinson, have composed for him or for the ensembles in which he plays.

Jukka Savijoki is currently a senior lecturer at the Sibelius Academy in Helsinki.

SELECTED RECORDINGS
Baroque Suites for Guitar.	BIS LP 176
Contemporary Finnish Guitar.	BIS LP 207
Guitar Music by Manuel Ponce.	BIS LP 255
Giuliani: Complete works for flute & guitar (with Mikael Helasvuo): 3 vols.	BIS CD-413
Plays Britten/Lennox Berkeley.	Ondine ODE 779-2 CD

SELECTED READING
Interview.	Guitar, September 1983
Interview.	Classical Guitar, April 1986
Interview.	Guitar International, November 1986

RICHARD SAVINO
Born -
New York City, USA
3 April 1956

SELECTED RECORDINGS
Boccherini Guitar Quintets 1-3
　　　　　　　　　Harmonia Mundi HMU 907039 CD
Boccherini Guitar Quintets 4-6
　　　　　　　　　Harmonia Mundi HMU 907026 CD
Boccherini Guitar Quintets 7-8
　　　　　　　　　Harmonia Mundi HMU 907069 CD
Bardic Sounds - Mertz   Harmonia Mundi HMU 907115 CD
Giuliani & Paganini Duos w/ Monica Huggett
　　　　　　　　　Harmonia Mundi 907116 CD
Carulli Sonatas　　　　　　　　Naxos 8.553301 CD

Richard Savino

Richard Savino gained his Bachelor of Arts in 1980 and Master of Music degree in 1981 from SUNY at Stony Brook. He went on to study privately with Eliot Fisk, Oscar Ghiglia, Timothy Walker and Jerry Willard. In 1982 he took part in master classes given by Andrés Segovia in Geneva and New York City. He also attended masterclasses given by Ernesto Bitetti, Angel Romero, Christopher Parkening and Narciso Yepes. In 1985 he was the first solo guitarist to win the Artists International Carnegie Recital Hall debut Competition.

Since 1987 Savino has directed the California State University Summer Arts Guitar and Lute Institute. In 1992 he received the Doctor of Musical Art degree from the State University of New York at Stony Brook. He is currently the Professor of Music at the California State University at Sacramento.

Richard Savino is a frequent lecturer at music colleges and performs extensively both as a soloist and accompanist. He is a regular broadcaster on radio and television, and has worked with Paul Hillier, Judith Nelson, Monica Huggett, and the Artaria Quartet.

ISAIAS SAVIO

Born – Montevidedo, Uruguay

1 October 1902

Died – São Paulo, Brazil, 12 January 1977

Isaias Sávio

Isaias Sávio began his musical education at the age of nine. After studying the piano for four years, he began to study the guitar. He made rapid progress on the instrument, and it was soon obvious that he had very special talents.

He became a highly successful concert artist, playing throughout South America. In 1931 he went to Brazil and decided to make his home there. He continued an active career as a guitarist, promoting the classical guitar throughout Brazil's cities, towns and villages.

Isaias Sávio was also a fine composer. Over one hundred of his original works for the guitar have been published. Many of his compositions are based on Brazilian folk melodies that he had heard and learnt while visiting Brazilian country villages.

Towards the latter part of his life, Sávio devoted most of his time to teaching. He was professor of guitar at the Conservatorio Dramático e Musical de São Paulo, the first person to hold this post. He was also the director of the Escola Violinistica Jose do Patrocinio.

SELECTED MUSIC

A Casinha Pequenina and Minha Terra Tem Palmeiras.	BR 150
Cajita de Música.	BA 11505
Cênas Brasileiras, 1st series (seven pieces).	BR 1593
2nd series (two pieces).	MCM 0271
Celeste y Blanco: Estilo.	BR 2301
Duas Guitarras: Canção Cignana.	BR 1811
Nesta Rua: Theme & Variations.	BR 2252
Ojos Negros (Dark Eyes – Russian song) & A Casinha Pequenina.	BA 11217
Para Nilo Brincar: 9 popular children's songs.	BR 1079
Pensamientos, op.3 (short works).	R & F
Pequeña Romanza.	RF 7448
Preludes Nos.3, 4, 5, 6.	BR 3193
Four Preludes Pitorescos.	BR 1808
Sarabande & Gigue.	BR 2170
Three Original Pieces, 1927.	BR 3076
Two Pieces, Vidalita Popular, Dança de Boneca.	BR 2337
Variações de Gato.	BR 2302
Variations on an Infant's Theme.	R & F

SELECTED RECORDING

Yone Perreira Interpreta Isaias Sávio.	Brasidisc LP 14037

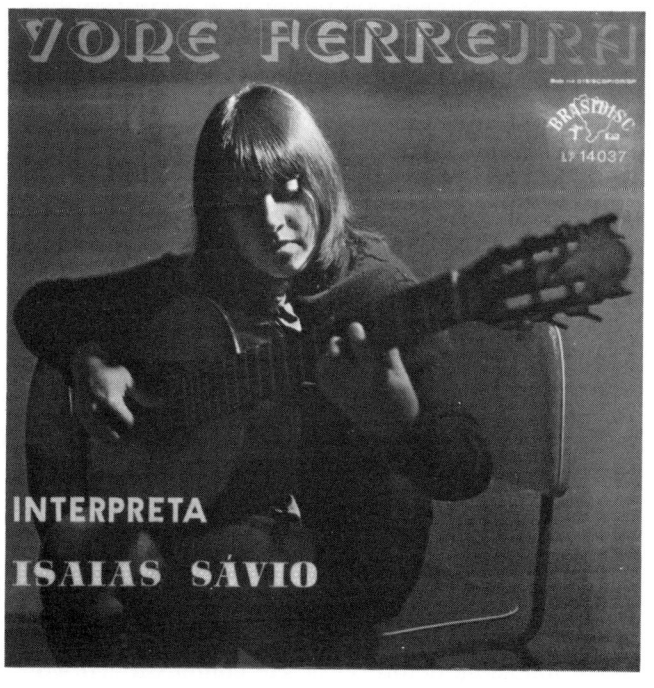

KARL SCHEIT

Born – Schönbrunn, Austria
21 April 1909
Died – Vienna, Austria, 22 November 1993

Karl Scheit

Karl Scheit's musical studies began on the violin at an early age. Although his father was a military band conductor, he did not want his son to become a professional musician. Scheit joined a youth group when he was fifteen years old, and it was then that he began to study the guitar in order to accompany himself when he sang. Soon afterwards the young musician became aware of the guitar's full potential, and began to study the instrument in earnest.

Karl Scheit left his home for Vienna and began to study music theory and harmony on the guitar at the Academy of Music there. After hearing both Miguel Llobet and Andrés Segovia in concert, Scheit decided to make the classical guitar his career. He continued his music studies with the eminent Austrian composer N.David. At the age of twenty-four Scheit was appointed professor of the guitar at the Vienna State Academy. He was regarded as one of the foremost guitar teachers in Europe, and published many transcriptions for guitar in addition to a Method for Guitar in five volumes.

Karl Scheit was the first guitarist to perform an entire Bach lute suite before 1939. He commissioned works for the guitar from several contemporary composers including Hans Erich Apostel, Franz Burkhardt and Roman Haubenstock-Ramati.

SELECTED RECORDING
Music for Guitar.   Turnabout TV 341238 LP

SELECTED READING
Karl Scheit. Ein Portrait – Erik Partsch.
                                    Doblinger, Vienna, 1994

STEPHAN SCHMIDT

Born - Villingen-Schwenningen,
Germany
10 September 1967

Stephan Schmidt

Stephan Schmidt studied with Gerhard Schlempp and Luis Martin Diego at the Musikhochschule in Trossingen (1982-86). After showing great promise he obtained a grant from the Studienstifung de Deutches Volkes to study with Alberto Ponce at L'Ecole Normale de Musique in Paris (1985-87), and then with Manuel Barrueco at the Manhattan School of Music in New York (1987-88). Schmidt also studied with Oscar Ghiglia in Siena (1983), and Betho Davezac in Meudon, France (1983-84). He won many awards during his student days.

In 1987 Stephan Schmidt won the Emilio Pujol Prize at the Carpentras International Guitar Competition, organised by Radio France, and first prize at Mettmann International Guitar Competiton in Germany. In 1988 he won first prize at the 30th International Radio France Guitar Competition in France. In the same year he was appointed to the teaching staff at the Conservatory of Music in Berne, Switzerland where he is now Chairman of the Guitar Department, and Professor of Classical Guitar and Methodology for professional students.

Stephan Schmidt was introduced to the composer Maurice Ohana by his teacher Luis Martin Diego. In 1991 Schmidt, who usually plays a ten-string guitar, began to record the complete solo guitar works of Maurice Ohana under the direction of the composer. Ohana was greatly impressed by Schmidt's musicianship and chose him to make the recording. The recording won six press awards. Schmidt combines his academic career with a busy career as an international concert recitalist, and also broadcasts frequently on television and radio.

SELECTED RECORDINGS
Maurice Ohana - L'Oeuvre pour Guitare
                                                    Astree/Auvidis E 8513CD
Scarlatti - Sonatas   Valois/Auvidis V 4750

JOHN SCHNEIDER

Born –

Pasadena, California, USA

8 November 1950

John Schneider

John Schneider began to play the guitar at the age of nine after having experimented with the ukulele and the banjo. During his teenage years he performed in various amateur folk, rock and jazz groups before turning to the classical guitar. He first studied the instrument with Vincenzo Macaluso. Schneider went on to study composition at the University of California. From California he went to the University of Wales in Cardiff, where he earned a Masters Degree in Electronic Music and a Ph.D. in Physics and Music in 1977. He also studied the guitar at the Royal College of Music, London.

Upon his return to the USA John Schneider began producing and hosting his weekly two-hour radio programme SOUNDBOARD, the longest running guitar series in the USA. Schneider served as President of the Guitar Foundation of America from 1979 to 1983.

Since the early 1980s Schneider has performed almost exclusively on the 'well-tempered guitar', an instrument which uses a system of interchangeable fingerboards that attach to the neck of the guitar by magnetic means. Each fingerboard uses a different pattern of fretting which produces acoustically pure intervals (unlike the standard equally tempered system) that are tuned according to either the key or the tuning system desired. With this unique capability Schneider interprets music from past eras in their original temperaments, as well as the modern quartertone music of Alois Haba and Juan Carrillo, and the repertoire specifically written for the instrument by Lou Harrison and LaMonte Young. His chamber group 'Just Strings', consisting of guitar, harp and percussion, has enjoyed success both in the USA and Japan.

John Schneider has written widely on the history and repertoire of the guitar for Guitar Review, Soundboard and Guitar & Lute. He is a specialist in contemporary music, and his book, The Contemporary Guitar, has become a standard text in this field of music. He is currently on the editorial staff of Soundboard magazine and teaches at Pierce College in Los Angeles.

SELECTED RECORDING
Sonic Voyage. El Maestro Records EM 8004 LP
Lou Harrison – Music for Guitar and Percussion.
Etcetera CD KTC 1071
Just West Coast. Bridge BCD 9041

SELECTED READING
The Contemporary Guitar. University of California, 1985
Article: The Well Tempered Guitar. Guitar, November 1983
Interview. Classical Guitar, July/August 1984

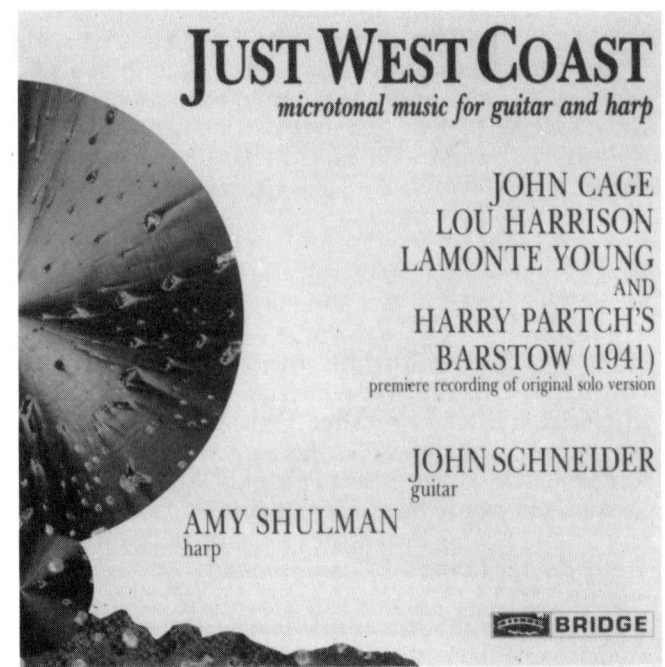

FRANZ SCHUBERT

Born – FRANZ PETER SCHUBERT

Lichtental, near Vienna, Austria, 31 January 1797

Died – Vienna 19 November 1828

Franz Schubert

Perhaps the greatest composer ever to have played the guitar, Franz Schubert produced an enormous amount of music, but unfortunately nothing of any consequence for the guitar.

He was given a sound music education by his father, a schoolteacher, who recognised his son's musical talents at a very early age. From him, Franz learned to play the violin; from his brother Ignaz, the piano. He learned to sing at the Chapel of the Court. He befriended the poet Theodor Korner, who was an enthusiastic guitarist. Much impressed with the instrument, Schubert decided that he would master it, and in a short time had become an accomplished guitarist.

The classical guitar became Franz Schubert's main instrument during the early part of his career. Before he could afford to buy a piano, he conceived all his vocal compositions on the guitar, and most of his songs at that time were written with a guitar accompaniment.

Franz Schubert lived in virtual poverty, achieving little success or recognition during his short life. His activities as a song writer lasted for almost seventeen years, yet it was not until 1819 that one of his songs was publicly performed, and it was not until 1821 that the first one was published.

There has recently been a revival of interest amongst guitarists in the guitar accompaniments of Schubert, the master of the Lied. Some of his other compositions include a guitar part. The Kantata zur Namensfeier des Vaters, for two tenors and bass, has an arpeggio accompaniment for guitar. In 1819 his 15 Original Dances for flute, violin and guitar were published by Diabelli, and he adapted a trio by Matiegka for flute, viola and guitar, adding a cello and turning it into a quartet.

Franz Schubert suffered ill health for many years. He died on 19 November 1828 at the age of thirty-one. One of his guitars, bearing his name, is on display in the Vienna Museum.

SELECTED MUSIC
Terzetto for male voices & guitar: ed.Scheit.   Doblinger
Die Nacht (voice & guitar).   Universal UE 18 957

SELECTED RECORDINGS
Guitar Quartet – Fred Jacobs (guitar) and Ensemble.
     Globe GLO 5040 CD
Der Winterreisse (Op. 89).
Tadashi Sasaki with Peter Ziethen (baritone).
     Globe VMK 63-41 213 CD

SELECTED READING
Schubert – A biography. Peggy Woodford.
     Omnibus Press Op. 42415

Andrés Segovia

ANDRÉS SEGOVIA

Born – ANDRÉS TORRES SEGOVIA

Linares, Granada, Spain, 21 February 1893

Died – Madrid, Spain, 2 June 1987

Andrés Segovia was one of the greatest musicians of the twentieth century, and certainly the most important guitarist the world has ever known. His exceptional genius and determination overcame very heavy prejudices against the guitar, and the instrument is now widely accepted as the equal of any other. There is not one classical guitarist alive today who has not been influenced by Andrés Segovia in one way or another.

At the age of five, Andrés Segovia was taken to live with his uncle in Granada. The uncle tried to encourage his nephew to learn the violin, but with little success. Andrés Segovia became fascinated with the sound of a guitar played by a flamenco guitarist who happened to be in his uncle's house. At the age of ten, Segovia received his first guitar, and from that moment, despite his uncle's opposition, he devoted every spare moment to it. After his uncle's death, Segovia, then twelve years old, went to live with his mother and brother in Córdoba. A little later, the young guitarist decided to rent his own room, so that he could fully develop his study of the guitar and music. He made friends with several musicians, including a pianist, Luis Serrano, who introduced him to a young pianist, Rafael de Montis. Montis was much impressed by Segovia's transcriptions of classical music for the guitar.

At the age of sixteen Andrés Segovia left school, determined to make the guitar his life. In 1909 he gave his first public recital, at the Granada Art Centre. The young guitarist then went to Seville to the home of Rafael de Montis. There he met and impressed many influential people who would patronise his future concerts. Segovia stayed in Seville for over a year, and played sixteen recitals while he was there. He then went to play in other major cities in Spain, but found enormous opposition to the classical guitar from musicians and critics alike.

In 1912 Segovia went to Madrid to make his debut in Spain's capital. There he met the luthier Manuel Ramírez, who was so impressed with the guitarist's ability that he gave him one of his finest guitars as a gift. Segovia's Madrid concert, despite an excellent performance, was not well received.

He went to Valencia, where he made contact with Tárrega's most prominent pupil, Miguel Llobet. They became good friends, and Llobet invited Segovia to his home in Barcelona. Segovia played three concerts in Barcelona, and they were generally well received.

On his return to Madrid Segovia was introduced to the concert promoter Ernesto de Quesada. Quesada was greatly impressed by Segovia's musicianship and technical ability, and offered to be his concert agent. The first booking arranged by Quesada was a tour of South America. It was highly successful. In 1920 Segovia was invited to play for Queen Victoria of Spain at the Palace of Madrid, a positive sign of the young guitarist's growing reputation and great musical talent.

From 1920 to 1935 Andrés Segovia gave concerts throughout the major cities of Europe. He appeared in London and Paris in 1924, and in Moscow in 1926. In 1928 he crossed the Atlantic again to make his United States debut in New York's Town Hall. Everywhere he went, he astounded his audiences with his performances. It was during this period that Segovia began his campaign to encourage leading composers to write for the guitar. The first to reply was Federico Moreno Torroba. Many more prominent composers, including Manuel Ponce, Heitor Villa-Lobos, Joaquín Turina, Mario Castelnuovo-Tedesco and Joaquín Rodrigo, were to compose original music for solo guitar and guitar and orchestra.

At the beginning of the Spanish Civil War in 1936, Segovia left Spain. His home in Barcelona was looted. He did not return until after the end of World War II. During these years he made his home in New York and Montevideo, Uruguay.

After the end of World War II, Segovia was instrumental in bringing about a revolution for classical guitarists. For many years he had suffered from the unreliability of gut strings. With the help of his friend Albert Augustine, Segovia persuaded the chemical company Du Pont to investigate the possibility of producing a nylon guitar string. Augustine took charge of the project, and in 1947 the first nylon guitar strings were made. Another big step forward, instigated by Andrés Segovia, had been made for the classical guitar.

During the 1950s and 1960s, Segovia continued a highly successful career as a concert and recording artist. Averaging one hundred concerts a year during this period of his career, he also recorded thirty albums for the Decca label. It was during this time that he began his annual masterclasses in Siena, Italy, and Santiago de Compostela, Spain. Many of the guitarists who attended them are among the leading players today.

Up to the time of his death, Segovia still held occasional masterclasses, in countries as far apart as the USA and Japan. The teaching movement instigated by him has ensured more guitar virtuosos than ever before. Segovia also encouraged colleges and conservatories of music in the major cities of the world to include the guitar in their curriculum, and today there are few colleges that do not have a professor of guitar.

Early in his career, Andrés Segovia set himself several goals, all of them designed to raise the level of the classical guitar. The seeds which had been sown by Franciso Tárrega and Miguel Llobet were cultivated and brought to full bloom by the superhuman efforts of Andrés Segovia. There is little doubt that he achieved all his goals, and more. The classical guitar now enjoys worldwide acceptance and popularity in all musical circles.

SELECTED MUSIC

Five Short Works for the Guitar-Impromptu, Tonadilla, 3 Preludes.	Kalmus
From 'Follies of My Youth': Five Anecdotes	Belwin Mills
Lessons Nos.11 and 12	Belwin Mills
Macarena	Belwin Mills
Neblina (a Olga)	Belwin Mills
Prelude on Chords.	Celesta

SELECTED LP RECORDINGS

The Art of Segovia 1927-1939 (2 LPs).	EMI RLS 745 LP
Andrés Segovia 1949.	EMI HLM 134 LP
Concerto.	MCA S-26044 LP
International Classics.	MCA MACS 2359 LP
Andrés Segovia Plays.	MCA MACS 1354 LP
Recuerdos de la Alhambra: Tárrega and Sor.	MCA S26091 LP
Interprete les Italiens.	MCA MACS 6123 LP
Segovia and the Guitar.	MCF 3073 LP
Golden Jubilee Set (3 LPs).	Decca DXT 148 LP
Maestro.	Brunswick SXA 4535 LP
Boccherini/Cassado and Bach Suite.	MCA MACS 125 LP
Five Pieces from 'Platero and I'.	MCA MACS 1967 LP
Granada.	MCA MACS 1968 LP
Sonata Romantica.	MCA S-26087 LP
Tansman & Mompou.	Brunswick AXA 4532 LP
On Stage.	Brunswick SXA 4550 LP
Mexicana.	MCA MACS 100 LP
España.	MCA S-26-037 LP
Castles of Spain.	MCA MACS 3045 LP
The Unique Art of Andrés Segovia.	Decca DL 71067 LP
The Guitar and I: Volume One.	MCA MACS 3965 LP
The Guitar and I: Volume Two.	MCA MACS 6281 LP
Nocturno.	Intercord INT 160 815 LP
The Intimate Guitar: Volume One.	RCA ARL 1-0864 LP
The Intimate Guitar: Volume Two.	RCA ARL 1-1323 LP
Reveries.	RCA RL 12602 LP

SELECTED CD RECORDINGS

Centenary Celebration (4 CD set).	MCA 11124
Complete 1949 Recordings.	Testament SBT 1043
EMI Recordings (1927-39) Vol.1.	CAPITOL 61048
EMI Recordings (1927-39) Vol.2.	CAPITOL 61049
Segovia Collection Vol.1. Bach.	MCA 42068
Segovia Collection Vol.2. Rodrigo/Ponce/Torroba.	MCA 42067
Segovia Collection Vol.3. My Favourite Works.	MCA 42069
Segovia Collection Vol.4. Baroque Guitar.	MCA 42070
Segovia Collection Vol.5. Five Centuries Spanish Guitar.	MCA 42071
Segovia Collection Vol.6. Ponce Sonatas.	MCA 42072
Segovia Collection Vol.7. Guitar Etudes.	MCA 42073
Segovia Collection Vol.8. Castelnuovo-Tedesco.	MCA 10056
Segovia Collection Vol.9. Romantic Guitar.	MCA 10281

SELECTED VIDEO RECORDINGS

Segovia at Los Olivos 1967.	Video Argos
Andrés Segovia.	Kultur 1103
The Segovia Legacy.	Kultur 1290

SELECTED READING

Andrés Segovia.	Guitar, December 1972
Andrés Segovia.	Guitar, December 1974
Andrés Segovia.	Guitar, October 1976
Andrés Segovia.	Guitar, June 1977
Andrés Segovia.	Guitar, December 1977
Andrés Segovia.	Guitar Player, June 1971
Andrés Segovia.	Guitar Player, October 1971
Andrés Segovia.	Guitar Player, February 1972
Andrés Segovia.	Guitar Player, April 1974
Andrés Segovia.	Guitar Player, June 1978
Andrés Segovia.	Frets, December 1981
Andrés Segovia.	Guitarra, January 1979
Andrés Segovia.	Guitarra, September 1980
The Sound of Segovia.	Guitar Review No.42, 1977
A Conversation with Segovia.	Guitar Review No.43, 1978
Andrés Segovia: Bernard Gavoty.	Kister, 1955
Andrés Segovia: ed. Clinton.	Musical New Services, 1978
Segovia: An Autobiography 1893-1920.	Macmillan, 1976
Andrés Segovia: Contributions to the World of Guitar: Ronald C. Purcell.	Belwin Mills, 1975
The Segovia Technique: Vladimir Bobri.	Macmillan, 1972
The Guitar and Myself: Series of articles,	Guitar Review Nos.4, 6, 7, 8, 10, 13.
Andrés Segovia: M. Vaisbord.	Musika, Moscow, 1981
Interview.	Classical Guitar, Jan/Feb 1983
Reminiscences: Alice Artzt.	Classical Guitar, Jan/Feb 1983
Special Issue.	Guitar International, April 1986
Segovia: A Celebration of the Man and his Music – Graham Wade.	Allison & Burby, 1983
Maestro Segovia – Graham Wade.	Robson Books 1988
Segovia's Strings of Destiny: Julian Bream.	The Guardian, reprinted in Classical Guitar, August 1987
The Father of Them All: Vollers.	Classical Guitar, August 1987
Segovia and Falla: Graham Wade.	Classical Guitar, April 1988
Andrés Segovia and Guitar Art in the 20th Century: M. Vaisbord.	Soviet Composer, Moscow 1989
The Segovia-Ponce Letters.	Editions Orphée, 1989
Tras la Huella de Andrés Segovia – Pérez-Bustamente de Monasterio.	University of Cádiz, Spain 1990
Article.	Guitar Review, Spring 1992
Centennial Tribute Issue.	Classical Guitar, February 1993
Centennial Tribute Issue.	Guitar Review, Spring 1993
A New Look at Segovia, His Life, His Music.	Wade/Garno Mel Bay Publications, 1996

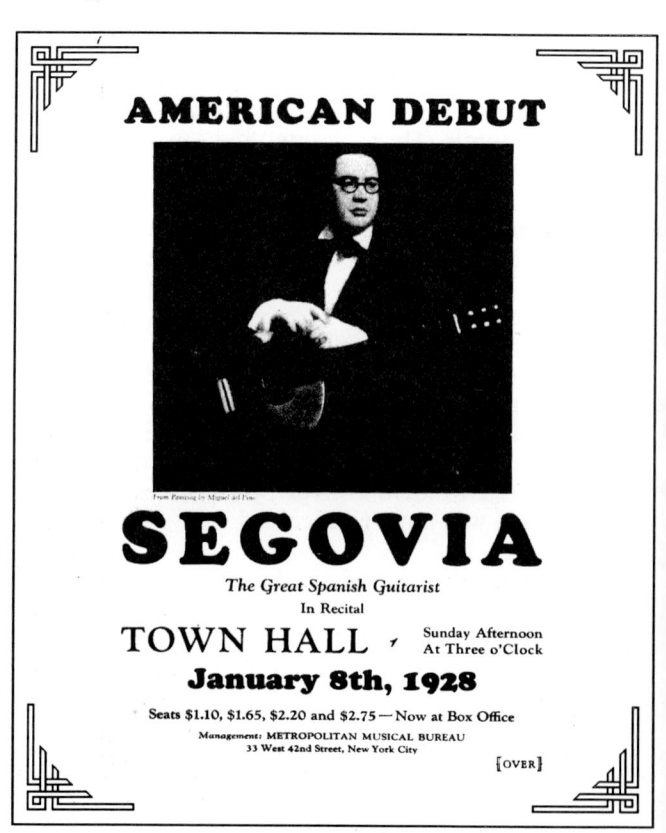

EMANUELE SEGRE
Born -
Locarno, Italy
2 November 1965

Emanuele Segre

Emanuele Segre studied under Ruggero Chiesa at the Milan Conservatory. He gained his diploma there with the distinction of 'summa cum laude'. Segre, who has also studied violin and composition, attended masterclasses given by John Williams and Julian Bream.

Segre went on to win several international guitar competitions, including the East and West Artists Prize in New York in 1987. He made his USA debut at the Carnegie Recital Hall in 1987. In 1989 he was selected for the UNESCO 'International Rostrum of Young Performers'.

Regarded as one of Italy's finest classical guitarists, Emanuele Segre has played with the English Chamber Orchestra conducted by Salvatore Accardo, and with Yuri Bashmet and the Moscow Soloists. The prominent French composer Jean Françaix dedicated his guitar concerto to Segre.

SELECTED RECORDINGS
Baroque Concertos	Pickwick CD 979
Baroque Concertos	Pickwick CD 993
Jean Françaix Guitar Concerto	Wergo CD 6198-2
Giuliani/Rossini/Paganini	Claves CD 50-9303
Guitar Concertos Rodrigo/Villa-Lobos/Castelnuovo-Tedesco	Claves CD 50-9516

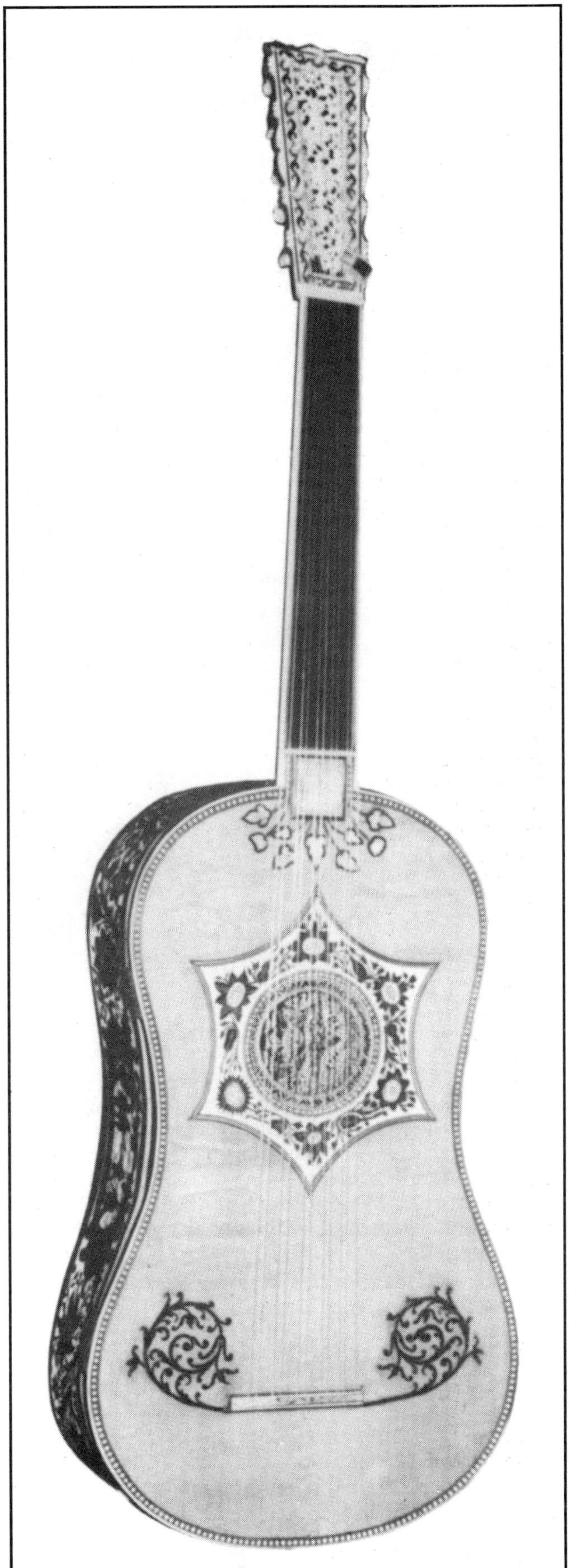

Joachim Tielke guitar, Hamburg 1693

PETER SENSIER

Born – Ealing, London, England
20 January 1918
Died – Gateshead, England, 24 September 1977

Peter Sensier

Peter Sensier was one of the most important guitar personalities in Britain for many years. Although his playing was generally restricted to a popular South American vocal duo 'Dorita y Pepe' for most of his career, Sensier was an authority on the classical guitar repertoire. He made many transcriptions of early lute music and classical melodies for the guitar, and he was also the original presenter of the BBC Radio 3 programme 'The Classical Guitar'. He was also a fine constructor of guitars and vihuelas. His journalism embraced regular contributions to B.M.G. magazine for many years, and a wide range of articles for various other periodicals and reference books.

Peter Sensier's first music studies were on the piano at the age of eight. After leaving school he took up the plectrum guitar, and by the age of nineteen was playing professionally in dance bands. During World War II he served with the Royal Signals. He continued to play the guitar in an army dance band, and also studied the oboe and clarinet.

In 1945 Peter Sensier returned to a career as a professional guitarist, playing in several London night-clubs. In 1948 he began to take an interest in the classical guitar, and studied it with Geoffrey Sisley, Desmond Dupré and Angel Iglesias. In 1952 his wide knowledge resulted in an invitation to give a series of lecture-recitals in Middlesex County Schools.

In Dorothy Holcombe, whom he met in 1956, Sensier found a mutual interest in South American music and the guitar, and over the next five years the couple collected and built up an extensive repertoire of South American vocal and instrumental music. As 'Dorita y Pepe', they made their recital debut at the Wigmore Hall in 1961. It was a great success. In the same year they visited Mexico, where they were awarded a diploma, a silver plaque and a gold statuette, the much coveted 'El Pipila', for their work in spreading and popularizing Latin American folk music. About this time they became much in demand for radio and televison programmes, in mainland Europe as well as Britain (where they had a 39-week series on Southern TV).

In 1964 Dorita y Pepe went to Argentina and Paraguay. They were invited back to Argentina in 1965 for the Fifth National Festival of Argentine Folklore in Cosquín, where they appeared beside the great folk artists of Argentina on equal terms and with great success. During that visit they also appeared in the National Festival of Poetry and Folk Music at Carlos Paz, and in the first Festival of Latin American Folk Music at Salta, where they were a part of the delegation of professional Argentine folk artists.

Despite the burden of failing health, Peter Sensier continued to write about the guitar in various journals, construct many fine fretted instruments, and also broadcast for the BBC on guitar matters, until his death in 1977 at the age of fifty-nine.

SELECTED RECORDINGS
Latin American Folk: Dorita y Pepe.	Pye NSPL 18215 LP
Si! Dorita y Pepe.	Argo ZFB 24 LP
Dorita y Pepe in Buenos Aires.	Parlophone PCS 7007 LP
Dorita y Pepe.	Hallmark HM 546 LP
Dorita y Pepe.	Society SOC 954 LP

ERNEST SHAND

Born – ERNEST WATSON

Hull, England, 31 January 1868

Died – Birmingham, England, 30 November 1924

Ernest Shand

Ernest Shand was best known to the British public as an actor and comedian, but he was also one of the best guitarists in Britain at the end of the nineteenth century.

Shand studied the violin for five years, then began to teach himself the guitar. He later studied with Madame Sidney Pratten, and with her guidance made great progress on the instrument. Before he was thirty years old, he had written one hundred and fifty compositions for the guitar, many of which were published by Barnes & Mullins, Schott & Co., Weekes and Co., and Essex & Cammeyer.

In 1896 Shand opened a guitar teaching studio in Bryanston Street, London, but he could not get enough pupils and it was not a success. Although he continued to play the guitar, he never used it in his theatre appearances. He would occasionally play the guitar at concerts, some of which took place at the London Conservatoire of Music.

Ernest Shand was one of Britain's most prolific composers for the guitar. At the time of his death he had composed nearly two hundred and fifty works for the guitar, the most important of which was his Premier Concerto pour Guitar, op.48. He performed this work for the first time at the Glasgow Arts Club in February 1896. He was also the author of a guitar method, published by Barnes & Mullins of London.

SELECTED READING
Ernest Shand.   Classical Guitar, May 1985

MARIA ISABEL SIEWERS

Born –

Buenos Aires, Argentina

22 October 1950

Maria Isabel Siewers

Maria Isabel Siewers studied music and the guitar at the Manuel de Falla Conservatory in Buenos Aires. Her teacher was Maria Luisa Anido. She graduated with honours in 1974. She earned grants from the Spanish and Italian governments, enabling her to study with Andrés Segovia and José Tomás in Santiago de Compostela, and with Oscar Ghiglia, Ruggiero Chiesa and Alan Meurnier at the Accademia Musicale Chigiana in Siena, from which she received a diploma with honours.

In 1974 Maria Isabel Siewers won several prizes in Argentinian music competitions, and also won second prize in the 16th International Classical Guitar Competition held in Paris by Radio France under the direction of Robert Vidal. In the same year she gave concerts throughout Europe, the USA and Latin America, and since that time has maintained a busy international concert schedule.

Maria Isabel Siewers has also played in many radio broadcasts, and has presented a series of radio programmes on the classical guitar in Argentina. A fine teacher, she has taught at the Manuel de Falla Conservatory in Buenos Aires and at the Morón Conservatory. She is currently professor of guitar at the Musikhochschule Mozarteum in Vienna, Austria.

SELECTED RECORDINGS
Music of Argentina.	Guitar Masters GMR 1003 LP
Amigos.	Aurophon AV340952 CD
Guastavino Guitar Music.	ASV CD DCA 933

SELECTED READING
Interview.	Classical Guitar, Jan/Feb 1984
Interview.	Classical Guitar, April 1986

SEPPO SIIRALA

Born –

Helsinki, Finland

29 February 1952

Seppo Siirala

Seppo Siirala's first musical instrument was the violin, which he began to play at the age of six. He began to play the classical guitar after a short time, playing both the electric and the folk instrument. In 1972 he won first prize at the Lanchester International Guitar Competition, England. He made his debut in London in 1975, and since that time has performed throughout Scandinavia, Europe, Australia and the USA. He has made several recordings which reflect his interest in ensemble music and his wide variety of musical styles.

Since 1977 Seppo Siirala has been teaching classical guitar at the Sibelius Academy in Helsinki, and since 1981 he has been chairman of the Helsinki Guitar Society. He is the author and co-author of a number of pedagogical and performance publications, and is regarded as one of Finland's finest players and foremost teachers. He appears frequently as both teacher and performer at international guitar events, including the Scandinavian Guitar Festival, the Danish festivals in Aalborg and Aarhus, Gdansk in Poland, the Esztergom Guitar Festival in Hungary and the GFA Festival in Lubbock, Texas, USA.

SELECTED RECORDINGS
Seppo Siirala and Ilari Lehtinen.	Love 140 LP
Rantalaitumella: Siirala & others.	Ponsi 12 LP
Zingara: Siirala & others.	Beta 4016 LP
Lorca, Granados etc. Siirala and Airas.	Beta 4018 LP
Guitar Souvenir: Finnish Music.	Chorus CH 8702 LP

RONOEL SIMÕES

Born –

São Paulo, Brazil

24 March 1919

Ronoel Simões

PHOTO: RICO STOVER

Ronoel Simões began to play the guitar in 1939. In 1941 he began to study the classical guitar seriously with Attilio Bernardina. He studied with this well-known guitarist for six years, after which he went on to perform, mainly in guitar duos and trios. He also began to teach, and in 1953 opened his guitar school, the Academia Brasileira de Violão.

Simões' passion for the guitar led him to become a collector of records, music books and guitar memorabilia. He is reputed to have one of the largest collections of such material in the world. For many years he had a weekly programme of guitar music, 'Solos de Violão', on Radio Gazeta in São Paulo. He also wrote a regular guitar column in the São Paulo newspaper, 'A Gazeta'. Over the years Simões' home became the centre of guitar activity in Brazil.

Ronoel Simões closed his Academy in 1984 and retired from teaching altogether, but continues to devote his energies to the guitar. No one has contributed more to the advancement of the guitar in Brazil in the last fifty years.

SELECTED READING
Ronoel Simões: A Profile.	Guitar Review, Summer 1988

PER SKARENG
Born -
Gaule, Sweden
28 June 1959

Per Skareng

Per Skareng played the trombone and the electric guitar in his youth. He was attracted to classical music after hearing some music by Bartók and Stravinsky. In 1979 Skareng studied with Per-Olof Hedlund and Rolf la Fleur at the Music Academy in Stockholm. He became the first guitarist to receive a Recital Diploma from the Academy in Stockholm. Skareng attended masterclasses given by Julian Bream and Alirio Díaz. In 1985, after gaining his soloist diploma, he made his concert debut as a soloist with the the Swedish Radio Symphony Orchestra under Jorma Panula. In recent years he has established himself as one of Scandinavia's foremost classical guitarists.

A winner of international guitar competitions in Paris, Berlin and Havana, Per Skareng made his London debut at the Wigmore Hall in 1993. Since that time he has given concerts in many countries including Cuba, Argentina, Switzerland and Estonia.

Per Skareng currently teaches at the Music College in Vaasa, Finland. He is also a guest lecturer at music colleges in Stockholm, Oslo and Copenhagen.

SELECTED RECORDINGS
El Colibri　　　　　　　　　　　Caprice CAP 21392 CD
Italian Music w/ Tobias Carron (flute)
　　　　　　　　　　　　　　　　Caprice CAP 21436 CD

NEIL SMITH
Born –
Horwich, Lancashire
6 January 1945

Neil Smith

Neil Smith began to play the plectrum guitar at the age of sixteen. He was self-taught on this instrument, and soon became a well-known dance band and session guitarist in the Lancashire area.

At the age of twenty-two, Neil Smith heard some records by Andrés Segovia, and decided that he wanted to make his career on the classical guitar. He took lessons with the guitarist Michael Strutt in Manchester, and lessons in theory and harmony with the pianist Robert Marsh. He went on to study in London with the composer/guitarist John W. Duarte, and later with professors at the Royal College of Music and the Guildhall School of Music. He gained a fellowship of the London College of Music at the end of his course. In 1975 he was the only English guitarist invited to study in Canada with the Venezuelan guitarist Alirio Díaz in a masterclass recorded by CBC.

Since 1975 Neil Smith has established himself as one of Britain's finest classical guitarists. He has made many broadcasts on BBC radio and television, and continues an active career as a recitalist and teacher throughout Great Britain and Europe.

SELECTED RECORDINGS
Classical Guitar.　　　　　　　Pennine Sound PS 186 LP
Neil Smith plays John W. Duarte.
　　　　　　　　　　　　　　　Guitar Masters GMR 1006 LP
Virtuoso – Neil Smith　　　　　　　　　LCR 1 (Cassette)
La Danza.　　　　　　　　　　　　　Apoyo APOY 001 CD

SELECTED READING
Interview.　　　　　　　　　Classical Guitar, January 1985
Various contributions.　　　　　Classical Guitar, from 1982

REGINALD SMITH BRINDLE

Born –

Preston, England

5 January 1917

Reginald Smith Brindle

Reginald Smith Brindle studied at the Bangor College of the University of Wales under D.E.Parry Williams and was awarded the Gynnedon Scholarship.

His first interest in the guitar began before World War II, when he played in jazz bands. His main instruments were the saxophone, the clarinet, the guitar, the organ and the double bass. He realised the full potential of the guitar when he heard some records by the Gypsy jazz guitarist Django Reinhardt. In 1939 he joined the army, and during his military service (until 1946) took the guitar with him everywhere to continue his music studies. He became aware of the classical guitar in early 1946 when he went to Florence and met Professor Giuseppe Gullino, who introduced him to the classical literature of the guitar. Smith Brindle was particularly impressed by the many records of Segovia he heard at this time.

A university fellowship had enabled Reginald Smith Brindle to continue his studies under Ildebrando Pizzetti at the Santa Cecilia Academy in Rome. Here he received a diploma for advanced composition, and also the Luigi Sturo Prize. He studied twelve-tone technique with Luigi Dallapiccola for a period of two years.

Reginald Smith Brindle lived for much his life in Italy, writing music for documentary films, conducting British music and writing as a music critic. He has composed over sixty original works for guitar, which have made him one of the most important composers for the classical guitar in the twentieth century.

SELECTED MUSIC

Danza Pagana	Schott
Do Not Go Gentle.	SZ 8021
El Polifemo de Oro.	Bruzz
Etruscan Preludes.	Schott
Four Poems of García Lorca.	Schott
Fuego Fatuo.	Schott
Guitarcosmos: Progressive Pieces for Guitar.	Schott
Memento in Two Movements.	Bèrben 1986
Nocturne.	Schott
November Memories.	SZ 8020
Sonata: El Verbo.	G21
Sonatina Fiorentina.	Schott
Ten Simple Preludes, ed. Duarte.	UIE 29162
Variants on Two Themes of J. S. Bach.	Peters 7131
Vita senese.	Schott

For two guitars:

Las Doces Cuerdas.	Schott
The Pillars of Karnak.	Schott

For four guitars:

Concerto de Angelis.	Schott

SELECTED RECORDINGS

El Polifemo de Oro: Julian Bream. RCA Victor RB 6723 LP
Trio Chitarristico Italiano. RCA RL 31277 LP
Sonata 'El Verbo': Forbes Henderson. Musical New Services G121 LP
Reverie: Minoru Inagaki. Super Nova SNLD-003 CD

SELECTED READING

Reginald Smith Brindle: Article. Guitar, June 1973
Reginald Smith Brindle: Article. Guitar & Lute, October 1980
Interview. Classical Guitar. January & February 1988
Autobiography. Classical Guitar January and February 1989

RAPHAËLLA SMITS

Born –

Mortsel, Antwerp, Belgium

1 February 1957

Raphaëlla Smits

Raphaëlla Smits was brought up in an artistic environment. She studied at both the Antwerp and Brussels Royal Conservatories of Music in Belgium. In 1978 she received the first prize in the Antwerp Conservatory annual awards, and in 1981 she received the Diploma Superior from the Brussels Conservatory. She studied with José Tomás at the Andrés Segovia classes in Spain, and in 1986 won first prize in the 10th Certamen Internacional de Guitarra Francisco Tárrega Competition.

Raphaëlla Smits began her professional performing career in 1975, since when she has given many concerts throughout Europe and the USA. She has established a fine reputation as a teacher, giving masterclasses at many important centres as well as her own summer course in Belgium. She is currently teaching guitar and chamber music at the Louvain Lemmens Institute in Belgium.

SELECTED RECORDINGS
Fernando Sor: Guitar Duets with David Russell.
                                                Poketino PL0008 LP
Napoléon Coste: Guitar Music.   DOR 1 LP
Romantic Guitar: Mertz & Giuliani.
                                        CD Accent ACC2 8863D
20th Century Guitar Music   CD Accent ACC2 8966D
Sor and Coste.   CD Accent ACC2 9182
Bach and Weiss.   CD Accent ACC2 93100

MARCO SOCIAS

Born -

Malaga, Spain

6 June 1966

Marco Socias

Marco Socias was born into a family of pianists. He studied guitar at the Conservatory of Music in Málaga with Carmen Gallardo and Antonio Company. He went on to study privately with José Tomás, David Russell, and José Miguel Moreno. He earned a grant from the autonomous Andalucian government, together with the Alexander von Humboldt Foundation in Bonn, to study with Hubert Käppel at the Musikhochschule in Cologne, Germany. Socias went on to win prizes in several international guitar competitions, including 1st prize in the 6th 'Infanta Christina' International Guitar Competition in Madrid, 1990.

At the age of 21 Marco Socias was awarded a professorship in the Conservatory of Málaga, the youngest person to hold such a position in Spain. As well as teaching he maintains a busy career as a concert recitalist in Europe. He has also broadcast on televison and radio stations in several European countries.

SELECTED RECORDINGS
Giuliani & Domeniconi Concertos   Gailly CD-87505
Pujol, Llobet & Mompou Sonatas
                                        Opera Tres CD 1015 OPE

MAREK SOKOLOWSKI

Born - Marek Konrad Sokolowski Pohrebyszcze, Ukraine 25 April 1818

Died - Rossa, Vilnius, Lithuania 25 December 1883

Marek Sokolowski

Marek Sokolowski was born of Polish/Jewish parentage in a small village situated near Zytomierz in the Ukraine. Recent research has confirmed that he was one of the great guitar virtuosos of the 19th century.

Sokolowski suffered ill health as a child. He began to play the guitar at the age of six, and developed a life-long passion for music. Although he also studied the violin, piano and cello, the guitar became his favourite instrument. Sokolowski made his professional debut on the 28 May 1841, when he performed Carulli`s Concerto in E minor. His perfomance was well received and he went on to play throughout the Ukraine, and then in Moscow. It is reputed that he attracted an audience of four thousand to one of his Moscow concerts.

Sokolowski experimented with various guitars, including a 17-stringed instrument, but finally settled on a 10-string guitar. He claimed this instrument was most suited to his guitar transcriptions of the music of Chopin, Schubert sond Mendelssohn. When Sokolowski met Giulio Regondi it is reported he tried to persuade the Italian virtuoso, without success, to play the 10-string guitar.

In the mid-19th century, even though solo guitar recitals were declining in popularity, Sokolowski continued to get excellent reviews for his concerts in Germany, France , Russia and England. It seems from contemporary reports that he was also a prolific composer for the guitar, but at this time only a few of Sokolowski's works are known.

SELECTED READING

| Article. | Soundboard, Summer 1992 |
| Article. | Classical Guitar, April 1994 |

Two Russian guitarists, Boris Perott (right) and V. Ivanoff in St Petersburg, 1905

GÖRAN SÖLLSCHER

Born –

Vaxjo, Sweden

31 December 1955

Göran Söllscher

Göran Söllscher grew up in Kalmar on the east coast of Sweden. He started to play the guitar at the age of seven, and studied at the Kalmar Municipal School of Music from 1965 to 1970. His studies continued under Professor Per-Olof Johnson, privately at first, and later at the Malmö Conservatory (from 1975 to 1977) and the Copenhagen Conservatory (from 1976 to 1979).

Göran Söllscher's recital debut took place in Kalmar in 1973, and he made his first appearance on Swedish television in 1975. In 1978 he won first prize at the Concours Internationale de Guitarre in Paris. This led to an important recording contract with Deutsche Grammophon. Since that time, he has established himself as one of the guitar's finest exponents. He has a wide repertoire, playing on both the regular six-string guitar and an eleven-string alto guitar. He has given numerous concerts throughout Scandinavia, Europe, North America, Eastern Europe and China.

SELECTED RECORDINGS

Bach & Sor.	Deutsche Grammophon DG 2531-195 LP
Bach Works for Lute Vol.1.	Deutsche Grammophon DG 413 719-1 CD
Bach Works for Lute Vol.2.	Deutsche Grammophon DG 413 719-2 CD
Cavatina.	Deutsche Grammophon DG 413 720-1 CD
Rodrigo: Concierto de Aranjuez; Fantasía para un Gentilhombre. Villa-Lobos Concertos.	Deutsche Grammophon 429-232 2 CD
Paganini for Two with Gil Shaham (violin).	Deutsche Grammophon 437 837 2 CD
Goran Sollscher.	Caprice CAP 21514 CD

SELECTED READING

Interview. Guitar International, April 1985

Fernando Sor

FERNANDO SOR

Born – JOSEPH FERNANDO MACARI SORS

Barcelona, Spain 14 February 1778

Died – Paris, France, 8 July 1839

Fernando Sor, one of the guitar's greatest composers and performers, received his first musical education in singing, harmony and counterpoint at a monastery, the Escolania at Montserrat. His tutor was Father Anselmo Viola. As a child, Sor had played his father's guitar, and in the monastery he studied the organ and the violin as well as singing.

After completing his studies at the age of sixteen, Sor left the monastery and returned to Barcelona. There he joined the military academy in which he was to spend the next four years. During this time he never lost his interest in music, and at the age of nineteen he presented his first opera in a Barcelona theatre. By that time he was already accepted as one of Spain's most brilliant young musicians. After hearing some guitar music by Moretti, he decided to make the guitar his main instrument.

On a visit to Madrid, Sor was commissioned by the Duke of Medina and the Duchess of Alba to write music. When the French invaded Spain, Sor wrote patriotic songs. He became a captain in the Cordoban Volunteers, but later, when virtually the whole of Spain was occupied and many thoughtful Spaniards had come to admire the ideals of the French Revolution, he made contact with French musicians in Madrid. It made his position impossible after the defeat of the French armies by Wellington, and when the French left Spain in 1813, Sor left too and made his home in Paris. Here, encouraged by Cherubini, Méhul and Berton, he resumed his musical career.

From 1815 to 1823 Fernando Sor lived in London, where his great talent on the guitar was recognized, and where he was highly successful as a guitarist, teacher and composer. His singing was also appreciated by London audiences, and while there he published more compositions for the voice than for any other instrument. His ballet Cendrillon was performed for the first time at the Kings Theatre in 1822. It was a great success, and in the following year it was performed in Paris, and later in Moscow.

From 1823 to 1826 Sor lived in Russia. Here, as in London, he enjoyed enormous popularity. In 1827-28 he was once again living in Paris, and there he decided to devote his life totally to the guitar. Other great nineteenth century guitarists were living in Paris at the same time, and Sor appeared often in concerts with Aguado and Coste.

Fernando Sor was to spend the remaining years of his life in Paris. It was during this period that he wrote his famous guitar method. It was originally published in France in 1830, and the first English translation was made by the organist and professional translator Arnold Merrick. This English edition was published in 1832 by Robert Cooke Co., London. It is one of the most remarkable guitar methods ever published, and is a lasting memorial to the genius of its author.

Fernando Sor composed over four hundred pieces for the guitar including studies, fantasies, themes with variations, and sonatas.

SELECTED MUSIC
Complete Works for Guitar, facsimile editions, ed. Jeffery.
Tecla Editions
Sor – Complete Studies for Guitar.　Chanterelle ECH 491

SELECTED RECORDINGS
Diego Blanco plays Sor.　BIS LP 133 LP
Alice Artzt plays Sor.　Meridian E 77006 LP
Turibio Santos plays Sor.　Erato STU 71268 LP
Segovia plays Sor and Tárrega.　MCA S 26091 LP
La Guitarre en Duo: Lemaigre/Lukowski.
Pavanne ADW 7016 LP
Rey de la Torre plays Sor.　SMC 517 LP
Fernando Sor: Complete Works for Guitar.
Kazuhito Yamashita.　RCA VDC-14 to VDC-29 CD
Adam Holtzman plays Sor.　Naxos 8-554430 CD
Eduardo Fernandez plays Sor.　Decca 425 821-2 CD
Tania Chagnot plays Sor.　Opera Tres CD1017
Sor – Complete Works for Two Guitars (2 CD set).
Ros/Ferrer Duo.　Opera Tres CDS 1008/9
Sor – Complete Studies for Guitar (3 CDs) – Alain Prevost.
De Plein Vent 9124/5/6
Tilman Hoppstock plays Sor.　Signum SIGX 14-00 CD

SELECTED READING
Fernando Sor: Composer and Guitarist. Brian Jeffery.
Tecla, 1977
Fernando Sor: Article.　Guitar Review No.26, 1962
Fernando Sor: Article.　Guitar Review No.39, 1974
The Significance of Fernando Sor: Stuart Button.
Article in 'The Guitar in England 1800-1924', Garland, 1989
Article.　Soundboard, Winter 1994

Fernando Sor's grave in Paris

ROBERT SPENCER

Born -
Ilford, Essex, UK
9 May 1932

Robert Spencer

PHOTO: COLIN COOPER

Robert Spencer began to play the guitar at the age of eighteen. Inspired by folk-singer Burl Ives, Spencer originally sang folk songs and accompanied himself on the guitar.

After a short career as a librarian, he began to study the lute in 1955 with Walter Gerwig at the Haslemere Festival, and with Julian Bream at the Dartington School of Music (1957-60). In 1961 he played for the Royal Shakespeare Company at Stratford-upon-Avon, and in the same year joined the Julian Bream Consort as a founder member. Spencer built up a solo career specialising in self-accompanied English song and lecture-recitals. He played theorbo continuo for, among others, Raymond Leppard`s Glyndebourne productions of operas (1961-71). Spencer accompanied many solo singers in recital, and on recordings, including Janet Baker, James Bowman, Alfred Deller and Michael Chance. He married actress -singer Jill Nott-Bower in 1960, and as a duo they gave over 3000 performances in Europe, Japan and North America. They specialised in programmes mixing songs, spoken word, lute and guitar. He has been a professor at the Royal Academy of Music in London since 1974. Specialising in Early English Song, he has also taught at other music colleges and many international summer schools.

Robert Spencer has made a unique contribution to the classical guitar in that, since 1958, he has built up an extensive library of original editions and manuscripts of guitar and lute music, from which many facsimile editions of 19th-century guitar and 17th-century lute music have been printed. These have helped rehabilitate into the current guitar repertory the music of Sor, Giuliani, Coste, Regondi, Zani de Ferranti, Merz, Sagreras, Ferrer, among others. Spencer has also written articles on guitar and lute music music for The New Grove Dictionary of Music 1980, Early Music and for other scholarly journals and books since 1958. A prominent performer, Robert Spencer has a fine collection of historic lutes and guitars, all in playing order.

SELECTED RECORDINGS
Elizabethan Serenade - Bream Consort   RCA 5687/88
English Ayres - London Camerata   Hyperion CD A 66003

SELECTED READING
Interview   Guitar International, March & April 1990

DAVID STAROBIN

Born – DAVID NATHAN STAROBIN

New York City, USA

27 September 1951

David Starobin

David N. Starobin began his guitar studies at the age of seven with Manuel Gayol in New York. From 1963 to 1967 he studied with Alberto Valdes Blain, going on to study with Aaron Shearer at the Peabody Institute in Baltimore, 1967-73.

It was during his student years at the Peabody Institute that Starobin first became involved with ensemble music. He was invited to make a recording with the Chamber Players of the Kennedy Centre in Washington D.C. Aaron Shearer, who had recommended Starobin to play the guitar with this group, soon put the young guitarist in charge of Peabody's Guitar Ensemble, 1971-73. Starobin's passion for and dedication to the advancement of the guitar in ensemble music has continued since that time.

David Starobin moved back to New York in 1974, where he joined the faculty at Brooklyn College in 1976 as Adjunct Assistant Professor. He also held associate positions at several other USA colleges, and gave masterclasses and seminars throughout the USA and Europe. In the fall of 1993 Starobin was named chairman of the guitar department at the Manhattan School of Music. Awarded the Andrés Segovia chair, Starobin continues in this post and is a vital force in the success of this prestigious college. He has also led an important career as a solo performer, both in the USA and in Europe. He has given première performances of over one hundred new works written and dedicated to him, including works by Elliott Carter, David Del Tredici, Poul Rouders and Charles Wuorinen.

David Starobin has also made an important contribution to Bridge Records, both as performer and as producer. He is also a music editor for numerous guitar publications for companies such as Boosey & Hawkes and G. Schirmer.

SELECTED RECORDINGS

New Music with Guitar Volume 1, 2 and 3.	Bridge BCD 9009
A Song from The East.	Bridge BCD 9004
New Music with Guitar Volume 4.	Bridge BCD 9022
Solo Guitar Works of Mauro Giuliani.	Bridge BCD 9029
Poul Rouders Psalmodies.	Bridge BCD 9037
Eliot Carter.	Bridge BCD 9044
The Great Regondi Vol.1.	Bridge BCD 9039
The Great Regondi Vol.2.	Bridge BCD 9055
Romantic Guitar.	GHA 126-022 CD

SELECTED READING

Interview.	Guitar International, March 1985
David Starobin.	Classical Guitar, November 1985
David Starobin.	Guitar Player, May 1986
David Starobin.	Guitar Review, Autumn 1986
David Starobin.	Guitar Review, Winter 1986
Interview.	Guitar International, June 1987
David Starobin.	Guitar Player, August 1987
David Starobin.	Gramophone, August 1987
Interview.	Classical Guitar, November 1989
Interview.	Guitar Review, Summer 1992
Interview.	Classical Guitar, December 1991
Interview.	Classical Guitar, October 1995
Interview.	Acoustic Guitar, June 1996
Article.	Guitar Review, Winter 1996

PAVEL STEIDL

Born -
Rakovnik, Czech Republic
24 June 1961

Pavel Steidl

PHOTO: HILDE VAATSTRA

Pavel Steidl first began to play the guitar at the age of eight. His first teacher was his brother. He then studied with Milan Zelenka and Arnost Sadlik at the Prague Conservatory. Steidl graduated from the conservatory in 1983 and went on to study with Stepan Rak for a further four years at the Academy of Musical Arts in Prague. He also attended masterclasses given by David Russell and Abel Carlevaro.

In 1982 Steidl won the Radio France Competition in Paris, and this success put him on the road to a busy career as an international concert recitalist and recording artist. He has also made many radio and television broadcasts.

Pavel Steidl now lives in Holland, where he leads an active career as a concert recitalist and teacher.

SELECTED RECORDINGS
Debut - Pavel Steidl Panton 8111 0578 LP
Losy/Weiss/Mertz Recital Panton 1227 - 2131 CD
Masters of Czech Classical Guitar Pehy 0001-2231 CD
Cantabile w/ Jan Opsitos (violin) Erasmus WVH 12

To Jane, With a Guitar

By

PERCY BYSSHE SHELLEY

The artist who this idol wrought,
To echo all harmonious thought,
Felled a tree, while on the steep
The woods were in their winter sleep
Rocked in that repose divine,
On the wind-swept Appennine;
And dreaming some of Autumn past
And some of Spring approaching fast,
And some of April buds and showers
And some of songs in July bowers
And all of love; and so this tree,—
O that such our death may be!
Died in sleep, and felt no pain,
To live in happier form again;
From which, 'neath Heavens fairest star,
The artist wrought this loved Guitar
And taught it justly to reply,
To all who question skilfully
In language gentle as its own
Whispering in enamoured tone
Sweet oracles of woods and dells
And summer winds in sylvan cells;
For it had learnt all harmonies
Of the plains and of the skies,
Of the forests and the mountains
And the many-voicèd fountains
The clearest echoes of the hills
The softest notes of falling rills
The melodies of birds and bees
The murmuring of summer seas
And pattering rain, and breathing dew
And airs of evening; and it knew
That seldom heard mysterious sound
Which, driven in its diurnal round
As it floats through boundless day
Our world enkindles on its way
All this it knows, but will not tell
To those who cannot question well
The spirit that inhabits it—
It talks according to the wit
Of its companions; and no more
Is heard than has been felt before
By those who tempt it to betray
These secrets of an elder day
But sweetly as it answers will
Flatter hands of perfect skill,
It keeps its highest, holiest tone
For our beloved friend alone —.

ERIK STENSTADVOLD

Born –

Oslo, Norway

10 March 1948

Erik Stenstadvold

Erik Stenstadvold began playing the guitar at the age of eleven. He studied first with a local teacher and then with Per-Olof Johnson. From 1970 to 1973 he studied at the Royal College of Music in London, where his teachers were John Williams (guitar) and Diana Poulton (lute). From 1975 to 1976 he continued his lute studies at the Schola Cantorun Baseliensis in Basle, Switzerland, with Eugen Dombois, and also medieval music under Thomas Binkley.

In 1973 Erik Stenstadvold was appointed professor of guitar at the Norwegian State Academy of Music in Oslo. He has been active as a concert performer, both as a soloist and in chamber groups, on both guitar and lute. He has performed with several of the major Norwegian orchestras and appears frequently on Norwegian radio and television. His scholarship is also impressive, and has resulted in many well-researched articles.

SELECTED RECORDINGS
Visions: Duo with Lars Klevstrand.   Fugitive ALP 11001 LP
Norwegian Guitar Music.   Veps CD 1012 LP

SELECTED READING
Coste's Contribution to Sor's 20 Studies.
                              Soundboard Vol. XI, No. 2, 1984
Giuliani's Sixth Finger.   Guitar International, August 1985
The Bother over Broken Chords. Classical Guitar, May 1987
The Guitar Methods of Dionisio Aguado.
                            Classical Guitar, March & April 1990

ICHIRO SUZUKI

Born –

Kobe, Japan

9 May 1948

Ichiro Suzuki

Ichiro Suzuki began to play the guitar at an early age. He gave his first public recital in Kobe, Japan, in March 1965 at the age of sixteen. He showed great talent, and won second prize in both the 11th and 12th Tokyo International Guitar Competitions, held in 1968 and 1969.

Since 1970 Ichiro Suzuki has lived in Europe, where he studied guitar with Andrés Segovia, José Tomás, Oscar Ghiglia and Leo Brouwer. At present he is music director of the Palamós International Music Festival. He lives in Paris, and gives fifty to sixty concerts annually in many countries, including Czechoslovakia, Hungary, Poland, Yugoslavia, the USSR, Japan, Australia, Africa, North and South America, Asia and the Caribbean countries. As a soloist he has performed with the Paris Concerts Colonne Orchestra, the Lyon Symphony Orchestra, the Orchestra Solistas de Cataluña, and the Tokyo Philharmonic Orchestra, amongst others. He has also accompanied the soprano Victoria de los Angeles in many of her concerts of Spanish songs.

SELECTED RECORDINGS
Suzuki plays Britten's Nocturnal.   CMT 1045 LP
Concertos by Hirayoshi & Tedesco. Camerata CMT 4015 LP
From Yesterday to Penny Lane   Codep-Auvidis A4846 LP

SELECTED READING
Interview.   Classical Guitar, May 1988

LASZLO SZENDREY-KARPER

Born –
Budapest, Hungary 28 January 1932
Died – 12 February 1991, Budapest

SELECTED RECORDINGS
Guitar Recital.	Qualiton LPX 1161 LP
Guitar Recital.	Hungaroton LPX 1162 LP
Vivaldi Guitar Concertos	Hungaroton SLPX 11970 LP
Geminiani: Six Sonatas.	Hungaroton SLPX 12013 LP
Guitar Music of Mertz.	Hungaroton SLPD 12894 LP
Boccherini Guitar Quintets.	Hungaroton HRC 055 CD

SELECTED READING
Interview.   Classical Guitar, July 1986

László Szendrey-Karper

László Szendrey-Karper began to play the guitar at the age of seven. He studied the guitar with E. Kaparti and Barna Kovats, and music with Janos Hammerslag, Aladar Racz, Ede Zathureczy and Rezso Sugár. His first public appearance as a soloist took place in 1948 in a Hungarian radio broadcast.

Szendrey-Karper was awarded first prize at the Warsaw World Youth Festival in 1955. He was also well placed in the Radio France Competition in Paris in both 1961 and 1962. In Hungary in 1962 he was awarded the Second Degree of the Liszt Prize, and in 1973 the First Degree of the same prize.

From 1957 Szendrey-Karper performed widely and made several recordings. He began teaching the guitar in 1962 at the Liszt Academy of Music in Budapest. In 1972 he wrote a method for teaching classical guitar, now the basis of the curriculum for the guitar department at the Academy of Music. László Szendrey-Karper was also an important figure in the organisation of the Esztergom International Guitar Festival, which he directed from its inception in 1972 to 1990.

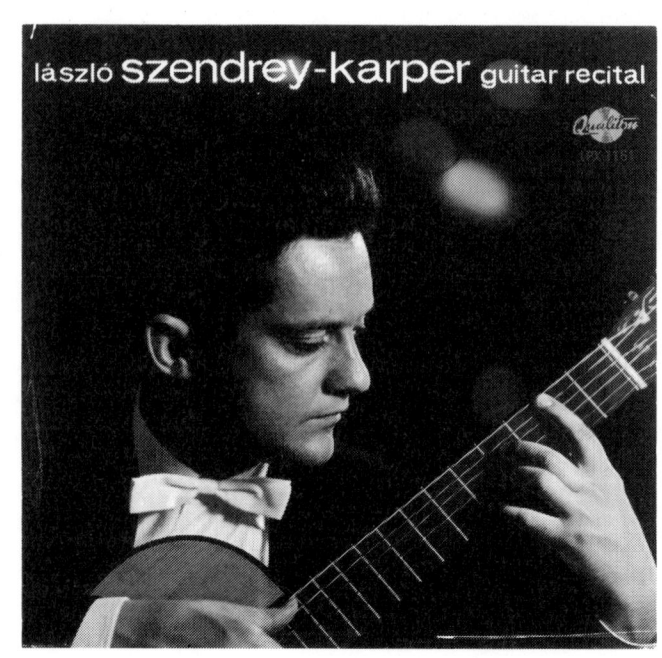

DAVID TANENBAUM

Born –

New York City

10 September 1956

David Tanenbaum

David Tanenbaum is the son of two classical musicians. He studied both the piano and the cello when very young but gave them up in favour of the electric guitar at the age of ten. A year later, after hearing Segovia play, he began classical guitar studies with Rolando Valdes-Blain in New York. He made his solo debut at the age of sixteen, and began touring the USA as a guest soloist with the Joffrey Ballet. He then studied with Aaron Shearer at the Peabody Conservatory.

After completing his studies, Tanenbaum won the first prize at the 1977 Carmel Classical Guitar Competition, and second prize at the 1978 Toronto International Competition. Since then he has appeared on concert platforms throughout the USA, Canada and Europe. He has been heard with the London Sinfonietta, the Kronos Quartet and the Steve Reich Ensemble, and has been a soloist at many festivals, including those in Bath, Lucerne, Frankfurt and the 2nd American Classical Guitar Congress, of which he was the President. He has had important new works written for him, including a guitar concerto by Hans Werner Henze entitled An Eine Aeolsharfe. David Tanenbaum has also recorded the complete Royal Winter Music by Henze on the Audiofon label. His transcriptions of Scarlatti sonatas and a Mozart Divertimento have been published by Guitar Solo Publications.

David Tanenbaum is a recipient of grants from the Martha Baird Rockefeller Fund and the NEA, and has given masterclasses at many leading universities. Since 1987 he has been chairman of the guitar department at San Francisco Conservatory of Music, and is also an artist-in-residence of Manhattan School of Music.

Tanenbaum is a frequent contributor to Guitar Review magazine, and has produced several study books for GSP of San Francisco. In 1995 he received the Outstanding Professional Award at the San Francisco Conservatory of Music.

SELECTED MUSIC
The Essential Studies: Carcassi, Sor, Brouwer. 3 Vols. GSP

SELECTED RECORDINGS
Royal Winter Music: Henze.	Audiofon CD 72029
Lute Masterworks.	Innova Digital Archive IDA 1001-1
Estudios: The Essential Recording.	Guitar Solo GSP 1000C (cassettes), GSP 1000CD
Acoustic Counterpoint.	New Albion Records NA 032 CD
Perilous Chapel: Lou Harrison.	New Albion NA 055 CD
El Porteno: Piazzolla.	New Albion NA 065 CD
Great American Guitar Solo.	Neuma 450-84 CD

SELECTED READING
Interview.	Guitar International, July 1987
Interview.	Classical Guitar, October & November 1987
Article.	Guitar Player, September 1986
Article.	Guitar Player, September 1987
Interview.	Acoustic Guitar, March/April 1993
Interview.	Guitar Player, December 1993
Interview.	Guitar Review, Fall 1995

RENATA TARRAGO

Born –

Barcelona, Spain

1927

Renata Tarragó

Renata Tarragó was first taught the guitar by her father, Graciano Tarragó, a well-known professor of guitar in Barcelona. She gave her first public recital at the age of fourteen. At sixteen she won a silver medal in the Premio del Conservatorio del Liceo. She was soon regarded as one of Spain's most leading guitar recitalists. In 1944 she finished her studies at the Conservatory of Music in Barcelona, and was appointed Assistant Professor of Guitar to her father at the same conservatory.

In 1948 Renata Tarragó appeared in London to take part in the BBC's presentation of Manuel de Falla's La Vida Breve. She also appeared in London in a recital of popular Spanish songs in collaboration with her father and the soprano Victoria de los Angeles. In 1951 she won the Premio Extraordinario award for unusual achievement created by the Conservatorio del Liceo of Barcelona. Following this, she embarked on a highly successful concert tour of Europe. In 1960 she made her first tour of the United States, her performances there receiving high critical acclaim. She officially represented Spain in the International Guitar Congress in Tokyo in 1962, receiving the award of a gold medal for her performances. In 1963 she returned to Japan for a highly successful concert tour. During the next three years she continued to give guitar recitals in most countries of the world.

In 1968 Renata Tarragó was featured with the London Philharmonic Orchestra on the soundtrack of the British film thriller Deadfall. In recent years she has spent most of her time teaching in the Barcelona area.

SELECTED RECORDINGS

La Guitarra de Renata Tarragó.   Philips (Spain) 843 138PY LP
Romance for Guitar and Orchestra (J. Barry).
　　　　　　　　　　　　　　　　　Stateside SL 10263 LP
Torroba: Concerto de Castille.   Erato EFM 8080 GU LP
Rodrigo Concerto: MorenoTorroba Suite.
　　　　　　　　　　　　　　　　　Columbia ML 5345 LP
Music of Francisco Tárrega.   Columbia ML 5454 LP
Renata Tarragó.   Columbia ML 5722 LP

A selection of B. M. G. magazine, a guitar magazine of the past

Francisco Tarrega

FRANCISCO TARREGA

Born – FRANCISCO DE ASSIS TARREGA EIXEA
Villareal de los Infantes, Castellón, Spain
21 November 1852
Died – Barcelona, Spain, 5 December 1909

Francisco Tarrega

Francisco Tárrega's first teacher was a local player, Manuel González. The young guitarist's talent was first recognized when he played in public, in Villareal, a guitar concerto by Julián Arcas. In October 1874 Tárrega entered the Madrid Conservatory of Music as a student of harmony and composition. In 1875 he was awarded the first prize in these subjects. It has been recorded that at one of his early recitals he played half of the programme on the piano and the other half on the guitar, asking the audience to choose which they preferred. They chose the guitar, so Tárrega decided to dedicate his life to that instrument.

Francisco Tárrega then began a highly successful career as a recitalist and teacher. He toured throughout Europe, and audiences in most of the continent's major cities were able to hear his virtuoso guitar playing. He became Professor of Guitar at the Conservatories of Madrid and Barcelona. Among his many pupils were Emilio Pujol, Miguel Llobet, Daniel Fortea and Alberto Obregón.

Tárrega's vast knowledge of music enabled him to do two major things for the guitar. He improved sitting posture and the position of legs, arms and hands; he advocated the use of a footstool, and generally prepared the body to meet the demands imposed by not only the larger Torres guitar that he used but also the greatly expanded repertoire, to the creation of which he had devoted a large part of his energies. Particular attention was paid to improving the action of the fingers of each hand; and there seems little doubt that he drew on his expert knowledge of piano playing techniques, adapting their principles to the guitar.

Francisco Tárrega's other great contribution to the classical guitar was the improvement of the repertoire. Almost all other professional guitarists at that time played nothing but their own compositions. Napoléon Coste, one of Sor's pupils, made a few arrangements for the guitar of music written for other instruments, whereas guitarists of an earlier age, notably Giuliani and Carulli, had made many transcriptions. Tárrega continued and extended that tradition, transcribing works by Schumann, Chopin, Beethoven, Bach and other composers, including contemporary ones. He was especially successful with piano solos by Granados and Albéniz. It is said that Albéniz, on hearing Tárrega play one of his piano pieces on the guitar, declared that he preferred the guitar version to the original.

Francisco Tárrega has often been called the founder of the modern guitar school, a title well earned, although he did advocate the right-hand 'no nail' technique, a technique which today is not employed by most of the world's foremost guitarists. A man of great modesty and humbleness, Francisco Tárrega maintained his intense devotion to the guitar and music throughout his life. He died of apoplexy in 1909 at the age of 55.

Without doubt Francisco Tárrega was one of the greatest classical guitarists of all time. It was due to his commitment and energy through the latter half of the nineteenth century that the way was opened for the great guitarists of the twentieth century, in particular Andrés Segovia, to demonstrate to the world the enormous musical potential of the classical guitar.

SELECTED MUSIC

Capricho Arabe.	Bèrben
The Carnival of Venice.	EMB
Complete Preludes.	Universal 13408
Danza Mora.	Ricordi (BA) 9900
Gavotta, Pavana, Mazurka	Bèrben
Gran Jota Aragonese.	Ricordi (BA) 7924
Gran Vals.	Ricordi (BA) 7321
La Alborada (Music Box).	Ricordi (BA) 7923
Maria.	Ricordi (BA) 9068
Marieta.	Ricordi (BA) 12075
Danza Mora & Capricho Arabe	GA Schott 451
Danza Odalisca.	Ricordi (BA) 12074
Eighteen Original Studies.	Ricordi (BA) 11365
Pavane, ed. Savio.	Ricordi (BA) 3215
Recuerdos de la Alhambra.	Ricordi 2001
Rosita: Polka.	Ricordi (BA) 12076
Sueño!	Ricordi (BA) 11393
Thirty Original Preludes.	Ricordi (BA) 12720

SELECTED RECORDINGS
Alice Artzt plays Tárrega.   Meridian E77026 LP
Segovia plays Tárrega.   MCA S 26091 LP
Leif Christensen plays Tárrega.   Paula PACD 59
Tarrega: Integral de Guitarra: David Russell.
                                      Opera Tres CDS 100314

SELECTED READING
Tárrega: Ensayo Biographico.
                Emilio Pujol: Ramos and Alfonso, 1960
Is There a School of Tárrega?
                                  Guitar Review No.1, 1946
Complete list of works.   Guitar and Lute No.5, 1977

A sketch of Francisco Tarrega drawn by Miguel Llobet

Tarrega playing to an audience of his disciples

SCOTT TENNANT

Born -
Detroit, Michigan, USA
2 March 1962

Scott Tennant

Scott Tennant began to play the guitar at the age of six. He moved to Los Angeles in 1980 to study at the University of Southern California. He studied there with Pepe Romero and James Smith. Whilst a student he received numerous awards, and was selected to perform in masterclasses of Andrés Segovia and Joaquín Rodrigo.

Tennant is a founding member of the Los Angeles Guitar Quartet, but still maintains a busy solo career. He won first prize in the 1989 Tokyo International Guitar Competition. He also won second prize in the 1984 Toronto International Competition, and a silver medal in the 1988 Concours International de Guitare of Radio France.

Scott Tennant is a respected teacher. He was a faculty member of the San Francisco Conservatory of Music from 1989 -93, and currently is on the faculty of the University of Southern California.

SELECTED RECORDINGS
Guitar Recital	GHA CD 126.011
Complete Guitar Works of Rodrigo	GHA CD 126.026
El Amor Brujo LA Guitar Quartet	GHA CD 126.001
Recital LA Guitar Quartet	GHA CD 126.016
Dances LA Guitar Quartet	Delos DE 3132 CD
Evening in Granada LA Guitar Quartet	Delos DE 3144 CD
Labyrinth LA Guitar Quartet	Delos DE 3163 CD

SELECTED MUSIC
Pumping Iron -Guitar Technique Method	Alfred/GSW

MILAN TESAR

Born -
Prague, Czech Republic
30 March 1938

Milan Tesar

Milan Tesar completed his music education at the Prague Conservatory in 1964. He became a teacher at the Prague Volskonservatorium. In 1967 he went to Italy to teach and give concerts. He returned to Prague in 1971, and taught at the Prague Conservatory 1974-77. Since 1973 Tesar has concentrated on composing, although he currently teaches at the Jaroslav Jezek Conservatory in Prague. His works have been published by Editions Lemoine in Paris, Gendai in Tokyo, Supraphon in Prague, and Daminus in Walsrode, Germany.

SELECTED RECORDINGS
The Ballad Stories w/ Milan Tesar	Supraphon CD
Suite Perestroika	Daminus DR 902 CD
Vladimir Mikulka	Supraphon 111418 CD
Milan Tesar - Czech Colours	Monitor CD 660355-2

SELECTED MUSIC
Milan Tesar - Guitar Solos ed. Mikulka	Gendai Guitar
Five Menuets	Gendai Guitar
Ten Pieces for Solo Guitar Vols 1 & 2	Lemoine
Czech Song for Two Guitars	Lemoine
Pastoral for Two Guitars	Lemoine
Divertimento for Four Guitars	Lemoine

JOSÉ TOMAS
Born – JOSÉ TOMAS PEREZ SELLÉS

Alicante, Spain

26 August, 1934

José Tomás

Encouraged by his father, José Tomás was originally self-taught on the guitar. His first serious musical education was with the Spanish pianist Oscar Esplá.

It was soon realized that Tomás was a talented player, and he went to Madrid to study with Regino Sainz de la Maza. In Madrid he met Alirio Díaz who, after hearing the young guitarist play, advised him to go and study at the Guitar School in Siena, Italy. José Tomás went to Siena in 1955, and it was there that he first met Andrés Segovia.

From 1956 to 1957 José Tomás was in the Spanish army. In 1958 he went for two years to Santiago de Compostela, where he worked with Emilio Pujol. He had kept contact with Andrés Segovia since their first meeting in Siena, and Segovia, having recognized Tomás's exceptional teaching ability, asked him to be his assistant at his masterclasses. Since that time Tomás has devoted most of his career to teaching, although he is a fine recitalist and has appeared in concerts throughout Europe, the Middle East, Japan and the United States of America.

Around 1974 José Tomás changed to an 8-string guitar built by José Ramírez. The 7th string is tuned D below E, and the 8th string is tuned F above low E.

José Tomás lives in his native town of Alicante, where he teaches at the Oscar Esplá Conservatory and directs the guitar programme there. For many years he spent his summers at Santiago de Compostela directing Segovia's masterclasses.

SELECTED READING

José Tomás.	Guitar Player, March 1981
Interview.	Nova Giulianiad, 9/10 1986
Interview.	Classical Guitar, March 1987
Profile.	Classical Guitar, August 1990
Interview.	Classical Guitar, March 1993

SELECTED RECORDING

José Tomás – Guitar Recital.	Crown (Japan) SW-2001

A classical guitar with a revolutionary design by guitarist Abel Carlevaro and constructed by Manuel Contreras since 1984.

REY DE LA TORRE

Born – JOSÉ REY DE LA TORRE

Gibara, Cuba, 9 December 1917

Died – San Jose, California, USA, 21 July 1994

SELECTED RECORDINGS

20th Century Music for Guitar.	Elektra EKL 244 LP
Plays Classical Guitar.	Epic LC 3418 LP
Virtuoso Guitar.	Epic LC 3479 LP
Romantic Guitar.	Epic LC 3564 LP
Music for One and Two Guitars.	Epic LC 3674 LP
Recital.	Epic LC 3815 LP
Spanish Music for the Classical Guitar.	Nonesuch 2590-001 LP

SELECTED READING

Rey de la Torre.	Guitar Player, October 1975
Appreciation.	Guitar Review, Fall 1994

Rey de la Torre

Rey de la Torre began studying music and the guitar as a child in Havana, Cuba. His first teacher was Severino Lopez. After five years of study he astounded audiences with his ability after he had given several public recitals and some radio broadcasts.

Such was his success that the young guitarist travelled to Spain to continue his studies with Miguel Llobet in Barcelona. In 1933 he appeared in concert with great success at the Granados Academy.

In 1939 Rey de la Torre moved to New York, and established himself there as a leading recitalist and teacher of the guitar. His Town Hall concert in 1941 was widely acclaimed. From that time he made the USA his home, although he appeared in concerts all over the world. He appeared on numerous occasions on radio and television, and performed Rodrigo's Concierto de Aranjuez with the Cleveland Symphony Orchestra. He had several pieces specially written for him by prominent contemporary composers including Julian Orbón, José Ardevol and Joaquín Nin-Culmell.

Towards the end of his life ill health (degenerative arthritis) compelled Rey de la Torre to give up performing, but he continued to teach for his last thirty years.

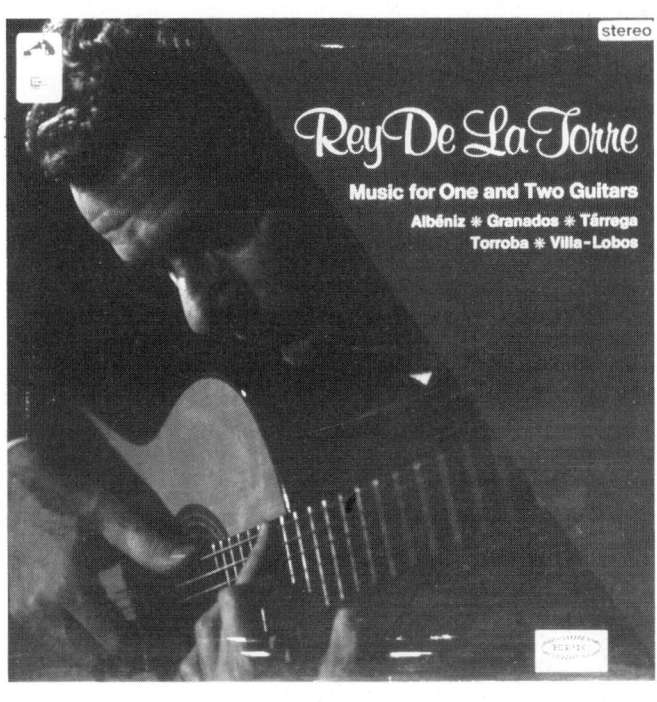

MICHAEL TRÖSTER

Born –
Schweinfurt, West Germany
26 October 1956

Michael Tröster

Michael Tröster first studied the guitar with Gerhard Vogt in his home town of Schweinfurt, in 1966. He showed great promise and went on to study with Siegfried Behrend, Konrad Ragossnig, Karl Scheit and others. In 1972 he was a prizewinner in a national competition, Jugend Musiziert. In 1973 he won the first prize in his category in the Bavarian Guitar Competition.

Tröster continued his competition successes, winning a prize in 1977 in the 22nd national selection of young artists, Podium Junger Solisten. In 1980 he won first prize in the Deutschen Musikwettbewerb (German Music Competition), and in 1981 first prize at the Wettbewerb der Deutschen Musikhochschulen (German Music Colleges Competition). In 1983 he won a national award for the encouragement of young artists; and in the following year he won first prize at the 19th Milan International Guitar Competition and first prize in the Villa-Lobos Competition held in Milan.

Since that time Michael Tröster has performed throughout Europe, Australasia and Japan, and made many recordings for several companies. From 1980 to 1986 he was a teacher at the College and Conservatory of Würzburg. Since 1986 he has been director of a class at the Kassel Academy of Music.

SELECTED RECORDINGS
Etuden meisterhaft gespielt: Die Gitarre.
　　　　　　　　　　　　　　Schwann VMS 712/13 LP
Repertoire für junge Gitarristen.　Calig CLG 30 902 LP
Mertz, Carulli, Chopin, Mozart, Sor.　EMI 567 747 5882 LP
Berlin Guitar Ensemble & Michael Tröster.
　　　　　　　　　　　　　　Electrola ASD 308 222 LP
Walton, Sor, Legnani and Giuliani.
　　　　　　　　　　　　　　Electrola ASD 308 223 LP
Berlin Guitar Ensemble & Michael Tröster.
　　　　　　　　　　　　　　Electrola ASD 741 LP
Michael Tröster plays Villa-Lobos.
　　　　　　　　　　　　　　Thorofon CTH 2052 CD
Music for Mandolin & Guitar
(with Gertrud Weyhofen): Vivaldi etc.
　　　　　　　　　　　　　　Thorofon CTH 2092CD
Michael Tröster plays Sonatas by Ponce, Berkeley, Rodrigo, Turina, Tedesco.　　Thorofon CTH 2171CD
Recuerdos de la Alhambra.　　JP Records 1002 CD
Salonaden.　　Harmonia Mundi HM872-2 CD
Concertos for Guitar.　　Thorofon CTH 2171 CD
Terremoto Con Variazioni.　　Thorofon CTH 2205 CD
Troster plays Llobet.　　Super Nova SNCD-0031

SELECTED READING
Interview.　　　　　　　　Gitarre & Laute, Winter 1988

JAMES TYLER

Born – JAMES HENRY TYLER
Hartford, Connecticut, USA
3 August 1940

James Tyler

James Tyler studied at the Hartt College of Music and the University of Connecticut. He took private tuition on the lute with Joseph Iadone. He made his concert debut at the Library of Congress, Washington D.C. in 1961, and played at the White House a year later. During this period he also performed as guest soloist with the New York Pro Musica, with whom he also recorded.

Tyler left the USA in 1967 for Germany to continue his research into the history of the lute and its music. In 1969 he came to London and soon established himself as one of the finest lutenists and early musicians around. He joined the Early Music Consort of London and Musica Reservata, and performed with them throughout the world.

For many years James Tyler has been a prominent member of The Julian Bream Consort. In 1976 he formed the London Early Music Group, an ensemble specializing in the performance of medieval and Renaissance music. Recognized internationally as an authority on early plucked instruments, Tyler has contributed articles to many learned journals, including Grove's Dictionary of Music & Musicians and Early Music magazine. His book The Early Guitar, published in 1980, is regarded as the definitive work on the instrument and its music.

SELECTED RECORDINGS
Music of the Renaissance Virtuosi.	Saga 5438 LP
The Early Guitar	Saga 5455 LP
English Social Music (with Barry Mason).	Saga 5467 LP
Italian Bel Canto Arias (with Barry Mason).	Hyperion A 66153 LP

SELECTED READING
The Early Guitar.	Oxford University Press, 1980
A Brief Tutor for Baroque Guitar.	Chorus, 1984

TERRY USHER

Born – TERENCE FLETCHER USHER

Manchester, England, 7 May 1909

Died – Manchester, 12 April 1969

Terry Usher started to play the guitar in 1932. In 1936 he began to teach and write about the guitar for the musical press. In the same year he broadcast for the first time, and was then frequently heard on the radio playing guitar solos and with various instrumental ensembles. In 1937 he heard Andrés Segovia play at a concert in Liverpool, and was so impressed that he began a serious study of the classical guitar soon afterwards. Usher soon came to be regarded as one of Britain's authorities on the instrument and its music.

In 1945 Terry Usher began teaching the classical guitar, and embarked on a series of lecture-recitals to music societies under the auspices of the Hallé Concerts Society and the Arts Council of Great Britain. On 24 March 1954 he was appointed Tutor for the Guitar to the Royal Manchester College of Music.

Terry Usher

COURTESY: JOHN W. DUARTE

Terry Usher wrote and arranged extensively for the guitar. His published compositions include Impromptu and Minuet, Canzoncina and Arabesque and Epitaph for Manuel Ponce. He was a member of the editorial board and editor of the academy section of Guitar Review, New York. He was also a regular contributor on the classical guitar to BMG magazine, and a founder member of the Manchester Guitar Circle.

Terry Usher continued his total involvement with the guitar until his death after a stroke in April 1969.

SELECTED MUSIC
Impromptu and Minuet.	Schott
Canzoncina and Arabesque.	Schott

SELECTED READING
The Spanish Guitar in the Nineteenth and Twentieth Centuries: Usher.
The Galpin Society Journal No.IX, June 1956

ALBERT VALDES BLAIN

Born –

Havana, Cuba

10 April 1921

Roland and Albert Valdes Blain

In 1924 Albert Valdes Blain's parents moved to the United States of America and settled in New York. Blain's enthusiasm for the classical guitar was aroused by the early concerts of Andrés Segovia in that city.

Blain studied with the Uruguayan concert guitarist Julio Martínez Oyanguren for three years. He also studied piano and composition at the Greenwich House Music School and the Juilliard School of Music, New York.

For many years Albert Valdes Blain was regarded as one of the foremost classical guitar recitalists in the United States. He made his debut in 1941 at the Carnegie Chamber Music Hall, and appeared in concerts throughout the North American continent for many years. He has also broadcast on both radio and television on most of the important American networks.

It is as a teacher that Albert Valdes Blain has been one of the most important figures in the American guitar scene in recent years. He has taught the classical guitar at the Greenwich House Music School, The School for Musical Education, and at the Brooklands Conservatory for Music. He also has his own studio in New York, and many of today's best-known American guitarists have studied with him.

SELECTED READING
Albert Valdes Blain.   Guitar Player, November 1979

ROLAND VALDES BLAIN

Born –

Havana, Cuba

1922

The younger brother of Albert Valdes Blain, Roland Valdes Blain originally studied with the Uruguayan guitarist Julio Martínez Oyanguren. He later went to Spain to give concerts and to work in advanced study with Regino Sainz de la Maza at the Royal Conservatory of Madrid, from which he graduated with the Grand Prize Award for concert guitar playing.

Since that time he has toured extensively throughout the main cities of the United States, Canada, South America and Spain. He has also appeared on the major radio and television networks in the United States, played and composed for various Broadway theatrical productions and appeared with several major symphony orchestras as guest soloist.

Roland Valdes Blain currently lives in New York, and maintains a busy career as a guitar recitalist and teacher.

SELECTED RECORDING
La Guitarra.   Roulette SR-25055 LP

BENJAMIN VERDERY

Born – BENJAMIN FRANCIS VERDERY

Danbury, Connecticut, USA

1 October 1955

Benjamin Verdery

Benjamin Verdery graduated in 1978 at The State University of New york at Purchase. He studied guitar with Frederic Hand and Phillip de Fremery.

Since his duo debut recital with his wife, the flautist Rie Schmidt, in New York in 1980, Benjamin Verdery has performed extensively throughout the USA, Canada and Europe. He has appeared at many major festivals, given masterclasses, and appeared on both radio and television. He has commissioned and performed several new works for guitar by Anthony Newman, Alvin Brehm, David Leisner, Frederic Hand, Roberto Sierra and Ernesto Cordero.

Verdery has appeared at the South Bank Festival in London with John Williams and Paco Peña. He has also performed or taught at other leading European festivals, including Paco Peña's International Guitar Festival in Córdoba, Spain.

A member of the roster of Affiliate Artists, Benjamin Verdery is also on the faculty at Yale University, the Artistic Director of the D'Addario Foundation for the Performing Arts and was for some years a regular columnist for Guitar Player magazine was for some years.

SELECTED RECORDINGS
Music by Anthony Newman.	Cambridge CRS B 2833
Bach Transcriptions for Guitar.	Guitarra GRICD 002 CD
French Music for Flute & Guitar.	Newport Classics NC 0010 (cassette & CD)
Bach: Two Generations.	Musical Heritage Society 7397A (cassette, CD, LP)
American Guitar Music.	Newport NPD 85509 CD
Some Towns and Cities.	Newport NPD 85519 CD

Essentials of Classical Guitar – Instructional Video.
Workshop Arts, USA

SELECTED READING
Interview.	Guitar International, December 1984
Article.	Classical Guitar, May/June 1984
Interview.	Guitar Player, August 1984
Interview.	Classical Guitar, March 1985
Interview.	Guitar Player, June 1985
Interview.	Acoustic Guitar, September/October 1992
Interview.	Classical Guitar, May 1994

SELECTED MUSIC
Some Towns and Cities.   Alfred Publishing Company
The Verdery Guitar Series (Vols.1 and 2).
Frederick Harris Music

ANDRE VERDIER

Born – Paris, France

1 November 1886

Died – Paris, 13 December 1957

André Verdier

André Verdier studied music from the age of six. He had a fine soprano voice as a child, and became a soloist in Paris churches. When his voice broke he studied the flute at the Paris Conservatoire. Later he studied the guitar under Rodriguez Aravena. Verdier met Miguel Llobet in Paris, and this great guitarist introduced him to the Tárrega method of playing.

At the age of eighteen André Verdier decided to enlist in the army to make his career as a military musician. He remained in this occupation until he was twenty-three, working at perfecting his flute playing and also studying harmony, but on returning to civilian life he could not make a living either as a flautist or a guitarist. He learnt to play the banjo, and within a relatively short time was known all over Paris for his virtuoso banjo playing in night clubs and cabarets.

Verdier's great contribution to the classical guitar in France was his foundation, in collaboration with Emilio Pujol, of 'Les Amis de la Guitare' in 1936. Verdier arranged regular meetings in his house in Ile St Louis, Notre Dame, Paris. One of the first important acts of the society was a pilgrimage to the tomb of Fernando Sor, which had been rediscovered by Verdier and the Danish guitarist W. Ostergoart in 1934. They arranged for a commemorative plaque to be placed on the tomb, and homage was thus paid to the great nineteenth century guitarist.

In 1939, during a recital of 'Les Amis de la Guitare', Verdier presented the child prodigy Ida Presti. The society made her an honorary member and greatly helped her in her career. It was in Verdier's house that Ida Presti met Alexandre Lagoya years later.

André Verdier was a teacher of music who specialised in teaching the guitar. He was also an enthusiastic collector of classical guitars and of guitar music and manuscripts. No single person did more to promote the classical guitar in France than André Verdier.

SELECTED READING
André Verdier.   Guitar Review, No.22, 1958

ROBERT J. VIDAL

Born –

Paris, France

6 May 1925

Robert Vidal is one of the most notable guitar personalities in the classical guitar world today. For almost forty years his promotions on behalf of the guitar have been prolific in number and generally excellent in quality. He has presented programmes on French radio and television devoted exclusively to the guitar. He has also produced an excellent series of classical guitar records for the RCA and Erato labels, featuring such famous guitarists as Turibio Santos, Oscar Cáceres, Leo Brouwer, Maria Luisa Anido, Betho Davezac and the Pomponio-Zarate Duo.

Robert Vidal

PHOTO: COLIN COOPER

Vidal's Concours International de Guitare, held in Paris and sponsored by ORTF, became one of the most important annual international classical guitar events. The first was held in 1958. The event went from strength to strength, and was an important stepping-stone in the career of many of today's leading classical guitarists. The series ended in October 1993.

Robert Vidal continues to travel widely, attending guitar festivals, lecturing and adjudicating. In 1976 he organised the Festival Mondial de la Guitare in Martinique, in which guitarists from twenty-three countries participated.

Robert Vidal's exceptional efforts on behalf of the guitar have been applauded by Andrés Segovia, Emilio Pujol, John Williams and Leo Brouwer among many other prominent classical guitarists who have recognized his vital contribution to their instrument.

SELECTED READING
Notes sur la Guitare: Robert Vidal.   EMT 1779
Interview.   Classical Guitar, September 1994

COURTESY: JOHN W. DUARTE

Philharmonic Society of Guitarists, London, 1947. Julian Bream in front row, 3rd from right: Dr Boris Perott. Also in front row, A. P. Sharpe (editor of B. M. G.), 2nd from left. 4th from right. On his left, Victoria Kingsley, Wilfrid Appleby and centre, Johanna Vollers (secretary P. S. G.) Harry Bream, Julian's father, is on the right at the end.

Heitor Villa-Lobos

HEITOR VILLA-LOBOS

Born – Rio de Janeiro, Brazil

5 March 1887

Died – Rio de Janeiro, 17 November 1959

Heitor Villa-Lobos began his musical studies at the age of six with his father, a writer and amateur musician. Encouraged by his father, he learnt to play cello, guitar, clarinet and piano. After his father's death, when he was eleven years old, Villa-Lobos became almost entirely self-taught in all aspects of music. At a very early age he began to improvize on popular Brazilian melodies, but his first original composition was a piece for the guitar, Panqueca. He began to play the guitar in one of the small music groups known as 'chôros', and at the age of seventeen played the cello in theatres, cinemas, cabarets and other small and large orchestras in Rio. About this time he enrolled in the National Institute of Music. He had intended to study composition but soon found that he did not like formal study, and left the institute. For five years he travelled in Brazil, studying the music of the people and absorbing the varied landscape and picturesque style of life, and recognizing it as something of his own which he would incorporate into his compositions.

In 1928 Villa-Lobos met the pianist Artur Rubinstein and the composer Darius Milhaud. This meeting, and his love of the music of Debussy, influenced Villa-Lobos in his decision to go to Paris in 1923. It was presumed that he was going there to study European music, but he made it known that he was going there to show European musicians what he had done. His music caused excitement in Paris, and attracted worldwide attention to him.

Villa-Lobos lived in Paris until 1929. It was during this period that he met Andrés Segovia. The result of their meeting was that Villa-Lobos would compose some of the most beautiful music in the modern guitar repertory.

Upon his return to Brazil, Villa-Lobos played an important part in the national campaign to provide general education. In 1932 he was appointed Supervisor and Director of Musical Education in Brazil, and became an educator and illustrator. He invented revolutionary ideas for musical instruction and was especially interested in the development of community singing. In recognition of his achievements and instruction in choral singing, the Federal Government of Brazil in 1943 made him Director of the newly founded Conservatorio Nacional de Canto Orfeônico.

Villa-Lobos received an impressive number of honours. In addition to a citation presented to him by the Mayor of New York for distinguished and exceptional service, he was awarded honorary degrees from several universities, was an Officer of the Legion of Honour in France, and an honorary member of the French Institute. He was an honorary member of the American Academy of Arts and Letters, and of the Accademia de Santa Cecilia in Rome. He was also President of the Brazilian Academy.

Villa-Lobos composed around 2,000 works. The best known of his guitar works are Suite Populaire Brésilienne (written in 1912, published in 1955); Twelve Studies (written in 1929, published in 1952); Five Preludes (written in 1940, published in 1954); and Concerto for Guitar and Small Orchestra (written in 1951).

SELECTED MUSIC

Chôros No.1.	ESC 7418
Five Preludes.	ESC 6731-35
Suite Populaire Brésilienne.	ESC 6737, 6738, 6793, 6794, 6817
Twelve Studies.	ESC 6679
Mystic Sextet (1917).	ESC 6679
Concerto for Guitar and Small Orchestra.	ESC 7993

SELECTED RECORDINGS

Concerto for Guitar and
Small Orchestra: Laurindo Almeida. (Capitol) Master 8638 LP
Villa-Lobos Music for the Spanish Guitar:
Laurindo Almeida. (Capitol) Master 8497 LP
Manuel Barrueco: Etudes,
Suite Populaire. Turnabout TV 34676S LP
Barrueco plays The Music of Brazil. Vox FSM 53-043 LP
Guitar Music of Villa-Lobos and Torroba: Julian Bream.
HMV CLP 1763 LP
Sexteto Místico, Bachianas Brasileiras No.5: Bergström.
Proprius PRCD 9021 LP
Julian Bream plays Villa-Lobos:
Concerto, Preludes, Suite Populaire). RCA SB 6852 LP
Twelve Etudes & Suite Populaire: Julian Bream.
RCA RL 12499 LP
Eduardo Fernández: 5 Preludes, 12 Studies.
Decca 414 616-1 LP
Eliot Fisk plays Villa-Lobos etc. EMI 14-6757-1 LP
Guitar Music of Villa-Lobos: Eric Hill. Saga 5453 LP
Lagoya plays Villa-Lobos & Sor. Philips 6504 131 LP
Thomas Müller-Pering: 5 Preludes, 12 Etudes.
Firebird K32Y 248 LP
Konrad Ragossnig: Preludes. Supraphon 1-11-1040 LP
Florilège de la Guitare 20: Brazilian Music:
Turibio Santos. Erato STU 70913 LP
Twelve Studies: Turibio Santos. Erato STU 1007 LP
Concerto/Sextuor Mystique/Preludes: Turibio Santos.
Erato STU 70566 LP
Maria Livia São Marcos: 12 Studies. Fermata 305-1039 LP
John Williams: Concerto CBS 76369 LP
Narciso Yepes: 5 Preludes. DGG 2530 140 LP
Villa-Lobos – Matt Bergstrom and Friends.
Proprius PRCD 9021
Frederic Zigante plays Villa-Lobos.
Stradivarius STR 33378 CD
Michael Troster plays Villa-Lobos. Thorofon CTH 2052 CD
Complete Solo Guitar Works – Turibio Santos.
Kuarup KCD-028
Alvaro Pierri plays Villa-Lobos. Anale KTA AN28751 CD
Wolfgang Lendle plays Villa-Lobos. Teldec 244 197-2 CD
Philippe Lemaigre plays Villa-Lobos.
Ricercar RIC 039012 CD
Pepe Romero plays Villa-Lobos. Philips 420 245-2 CD
Alexander-Sergei Ramirez plays Villa-Lobos.
Denon CO78931 CD

SELECTED READING

Villa-Lobos.	Guitar Review, No.21, 1957
I Met Villa-Lobos: Segovia.	Guitar Review No.22, 1959
Villa-Lobos.	Guitar Review No.29, 1966
Villa-Lobos: Marcel Beaufils (French edition).	Agir, 1967
Villa-Lobos.	Guitar & Lute, October 1980
Voice-leading: Towards a better understanding: Schaffer.	Soundboard, November 1980
Villa-Lobos.	Guitar Player, July 1981
Heitor Villa-Lobos and the Guitar: Turibio Santos (trans. Forde & Wade).	Wise Owl Music, 1985
Grosse Fugue Villa-Lobos: Brian Hodel.	Guitar Review, Fall 1987
Villa-Lobos and the Guitar: Brian Hodel.	Guitar Review, Winter 1988
The Guitar Works of Heitor Villa-Lobos: Jukka Savijoki.	Guitar International, May, June, July, August, September 1987, and March, April 1988.
Villa-Lobos: Lisa Peppercorn.	Omnibus Press, 1989
One world style of Villa-Lobos.	Guitar Review, Summer 1989
Article.	BBC Music Magazine, January 1996
Premiere Performance of Villa-Lobos' Preludes: Matanya Ophee.	Classical Guitar, June 1995

Segovia and Villa-Lobos and friends, Mrs Villa-Lobos is directly behind them

LUISE WALKER

Born –

Vienna, Austria

9 September 1910

Luise Walker

Luise Walker began to study the guitar at the age of eight. Her first teacher was the well-known Viennese guitarist Dr Josef Zuth. She subsequently studied at the State Musical Academy in Vienna under Professor Ortner. Luise Walker was also fortunate to be able to take lessons with Heinrich Albert and Miguel Llobet, both of whom were frequent guests at her parents' home in Vienna.

From 1940 Luise Walker devoted her life to guitar. Over the years she has made many concert tours of Europe, Russia and the United States. For many years she has been Professor of Guitar at the State Musical Academy of Vienna. She is also a highly respected composer, and many of her solos, studies and arrangements have been published, including Daily Studies for the Guitar and The Young Guitarist (published by V. Hladky, Vienna).

SELECTED RECORDINGS

Guitar Recital	Supraphon 1-11-1230 LP
Paganini Quartet & Terzetto.	Turnabout TV 34322S LP
Guitar Music in Vienna.	Turnabout TV 34171S LP
Ida Presti and Luise Walker.	Pavilion GEM CD9133

SELECTED READING
Ein Leben mit der Gitarre: Walker.
Zimmermann, Frankfurt a.M, 1989.

TIMOTHY WALKER

Born –

Durban, South Africa

13 May 1943

Timothy Walker

PHOTO: COLIN COOPER

Timothy Walker was born in South Africa of British parents. His father was a well-known journalist, writer, broadcaster and music critic.

Walker began playing the guitar at the age of twelve to accompany himself in the popular songs of the day. He eventually changed to the classical guitar, and when Narciso Yepes first toured South Africa he was invited by the Spanish guitarist to study with him in Madrid. This Walker did for two years before settling in London, where he gave his debut concert at the Wigmore Hall in 1970. He also studied with Ida Presti, Alexandre Lagoya and John Williams. The latter recommended him for work with the 'Fires of London', the modern classical group directed by Peter Maxwell Davies. Timothy Walker played regularly with this group until they disbanded in the middle 1980s.

Timothy Walker is currently the guitarist with the London Sinfonietta, and has played with the London Symphony Orchestra, the BBC Symphony Orchestra and the Royal Philharmonic Orchestra, amongst others. He has also appeared with small groups such as the Melos Ensemble and the Ensemble Musique Vivants. He has given concerts throughout Great Britain, Europe, South America and the United States.

Timothy Walker was the guitar soloist (playing electric guitar) in a 1977 Prom at the Royal Albert Hall, London. In 1978 he played duets with John Williams at the Queen Elizabeth Hall, London, in a Sor Bicentenary concert. His first solo tour of the United States took place in 1978, and was followed by a tour of South America with the soprano Mary Thomas. He has composed several original pieces for the guitar, including a concerto.

SELECTED MUSIC
African Light Suite.	Belwin Mills SI 115
Fantasia Celestina.	Belwin Mills SI 120
Prelude.	Belwin Mills SI 122

SELECTED RECORDINGS
Baroque Music.	Saga 5426 LP
Timothy Walker: Guitar.	Decca 6-42344 LP
Guitar Encores.	L'Oiseau-Lyre SOL 349 LP
Classical Folk Guitar.	Hyperion A66027 LP
Folk Songs and Music for Two Guitars.	Max Sound MSCB 27 CAS
Viennese Songs & Sonata: Giuliani.	Max Sound MSCB 28 CAS
Habanera! with Judith Hall (flute).	Collins 10132 CD

SELECTED READING
Timothy Walker.	Guitar, January 1974
Sir Peter Maxwell Davies with Timothy Walker.	Classical Guitar, December 1987 & January 1988
Technical Articles.	Classical Guitar, 1986 & 1987

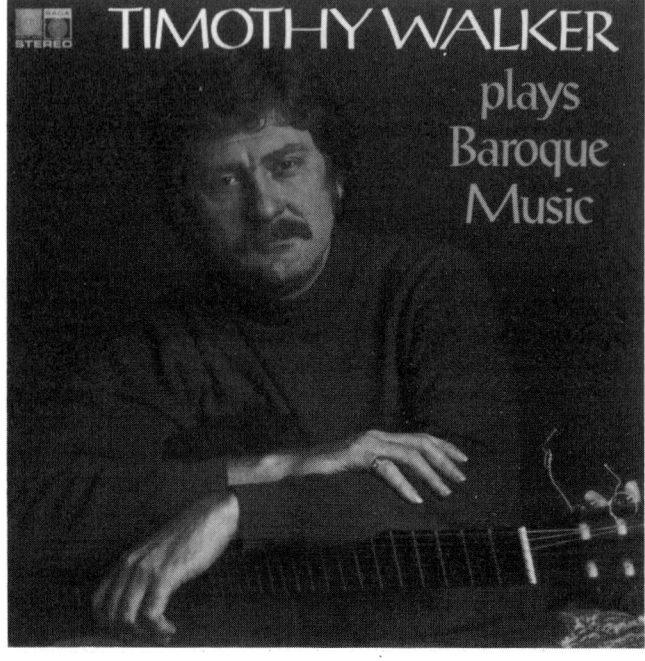

BUNYAN WEBB
Born – BUNYAN MONROE WEBB Jnr.
San Francisco, USA, 1936

Died – San Francisco, 14 November 1978

Bunyan Webb

Bunyan Webb received his Bachelor of Arts degree from South Western University in pre-medicine, then decided to pursue a career in music, in which he graduated at California State University at Fresno.

Webb then studied classical guitar at the Conservatory of Valencia, Spain, and later in masterclasses with Julian Bream, Andrés Segovia, Ida Presti and Alexandre Lagoya. Following this, he began a highly successful career as a guitar authority and teacher, giving concerts throughout the United States, Europe and Japan.

Webb made a valuable contribution to the promotion of the classical guitar in the United States of America as a member of the Affiliated Artists programme. He acquainted a large variety of audiences with the classical guitar, and performed and recorded with guitar in duos with viola, flute, voice and harpsichord. In addition to this active concert life, he held formal teaching positions at Blair Academy at Peabody in Nashville, the University of North Carolina at Raleigh, the Inter-American University in Puerto Rico, and held teachers' seminars for Guitar '78 in Toronto and for ASTA in New Orleans. He also held well-attended masterclasses and workshops for classical guitar throughout the United States.

Over the years Bunyan Webb collected an extensive library of manuscripts, books and records, now housed at the San Francisco Conservatory of Music. He died suddenly in 1978 while scuba diving in California.

A Grobert guitar originally owned by Paganini and then later by Berlioz. Now in the Paris Conservatoire museum

CARL MARIA VON WEBER

Born – Eutin, Nr. Lübeck, Germany

18 December 1786

Died – London, England, 4 June 1826

Carl Maria von Weber

Carl Maria von Weber was a founder of German national opera and is regarded as one of the most influential German composers of the early nineteenth century. The son of a travelling theatre director, he showed great musical talent from an early age. He wrote his first opera at the age of thirteen, and at seventeen was appointed as a conductor in Breslau. Later, after working for the Duke of Württemberg for a little while, the young composer had problems with his career and had to earn a living as a critic and writer, with some performing, in Darmstadt. In 1813 he was appointed conductor of the German theatre in Prague, and in 1816 he was appointed director of the court opera in Dresden. These appointments renewed Weber's success, and his operas continued to be acclaimed throughout Europe until his early death, of consumption, in London in 1826.

Weber, an excellent pianist (his large hands could stretch an interval of a twelfth), was also a very accomplished guitarist. He loved the instrument, and it was his constant companion. Many of his most beautiful songs were originally written with guitar accompaniment, and he wrote for the guitar throughout his short life. During his stay in Prague he wrote Five Songs with Guitar Accompaniment, Op.25, and in December 1816, whilst living in Berlin, he completed his Duo for Guitar and Pianoforte, Op.38. He also included a duet for two guitars in the incidental music he wrote in 1821 for Donna Diana, a musical version of a play by Moreto.

SELECTED READING
Weber – A Biography – Anthony Friese-Greene.
Omnibus Press, London 1991
Article.   BBC Music Magazine, June 1996

John Williams

JOHN WILLIAMS

Born – JOHN CHRISTOPHER WILLLIAMS
Melbourne, Australia
24 April 1941

John Williams began playing the guitar at the age of seven, receiving his first lessons from his father, Len Williams, the well-known guitarist and teacher. He quickly showed himself to be a most gifted pupil, and when the family moved to London in 1952 he was taken to meet Segovia, who was deeply impressed by the eleven-year old boy's talent.

Williams began studying with Segovia, and on his recommendation undertook a full musical education. He entered the Accademia Musicale Chigiana in Siena, Italy, where Segovia himself taught at the Summer School each year. John Williams held a scholarship at the school for the following five years. During that time he gained one of its most coveted prizes, receiving the unprecedented honour of giving the first complete solo recital by a student of any instrument. He also gave a performance of the Castelnuovo-Tedesco Concerto in Siena.

In England, John Williams attended the Royal College of Music from 1956 to 1959, studying piano and musical theory. On 6 November 1958 he made his London debut at the Wigmore Hall. Other highly successful debuts followed, with appearances in Paris in 1959 and in Madrid in 1961. In 1962 he toured the USSR and visited Japan and the United States for the first time in 1963.

In recent years the career of John Williams has developed along many diverse lines, and his constant striving to cross musical barriers has led to some interesting ventures and collaborations. One of the most notable was his appearance at Ronnie Scott's jazz club in London. In 1970 he became one of the artistic directors, with John Dankworth, Cleo Laine and Richard Rodney Bennett, of the Wavendon Theatre. In April 1970 he appeared again at Ronnie Scott's, on the same bill as the rock group 'Soft Machine'. Also in 1970 he took part in a concert at the Royal Albert Hall, held in aid of the families of Greek political prisoners. Later that year he recorded with the Greek singer Maria Farandouri an album of music by Mikis Theodorakis. During 1970 he also played on the soundtrack of the film The Raging Moon. In the studios he met the composer and arranger Stanley Myers, and this led to the making of John Williams's first popular album Changes, arranged and produced by Myers. Williams had already recorded several classical albums for the CBS label.

Several important composers have dedicated works to John Williams. André Previn's Guitar Concerto was given its first performance in November 1971 under the direction of the composer, at a London Symphony Orchestra gala concert. Stephen Dodgson has written several works for Williams, including Partita No.1 in 1964, Fantasy-Divisions in 1969 and, more recently, Stemma in 1988.

John Williams has managed to bridge more musical barriers than any other living guitarist. For some years his classical/rock fusion group 'Sky' achieved enormous popular success. Likewise his concert appearances and recordings with the popular jazz singer Cleo Laine have attracted vast audiences who had never previously appreciated the classical guitar. His group 'John Williams and Friends', an occasional ensemble with a strong Latin American content, attracts large audiences wherever it plays. John Williams has also performed duo concerts with another celebrated guitarist, Julian Bream, the result of which was three very successful recordings. For three years Williams was the artistic director of London's South Bank Summer Festival. In 1992 he formed a new contemporary music ensemble called 'Attaca'. This was made up of fellow Australian musicians.

John Williams currently spends part of each year in his native Australia, but continues to travel the world, make recordings and give a considerable number of concerts, a constant reminder that his ability and achievements with the classical guitar must be counted among the very highest the world has known.

SELECTED RECORDINGS

Guitar Recital: Volume One.
    Ace of Diamonds SDD R328 LP
Guitar Recital: Volume Two.
    Ace of Diamonds SDD R329 LP
Twenty Studies for Guitar: F. Sor.
    Pathé Marion C-065 93404 LP
Virtuoso Music for Guitar.   CBS 72348 LP
John Williams, Wilfred Brown: Songs and Poems with Guitar.   CBS 61126 LP
Two Favourite Guitar Concertos.   CBS 72439 LP
More Virtuoso Music for Guitar.   CBS 72526 LP
John Williams Plays Guitar Concertos.   CBS 72661 LP
Haydn Guitar Quartet: with Paganini Trio.   CBS 72678 LP
Virtuoso Variations for Guitar.   CBS 72728 LP
John Williams plays Spanish Music.   CBS 72860 LP
Songs and Guitar Pieces by Theodorakis (with Maria Farandouri).   CBS 72947 LP
Music for Guitar and Harpsichord.   CBS 72948 LP
Gowers: Chamber Concerto; Scarlatti: Six Sonatas.
    CBS 72979 LP
Gowers: Rhapsody; Villa-Lobos: Five Preludes.
    CBS 73350 LP
Previn: Guitar Concerto; Ponce: Concierto del Sur.
    CBS 73060 LP
Music from England, Japan and Latin America.
    CBS 73205 LP
Bach: Complete Lute Music.   Sony MK 42204 CD
Rodrigo Concerto, Villa-Lobos Concerto.   CBS 76369 LP
Duo: Paganini and Giuliani for Guitar and Violin (with Itzhak Perlman).   CBS 76525 LP
Castelnuovo-Tedesco/Dodgson/Arnold Guitar Concertos.
    CBS 76634 LP
John Williams plays Barrios.   CBS 76662 LP
Arnold and Brouwer Guitar Concertos.   CBS 76715 LP
John Williams plays Manuel Ponce.   CBS 76730 LP
Together: Duo with Julian Bream.   RCA 61452 CD
Together Again: Duo with Julian Bream.   RCA 61450 CD

Boccherini Quintets.   CBS 6671 LP
Bach for Guitar and Organ (with Peter Hurford).
                                                   CBS 37250 LP
Portrait of John Williams.   CBS Masterworks 37791 CD
Rodrigo: Concertos for Guitar.   Sony 37848 CD
Bach, Handel, Marcello Concertos.   Sony MK39560 CD
John Williams plays Paul Hart's. Concerto for Guitar and Jazz Orchestra.   CBS MK 42332 LP
The Baroque Album.   Sony SK44518 CD
Spirit of the Guitar.   Sony SK44898 CD
Iberia: Granados, Llobet and Rodrigo.   Sony SK 48480 CD
Takemitsu by John Williams.   Sony SK 46720 CD
The Seville Concert.   Sony SK 53359 CD
John Williams plays Barrios.   Sony SK 64396 CD
Echoes of Spain.   Sony SK 36679 CD
John Williams – from Australia.   Sony SK 53361 CD
John Williams plays Harvey and Gray Guitar Concertos.
                                                 Sony SK 68337 CD
John Williams and Timothy Kain Duo.   Sony SK 62007 CD
John Williams plays the Movies.   Sony SK 62874 CD
The Seville Concert Video.   Sony SHV 53 475

SELECTED READING

John Williams.	Guitar, August 1973
John Williams.	Guitar, September 1973
John Williams.	Guitar, August 1977
John Williams.	Guitar, August 1978
John Williams and Sky.	Guitar, July 1979
John Williams.	Guitar Player, February 1977
John Williams.	Guitar Player, November 1980
Interview.	Classical Guitar, February & March 1985
Interview.	Classical Guitar, August & October 1987
Interview.	Classical Guitar, December 1988
Interview.	Classical Guitar, December 1989, January & February 1990
Interview.	Classical Guitar, May 1992
Interview.	Guitar Review, Fall 1992/Winter 1993
Interview.	Classical Guitar, October 1993
Interview.	Acoustic Guitar, Nov/Dec 1994
Interview.	Guitar Review, Spring 1994
Interview.	Classical Guitar, May 1996
Interview.	Classic CD, June 1996

LEN WILLIAMS

Born – LEONARD ARTHUR WILLIAMS

London, England 11 August 1910

Died – Looe, England, 20 July 1987

Len Williams

Len Williams began to play the piano at the age of six, and by the time he was fourteen was already playing professionally in a dance band. After three years he gave up his career as a professional musician and became an assistant in the fretted instrument firm of John Alvey Turner in London. It was there that he became interested in the guitar after hearing recordings made by the jazz guitarist Eddie Lang.

Williams studied both plectrum and classical guitar, taking lessons on the latter with Mario Maccaferri, who was living in London at the time. It was Maccaferri who made Williams aware of Andrés Segovia, and soon he preferred playing the classical guitar, although professionally he played and taught the plectrum guitar.

In 1939 Len Williams emigrated to Australia, where he established himself as a teacher at Suttons, in Melbourne. He was house guitarist for radio station 3DB, and soon became very well known as a plectrum guitar soloist and teacher. His decision in 1946 to give up the plectrum guitar and concentrate on the classical guitar did much to popularize the instrument in Australia.

Williams returned to England in 1952, and established his famous Spanish Guitar Centre in London. Since that time hundreds of pupils have passed through his school, many of whom have become fine players and teachers of the classical guitar. There is no doubt that Len Williams's most famous pupil was his son John, who became one of the most successful guitar virtuosos of all time. In addition to his teaching activities, Len Williams developed a new classical guitar trio, consisting of bass guitar played by Desmond Dupré, standard classical guitar played by Robert Wilson, and the Tarina soprano guitar played by himself.

For the latter part of his life Len Williams devoted most of his time to the study of monkeys (specifically Humboldt's Woolly Monkey), having sold his interest in the Spanish Guitar Centre. He made his home close to his monkey sanctuary at Looe, in Cornwall, where he died in July 1987.

SELECTED READING

Len Williams.   Guitar, October 1978
Challenge to Survival: A Philosophy of Evolution: Len Williams.   Allison and Busby, 1971
The Dancing Chimpanzee – Len Williams.
                            Allison and Busby, 1980.

LEO WITOSZYNSKYJ

Born –

Vienna, Austria

23 June 1941

SELECTED RECORDINGS
International Guitar.   Music for Pleasure CFP 122 LP
Music for Guitar and Piano.   Turnabout TV 34728 LP
Folk Songs & Music for Two Guitars.
                                     Max Sound MSCB 27 LP

SELECTED READING
Interview.   Guitar, March 1975
Interview.   Classical Guitar, September/October 1983

Leo Witoszynskyj

Leo Witoszynskyj began to play the guitar at an early age. He completed his studies with Luise Walker at the Vienna Academy of Music, with honours. He later studied with Andrés Segovia and Narciso Yepes. At international competitions in Liège, Paris and Vercelli he was a finalist and prizewinner. In 1968 he won the 1st International Competition for Guitar in Alessandria, Italy.

Since that time Leo Witoszynskyj has maintained an active career as a recitalist in most countries of Europe, the Near East, Venezuela and the United States. He made his United States debut in 1974 in the Carnegie Recital Hall, New York. As a soloist, Witoszynskyj has played with many leading orchestras, including the BBC Concert Orchestra, the Birmingham Symphony Orchestra, and the Vienna Symphony Orchestra.

In 1974 Leo Witoszynskyj was appointed Professor at the Hochschule für Musik in Graz, Austria, and in 1980 elected as its Assistant Director. He combines his working year as a teacher at this important music establishment and as an international recitalist.

SIMON WYNBERG

Born –

Edinburgh, Scotland

4 October 1955

Simon Wynberg

Simon Wynberg studied initially with Fritz Buss in South Africa, later attending masterclasses with Narciso Yepes in Paris. He returned to the United Kingdom in 1978, where he completed a master's degree in musicology at Goldsmiths' College, London. After this, he began his researches into the guitar's neglected repertoire. This ultimately led to the publication of over fifty volumes of unknown guitar music by Faber Music and Chanterelle Verlag.

Among the editions researched and edited by Wynberg are the complete works of Coste, Regondi and Ferranti, selected works of Aguado, Mertz and Ferrer, ensemble works by Carulli, de Fossa, Gaude and Molino, and the Faber Music 'First Repertoire' series.

As a performer, Simon Wynberg has established himself as a keen advocate of chamber music with the guitar, and has worked with some of Europe's and America's top ensembles, singers and instrumentalists, including the English Chamber Orchestra and the Gabrieli String Quartet. He has performed in many British and European Festivals, and made his American debut at the Newport Music Festival in 1984, where he is now a regular visitor. He is the author of a biography of the nineteenth century guitarist Zani de Ferranti.

SELECTED RECORDINGS
Guitar Music of Ferranti & Ferrer. Chandos ABRD 1222LP, CHAN 8512CD
François de Fossa Guitar Quartets. Chandos ABRD 1109LP
Duo concert with Oboe at Castle Howard. Chandos ABRD 1083LP
Coste Music for Guitar & Oboe. Chandos ABR 1031LP
Coste & Mertz Guitar Duets (with David Hewitt). Meridian KE 77095
My Minstrel Love (with Anne Mackay, soprano). Meridian E 45 77076LP
Pot Pourri (with William Bennett, flute). ASV CD DCA692
A Bach Recital. Stradivari Classics SLD 6035 CD
Paganini Duos for Guitar and Violin (2 CDs) (with Scott St John, violin). Naxos 8-550690 and 8-550759
François de Fossa – Trio Concertante. Naxos 8-550760 CD

SELECTED READING
Interview. Classical Guitar, September 1985
Marco Aurelio Zani de Ferranti: A biography. Chanterelle, 1989
The Guitarist's ABC: Series. Classical Guitar, from April 1990

KAZUHITO YAMASHITA

Born –

Tokyo, Japan

25 March 1961

Kazuhito Yamashita

Regarded as one of the most remarkable guitar virtuosos that Japan has produced, Kazuhito Yamashita was a child prodigy. His first public recital in Japan was at the MY Studio in Tokyo in 1974.

Yamashita came to public notice when he won the Kyushu 18th Guitar Competition in 1972. In 1976 he won the 19th Tokyo International Guitar Competition, which was sponsored by the Japanese Federation of the Guitar. Following his successes in Japan, he went to Europe in 1977. Here, at the age of sixteen, he won first prize in three important competitions: the 'Ramírez' Guitar Competition, Santiago de Compostela, Spain; the 10th Concorso Internazionale Chitarra Classica, Alessandria, Italy; and the 19th Concours International de Guitare organized by Radio-Television France in Paris.

Kazuhito Yamashita now leads a busy life as a recitalist in Japan, the Far East, Europe and the United States. He has a recording contract with RCA Victor of Japan, and has released many recordings with this company.

SELECTED RECORDINGS

Romance de Amor.	RACE RDC-8 LP
Guitar Recital.	Victor SJX-9538 LP
Concierto de Aranjuez.	RCA RUC-2280 LP
Guitar Recital II.	Victor SJX-9544 LP
Yamashita plays Bach.	RCA RCL-8014 LP
Pictures at an Exhibition.	RCA RCL 8042 LP
Duo with James Galway.	RCA RL 60355 LP
Castelnuovo-Tedesco Guitar Concerto.	RCA RVC-2280 LP
Complete Works of Fernando Sor.	16 CD Set Victor 14-29
Yoshimatsu/Noda Guitar Concertos.	RCA BVC-2524 CD
Boccherini/Castelnuovo-Tedesco Guitar Quintets.	RCA BVCC-59 CD
Bach Lute Suites.	Crown Classics CRCC-12 CD
Mozart Opera Arias (Duos with Naoka Yamashita).	Crown Classics CRCC-10 CD
Yamashita plays His Favourites.	Crown Classics CRCC-8 CD
Giuliani Duos with James Galway (flute).	RCA 0902 60237 CD
François de Fossa.	RCA BVCC-719 CD

SELECTED MUSIC
Pictures at an Exhibition: Mussorksky arr. Yamashita.
Gendai Guitar

SELECTED READING

Interview.	Classical Guitar, September 1985
Kazuhito Yamashita.	Classical Guitar, August 1989
Interview.	Soundboard, Summer 1989

NARCISO YEPES

Born –

NARCISO GARCIA YEPES

Lorca, Spain, 14 November 1927

Narciso Yepes was given his first guitar at the age of four by his father, and took his first real lessons on the instrument at the age of six.

In 1940 he began his studies at the Conservatory of Music in Valencia, and in 1943 the pianist and composer Vicente Asencio became his teacher. Asencio's approach to music had a great influence in developing Yepes's guitar style.

In 1946 Ataulfo Argenta, the head of the Spanish National Orchestra, became aware of the nineteen-year old guitarist, and Yepes was invited to Madrid. The following year he made his debut as a soloist with the orchestra in a performance of Joaquín Rodrigo's Concierto de Aranjuez. By 1948 he was established as a guitarist of international standing, and made his first European tour. His highly acclaimed Paris debut took place in 1950, and in 1952 he achieved international fame as a composer and performer for the music to René Clement's film Jeux Interdits. During the next two years he continued to devote part of his career to composing more film music. The major part of his working year was devoted to expanding his concert career into nearly all countries of the world. In 1957 he made his first South American tour, in 1960 his Japanese debut, and in 1964 his first appearance in the United States of America.

Since 1963 Narciso Yepes has played a ten-string classical guitar of his own design. He commissioned José Ramírez to design a special instrument with four additional low-resonance strings tuned to c, b-flat, a-flat and g-flat. The purpose of this new instrument was to produce, through the extra bass strings, a more balanced or equalized group of sounds than with the traditional six-string guitar.

Since the middle 1960s Narciso Yepes has lived in Madrid, dividing his year between giving concerts and teaching. He is also a major recording artist for the Deutsche Grammophon company.

SELECTED RECORDINGS
Rodrigo Guitar Concerto and Fantasia.   Decca SPA 233 LP
Musique Espagnole Pour Guitare.
                                        Ace of Clubs ACL 907 LP
Narciso Yepes.   Decca 105-018 LP
Fernando Sor: 24 Studies.
                        Deutsche Grammophon 139 364 LP
Música Catalana.   Deutsche Grammophon 2530 273 LP
Bacarisse/Halffter Concertos.
                        Deutsche Grammophon 2530 326 LP
Ohana & Ruiz-Pipó: works with orchestra.
                        Deutsche Grammophon 2530 585 LP
Twentieth Century Guitar Music.
                        Deutsche Grammophon 2531 113 LP
Narciso Yepes.   Deutsche Grammophon 2531 113 LP
Telemann Guitar Duos.
                        Deutsche Grammophon 2531 350 LP
Domenico Scarlatti: Sonatas.   Deutsche Grammophon
                                        413 783-2 CD
Canciones Espanolas with Teresa Bergenza (2 CD set).
                        Deutsche Grammophon 435 848-2

SELECTED READING
Narciso Yepes and the 10-string Guitar. Guitar, August 1974
Interview.   Frets, February 1980
Interview.   Guitar Player, March 1978

Narciso Yepes

ANDREW YORK
Born -
Atlanta, Georgia, USA
31 August 1958

Andrew York

Andrew York grew up in Virginia. He studied the guitar at the James Madison University. In 1980 he was awarded a Bachelor of Music Degree in classical guitar performance from this university. He went on to complete his Master of Music Degree in Studio Guitar at the University of Southern California in 1986. Both degrees were magna cum laude. Whilst studying at this university he was the recipient of numerous awards, including the Jack Marshall Memorial Scholarship, the Manilow Scholarship and the Del Amo Foundation Grant for Study in Spain.

Andrew York is a talented composer. His compositions and arrangements for guitar have gained wide recognition among both musicians and audiences, particularly after John Williams recorded his 'Lullaby' and 'Sunburst' solos. He became a member of the Los Angeles Guitar Quartet in 1993, and has toured extensively with this famous quartet.

SELECTED RECORDINGS
Denouement	GSP 1007 CD
Perfect Sky	GSP 1011 CD
Dances	LA Guitar Quartet Delos DE 3132 CD
Evening in Granada	LA Guitar Quartet Delos DE 3144 CD
Labyrinth	LA Guitar Quartet Delos DE 3163 CD

SELECTED MUSIC
Sunburst	GSP
Lullaby	GSP
Chilean Dance	GSP
Evening Dance	GSP
Sunday Morning Overcast	GSP
Faire	GSP
Waiting for Dawn	GSP
Perfect Sky	Ricordi

SELECTED READING
Article	Acoustic Guitar, March/April 1993
Interview	Classical Guitar, December 1993

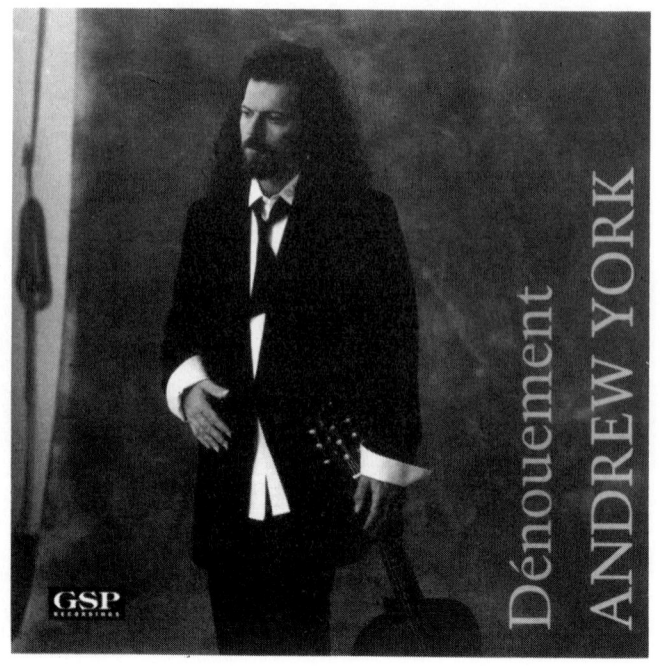

FABIO ZANON

Born - Fabio Pedroso Zanon
Jundia, near São Paulo, Brazil
6 March 1966

Fabio Zanon was exposed to diverse musical styles in his childhood. His first guitar teacher was his father, a talented amateur guitarist. He began his first formal lessons at the age of 13 with Antonio Guedes, and one year later gave his first concert.

Zanon went on to study with Henrique Pinto and Edelton Gloeden. Sergio Abreu was also an important early influence. After gaining his degree at the University of São Paulo, at the age of 18, Zanon decided to become a professional guitarist. After several concerts in São Paulo and other parts of Brazil, he won the coveted Rio de Janeiro Artists Award in 1986 and the Del'Arte Prize in 1987. In the following three years he won top prizes in international competitions. In 1996 Zanon won first prize at the Benicasim Competition, Spain, and also at the GFA Festival Competition held in St Louis, USA.

Fabio Zanon

PHOTO: JORG WAGNER

COURTESY: FABIO ZANON

Brazilian Bank Note, honouring Heitor Villa-Lobos

LUIS ZEA

Born -
Caracas, Venezuela
21 March 1953

Luis Zea

Luis Zea first studied guitar in Caracas with Antonio Lauro and Leopoldo Igarza.

He came to England in 1975 and studied at King`s College, London and at the University of Reading. He also studied privately with John W. Duarte. In 1980 he received his Bachelor of Music degree, and in 1983 his Master of Music degree, from the University of Reading.

Since 1976 Luis Zea has concertised widely, and given many masterclasses in Europe, South America and the USA. From 1984 - 86 he was guitar instructor at the State University of New York. He has been a member of the jury of several international guitar competitions. He has worked with Alirio Díaz, who has had a seminal influence on his career.

Since 1987 Zea has worked for Mavesa, a leading Venezuelan private company whose Proyecto Cultural was created for the consolidation and renewal of the guitar tradition in Venezuela. He is married to the pianist Clara Marcano and lives in Caracas, from where he maintains a busy career as a teacher and recitalist.

Luis Zea has written numerous articles for several international guitar magazines, including Classical Guitar and Guitar Player.

SELECTED RECORDINGS
Recital - Sojo & Lauro	ARC 1014 LP
Vals Elegiaco - Recital	Proyecto Cultural Mavesa PCM 1 CD

SELECTED READING
Interview	Guitar International, August 1985
Interview	Classical Guitar, February 1995
The Guitar Works of Antonio Lauro - Series	Classical Guitar January 1995 to November 1996
The Guitarist's Hands (with John Duarte)	Universal Edition (1978)

MILAN ZELENKA

Born –

Prague, Czechoslovakia

4 June 1939

Milan Zelenka

SELECTED MUSIC
Interval Studies: M. Zelenka & J. Obrovská. B 1508

SELECTED RECORDINGS
Guitar Concerto. Rediffusion ROY 2004
Moderni Ceske Skaldby. Supraphon 1-11-0969
Guitar Recital. Supraphon SUB 10373
Bellefleur. Opus 3 8405
Zelenka plays Bach. Supraphon 1111-2263
Obrovská: Concerto for two Guitars. Panton 8110-0185
Paganini: Works with Guitar. Supraphon 1111-3647
Suite Perestroika, Duo with Miloslav Matousek.
  Daminus DR 902CD
Caro Mio Ben – Prague Chamber Trio.
  Standard Agency 02 001-2 CD
Hommage to Segovia. Supraphon II 1855-2 131 CD
Castelnuovo-Tedesco Guitar Concertos.
  Supraphon SU 0038-2 0931 CD

Milan Zelenka is regarded as one of Czechoslovakia's leading guitarists. As a student he won first prizes and medals in the Moscow (1957) and Vienna (1959) international guitar contests. Since 1957 he has been constantly performing in Czechoslovakia, Russia, Hungary, Germany and elsewhere in Europe.

Zelenka is a graduate of the Prague Conservatory of Music. He frequently performs modern Czechoslovakian music, much of which has been specially written for him. Much of his year is spent in teaching the guitar. He is a member of the Concert Artists Union, and has made recordings with the State Music Editor and Artia. Also active as an editor and lecturer on his chosen instrument, he is currently Professor of Guitar at the Prague Conservatory of Music.

Milan Zelenka was married to the composer Jana Obrovská (1930-1987).

FRÉDÉRIC ZIGANTE

Born -
Roubaix, France
2 May 1961

Frédéric Zigante

Frédéric Zigante's parents were amateur musicians. His Italian father was a pianist, and his Belgian mother a singer. As a child Zigante played the piano for three years but changed to guitar. His parents were friends of Ida Presti and Alexandre Lagoya, and they introduced their son to the famous guitar duo. Zigante's first guitar teacher was Bruno Mattioli. He went on to study with Ruggero Chiesa and graduated in guitar at the 'Giuseppe Verdi' Conservatory in Milan, Italy. He also studied privately with Alexandre Lagoya and Alirio Diaz.

Zigante has given concerts thoughout Europe, and in Japan, China and Singapore.

He has also appeared at several international guitar festivals, and on many radio and television broadcasts. He has recorded extensively, including the complete guitar works of Nicolo Paganini, and Giuliani's Rossiniane. Zigante frequently works with the Arditti String Quartet. He has performed several world premieres including Alexandre Tansman's 'Concertino pour guitare et orchestre, Franco Donatoni's 'Marches II'.

Frédéric Zigante is currently a professor at the Conservatory in Trieste, Italy and holds masterclasses in Vigo, Spain, Beijing, China and Lausanne, Switzerland. He edits 19th century guitar works for the French publishers Max Eschig, and is a member of the editorial committee of the prestigious Italian guitar and lute journal, Il Fronimo.

SELECTED RECORDINGS
New Chamber Music with the Arditti Quartet
　　　　　　　　　　　　ADDA 581 157 CD
Recital　　　　　DRUMS CLASSIC EDLC 2175 LP
Mauro Giuliani　　　　Frequenz Amadeus 031-033 CD
Paganini - Complete Guitar Works
　　　　　　　　　　4 CDs Europa Music 350-205
Giuliani - Complete Rossiniane　2 CDs ARTS 447 146/7-2
Villa-Lobos - Complete Solo Works for Guitar
　　　　　　　　　　　　Stradivarius STR 33378CD

SELECTED READING
Profile　　　　　　　　Classical Guitar, January 1987
Interview　　　　　　　　Gendai Guitar, January 1992
Interview　　　　　　　　　Il Fronimo, April 1994
Interview　　　　　　　　Gendai Guitar, November 1994
Interview　　　　　　　Classical Guitar, September 1995

THE CLASSICAL GUITAR
ITS DUOS, TRIOS, QUARTETS
AND MORE

The Assad Brothers

THE CLASSICAL GUITAR
ITS DUOS, TRIOS, QUARTETS
AND MORE

The main section of this book has dealt with the foremost classical guitarists and guitar personalities since 1800. A prominent feature of the instrument's development since that time has been guitarists playing in duos, trios and quartets and other combinations of the instrument.

In the nineteenth century Dionisio Aguado appeared in concert several times in a duo with Fernando Sor. The twentieth century has seen a succession of great guitarists performing as duos. Francisco Tárrega with Daniel Fortea, Miguel Llobet and Maria Luisa Anido, Emilio Pujol and Mathilde Cuervas, Renata and Graciano Tarragó, and, regarded by many as the greatest guitar duo of all time, Ida Presti and Alexandre Lagoya. The Romero family quartet, often called the 'royal family of the guitar', achieved worldwide fame in the 1950s. Since then, this remarkable family of guitarists have established themselves as one of the most outstanding guitar quartets of all time.

In more recent times Turibio Santos has recorded and performed with Oscar Cáceres, and likewise Julian Bream with John Williams. All these great guitarists are included individually in the main section of the book.

This section of the book deals with the most important of those groups of guitar players not previously mentioned, who have established themselves as a vital part of the evolution of the classical guitar outside the sphere of the solo guitar.

Niibori 400 piece Guitar Ensemble, 1996.

SERGIO AND EDUARDO ABREU

Sergio and Eduardo Abreu

The Brazilian brothers, Sergio (born 5 June 1948) and Eduardo (born September 1949), originally studied the guitar with their grandfather Antonio Rebello. They were then tutored by the Argentinian guitarist and lutenist Adolfina Raitzin Tavora, who had studied with Andrés Segovia.

Their duo playing began in 1963, when they enjoyed enormous success in tours sponsored by the Brazilian Government. Individually, both brothers won high honours in competions both in Brazil and in Europe.

This duo, regarded by many critics as the finest since Presti and Lagoya, split up after Eduardo decided to make his career in another profession (at the time of going to press, he was studying for a Ph.D. in computing). Sergio Abreu, whose biography is shown earlier in this book, was, for a time, a guitar soloist of international renown, but now devotes his career mainly to the construction of guitars.

SELECTED RECORDINGS
The Guitars of Sergio and Eduardo Abreu.   CBS 61262 LP
The Guitars of Sergio and Eduardo Abreu.
                             Ace of Diamonds SDD 219 LP
Two Concertos for Two Guitars.   CBS 61469 LP

NICOLAS AND ILSE ALFONSO

Nicolas and Ilse Alfonso

Nicolas Alfonso (born 6 December 1913, Santander, Spain) studied music and the guitar in both Madrid and Barcelona. He became a successful recitalist in Spain and throughout Europe. In 1950 he settled in Brussels, establishing himself as a highly successful teacher, composer and editor of guitar works. Schott Frères of Brussels have published most of his original works and transcriptions, including a two-volume guitar method. In 1965 he was appointed professor of the newly founded Guitar Department of the Royal Academy of Music in Brussels.

For many years Nicolas Alfonso has performed and recorded in a successful guitar duo with his wife Ilse (born 15 February 1933).

SELECTED RECORDINGS
Concerto pour Deux Guitares.   Erato EFM 8040 LP
Musique Espagnole pour Deux Guitares.   Zephyr Z05 LP

AMADEUS GUITAR DUO

SELECTED RECORDINGS
Amadeus Guitar Duo	FSM FONO 97 762CD
Amadeus Guitar Duo Concertos for Two Guitars	
	FSM FONO 97 763CD
Amadeus Guitar Duo Concertos for Two Guitars	
	FSM FONO 97 767CD
Genzmer Concerto for Two Guitars	
	FSM FONO 97 767CD
Dale Kavanagh plays Lyrical Music	
	FSM FONO 97761CD
Dale Kavanagh plays Ponce and Britten	
	FSM FONO 97768CD

Amadeus Guitar Duo

Dale Kavanagh (born 15 April 1958, Halifax, Canada) and Thomas Kirchhoff (born 4 September 1960, Iserlohn, Germany) formed the Amadeus Guitar Duo in 1991. Both guitarists were already established as successful solo recitalists. Since that time the duo have established themselves as one of Europe's best.

Kavanagh gained her Bachelor of Music degree at Dalhousie University in Canada. A student of Eli Kassner in Toronto she went on to complete her graduate studies at the Musik Akademie der Stadt Basel in Switzerland. Here she studied with Oscar Ghiglia. From 1986-88 she was a prizewinner at several important international guitar competitions including the Segovia International Competition in Spain, the Neuchatel Competition in Switzerland, and the Scandinavian International Competition held in Finland.

Kirchhoff began to play the guitar at the age of seventeen. He studied privately with David Russell in London. He also attended masterclasses given by Manuel Barrueco, Eliot Fisk and Carlos Bonell. He has worked in a duo with flautist Doris Dietz.

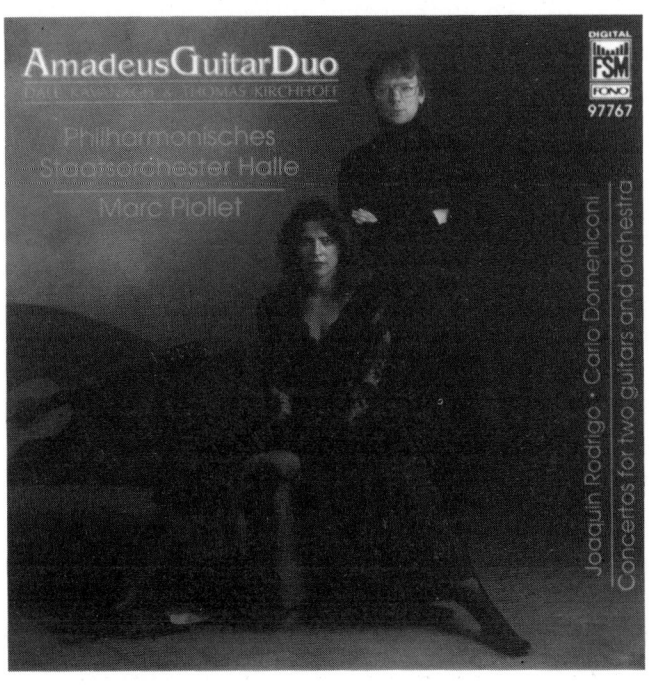

ASSAD BROTHERS

Sergio and Odair Assad

Sergio Assad (26 December 1952) and Odair Assad (24 October 1956) were both born in São Paulo, Brazil. Their father's encouragement led them to take up the study of the guitar. After only two years they won São Paulo's most important guitar competition. One year later they moved to Rio de Janeiro to begin seven years of study with the renowned Argentine guitarist, Monina Tavora, a former student of Andrés Segovia.

In 1973 the Assad Brothers won the Brazilian Symphony Orchestra's first prize for young soloists. Following this success, they began a brilliant concert and recording career with their recital at the Municipal Theatre of Rio de Janeiro. Their superlative work has attracted many prominent composers, and among those who have dedicated works to them are Mignone, Nobre, Piazzolla, Gnattali and Lemaigre.

In recent times the Assad brothers have lived in Europe, from where they lead their highly successful international career. Sergio Assad is also a gifted composer and arranger.

Their younger sister Badi is also a talented singer/guitarist specialising in the popular music of Brazil. She often appears in concert at international classical guitar festivals.

SELECTED RECORDINGS
Sergio & Odair Assad.	GHA 126-021 CD
Sergio & Odair Assad.	Warner/Nonesuch 79116 CD
Alma Brasileira.	Warner/Nonesuch 79179 CD
Baroque Duos.	Elektra/Nonesuch 79292 2CD
Natsuo No Niwa.	GHA 126-029 CD
Saga Dos Migrantes.	Elektra/Nonesuch 79365 2CD

SELECTED MUSIC
Aquarelle (Sergio Assad)

SELECTED READING
Interview.	Classical Guitar, January 1986
Interview.	Classical Guitar, January 1994
Interview.	Acoustic Guitar, May/June 1995

Badi Assad

CASTELLANI-ANDRIACCIO DUO

Castellani-Andriaccio Duo

Since forming their duo at the Guitar '75 International Festival in Toronto, Joanne Castellani and Michael Andriaccio have established themselves as one of America's foremost classical guitar duos.

Both guitarists, now husband and wife, were born in Buffalo, New York (Castellani on 23 June 1952, Andriaccio on 25 September 1952), and led parallel careeers on the guitar. They began their studies with Oswald Rantucci. They both earned a B.A. degree in Fine Arts in Applied Music cum laude in 1974 at SUNY in Buffalo. They performed for masterclasses of Oscar Ghiglia, Angelo Gilardino, Gilbert Biberian and Sergio Abreu. On the recommendation of Andrés Segovia they were both awarded scholarships to study at Musica en Compostela.

Since 1975 Castellani and Andriaccio have concertized internationally as a classical guitar duo. In 1982 they were recipients of National Endowment for the Arts Recitalist Fellowships, and both are faculty members of the SUNY in Buffalo. Castellani is Chair of the String Faculty. Both guitarists have served as board members of the Guitar Foundation of America.

SELECTED READING
Interview. Classical Guitar, April 1988

SELECTED RECORDINGS
Joanne Castellani & Michael Andriaccio. Icarus 1002 LP
Danzas and More for Two Guitars. Fleur de Son 57916-2 CD
1685 – A Glorious Trilogy. Fleur de Son 57917-2 CD
Under the Palms. Fleur de Son 57918-2 CD

HENRY DORIGNY AND AKO ITO

Henri Dorigny and Ako Ito

Henry Dorigny was born in France in March 1939. He studied the guitar in Nice with the Presti-Lagoya Duo at the Academie Internationale d'Et. He attended various masterclasses and in 1963 was appointed Professor of Guitar at the Conservatoire Regional de Musique of Nice. He also began to perform widely as a guitar soloist. In 1966, while still attending the masterclasses of Presti-Lagoya, he met Ako Ito, whom he later married. They began performing as a guitar duo throughout France. They made many appearances on radio and television and have made several recordings.

Ako Ito was born in Japan, December 1942. She began to study the guitar as well as the piano and voice at an early age. Her talent soon became evident, and at the age of eighteen, she went to the United States to continue her music studies and to give numerous concerts as a guitar soloist. She studied in France and in Canada with the Presti-Lagoya Duo, and in the United States and Spain with Andrés Segovia. She married Henri Dorigny in 1967, and they now live in Nice. She was made Professor of Guitar at the Academie de Musique Rainier III in Monaco.

In 1970 the duo made their first international tour of Japan, including an appearance with the Tokyo Philharmonic Orchestra. Since then they have appeared regularly throughout Europe, the United Kingdom, the United States and Canada.

SELECTED RECORDINGS
Danses Espagnoles pour Deux Guitares. SFP 31-102 LP
Compositions for Two Guitars. Delos FY 008 LP

DUO BATENDO

Duo Batendo

The Duo Batendo consists of the Dutch guitarists Ton Huijsman, born 1954 in Zaandam, and Sjaak van Vugt, born 1956 in Rotterdam.

Ton Huijsman began to play the guitar at fifteen. From 1971 to 1977 he studied with Dick Hoogeveen at the Twents and Rotterdam Conservatories. He also attended masterclasses given by Abel Carlevaro and Baltazar Benitez. Sjaak van Vugt began to play the guitar at eleven. From 1972 to 1980 he studied with Hans van Goch at the Rotterdam Conservatory.

It was during their studies at the Rotterdam Conservatory that Huijsman and van Vugt met and, in 1983, formed the Duo Batendo. Since that time they have given many concerts and made several radio broadcasts. Their special interest is the performance of neglected or little-known works.

SELECTED RECORDING
The Well-Tempered Guitars Op.199: Castelnuovo-Tedesco.
Etcetera ETC 2009 LP

DUO SONARE

Duo Sonare

The Duo Sonare was formed by Thomas Offerman and Jens Wagner in 1984. They are now regarded as being one of the best international classical guitar duos, and have a busy recital and recording career.

Thomas Offerman was born in Mainz, Germany, 2 April 1959. He studied the guitar at the conservatories of music in Cologne, Aachen and Basle. He gained his diploma for performance from the conservatory in Basel. He was a prizewinner and finalist at the Second Scandinavian Guitar Competition, the Twelfth Tarrega Competition and Sixth Segovia Competiton in Spain. When not performing with the Duo Sonare, Offerman teaches at the Hanns Eisler Music Conservatory in Berlin, and the Franz Liszt Music Conservatory in Weimar.

Jens Wagner was born in Gottingen, Germany, 18 March 1958. He studied the guitar at the music conservatories of Vienna, Essen and Bremen. He gained diplomas for performance with distinction in both lute and guitar, and also a music teaching diploma. When not performing in the duo, Wagner teaches at the music conservatories in Essen and Bremen.

SELECTED RECORDINGS
Duo Sonare Play Bach, Haydn, Spohr and Corea SST 30204
Duo Sonare Play Giuliani, Sor, Mertz and Coste SST 31110
Duo Sonare Play Zappa, Debussy, Albéniz, Piazzolla
SST 31111
Duo Sonare Play Mike Oldfield's Tubular Bells
MDG 630 0628-2

EVANGELOS AND LIZA

Evangelos and Liza

The duo of Evangelos Assimakopoulos (born Agrinio, Greece, on 10 September 1940) and his wife Liza Zoi (born Messologi, Greece, on 8 August 1940) was previously known as the Athenian Guitar Duo.

Both began their advanced studies on the guitar in 1954 at the National Conservatory of Athens under the direction of Dimitri Fampas. Each graduated and took First Prize with honours. Both guitarists gave their debut solo recitals in Athens in 1959. One year later they took the first two prizes in the international contest in Naples, and in 1962 both were appointed professors of the guitar in the National Conservatory in Athens.

The duo was formed in 1963, and Evangelos and Liza married in 1965. For three years they were awarded scholarships to study with the Presti-Lagoya duo in France, and in Spain with Andrés Segovia, who encouraged composers such as Castelnuovo-Tedesco to write works especially for them. Since their arrival on the international music scene in 1967, Evangelos and Liza have played concerts in the major cities of Great Britain and Europe, in addition to Greece. They have also appeared regularly on television and radio. Since 1969 they have made several extensive tours of North America.

SELECTED RECORDINGS
Musique Baroque pour Deux Guitares.   Edici Ed 21290 LP
Evangelos and Liza play the Romantics.
Minos EMI 80047-2 CD
Evangelos and Liza play Solo Music.
Minos EMI 80021-2 CD

SELECTED READING
Interview.	Guitar, August 1977
Interview.	Guitar, August 1980
Interview.	Guitarra, July 1980
Interview.	Classical Guitar, November 1984

GARAU-MILLET DUO

Garau-Millet Duo

Miguel Garau and Fernando Millet were both born in Buenos Aires, Argentina, in 1957 and 1956 respectively. They both hold diplomas from the Juan Jose Castro Conservatory in Buenos Aires, and both received the title of Senior Professor of Guitar with distinction.

Garau and Millet have performed regularly throughout South America and Europe. They made their first European tour in 1981, with a second in 1985. Since then they have lived in France, from where they follow an intensive schedule of concerts, also appearing on radio and television. They are now recognized as one of the finest classical guitar duos, having won first prize in a number of competitions including the Asociacón Estimulo Cultural 1978, Promociones Musicales 1979, and the Grand Prix and Médaille d'Or at the Festival de Jeunes Solistes, Bordeaux, in 1986.

SELECTED RECORDING
Piazzolla, Villa-Lobos, Smith Brindle.	G-M 3336 LP
Recital.	Pyramid NON 13508 CD

SELECTED READING
Article.	Classical Guitar, February 1988

GRONINGEN GUITAR DUO

Groningen Duo

Erik Westerhof and Remco de Haan studied at the Municipal Conservatory of Groningen (The Netherlands) with Willem van Lier. Both guitarists graduated in 1983 with a diploma for excellent performance. In the same year the duo gave the Dutch première of the Concerto for Two Guitars and Orchestra Op. 201 by Mario Castelnuovo-Tedesco.

In 1987 they reached the finals of the Concours for Chamber Music organized by Netherlands Impresariaat. In 1988 they won first prize at the 3rd International Guitar Duo Competition in Montélimar. In the same year they were invited by ORTF to give the first performance of the Concerto for two guitars and orchestra by Ton de Leeuw, with the orchestra of ORTF conducted by Leo Brouwer. They have recorded for the BBC, ORTF and NOIS.

As well as giving many concerts, the Groningen Duo have made several broadcasts on Dutch radio.

SELECTED RECORDINGS
Bach, Brahms, Albéniz, Petit.	GG-Records GG 8501 LP
Duo Recital.	Ottavo OTR 118 818 LP
Danzas Espanolas.	Ottavo OTR 48710 LP
Reverie.	Ottavo OTR C49135 CD
Scarlatti for Two Guitars.	Ottavo OTR C29445 CD

HILL-WILTSCHINSKY DUO

Hill-Wiltschinsky Duo

Robin Hill (born 1953, Huddersfield, Yorkshire) and Peter Wiltschinsky (born 1955, Doncaster, Yorkshire) formed their duo in 1979 after meeting and giving their first public recital at a music college in 1983.

Both guitarists studied with David Taplin at the Huddersfield School of Music. Robin Hill attended masterclasses given by Alirio Díaz.

In 1987 the duo made their debut at the Wigmore Hall, London, and since that time they have given many concerts throughout Europe, establishing themselves as one of the finest classical guitar duos.

SELECTED RECORDINGS
Virtuoso Music for Two Guitars.   Hyperion A66113 LP
Sound of Strings.   Teldec 8.44140 ZK 243 716-2 CD
Les Deux Amis Music for 2 Guitar
   Teldec 8.44141 ZK 244 181-2 CD
Art of Hill-Wiltschinsky Duo (2 CDs).   Teldec 0630-10011-2
Danza.   ASV CD WHL 2094

SELECTED READING
Interview.   Classical Guitar, November 1988
Interview.   Classical Guitar, April 1994

DUO MONTES KIRCHER

Duo Montes Kircher

The Duo Montes Kircher is made up of the husband-and-wife partnership of Alfonso Montes and his wife Irina Kircher.

Irina Kircher was born on 6 April 1966 in Stuttgart, West Germany. She began to play the guitar at the age of six, and later studied music and the guitar at the Hochschule für Musik und Darstellende Kunst in Stuttgart, where she studied with Mario Sicca. At the age of ten she won the German 'Young Musician of the Year' contest, a feat she repeated on the next occasion. In 1983 she moved to Caracas to study for a year with Antonio Lauro.

Alfonso Montes was born on 9 February 1955 in Ciudad Bolivar, Venezuela. His early involvement with folk music eventually developed into formal study with Leopoldo Igarza in Caracas. In 1976 he won a scholarship to study in London with John W. Duarte from 1976 to 1982, during which time he obtained the performance diploma of the Royal College of Music. Montes is also a composer, with many published works for theatre groups, ensembles and guitar.

Since 1983 Irina Kircher and Alfonso Montes have worked together as a duo, making their debut in 1984 at the Ateneo de Caracas. They now live in Germany, enjoying a busy career giving many concerts and appearing at international festivals.

SELECTED RECORDING
Guitar Duets.	Vest-Norsk VNP 0086-11 LP
Guitar Duets.	Vest-Norsk VNP 0086-17 LP
Dialogo.	W.H.Ziefle 22 33 44 LP
Duo 'Montes Kircher plays Montes.	KMK 66-55-11 CD
El Cielo Que Esta.	KMK 66-55-02 CD

SELECTED READING
Interview.	Classical Guitar, March 1990
Interview.	Classical Guitar, August 1995

POMPONIO-ZARATE DUO

Pomponio-Zárate Duo

Jorge Martínez Zárate was born in Buenos Aires, Argentina, on 1 October 1923 and died there on 1 March 1993. He became interested in music at an early age, and later began to study at the National Conservatory of Music in Buenos Aires, where he studied guitar with Maria Luisa Anido. Soon after he left the Conservatory, he married the guitarist Graciela Pomponio, and they gave their first duo concert shortly afterwards.

As well as appearing throughout the world in duo performances with his wife, Jorge Martínez Zárate was a highly respected teacher of the guitar. He was appointed Professor of the Guitar at the Music School of Santa Fé, and later became Professor of the Guitar at the National Conservatory of Music in Buenos Aires. Zárate was also a composer, and made over 600 transcriptions for one, two and four guitars.

Graciela Pomponio was born on the outskirts of Buenos Aires, Argentina, on 12 April 1926. Like most of the talented classical guitarists in Argentina at that time, she studied with Maria Luisa Anido. Pomponio performed her first public guitar recital at the age of eight.

She entered the National Conservatory of Music in Buenos Aires and studied the guitar, harmony and the theory of music. After completing her studies, she became the Professor of Guitar at the Music School of the National University of Littoral.

While studying at the National Conservatory of Music in Buenos Aires, Graciela Pomponio met Jorge Martínez Zárate. They married in 1948, and from that time appeared together throughout the world for many years, as the Pomponio-Zarate Duo.

SELECTED RECORDINGS
Moreno Torroba.	Erato STV 70549 LP
Masters of the Guitar – Volume Two.	RCA RB 6599 LP
Masters of the Guitar – Volume Three.	RCA SB 6610 LP
Musique de Amerique-Latine.	Mandala MAN 4804 CD
Cuarteto Martinez Zarate.	Mandala MAN 4846 CD

SELECTED MUSIC
Pequena Suite.	Ricordi BA
Preludios 1 and 2.	Ricordi BA
Danza No. 1.	Ricordi BA
Introducion y Allegro (2 guitars).	Ricordi BA
Preludio y Danza.	Columbia USA
Guitare and Education Musicale (3 Vols).	Edition Lemoine

AMSTERDAM GUITAR TRIO

The Amsterdam Guitar Trio was formed in 1978 at the Sweelinck Conservatorium in Amsterdam by Johan Dorrestein, Olga Franssen and Helenus de Rijke. Their London concert debut in 1981 and their outstanding recording of Vivaldi's Four Seasons in 1985 established them as one of the world's foremost guitar ensembles. In 1990 John Dorrestein was replaced by Edith Leerkes.

Johan Dorrestein (born Amsterdam, Holland, 1950) began to play the guitar at the age of twelve, yet only began to take it seriously when he was a drama student at the age of eighteen. Inspired by some of Narciso Yepes's recordings, he gave up drama and entered the Conservatory in Amsterdam.

Helenus de Rijke (born Holland 1954) was introduced to the guitar by his father, a jazz guitarist. After hearing, as a teenager, some of Segovia's recordings, he studied privately with Gerar Gest. At sixteen he decided to concentrate on his schooling, going on to study Latin and Greek at the University of Amsterdam. Whilst there his interest in the classical guitar was renewed, and under the guidance of Guido Topper he developed a serious interest in contemporary music and ensemble playing.

Olga Franssen (born Eindhoven, Holland, 1954) is from a musical family. She began to play the guitar at the age of nine. She also played piano, violin and oboe to a high standard. Her parents are musicians, and four of her brothers and sisters are professional musicians. She studied guitar with Hans Lutz Niessen and Guido Topper, and met the other members of the Amsterdam Trio while studying at the Conservatory in Amsterdam.

SELECTED RECORDINGS
Vivaldi's Four Seasons.	RCA RD 70220 CD
J.S.Bach – Brandenburg Concertos 2, 3, 5, 6.	RCA RL 70903 CD
Ravel/Debussy/Poulenc.	RCA RD 87800 CD
Music of Chiel Meijering.	RCA RD 60165 CD
Fandango.	Fidelio FID 8853 CD
Bach Concertos.	Emergo EC3989 2 CD
Scarlatti Sonatas.	Emergo EC3959 2 CD

SELECTED READING
Interview.	Classical Guitar, June 1985
Interview.	Classical Guitar, April 1989

Amsterdam Guitar Trio – (left to right): Helenus de Rijke, Edith Leerkes and Olga Franssen

THE FALLA TRIO

Original Falla Trio

The Falla Trio, formerly known as the De Falla Trio, consists of three excellent guitarists who have a common love of chamber music. In the tradition of string quartets and piano trios, Terry Graves, Ian Krouse and Kenton Youngstrom originally formed the group and established themselves internationally as a virtuoso guitar trio.

The three guitarists met initially at the University of Southern California in 1979 where they were all studying for their advanced music degrees. Since 1985 Dusan Bogdanovic, who studied at the Geneva Conservatory, Switzerland, has replaced Ian Krouse in the trio. All three guitarists mix a busy concert schedule, teaching and fulfilling an important recording contract for the Concord label.

SELECTED RECORDINGS
Virtuoso Music for Three Guitars.
　　　　　　　　Concord Concierto CC 2007 LP
The De Falla Trio.　　Concord Concierto CDJ 42011
West Side Story/Pulcinella/Jazz Sonata.
　　　　　　　　Concord Concierto CDJ 42013

PRO ARTE TRIO

Pro Arte Trio

The Pro Arte Trio was formed in 1987, and has established itself as one of the foremost guitar ensembles in the UK, with a busy concert and recording career. The trio was originally made up of Peter Rueffer, Cornelius Bruinsma and Simon Munting. Munting left in 1991 and was replaced by Daniel Thomas, who was in turn replaced by Raymond Burley in 1993. The combination of eight-string and requinto guitars, together with the standard tenor instrument gives the trio a distinctive sound.

Peter Rueffer (born - Portsmouth, UK. 16 April 1948) has had a wide experience of chamber ensembles involving the guitar. These include a duo with Raymond Burley, and as a member of Gilbert Biberian's Omega 2 group.

Cornelius Bruinsma (born- London, UK. 22 January 1956) studied at Colchester Institute and the Guildhall School of Music and Drama. He has performed as a soloist and as an ensemble player.

Raymond Burley (born - Reading, UK. 7 November 1948) is well known as a soloist, and also in duos with guitarist John Mills, and mezzo-soprano Jaqueline Fox. He is also a music editor for the publishers Schott & Co., and is on the reviewing staff of Classical Guitar magazine.

SELECTED RECORDINGS
Three Guitars - Albéniz & Granados	ASV CD WHL 2061
Arabesque	ASV CD WHL 2063
Brasilera	ASV CD WHL 2079
Americana - Gershwin & Bernstein	ASV CD WHL 2099

SELECTED READING
Interview　　　　　　　Classical Guitar, April 1993

TRIO CONCENTUS

Trio Concentus

The Trio Concentus began its career as a concert ensemble with a tour of the former Yugoslavia in 1984. The trio's first members were Vicenzo Di Benedetto, Stefano Palmidessi and Francesco Sorti. Sorti's place was taken by Claudio Marcotulli, and in the summer of 1996 Marcotulli left and was replaced by Arturo Tallini.

The Trio, now acknowledged as one of Europe's best, concertise regularly throughout Europe and Scandinavia.

SELECTED RECORDINGS
Original Works for Three Guitars   Nuova Era 68096 CD
Transcriptions & Original Works for Three Guitars
    Nuova Era 71109 CD

SELECTED READING
Interview   Classical Guitar, September 1996

ZAGREB GUITAR TRIO

Zagreb Guitar Trio

The Zagreb Guitar Trio consists of Darko Petrinjak, (b. 1 December 1954, Zagreb, Yugoslavia), Goran Listes (b. 1961) and Istvan Römer (b. 17 August 1962, Zagreb).

Petrinjak graduated from the Zagreb Music Academy in 1975, where he studied both guitar and double bass. He often includes this instrument in the Trio's repertoire. He went on to take post-graduate studies under Hector Quine at the Royal Academy of Music in London. He also studied lute under Robert Spencer. He was awarded the Julian Bream Prize and recital diplomas for both guitar and lute. After teaching for three years at the Birmingham School of Music, he returned to Yugoslavia in 1981 to become Professor of Guitar at the Zagreb Music Academy.

Listes and Römer were two of his best pupils at the Zagreb Academy, and they teamed up with Petrinjak in 1984 to form the now highly-regarded Zagreb Guitar Trio. All three guitarists are also established solo recitalists with many competition successes and recordings to their names.

SELECTED RECORDING
Zagreb Guitar Trio.   Jugoton LP-6-S 2 021949
April is the Cruellest Month.   MB2 CD 2009

SELECTED READING
Interview.   Classical Guitar, February 1990
Article.   Classical Guitar, April 1992

AIGHETTA QUARTET

Aighetta Quartet

The Aighetta Quartet was formed in 1979 in Monte Carlo by André-Michel Berthoux, Alexandre del Fa, Philippe Loli and François Szonyi. They were all students of Pier Domenico Amerio at the Academie de Musique Rainier III in Monaco.

The Aighetta Quartet gave their first public concert in February 1980. Since 1982 the Aighetta Quartet has been recognised as one of the most important guitar ensembles in Europe. They have concertised throughout Europe, and made many television and radio broadcasts. Pascal Rabati recently replaced Andre-Michel Berthoux in the quartet. In 1989 they gave the first performance of Quartet No.2 and other music by Anthony Burgess, the distinguished novelist and man of letters.

SELECTED RECORDING
Oeuvres pour Quatuor de Guitares – Burgess.
L'empreinte digitale ED 13049 CD
Oeuvres pour Quatuor de Guitares: Burgess, Delanoff, Torroba. REM 311111 XCD
Paul Robert Delanoff. L'empreinte digitale ED 13037 CD

ENGLISH GUITAR QUARTET

English Guitar Quartet

The original English Guitar Quartet was formed by Simon Munting (born 1947) early in 1978. Consisting of Peter Martin (born 1957), Alexander MacDonald (born 1950), Colin Thompson (born 1954) and Simon Munting, it built up a large and varied repertoire. Almost a quarter of a century later the English Guitar Quartet, now with new members, continues to achieve great success at home and abroad. Composers from several countries have written for the quartet; these have included Arthur Wills, Martyn Brabbins and Antonín Tucapsky.

Until recently the quartet consisted of Roland Gallery (born Coventry 7 April 1957), treble guitar; Tom Dupré (born Matfield, Kent, 9 May 1959), guitar; Andrew Marlow (born Teddington, Middlesex, 7 October 1961), guitar; and Tim Pells (born 8 June 1954), bass guitar. Each member of the quartet studied with Hector Quine at the Royal Academy of Music in London. In 1986 the British Council invited the quartet to tour Canada, where they were broadcast by CBC radio. In 1988 they toured Australia in connection with the bi-centennial celebrations. In 1995 Roland Gallery was replaced by Richard Hand.

SELECTED RECORDING
Romantic Guitar Quartets. Saydisc SDL 379 CD
Baroque Guitar Quartets. Saydisc SDL 386 CD
Spanish Guitar Quartets. Saydisc SDL 399 CD

LOS ANGELES GUITAR QUARTET

The Los Angeles Guitar Quartet was formed in 1980 by four young guitarists from the University of Southern California: Anisa Angarola, John Dearman, William Kanengiser and Scott Tennant. All four guitarists had been recognised as a talented soloists in their own right, and all four had been chosen to appear in Andrés Segovia's masterclass at USC in 1981. In 1990 the composer/guitarist Andrew York replaced Anisa Angarola in the quartet.

The Los Angeles Guitar Quartet are now recognized as one of the world's finest classical guitar quartets, and have toured extensively in North and South America and in Europe.

SELECTED RECORDING

Los Angeles Quartet.	GHA 126.001 CD
Recital.	GHA 126-016 CD
Dances – Renaissance to Nutcracker.	Delos DE 3132 CD
Evening in Granada.	Delos DE 3144 CD
Labyrinth.	Delos DE 3163 CD

SELECTED READING

Interview.	Classical Guitar, June 1988
Article.	Guitar Review, Summer 1990
Interview.	Classical Guitar, November 1995

Los Angeles Guitar Quartet

PHOTO: BLAKE LITTLE

PRAGUE GUITAR QUARTET

Prague Guitar Quartet

The Prague Quartet was founded in 1984. It is currently made up of four excellent guitarists, Marek Veleminsky, Vaclav Kucera, Jiri Mrhal and Martin Sauer, all of whom are graduates from the Prague Academy of Musical Arts. Three of the quartet's members have been finalists in the prestigious Radio France International Guitar Competition in Paris. The Prague Quartet tours extensively throughout Europe each year giving concerts at major music festivals and in important venues. They also appear frequently on television and radio, and have made some highly acclaimed recordings.

Marek Veleminsky (born - Prague, 6 February 1960) is the leader of the Prague Guitar Quartet. He graduated from the six-year course at the Prague Conservatory under Jiri Jirmal in 1985. In 1984 he won the Kutna Hora guitar Competition and in 1985 he was a finalist in the Paris Competition. In 1992 he graduated from the Prague Academy of Musical Arts under the tutelage of Stepan Rak.

Vaclav Kucera (born - Prague, 12 August 1954) is a 1975 graduate of the Prague Conservatory, where he studied with Milan Zelenka. He was a finalist in the 1974 Radio France Guitar Competition.

Jiri Mrhal (born - Prague, 28 March 1972) completed his studies at the Prague Conservatory in 1992 under Arnost Sadlik. In 1996 he graduated from the Prague Academy of Musical Arts where he was a student of Stepan Rak.

Martin Sauer (born Pilsen, 16 February 1965) also studied with Arnost Sadlik at the Prague Conservatory, and with Stepan Rak at the Prague Academy of Musical Arts. In 1982 he was a prize winner at the Kutna Hora Competition, and in 1985 was a finalist in the Paris Radio France Guitar Competiton.

Former members of the Quartet were Chaled Arman 1984-86, Jiri Voborsky 1984-90, and Marek Janda 1990-92.

SELECTED RECORDINGS
Prague Guitar Quartet Play Villa-Lobos, Gershwin, Torroba and Morel   Panton 810993-2 CD
Charles Bridge Variations   Bonton CD 710058-2131
Prague Guitar Quartet Play Corelli, Bach, Vivaldi
                                            Panton 811394-2 CD
Prague Guitar Quartet Play Rak & Duarte
                                            Panton 811273-2 CD

THE ROMEROS

The Romeros were a family guitar quartet consisting of the late Celedonio Romero and his three sons, Celin, Angel and Pepe. The main section of the book has already included biographies of Celedonio, Angel and Pepe, as they have all achieved individual success outside this famous guitar group. Celin, born in Málaga in 1936, has devoted his professional career to being an integral part of the quartet. When not working with the quartet, he is on the faculty of the University of California at San Diego. From 1993 Celin's son Celino took the place of Angel in the Romero Quartet.

From the time the Romeros settled in the United States of America in 1958, they were enthusiastically received throughout the North American continent for their solo, duo and quartet performances. In 1967, they commissioned Joaquín Rodrigo to compose his Concierto Andaluz for four guitars and orchestra. After that time several other important composers, including Federico Moreno Torroba, dedicated works to them. For almost forty years this outstanding group of guitarists entertained audiences all over the world.

SELECTED RECORDINGS

European Court Music.	Philips (Universo) 6582-001 LP
Compositions for Two Guitars.	Philips 9500-352 LP
Classical Music for Four Guitars.	Philips 9500-296 LP
Rodrigo: Conciertos Andaluz/Aranjuez.	Mercury 75021 LP
An Evening With the Romeros.	Mercury 75022 LP
Royal Family of the Guitar.	Mercury 75027 LP
Vivaldi Concertos.	Mercury 75054 LP
Spanish Guitar Favourites.	Philips 442 781-2 CD

SELECTED READING

Article.	Guitar Player, April 1972
Article.	Guitar & Lute, September 1978
Article.	Classical Guitar, Sept/Oct 1982
Article.	Classical Guitar, February 1985

The Romeros

THE TOKYO NIIBORI GUITAR ENSEMBLE AND ORCHESTRA

The well-known Niibori Guitar Music Academy in Japan conducts a full-scale academic guitar education, adopting graduate school, college and high school systems in its methods of education focusing on the guitar.

The Academy's 200 students, mostly aged between fifteen and twenty-three, are encouraged in ensemble work. The director of the Niibori Guitar Orchestra introduced the use of alto, contrabass, guitarron and bass guitars in order to achieve an orchestral sound.

The Niibori Guitar Ensemble and Orchestra, under the direction of its founder and principal Dr Hiroki Niibori has achieved popular success in Japan, playing over hundreds of concerts a year. They have made several recordings, including one of Vivaldi's Four Seasons arranged for the ensemble.

Dr Hiroki Niibori

SELECTED RECORDINGS
The Four Seasons/Vivaldi.	Fontec 5016 LP
Niibori 'Live' with Jorge Cardoso.	Apassionato 8009 LP

The Tokyo Niibori Guitar Ensemble and Orchestra

THE CLASSICAL GUITAR
THE OTHER
CLASSICAL GUITARISTS

The early nineteenth century has often been called the golden age of the guitar but few musicologists would disagree that the real golden age of the classical guitarist is now.

The major part of this book deals with the most important classical guitarists and guitar personalities since 1800. Needless to say, the classical guitar scene is now so vast that there are thousands of guitarists all over the world who, for one reason or another, have not yet received wide public recognition for their contribution to the instrument.

This section of the book pays tribute to these guitarists by including photographs of a few of those who seem likely to achieve wider recognition and fame in the near future.

Tom Dupré and Richard Hand Duo

Julian Gray and Ronald Pearl Duo

Novacek-Bissiri Duo

The Strano Sisters

Andrzej Mokry

Pablo de la Cruz

Marcus Llerena

Michael Strutt

Ruben Riera

Christopher Berg

Uros Dojcinovic

Carlo Barone

Harold Micay

Frank Bungarten

Philip Hii

Lex Eisenhardt

Enno Voorhorst

Nicholas Hopper

Sven Lundestad

Guillermo Fierens

Hilary Field

Gérard Rebours

Erling Møldrup

Richard Durrant

Leonardo De Angelis

Nicholas Goluses

Oscar Ohlsen

Christian Chanel

Everton Gloeden

Yaron Hasson

Elena Papandreou

Adam Holzman

Yoram Zerbib

Berta Rojas

Russel Brazzel

Ana María Rosada

Javier Calderón

Celia Linde

Pablo Marquez

José Miguel Moreno

Andrew Keeping

Gary Ryan

Mark Ashford

Irina Kulikova

Ahmet Kanneci

Jean-Pierre Antaki

Adrian Walter

Taly Roth

Susan McDonald

THE CLASSICAL GUITAR
ITS COMPOSERS

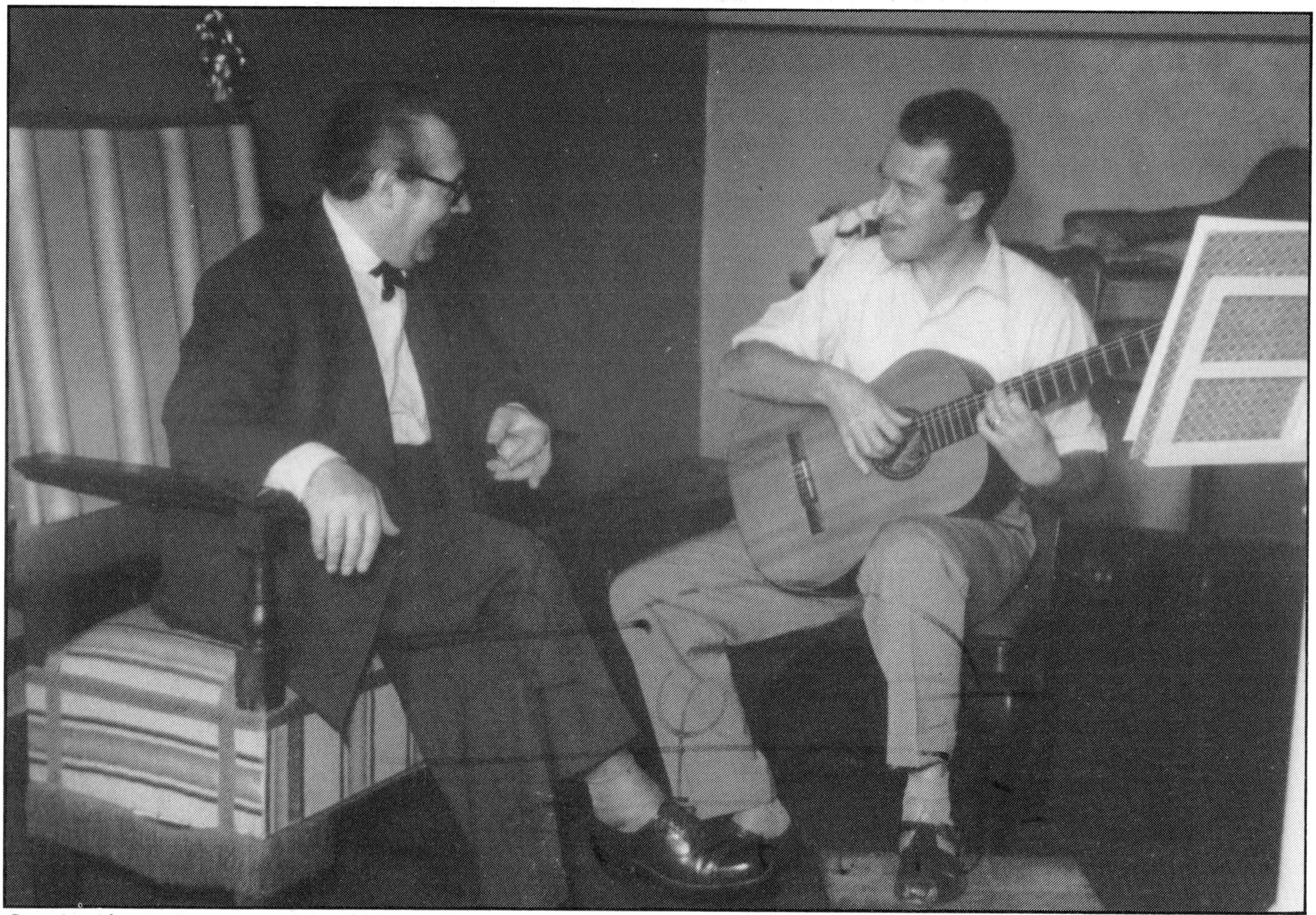

Segovia with guitarist composer Reginald Smith-Brindle

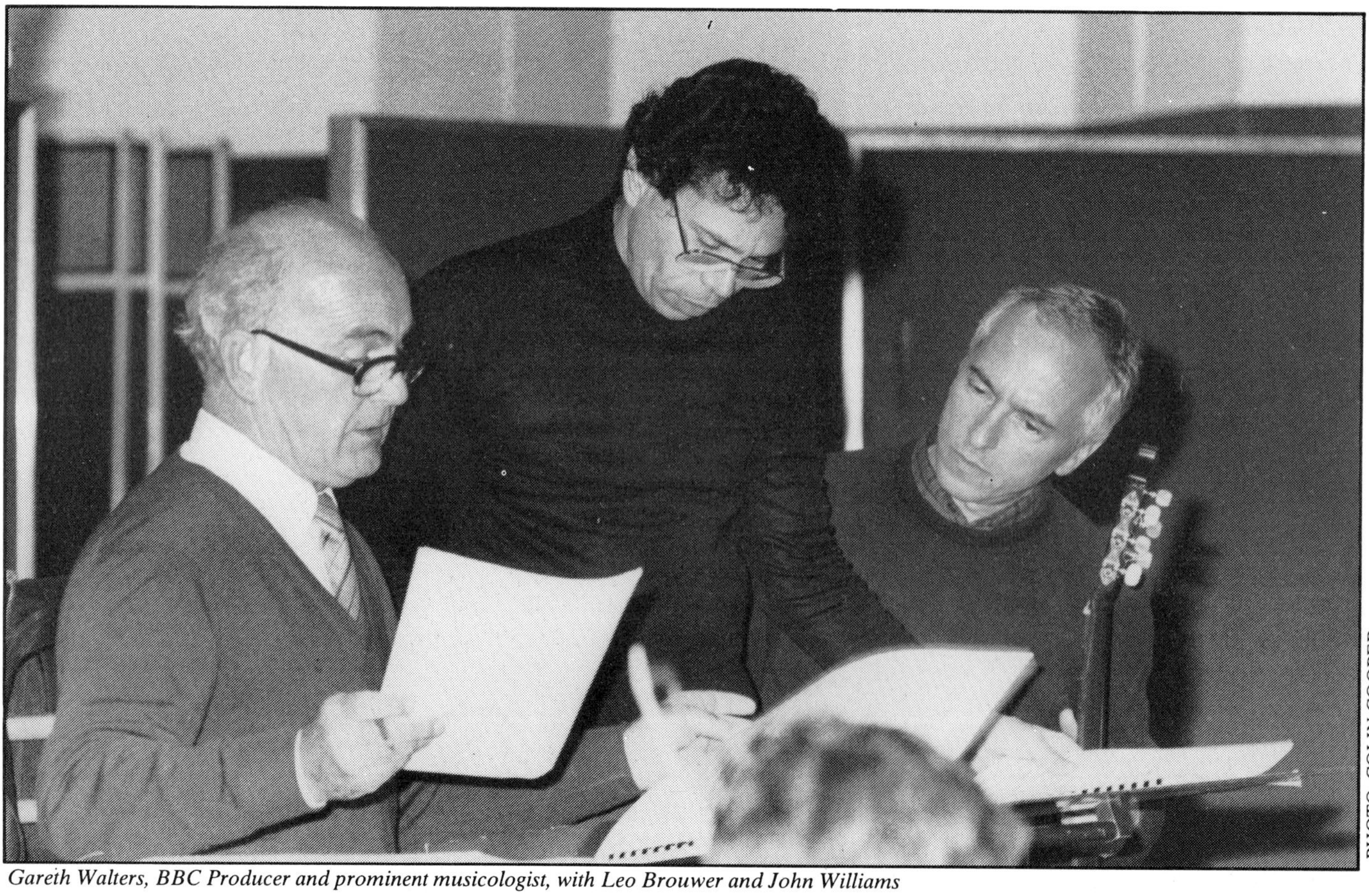

PHOTO: COLIN COOPER

Gareth Walters, BBC Producer and prominent musicologist, with Leo Brouwer and John Williams

THE CLASSICAL GUITAR
ITS COMPOSERS

During the nineteenth century the repertory for classical guitarists consisted mainly of their own compositions and those of other guitarists. Sor, Giuliani and Paganini were the most outstanding of these, and to a lesser extent Aguado, Coste and Regondi, among others, also proved themselves to be talented composers. Towards the end of the nineteenth century Francisco Tárrega extended the range of music considerably with his numerous transcriptions of works by composers such as Mendellsohn, Schumann, Albéniz and Granados, a lead that was followed in the twentieth century by Miguel Llobet and Andrés Segovia. Subsequently more and more classical guitarists made their contribution in this field, so that today a great portion of the guitarist's repertoire consists of transcriptions of works written for other instruments. The works of J.S.Bach (1685-1750), D.Scarlatti (1685-1757), I.Albéniz (1860-1909) and E.Granados (1867-1916) are among those which have been most successfully transcribed for the guitar. A vast library of music originally written for the lute, vihuela and early guitar has also been transcribed successfully for the classical guitar. The most important of these composers are John Dowland (1562-1626), Alonso de Mudarra (1508-1580), Francesco Corbetta (1612-1681), Gaspar Sanz (1640-1710), Luis Milán (1500-1561), Enriquez de Valderrábano (1500-1547), Adrian de Roy (1520-1598), Diego Pisador (1509-1557), Franıois Campion (1686-1748), Sylvius Leopold Weiss (1686-1750), Robert de Visee (1660-1720) and Luis Narváez (1500-1551). Their works are often included in the concert programmes of guitarists today.

As we have seen, Andrés Segovia campaigned during the 1920s for new guitar music from prominent contemporary composers. Manuel de Falla had already written Homenaje pour le Tombeau de Claude Debussy for Miguel Llobet in 1920, and now Joaquín Turina and Federico Moreno Torroba answered Segovia's call. Turina's Fandanguillo and Moreno Torroba's Suite Castellana were both published in 1926, and were the first of many important works written by these Spanish composers especially for the guitar. Since that time more and more prominent contemporary composers have written for the guitar. These compositions, together with those written by the great twentieth century guitar-composers like Agustín Barrios, Antonio Lauro and Heitor Villa-Lobos, have now given the guitar a repertory equal to that of most other solo instruments.

This section of the book is devoted to biographies of the most important of these twentieth century composers, who have made such a vital contribution to the evolution of the classical guitar since 1800.

Mario Castelnuovo-Tedesco with Vahdah Olcott Bickford at 40th Anniversary dinner of American Guitar Society

ANTON GARCIA ABRIL

Born –

Teruel, Spain

19 May 1933

Anton Garcia Abril

Anton Garcia Abril began his studies at the Conservatory of Music in Valencia. After earning the highest qualifications in piano and harmony, he went to the Madrid Conservatory of Music to complete his studies, after which he attended the Accademia Chigiana in Siena to study composition with Vito Frazzi, film music with Lavagino and conducting with Von Kempen. His composition Cantata a Siena for choir and orchestra won first prize at the Accademia.

Since that time, Abril has become one of Spain's foremost composers for theatre, film and television, with in addition many symphonic scores to his name. In 1971 his musical 'Un Million de Rosas' won the National Prize for Theatre. He has also won the National Prize for Film Scores several times.

Abril became interested in the guitar through Ernesto Bitetti. In 1979 Bitetti recorded Abril's Concierto Aguediano for guitar and orchestra, dedicated to Bitetti, for the Hispavox label. The recording was awarded the 1979 Premio Nacional para Empresas Fonográficas from the Spanish Ministry of Culture. The composer has gone on to write several more works for guitar, including Evocaciones, a solo work that won a prize in 1981 from the Spanish Ministry of Culture. Abril's second concerto for guitar and orchestra, Concierto Mudejar was completed in 1985 and premiered by Bitetti in 1986 with the Bilbao Symphony Orchestra.

Since 1974 Anton Garcia Abril has been Professor of Composition and Musical Forms at the Royal Conservatory in Madrid.

SELECTED READING
Concierto Aguediano.	Real Madrid
Fantasia Mediterranea.	Real Madrid
Vademecum Vols I & II.	Real Madrid
Planton y Tocata.	Real Madrid
Concierto Mudejar.	Real Madrid

SELECTED RECORDING
Concierto Aguediano – Homenaje a Sor.
    Bitetti Hispavox S 60.294 LP
Abril and Torroba Guitar Concertos – Remi Boucher.
    Analekta AN 2 9502 CD

SELECTED READING
Interview. Guitar International, October 1986

MALCOLM ARNOLD

Born – MALCOLM HENRY ARNOLD

Northampton, England

21 October 1921

SELECTED MUSIC
Serenade Op.50.	Faber
Concerto Op.57.	Faber
Fantasy Op.107.	Faber

SELECTED RECORDINGS
Serenade – John Williams.	CBS 76634 LP
Guitar Concerto – Julian Bream.	RCA SB 6826 LP
Guitar Concerto – Eduardo Fernandez.	Decca 430-233-2 CD

Malcolm Arnold

As a child Malcolm Arnold studied the violin and the trumpet. He won a scholarship to the Royal College of Music, and joined the London Philharmonic Orchestra as a trumpet player. He studied orchestration with Gordon Jacob, and in 1943 the great success of his overture Beckus the Dandipratt established him as a gifted composer. Later in 1948 he was awarded a Mendelssohn Scholarship, which enabled him to study in Italy for one year.

Since that time Malcolm Arnold has composed much orchestral music, including several symphonies, a great deal of highly successful incidental music for films (including 'The Bridge on the River Kwai') and fifteen solo concertos, including one for guitar (Op.67, written for and dedicated to Julian Bream) in 1959. Before that came his Serenade for Guitar and Strings in 1955.

Malcolm Arnold was awarded a knighthood in 1993, and given honorary doctorates in the United Kingdom and the USA.

Malcolm Arnold with Julian Bream

VICENTE ASENCIO
Born - Valencia, Spain 29 October 1908
Died - Valencia, Spain
3 April 1979

Vicente Asencio

Vicente Asencio was one of the most important 20th century composers from the Valencia region of Spain. Between 1946 and 1950 he wrote three compositions for piano as homages to Scarlatti, Falla and Garcia Lorca. He later transcribed these works - *Sonatina*, *Elegia* and *Tango de la Casada Infiel* - for the guitar. Asencio wrote *Suite Mistica* for Segovia, and *Suite Valenciana* for Angelo Gilardino. Many guitarists regard his *Collectici Intim* as his most important work for the instrument. His *Dance Valencia* for guitar was published posthumously and first recorded by Susanne Mebes in September 1992.

Vicente Asencio, although born in Valencia, gave Catalan titles to nearly all his guitar works. Although he could not play the guitar he is reputed to have said that it was his favourite instrument. He was married to the pianist Matilde Salvador.

SELECTED RECORDINGS
Musica Catalana	Narciso Yepes	
	Deutsche Grammophon	2530 273LP
Recital Catalan	Susanne Mebes	
	Leman Classics	LC 44201 CD
Recital	Manuel Babiloni	
	EGT CLASICA	656-CD
Recital	Claudio Marcotulli	
	EGT CLASICA	523-CD

SELECTED MUSIC
Collectici Intimi	Schott
Dipso	Berben
Suite Valenciana	Berben
Tango de la Casada Infiel	SF

RICHARD RODNEY BENNETT

Born – Broadstairs, Kent, England

29 March 1936

Richard Rodney Bennett

Richard Rodney Bennett won a scholarship to the Royal Academy of Music in 1953, where he studied with Lennox Berkeley and Howard Ferguson. In 1957 he went to Paris to study with Pierre Boulez for two years, having been awarded a scholarship by the French Government. In 1965 he was elected Composer of the Year by the Composers' Guild of Great Britain.

In 1968 Richard Rodney Bennett composed five short Impromptus for solo guitar, and in 1970 he completed his Concerto for Guitar, which was dedicated to Julian Bream.

SELECTED RECORDINGS
Julian Bream '70.	RCA SB 6876 LP
Dedication – Julian Bream.	RCA RL 25419 LP

SELECTED MUSIC
Impromptus, ed. Scheit.	Universal
Sonata, ed. Bream.	Novello

LENNOX BERKELEY

Born – Boars Hill, Oxfordshire, England

12 May 1903

Died – London, 26 December 1989

Lennox Berkeley

Lennox Berkeley was partly of French descent. After receiving a general education at Oxford, he completed his music education in Paris as a pupil of Nadia Boulanger. Berkeley, who was knighted in 1974, was without doubt one of Britain's most important composers of the twentieth century. He wrote piano music, chamber and choral music, orchestral music, and several operas. For over twenty years he was a professor of composition at the Royal Academy of Music in London.

With the encouragement of Julian Bream, Berkeley wrote several works for the guitar, of which Sonatina (1957) was the first. Then followed Songs of the Half Light (for Peter Pears and Julian Bream), Theme and Variations and, in 1974, the Guitar Concerto, dedicated to and first performed by Julian Bream.

SELECTED MUSIC
Guitar Concerto Op.88.	JWC
Sonatina for Guitar Op.51.	JWC
Songs of the Half-Light Op.65.	JWC
Theme and Variations Op.77.	JWC

SELECTED RECORDING
Guitar Concerto – Bream/Monteverdi Orchestra.	RCA ARL 1 1181 LP
Sonatina – Bream.	RCA SB 6891 LP
Theme & Variations – Bream.	RCA SB 6876 LP
Berkeley/Rodrigo Concertos – Yamashita.	Erato R32E-1056 CD
Guitar Works – Jukka Savijoki.	Ondine ODE 779-2 CD

BENJAMIN BRITTEN
Born – Lowestoft, England
22 November 1913
Died – Aldeburgh, England, 4 December 1976

Benjamin Britten

Benjamin Britten started to compose at the age of five. He was taught the piano and the viola. By the time he was fourteen he had shown that he was a talented composer. In 1927 he studied composition with Frank Bridge, and a few years later won an open scholarship in composition to the Royal College of Music. Britten was soon recognized as a leading composer. In 1963 he composed Nocturnal, having promised Julian Bream some years earlier that he would write a work for the guitar. Based on a 16th century song of John Dowland, it was first performed by Bream at the 1964 Aldeburgh Festival.

Benjamin Britten was admitted to the Order of Merit in 1965, an honour accorded to few. In 1976 he became Lord Benjamin Britten, the first composer to be elevated to the British peerage.

SELECTED MUSIC
Nocturnal Op.70, ed. Bream.   Faber
Songs from the Chinese (guitar & voice) Op.58.
     B & H

SELECTED RECORDING
20th Century Guitar – Julian Bream.   RCA SB 6723 LP
Guitar Works – Jukka Savijoki.   Ondine ODE 779-2 CD

SELECTED READING
Benjamin Britten's Style –   Soundboard, May 1980
Britten's Nocturnal – Donley.   Classical Guitar, May 1987

MARIO CASTELNUOVO-TEDESCO

Born – Florence, Italy, 3 April 1895
Died – Beverly Hills, California, USA, 16 April 1968

Mario Castelnuovo-Tedesco

Mario Castelnuovo-Tedesco was of Spanish/Jewish origin. He began to study the piano with his mother at the age of nine, and almost immediately began to compose. At the age of thirteen he entered the Cherubini Conservatory in Florence, where he studied the piano with Edgar Samuel de Valle. He also studied composition with one of Italy's foremost composers, Ildebrando Pizzetti. Before he reached the age of twenty, the young composer was acclaimed throughout Europe.

In 1925 Castelnuovo-Tedesco won the National Prize for his opera La Mandragola, performed for the first time in Venice. His ballet Bacco in Roscanam was performed in Milan in 1931. At the International Festival of Venice in 1932 he met Andrés Segovia, who asked him to write a piece for the guitar. The result was Variations à Travers les Siècles (Variations across the centuries), Op.71. Over the next few years Castelnuovo-Tedesco continued to write several pieces for the guitar. His Concerto in D Op.99 for guitar and orchestra was written in 1938 at the request of Segovia, and was the last composition Castelnuovo-Tedesco wrote in Italy before the Fascist government's anti-Semitic campaign forced him and his family to leave Italy. They emigrated to the United States in 1939, settling in California. During his early years in Beverly Hills he wrote scores for motion pictures, but later devoted himself mainly to teaching composition and orchestration.

In 1971 Segovia introduced him to the guitar duo of Ida Presti and Alexandre Lagoya. They inspired him to produce a series of works for two guitars: the Sonatina Canonica Op.196, Twenty-Four Preludes and Fugues for 'The Well-Tempered Guitar' Op.199, and Concerto for Two Guitars and Orchestra Op.201.

Mario Castelnuovo-Tedesco was a prolific composer. Included among his works are six operas, five oratorios, numerous orchestral pieces (including overtures for eleven Shakespeare plays), over 100 piano works, over 400 songs, over 100 choral pieces, and a great amount of chamber music for various instrumental combinations. For the guitar he composed almost 100 works. One of his last and most beautiful is Platero y Yo Op.190, for narrator and guitar.

SELECTED MUSIC

Aranci in Fiore, ed. Segovia.	Ricordi
Aria da Chiesa.	Bèrben
Balleta, on the name of Christopher Parkening, Op.170/34.	Farfisa
Canción Cubana, on the name of Hector Garcia, Op.170/41.	Bèrben
Canción Venezolana, on the name of Alirio Diaz, Op.170/40.	Bèrben
Canzone Calabrese, on the name of Ernest Calabria, Op.170/48.	Bèrben
Canzone Siciliana, on the name of Mario Gangi, Op.170/33.	Bèrben
Capriccio Diabolico (Homage to Paganini)	Ricordi
Escarraman – A Suite of Spanish Dances from the 16th Century (after Cervantes).	Bèrben
Estudio, on the name of Manuel López Ramos, Op.170/2.	Bèrben
Homage to Purcell – Fantasia, on the name of Ronald and Henry Purcell, Op.170/46.	Bèrben
Japanese Print, on the name of Jiro Matsuda, Op.170/46.	Bèrben
Passacaglia, Omaggio a Roncalli, Op.180.	Bèrben
Platero y Yo, Op.190.	Bèrben
Rondo, Op.129.	GA168
Sonata (Omaggio a Boccherini).	GA 149
Suite, Op.133.	GA 169
Tarantella.	Ricordi
Tarantella Campana, on the name of Eugene di Novi, Op.170/50.	Bèrben
Tonadilla, Op.170/5.	GA 191
Tre Preludi al Circeo, Op.194.	Farfisa
24 Caprichos de Goya, Op.195.	Bèrben
Variations à Travers les Siècles.	GA 137
Variations Plaisantes, ed. Gilardino.	Bèrben
Volo D'Angeli, on the name of Angelo Gilardino, Op.170/47.	Bèrben.
Concerto for 2 Guitars and Orchestra, Op.210 (piano reduction).	Bèrben
Fantasia for Guitar and Piano, Op.145.	GA 170
Concerto No.1 for Guitar and Orchestra in D, Op.99 (piano reduction).	GA 166
Concerto No.2 in C, Op.160 (piano reduction).	GA 240
Sérénade, Op.118 (piano reduction), ed. Behrend.	GA 167

SELECTED RECORDINGS
Guitar Concerto No.1 – Andrés Segovia. EMI HLM 7134 LP
Concerto for Two Guitars – The Abreu Duo. CBS 61469 LP
Platero and I – Andrés Segovia. Vol.1. MCA MACS 1967 LP
Platero and I – Andrés Segovia. Vol.2. MCA S-26 087 LP
Music of Castelnuovo-Tedesco – Beppe Ficara.
C & M PNL 059 LP
Music of Castelnuovo-Tedesco:
Fantasia Op.145, Sonatina Canonica Op.196, 4 Preludes & Fugues etc. – David Russell, Raphaëlla Smits, Jos van Immerseel. AGLA AX 850218 LP
Platero und Ich – Sonja Prunnbauer.
Harmonia Mundi HM 723 D LP
The Well-Tempered Guitars:
Preludes and Fugues Op.199 complete – Duo Batendo.
Etcetera ETC 1057 CD
Sonatina, Op.205 – William Bennett, Simon Wynberg.
ASV CD DCA 692
24 Caprichos de Goya – Philippe Loli (2 CDs).
Ambitus 383 831
24 Caprichos de Goya – Lily Ashfar. Summit DCD 167
Guitar and Voice Works – Dick Hoogeven (guitar) with Roberta Alexander (soprano). Etcetera KTC1 150 CD

Castelnuovo-Tedesco Guitar Concertos – Kazuhito Yamashita. RCA V 60355 CD
Castelnuovo-Tedesco – Mats Bergstrom and Ensemble.
Proprius Musik PRCD 9124 CD
Castelnuovo-Tedesco Guitar Concertos – Milan Zeleka.
Supraphon SU 0038-2 0931 CD
Castelnuovo-Tedesco Solo Guitar Works – Susanne Mebes.
Leman LC 42501 CD
Fugas y Fandangos – Mebes/Freire Duo.
Leman LC 44401 CD

SELECTED READING
Mario Castelnuovo-Tedesco. Guitar, February 1978
Mario Castelnuovo-Tedesco. Guitar Review, No.37, 1972
Castelnuovo-Tedesco's 24 Caprichos de Goya
and their relation to Goya's etchings – Lily Afshar.
Guitar Review No.79, Fall 1989
Mario Castelnuovo-Tedesco:
su vida y su obra para guitarra – Corazón Otero.
Ediciones Musicales Yolotl, Mexico (1989)
24 Caprichos de Goya Guitar Review.
Fall 1989, Winter and Spring 1990

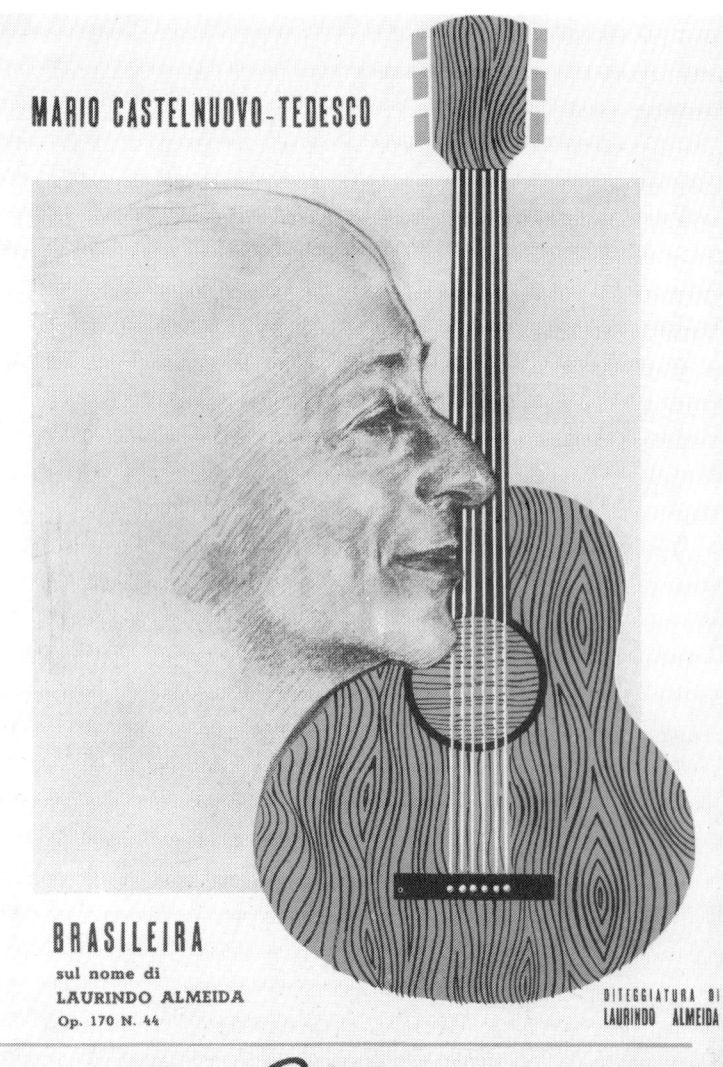

Fine drawing of Castelnuevo Tedesco on music cover

PETER MAXWELL DAVIES

Born –

Manchester, England

8 September 1934

Peter Maxwell Davies

Peter Maxwell Davies studied music at both the Royal Manchester College of Music (1952-56) and Manchester University. His fellow students included John Ogdon, Alexander Goehr and Harrison Birtwistle. Because of their common interest in presenting music from the European avant-garde, the young musicians became known as the 'Manchester Group'. In 1957 Davies received a grant from the Italian Government and went to Rome to study with Goffredo Petrassi. On his return to England he was appointed music director at Cirencester Grammar School (1959-62). In 1962 he went to the USA on a Harkness Fellowship to study with Roger Sessions at Princeton. After spending some time as composer-in-residence at the University of Adelaide, Australia, he returned to Britain in 1967. He teamed up with Harrison Birtwistle and formed the Pierrot Players, for whom Davies wrote his principal works. It was renamed The Fires of London in 1970, and the guitarist Timothy Walker became a prominent member.

In 1970 Davies moved to Orkney in Northern Scotland. This remote island has become his permanent home, and his compositions often reflect the stark beauty of the Orkney countryside. In 1977 he organized the annual St Magnus Festival there.

Peter Maxwell Davies has written several important works for the guitar, including Hill Runes for Julian Bream in 1981. His Sonata was first performed by Timothy Walker in the St Magnus Festival, 1987. He was knighted as Sir Peter Davies in 1987, and is now generally known as Sir Peter Maxwell Davies.

SELECTED MUSIC
For solo guitar:

Hill Runes.	Boosey & Hawkes
Lullaby for Ilian Rainbow.	Boosey & Hawkes
Guitar Sonata	

Works including guitar:

Dark Angels.	Boosey & Hawkes
Fiddlers at the Wedding.	Boosey & Hawkes
From Stone to Thorn.	Boosey & Hawkes
Tenebrae Super Gesualdo.	Chester Music
The Blind Fiddler.	Boosey & Hawkes
The Lighthouse.	Chester Music
The Martydom of Saint Magnus.	Boosey & Hawkes
Points and Dances from Taverner.	Boosey & Hawkes
Psalm 124.	Boosey & Hawkes
Renaissance Scottish Dances.	Boosey & Hawkes
Shakespeare Music.	Boosey & Hawkes

SELECTED READING
Interview.   Classical Guitar, December 1987/January 1988

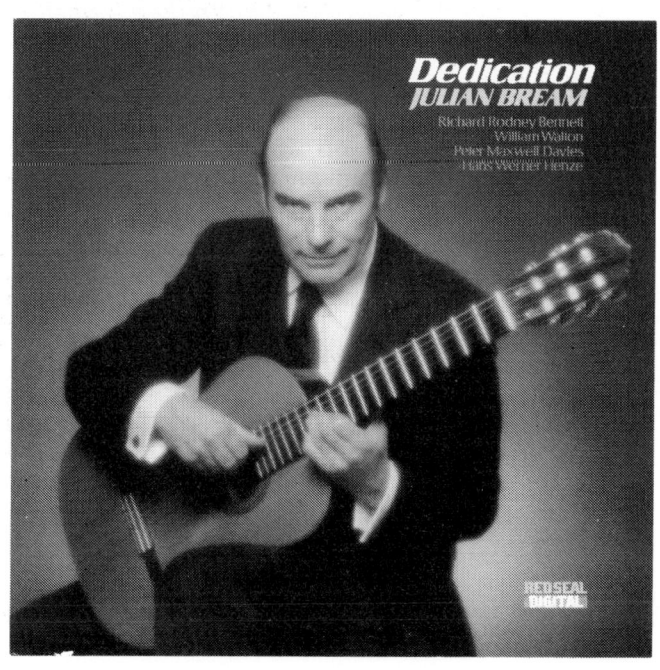

STEPHEN DODGSON

Born –

London, England

17 March 1924

Stephen Dodgson

PHOTO: COLIN COOPER

Stephen Dodgson studied at the Royal College of Music, which he left in 1950 after receiving a scholarship to study in Italy.

On his return to England he became active as a composer, teacher, lecturer and broadcaster, and is closely concerned with the work of the Composers' Guild of Great Britain. He has twice been the recipient of Royal Philharmonic Society prizes.

Stephen Dodgson's orchestral works include concertos for harpsichord, viola da gamba, viola, piano, cello and bassoon. He has written a large amount of chamber music, and his compositions for guitar include a trio with flute and cello, two concertos, a set of songs, four partitas and several other solo pieces.

SELECTED MUSIC

Fantasy-Divisions.	Bèrben
Legend for Guitar.	G 123
Partita No.1 for Guitar.	Oxford
Partita No.2 for Guitar.	Oxford
Partita No.3 for Guitar.	Bèrben
Merlin.	Moeck
Follow the Star (3 guitars).	B
Duo Concertante (guitar & harpsichord).	ESC
Capriccio (flute & guitar). Schott	
Sonata for Three (guitar, flute, viola).	Orphée

SELECTED RECORDINGS

Guitar Concerto No.1 – Williams.	CBS 61841 LP
Duo Concertante – Williams & Puyana.	CBS 61841 LP
Partita No.1 – Williams.	CBS 61841 LP
Fantasy-Divisions – Williams.	CBS 73205 LP
Four Poems of John Clare – Brown, Willliams.	
	CBS 61126 LP

SELECTED READING

Interview.	Guitar, March 1973
Stephen Dodgson at Prussia Cove.	
	Classical Guitar, November 1985
Stephen Dodgson at Dartington.	
	Classical Guitar, December 1985
The Guitar Works of Stephen Dodgson – Culf. 6 parts	
	Classical Guitar, 1990
Interview.	Soundboard, Winter 1991

304

MANUEL DE FALLA

Born – Cadiz, Spain, 23 November 1876

Died – Alta Gracia, Argentina
14 November 1946

Manuel de Falla

SELECTED MUSIC
Homenaje pour le Tombeau de Claude Debussy,
ed. Llobet, rev. Duarte.   JWC
Omaggio por le Tombeau de Debussy, ed. Llobet.
    Ric 129390
Miller's Dance and Dance of the Corregidor, ed. Behrend.
    JWC
Récit du Pêcheur and Chanson du Feu Follet,
from El Amor Brujo tr. Pujol.   JWC

SELECTED RECORDINGS
El Amor Brujo – Finnish Guitar Trio.   Chorus CH 8703 LP
El Amor Brujo – Los Angeles Guitar Quartet.
    GHA CD 126.001
Ritual Fire Dance – Hill/Wiltschinsky.   Teldec CD 8.44140
Manuel de Falla – Ernesto Bitetti.   Hispavox S60-20 LP
Homenaje/Debussy – Manuel Barrueco. EMI CDC 7 49228 2
El Sombrero de Tres Picos: Night, Miller's Dance, Dance of
the Miller's Wife – Manuel Barrueco.   EMI CDC 7 49228 2
Suite Populaire Espagnole – Kraft/Hornoy.   MMG 1144 CD
Seven Spanish Popular Songs – Christianson/Friebo.
    Danica DLP 8102

SELECTED READING
Manuel de Falla.   Guitarra, May 1979
Manuel de Falla.   Guitar Review No.41, 1976
Manuel de Falla: On Music and Musicians.   Boyars, 1979
Manuel de Falla – Ronald Crichton.   Chester, 1976
Article.   Guitar Review, Winter 1976
Manuel de Falla – Burnett James.   Gollancz, 1981
Falla's 'Homenaje' revisited – Duarte.   Guitar, August 1984
El Cante Jondo – Falla, tr. Martinez.
    Classical Guitar, November 1987

Manuel de Falla was a pupil of Felipe Pedrell, regarded as the founder of the Modern National Spanish school. Although he wrote only one piece for the guitar, Homenaje pour le Tombeau de Claude Debussy, several other of his compositions have been successfully transcribed for the guitar and have become part of the instrument's standard repertoire.

Falla's opera La Vida Breve won the prize for the best national opera. For eight years Falla lived in Paris, where he counted Debussy, Ravel and Dukas among his friends. Falla was a keen student of native folk song, and many of his compositions had a distinct Andalusian flavour. He arranged several festivals in Spain in order to maintain the cultivation of native folk song.

In 1939, horrified by the events of the Spanish Civil War and also suffering from ill health, Falla settled in Argentina, where he died in 1946 at the age of seventy.

ALBERTO GINASTERA

Born – Buenos Aires, Argentina, 11 April 1916

Died – Geneva, Switzerland

25 June 1983

Alberto Ginastera

Alberto Ginastera began his music studies in Buenos Aires, where he remained until 1930. He continued his studies in the USA, returning to Argentina to found a music conservatory in La Plata. A Guggenheim fellowship allowed him to travel to the USA in 1946-47. On his return to Argentina, he was appointed to a teaching post at the National Conservatory in Buenos Aires. He also served as dean of the faculty of arts and sciences at the Argentine Catholic University. From 1969 until his death in 1983, he lived mainly in Geneva, Switzerland.

Ginastera's contribution to the guitar's repertoire is limited to one composition, Sonata para guitarra Opus 47. It was commissioned by Robert Bialek, president of the Discount and Record and Book Shop in Washington, D.C. to celebrate the company's 25th year in business. Its first performance was given in that city by Carlos Barbosa-Lima on 27 November 1976, and received wide critical acclaim. Subsequent opinion has confirmed its reputation as one of the finest works written for the guitar in the twentieth century. It was first recorded by Maria Isabel Siewers on Guitar Masters Records.

SELECTED RECORDINGS
Music of Argentina – Maria Isabel Siewers: Sonata Op. 47
    Guitar Masters GMR 1003 LP
Timo Korhonen: Sonata op.47.   Ondine CD ODE 730-2 LP
Alexander-Sergei Ramirez: Sonata Op. 47.
    Demon CO-78975 CD
Carlos Barbosa-Lima: Sonata Op. 47.   Concord CCD-42015

SELECTED MUSIC
Sonata para guitarra Op.47.   Boosey & Hawkes

SELECTED READING
Alberto Ginastera.   Guitar Review, Spring 1985
Remembering Alberto Ginastera.   Guitar Review, Fall 1991

RADAMÉS GNATTALI

Born – Rio de Janeiro, Brazil, 27 January 1906

Died – Rio de Janeiro

3 February 1988

Radamés Gnattali

Radamés Gnattali, a virtuoso pianist in his youth, became one of Brazil's leading composers, well known for his synthesis of Brazilian popular music, jazz and twentieth century classical composition. He wrote many fine works for the guitar which, although played for many years by Laurindo Almeida and more recently by the Assad Brothers, are only now beginning to gain full recognition.

A popular figure in Brazil, Gnattali was for many years the conductor, composer and arranger for the National Radio Orchestra in Rio. His enormous contribution to modern Brazilian music laid the foundation of Brazilian popular music, including the bossa-nova style, from the 1930s to the 1950s.

SELECTED RECORDING
Rafael Rabello plays Radamés Gnattali.   Visom LPVO-006

SELECTED MUSIC
10 Studies for Guitar.   Chanterelle
3 Concert Studies for Guitar.   Chanterelle
Brasiliana No.13.   Eschig
Pequena Suite.   Eschig

SELECTED READING
Radames Gnattalli.   Classical Guitar, October 1990

CARLOS GUASTAVINO

Born –

Santa Fé, Argentina

5 May 1912

Carlos Guastavino

Carlos Guastavino began his working career as an engineer. His musical talent was quickly recognied, and he entered the Conservatorio Nacional de Musica y Arte Escenico in Buenos Aires, where he studied under Athos Palma. This he did on a scholarship from the government of the Province of Santa Fé. Guastavino soon established himself as one of Argentina's finest composers and pianists, but became best known for his solo songs and song cycles. At the end of the Second World War he went to London to study with the help of a grant from the British Council.

Although he has concentrated on vocal music, Guastavino has written several important works for the guitar, which have in recent times gained popularity.

SELECTED MUSIC
Bailecito.	BA 12611
Cantilena No.1.	BA 10893
Cantilena No.4.	BA 11733
La Tempranera (Baez).	LAG 203706
Sonata No.1 (Lara).	BA 12647
Sonata No.2 (Lara).	BA 12763
Sonata No.3 Ceballos).	BA 13020
Tres Cantilenas Argentinas (Lara).	BA 12532
Las Presencias No.6 Jeromita Linares' (string quartet).	BA 12512

SELECTED RECORDINGS
Music of Argentina:Sonata No.2 – Siewers.
  Guitar Masters GMR 1003 LP
La Rosa y el Sauce; Viniendo de Chilecito; En los Surcos del Amor – Lendle & Casares. TGF 20-8504 LP
Guastavino Guitar Works – Siewers. ASV CD DCA-933

HANS WERNE HENZE

Born –

Gütersloh, Germany

1 July 1926

Hans Werner Henze

Hans Werner Henze began to compose at the age of twelve before he actually received any formal music education. Over the years he has established himself as one of the world's foremost avant-garde composers. His chamber vocal works Kammermusik 1958 and El Cimarrón (1969) contain sections for solo guitar. In 1974 he composed Carillon, Recitatif and Masque for harp, guitar and mandolin. Henze's further interest in the guitar was stimulated by Julian Bream's request for a new major work for the instrument. The collaboration with Bream resulted in the First Sonata on Shakespearian Characters, Royal Winter Music, completed in 1976. The Second Sonata on the same theme was completed in 1979. His guitar concerto, An Eine Aeolsharfe, was first performed in 1987 by David Tanenbaum.

SELECTED MUSIC
Drei Tentos.	Schott
Memorias de El Cimarrón.	Schott
Royal Winter Music – First Sonata arr. Bream.	Schott
Royal Winter Music – Second Sonata arr. Evers.	Schott

SELECTED RECORDINGS
Dedication – Julian Bream.	RCA RL25419 LP
Royal Winter Music – Leif Christensen.	Paula 25 LP
Reinbert Evers.	EMI Electrola CD MD G1110
David Tanenbaum.	Audiofon CD 72029
Drei Tentos – Stefano Grondona.	Dynamic CDS 59
El Cimarron (2 CDs).	Schwann CD 314 032

SELECTED READING
Interview. Guitar, November 1982

ANTONIO JOSÉ

Born Antonio José Martinez Palacios

Burgos, Spain 12 December 1902

Died - Estepar, near Burgos, Spain 11 October 1936

Antonio Jose

Antonio José began his music studies in Burgos with Julian Garcia Blanco and José Maria Beobide. He moved to Madrid, where he completed his studies with Conrado del Campo and Emilio Vega. He lived in Paris in the summers of 1925 and 1926. The influence of his association with the many musicians in the French capital is heard in much of his work. José returned to Spain, where he worked as a music teacher at a Jesuit school in Málaga, and then as the conductor of the Burgos city choir.

José's musical output comprises around 150 works for various instruments. He wrote only two works for the guitar, both commissioned by his friend Regino Sainz de la Maza, *Romancillo infantil* and *Sonata*. The latter work, now regarded as one of the best 20th century works for guitar, was completed on 23 August 1933.

Antonio José included amongst his friends the poet Federico García Lorca, the painter Salvador Dali and the writer Adolfo Salazar. José's social and political associations led to his arrest and imprisonment in August 1936 by Falangist militia. They shot him two months later, prematurely ending the life of one of Spain's great contemporary composers.

SELECTED RECORDINGS

Sonata - Julian Bream	EMI Classics 5 55362 2 CD
Integrales Para Guitarra - Juan José Saenz	Tanidos SCD-812
Ponce/José - Andrea Dieci	MAP G-0024 CD
Carlos Trepat - Recital	la ma de guido MG1012G CD

SELECTED READING

Article   Seicorde   January/February 1992

SELECTED MUSIC

Sonata para guitarra   Bèrben

VACLAV KUCERA

Born –

Prague, Czechoslovakia

29 April 1929

Vaclav Kucera

Václav Kucera studied composition at the Moscow Conservatory of Music under Vissarion Shebalin. He has worked in Czechoslovakian Radio, headed the Cabinet of Contemporary Musical Studies affiliated to the Union of Czechoslovak Composers, and was active at the Institute of Musical Science in the Czechoslovakian Academy of Sciences. From 1969 to 1983 he was secretary of the Union of Czech Composers and Concert Artists. Since 1972 he has taught composition at the Prague Academy of Music and Dramatic Arts, and was appointed Professor there in 1988. In recognition of his achievements, he was in 1979 awarded the state distinction 'For Outstanding Work' and, in 1986, the title of Merited Artist.

Václav Kucera's output is extensive and varied, and includes stage works, symphonies, chamber works, and vocal and electronic works. His interest in the guitar has resulted in works for violin and guitar and for flute and guitar in addition to solo pieces, of which the best-known is Diario, a cycle of pieces based on five days in the life of Che Guevara.

Kucera's compositions have won a number of prizes, including the Italian Radio Prix d'Italia (1972). He is also the author of a number of books and studies, including a monograph on Mussorgsky.

SELECTED MUSIC
Diario – Homage to Che Guevara.	Panton
Capricci for guitar & violin.	Panton
Nouvelles.	Edition Moeck
Urgestalten – Homage to Hand Arp.	Ricordi
Aquarelles for flute & guitar.	Peters
Stilistisches bungen.	Hubertus Nogatz

SELECTED RECORDING
Diario – Stein-Erik Olsen.	Samt 184 LP
Diario – Vladimir Vectomov.	Panton 01/11 0415 LP

FRANK MARTIN

Born – Geneva, Switzerland, 15 September 1890

Died – Naarden, Holland

21 November 1974

Frank Martin

Frank Martin became interested in music at the age of twelve after hearing a performance St Matthew's Passion. After classical studies in Geneva, Zürich and Paris, he performed professionally on both piano and harpsichord. He taught at the Institut Jaques-Dalcroze. Later he became president of the Association of Swiss Musicians. His compositional style went through three distinct changes: from French Impressionism to a more Germanic contrapuntal style, then to the use of twelve-tone procedures. His best-known work is the oratorio In Terra Pax, written to celebrate the end of the Second World War.

In 1946 Martin moved to Holland and taught composition at the Cologne Hochschule für Musik in Germany. Over the years he was very prolific, composing many instrumental and vocal works. His most important work for the guitar, Quatres Pièces Brèves, was composed in 1933 and is one of the earliest guitar works to be written in a truly twentieth century style. Its importance as one of the finest twentieth-century repertoire pieces for the guitar is only now becoming fully recognized.

SELECTED MUSIC
Quatres Pièces Brèves ed. Scheit.	Universal Edition
Quant N'ont Assez Fait Dodo.	G + L 147

SELECTED RECORDINGS
20th Century Guitar – Julian Bream. CA Victor SB-6723 LP
Prestige de la Guitare au XX Siècle – Alberto Ponce.
Arion ARN 30 S 150 LP

SELECTED READING
Article.	Soundboard, Summer and Fall 1993

FRANCISCO MIGNONE

Born - São Paulo, Brazil 3 September 1897

Died - Rio de Janeiro, Brazil

February 1986

SELECTED RECORDING
Twelve Guitar Etudes - Carlos Barbosa-Lima   Philips (Brazil) 6598-312LP

SELECTED MUSIC
Modinha & Choro   Guitar Review
Twelve Etudes Two Volumes ed. Barbosa-Lima Columbia
Twelve Brazilian Waltzes   ed. Barbosa-Lima Columbia
Seven Valsas de Esquina ed. Barbosa-Lima   GSP

SELECTED READING
Article   Guitar Review, Fall 1992

Francisco Mignone

Francisco Mignone was a virtuoso pianist and one of Brazil's great composers. He was the author of a large catalogue of works including many operas, ballets, chamber music and orchestral pieces.

Mignone first studied music with his father in São Paulo. In 1920 he moved to Milan, Italy, to continue his music studies with Ferroni. He returned to Brazil and in 1929-32 was a professor at the São Paulo Conservatory. In 1934 he was appointed to the faculty of the Escola Nacional de Musica in Rio de Janeiro. He continued to teach there until 1967.

In 1953 Mignone composed two pieces for the guitar, *Modinha* and *Choro,* and these were published in Guitar Review, issue 22 in 1958. In 1970 the composer met Carlos Barbosa-Lima at the International Guitar Seminar in Porto Alegre. The composer developed a close relationship with the guitarist and over the next few years wrote several important works for the guitar including *Twelve Etudes*, and *Twelve Brazilian Waltzes* (dedicated to Isaias Savio). In 1975 Mignone completed his guitar concerto, and the world premiere was played by Barbosa-Lima at the Kennedy Centre in Washington DC.

FEDERICO MORENO TORROBA

Born – Madrid, Spain, 3 March 1891

Died – Madrid, Spain
12 September 1982

Federico Moreno Torroba

Federico Moreno Torroba had the distinction of being the first composer to heed Andrés Segovia's request for new guitar music from prominent contemporary composers.

Moreno Torroba's first music teacher was his father, the organist José Lopez Ballesteros. His musical talent was obvious at an early age, and he entered the National Conservatory of Music where he studied extensively with Conrado del Campo, a celebrated musical pedagogue of that period.

Moreno Torroba's compositions are regarded by some critics as milestones in Spanish music in the three creative media into which he chose to direct his talents: the orchestra, the guitar and the zarzuela (the traditional form of Spanish comic opera). The National Orchestra of Madrid has successfully and repeatedly presented such symphonic works of Moreno Torroba's as Capriccio Romantico and the Cuadros Castellanos.

Federico Moreno Torroba wrote many important works for the guitar after meeting Andrés Segovia in the 1920s. They include his Piezas Caracteristicas in two volumes, Sonatina in A Major, Burgalesa in F Sharp and the Castles of Spain Suite. In 1974 Moreno Torroba wrote Dialogos for guitar and orchestra, dedicated to Andrés Segovia, and in 1976 he wrote Concerto Iberica for four guitars and orchestra, dedicated to the Romero Quartet. Moreno Torroba also wrote Concierto en Flamenco for flamenco guitar and orchestra, which was dedicated to and played by Sabicas with the Concert Orchestra of Madrid. These compositions firmly established Moreno Torroba as one of the finest composers for the guitar of the twentieth century.

SELECTED MUSIC

Aires de la Mancha.	GA 235
Alpujarrena.	BA 10840
Burgalesa	GA 113
Castles of Spain.	Cadencia
Characteristic Pieces, Book I.	GA 113
Book 2.	GA 134
Contradanza.	AMP
Five Pieces: Zapateado, Capricho, Improvisación, Sevillana, Romancillo.	GA 234
Jaranera.	UME
Jota Levantina.	AMP
Madrileñas – Suite: Tirana, Copla, Bolero.	Música del Sur
Madroños.	AMP
Mi Farruca.	BA 10841
Molinera.	AMP
Nocturno.	GA 103
Preludio.	GA 114
Punteado y Taconeo Clásico.	ESC
Romance de los Pinos, ed. Segovia.	Cadencia
Scherzando.	BA 10041
Serenata Burlesca.	GA 115
Sonatina.	BA 10042
Sonatina (New Edition), ed. Segovia.	CO 168
Suite Castellana.	GA 104
Triptico: Pintoresca, Romance, Festiva.	UME
Verbenera.	UME
Vieja Leyenda.	UME

SELECTED RECORDINGS

Concierto Iberico/Dialogos – The Romeros.
　　　　　　　　　　　　　Philips 9500 749 LP
Piezas Caracteristicas – Angel Romero.　Angel 37312 LP
Julian Bream plays Torroba/Villa Lobos.
　　　　　　　　　　　　　HMV CLP 1763 LP
Moreno Torroba – Pomponio-Zarate Duo.
　　　　　　　　　　　　　Erato STV 70549 LP
Two Concertos For Guitar – Sabicas/Tarragó.
　　　　　　　　　　　　　Erato EFM 8080 LP
Segovia Collection (Vol.2).　　　MCA 42067 CD
Moreno Torroba Guitar Works (Vol.1 and 2).
　Escarpa/Trapaga/Viloria/Blanca Opera Tres CDS 1013/14
Torroba and Abril Guitar Works – Remi Boucher.
　　　　　　　　　　　　　Anale KTA AN 2 9502 CD

SELECTED READING
Federico Moreno Torroba.　　Soundboard, Spring 1983

MARLOS NOBRE

Born -
Recife, Pernambuco, Brazil
18 February 1939

Marlos Nobre

Marlos Nobre is regarded by many musicians as Brazil's foremost living composer. He has composed several important works for guitar.

Nobre studied piano and music theory at the Pernambuco Conservatory of Music (1948-59), and composition with H.J. Koellreutter and Guarnieri (1960-62). With a scholarship from the Rockefeller Foundation he followed advanced studies at the Latin American Centre in Buenos Aires (1963-64). His teachers included Ginastera, Messiaen, Malipiero, Copland and Dallapiccola. In 1969 Nobre studied at the Berkshire Music Centre in Tanglewood with Alexander Goehr and Gunther Schuller. In the same year he studied electronic music at the Columbia-Princeton Electronic Music Centre in New York.

Over the years Nobre has won numerous prizes, including many first prizes, at important international competitions. He has served as a jurist for several international competitions, and has received many commissions to write works for leading music organisations. He was composer-in-residence at the Brahm-Haus in Baden-Baden (1980-81), at the Deutscher Akademischer Austauschdienst in Berlin (1982-83), and in New York with a Guggenheim Fellowship (1985-86). He was Visiting Professor in Composition at Yale University, USA (1992).

Marlos Nobre also remains active as a pianist and conductor, working with many of the world's finest orchestras. He is currently President of the Brazilian Academy of Music, and President of the National Music Committee of UNESCO, as well as serving on other important committees. He has received Decorations from the Brazilian and French governments for his contribution to music. Marlos Nobre has written many excellent works for the guitar which are now earning the full recognition they deserve.

SELECTED RECORDINGS
Alma Brasileira - Assad Brothers
    Elektra Nonesuch 9 79179-2 CD
Joaquim Freire   Leman Classics LC 44601 CD
Marcus Llerena   Velas 65238320 CD
Guitar Favourites Marcelo Kayath
    IMP Classics PCD 1036 PK 515
Marcelo Kayath   Hyperion A 66203
In Memoriam for Orchestra   Leman Classics LC 44100
Sergio & Odair Assad   EMI Angel 31C-063422921
Oscar Caceres   ASTURIA CD DP 87003

SELECTED READING
The Music of Marlos Nobre
    Musical Opinion, November 1990
Interview   Les Cahiers de la Guitare (3eme) 1991
Interview   Classical Guitar, November 1993
Profile   Fanfare, May/June 1994
Interview   Fanfare, September/October 1994

SELECTED MUSIC
1.o Ciclo Nordestino	Editora Vitale
Momentos 1-4	Editions Max Eschig
Momentos 5-7	Musica Nova
Homenagem a Villa-Lobos	Editions Max Eschig
Entrada e Tango	Lemoine
Reminiscencias	Lemoine
Relembrando	Musica Nova
Rememorias	Lemoine
Tres Dancas Brasileiras	Boosey & Hawkes
Sonatina	Musica Nova
Fandango-Guitar Quartet	Musica Nova
Guitar Concerto	Tonos Verlag

JANA OBROVSKA

Born – Prague, Czechoslovakia

13 September 1930

Died – Prague, 9 April 1987

SELECTED MUSIC

Due Musici.	G & L Publications
Hommage à Choral Gothique.	G & L Publications
Hommage à Bela Bartók.	Max Eschig
Präludien für Gitarre.	Supraphon
Album für Gitarre.	Supraphon
Studii di Intervalli.	Broekmans & Van Poppel
Sonata in modo antiquo.	Van Teeseling
Four Images of Japan.	Lemoine

SELECTED RECORDINGS

Obrovksa – Concerto for Two Guitars. Zelenka/Brabec.	Panton 8110 0185 LP
Miloslav Matousek.	Panton 8111 0318 LP
Pavel Steidl – Debut.	Panton 8111 0578 LP
Alice Artzt – Musical Tributes.	Hyperion A 66146 LP

Jana Obrovska

COURTESY: MILAN ZELENCA

Jana Obrovska was one of Czechoslovakia's most gifted contemporary composers. Although not a guitarist herself, she was married to Milan Zelenka and as a result knew the instrument well.

Jana Obrovska was the first woman to participate in the ORTF Concours International de Guitare composer's competition in Paris. Her composition Hommage à Bela Bartók was selected as a compulsory work for the 18th ORTF Concours. A composer of several chamber and symphonic works, her output of guitar compositions in the years immediately preceding her death was quite prolific, and several of her works have now become standard repertoire pieces. Her early death from cancer at the age of 57 robbed the guitar of one of its finest contemporary composers.

MAURICE OHANA

Born – Casablanca, Morocco

12 June 1914

Died – Paris, France, 13 November 1992

Maurice Ohana

Maurice Ohana was born in Morocco. His parents were a Gibraltarian Sephardic family. He left Gibraltar for Bayonne, France, as a youth, and it was here he was educated. He went on to study architecture at the Sorbonne in Paris. At the same time he pursued his musical studies with Daniel Lesur, Alfredo Casella and the pianist Lazare-Levy. Ohana also studied in Barcelona with the distinguished pianist Frank Marshall. He in fact began his musical career as a pianist before turning his attention to composing.

In 1947 Ohana started a group called 'Zodiaque' in reaction to the serial intellectualism and academic neo-classicism movements in music. He coloured his compositions with the traditions of Andalusia, and at the same time took inspiration from North African and medieval music. These influences led to a most distinctive compositional style.

In 1950 he wrote his concerto for guitar, Trois Graphiques. This work, and subsequent compositions for the guitar, established Ohana as one of the few important twentieth-century composers who have taken a major interest in the instrument.

SELECTED MUSIC
Trois Graphiques (1950). Billaudot
Tiento (1955). Billaudot
Si Le Jour Paraît (1963). Billaudot

SELECTED RECORDINGS
Ohana: Works for Guitar – Alberto Ponce.
    Arion ARN 38240 LP
Ohana: Guitar Concerto – Narciso Yepes.
    Deutsche Grammophon DG2530 585 LP
Music of Spain – Julian Bream. RCA RL 45548 LP
Ohana: Complete Guitar Works – Stephen Schmidt.
    Astree Auvidis E8513 CD

GOFFREDO PETRASSI

Born –

Zagarolo, Italy

16 July 1904

Goffredo Petrassi

In his youth Goffredo Petrassi worked as an assistant in a music shop and studied music in his spare time, later having regular lessons in composition with Vincenzo di Donato and Alessandro Bustini. His early compositions were influenced by the work of the neo-classicist Alfredo Casella, but his later work, of which Nunc for solo guitar (written in 1971) is an example, reflects his interest in twelve-tone music.

SELECTED MUSIC
Nunc. SZ

SELECTED RECORDING
Nunc – Stefano Grondona. Dynamic CDS 59

SELECTED READING
Interview. Soundboard, May 1981

ASTOR PIAZZOLLA

Born – Mar del Plata, Argentina, 11 March 1921

Died – Buenos Aires, Argentina, 5 July 1992

Astor Piazzolla

SELECTED MUSIC
Five Pieces, ed. Aussel.	Editions Lemoine
Histoire du Tango.	Editions Lemoine
Adios Nonino, arr. Carlevaro.	GSP
Four Pieces, arr. Benitez.	Chanterelle ECH 725

SELECTED RECORDINGS
Baltazar Benitez plays Astor Piazzolla.
　Canal Grande CG 9322 CD
Roberto Aussel plays Piazzolla, Brouwer etc.
　Mandala Man 4827 CD
The Assad Brothers play Piazzolla, Gnatalli & Rodrigo.
　GHA 126-021 CD
Concerto for Bandoneon & Guitar, Histoire du Tango.
　Carrere CA 681.325 LP
Tango Futur – Astor Piazzolla Orchestra.
　RCA NL 70-142(2) LP
Recital – Krzysztof Pelech.　　Kos CD 11
Adios Nonino.　EMI Classics 5-44007-2 CD
Tango: An Anthology – Balthazar Benitez.
　Channel Crossings CCS 5393 CD
David Tanenbaum plays Astor Piazzolla.
　New Albion NA065 CD

SELECTED READING
Roberto Aussel & Astor Piazzolla.	Classical Guitar, March/April 1984
Ginastera & Piazzolla.	Classical Guitar, November & December 1985
Astor Piazzolla.	Classical Guitar, April 1992
Piazzolla Guitar Works.	Guitar Review, Spring 1995

Astor Piazzolla first studied the piano and then composition with Nadia Boulanger. He showed an exceptional talent on the bandoneon, a type of concertina, and also as a composer of music based on traditional tango rhythms. He was encouraged by his musical contemporaries, Boulanger in particular, to explore and develop his unique talent in this field of music. Today he is regarded by many as one of the most important composers of popular Argentinian music in recent times.

Piazzolla wrote works for quintet, octet, chamber orchestra, celesta, solo bandoneon and also several film scores. It was after hearing his fellow countryman Roberto Aussel play William Walton's Five Bagatelles that he decided in 1980 to write five original pieces for guitar. These were recorded by Aussel in 1982. After that time he wrote several more important works for guitar, including Tango Suite for the Assad Duo. Some of his more popular tangos have been transcribed for guitar by Baltazar Benitez and others.

Popularly known as the 'King of the Tango', Astor Piazzolla gave the familiar tango style new rhythmic and harmonic qualities which adapted very well to the classical guitar.

MANUEL PONCE

Born – Fresnillo, Mexico

8 December 1886

Died – Mexico City, 24 April 1948

Manuel Ponce

Manuel Ponce began composing at the age of seven and by the time he was twelve years old was playing a cathedral organ. After studying at the National Conservatoire of Music in Mexico City, he went to Italy and Germany in 1904 to study the piano and composition. On his return to Mexico in 1908 he was appointed professor at the Conservatory of Music. For a few years he had made a special study of the folk music of Mexico, and by 1912 the influence of this music was seen in some of his compositions. In 1925, he returned to Europe and lived in Paris, where he studied composition and orchestration with Paul Dukas. It was during his stay in Paris that he met Andrés Segovia, and his lifelong association with this great guitarist was to be the determining factor for most of his guitar compositions.

In 1931 the Mexican Government arranged for Ponce to make a tour of several South American Republics by aeroplane. It was during this tour that he conducted the first performance of his Concierto del Sur for guitar and small orchestra, on 4 October 1941 in Montevideo, Uruguay, with Segovia as the soloist.

In 1936-37, Manuel Ponce founded and edited the journal 'Cultura Musical' in Mexico City. His impressive guitar works laid the foundation and set standards for future Latin American composers.

SELECTED MUSIC

Mazurka, arr. Almeida.	No 93
Preludes 1-6.	GA 124
Preludes 7-12.	GA 125
Preludio.	GA 112
Scherzino Mexicano.	Southern
Six Short Preludes.	Southern
Sonata Clásica.	GA 122
Sonata Mexicana (Sonata No.1), ed. López Ramos.	Southern
Sonata Romántica.	GA 123
Sonata III.	GA 110
Sonatina Meridional.	GA 151
Suite: Preambule, Courante, Sarabande, Gavotte I and II, Gigue.	Southern
Thème, Varié et Finale.	GA 109
Three Popular Mexican Songs.	GA 111
24 Preludes for Guitar, ed. Alcázar from the original manuscripts.	Tecla
Two Pieces: Scherzino Mexicano, Giga Melancólica, ed. Papas.	CO 199
Valse.	GA 153
Variations on Folia de España, and Fugue.	GA 135

SELECTED RECORDINGS

John Williams plays Manuel Ponce.	CBS 76730 LP
Concierto del Sur – John Williams.	CBS 73060 LP
24 Preludes, Variations and Fugue on 'Las Folias de España' – Galbraith.	Watercourse WCRCD1
Ponce Sonatas – Andrés Segovia.	MCA 42072 CD
Horst Klee plays Manuel Ponce.	Koch Swann 310177 CD
Manuel Ponce – Jukka Savijoki and Diego Blanco.	BIS CD 255
Manuel Ponce – Susanne Mebes.	Leman LC 42701 CD
Recital. Joaquim Freire.	Leman LC 42601 CD
Ponce Sonatina Meridional – Timo Korhonen.	Ondine ODE 770 CD

SELECTED READING

Manuel Ponce – A Tribute.	Guitar Review No.7, 1948
Manuel Ponce – Corazón Otero.	Bold Strummer, 1995
The Segovia-Ponce Letters.	Editions Orphée, 1989
Manuel Ponce and the Mystery of the Cabezon Variations – J. Alberto Ubach.	Soundboard, Spring 1991
Harmonic Practice in the Guitar Music of Manuel M. Ponce – David J. Nystel.	Guitar Review, Spring 1991

Historic photograph of (left to right): Andrés Segovia, Daniel Fortea, Miguel Llobet and Emilio Pujol, c.1918.

Historic photograph of two of the greatest twentieth century composers for the guitar. Heitor Villa-Lobos (left) and Mario Castelnuevo-Tedesco with their wives, c.1947.

Joaquín Rodrigo

JOAQUIN RODRIGO

Born –

Sagunto, Province of Valencia, Spain

22 November 1902

Joaquín Rodrigo, though blind from early childhood, studied music in Valencia and later went to Paris, as had other famous Spanish musicians including Albéniz, Falla and Turina. In 1927 he entered the Ecole Normale de Musique as a pupil of Paul Dukas. At that time Dukas occupied, as a teacher and composer, a leading position among musicians in Paris, and together with Manuel de Falla and the Spanish pianist Ricardo Vines he exerted a lasting influence on the young composer.

Rodrigo continued to study with Dukas until 1932. In the next four years he travelled extensively, principally in Switzerland, Germany and Austria. On the outbreak of the Spanish Civil War in 1936, he returned permanently to live in his home land. He eventually took up residence in Madrid, and it was there in 1938 that he met the guitarist Regino Sainz de la Maza and the Marqués de Bolarque, a patron of a music. The outcome was his Concierto de Aranjuez, performed for the first time on 9 November 1940 in Barcelona by Regino Sainz de la Maza. The concerto, which was dedicated to Regino Sainz de la Maza, brought Rodrigo immediate world-wide fame, and over the years has become one of the most popular pieces of classical music.

Joaquín Rodrigo continued his association with other guitarists, and was to write some of the most beautiful guitar music of all time. In 1954 he composed another concerto, Fantasía para un Gentilhombre which he dedicated to Andrés Segovia. After this, an association with the Romero family, whom he knew in Madrid before they left for the United States, encouraged him to write in 1967 the Concierto Andaluz for four guitars, in 1968 the Concierto Madrigal for two guitars, and in 1971 Elogio de la Guitarra, which he dedicated to Angel Romero. In 1982 he was commissioned by William and Carol McKay of Fort Worth, Texas, to write a guitar concerto for the social debut of their daughters Alden and Lauri. The result was Concierto para una Fiesta, first performed on 9 March 1983 by Pepe Romero and the Fort Worth Chamber Orchestra conducted by John Giordani.

SELECTED MUSIC

Bajando de la Meseta	Ediciones Rodrigo
Concierto de Aranjuez (Guitar part only).	AP 425
Concierto de Aranjuez (Piano reduction): Score.	AP 424
Elogio de la Guitarra, ed. Gilardino.	Bèrben
Four Easy Pieces from the Album of Cecilia.	UME 19440
Invocation et Danse.	Ediciones Rodrigo
Junto al Generalife, ed. Behrend.	Bote & Bock
Pajaros de Primavera.	Ediciones Rodrigo
En Los Trigales, Entre Olivares.	Ediciones Rodrigo
Sarabande Lointaine.	ESC
Sonata à la Española.	Ediciones Rodrigo
Sonata Giocosa.	Chester
Three Little Pieces.	Ediciones Rodrigo
Three Spanish Pieces: Fandango, Passacaglia, Zapateado.	Schott GA 212
Two Preludes for Guitar.	Ediciones Rodrigo
Rodrigo Music Collection – 19 Pieces.	Schott

SELECTED RECORDINGS

Concierto de Aranjuez, Fantasía para un Gentilhombre – Regino Sainz de la Maza.	RCA VICS 1322 LP
Concierto de Aranjuez, Fantasía para un Gentilhombre – John Williams.	COL 48168 CD
Concierto de Aranjuez, Fantasía para un Gentilhombre – Alexandre Lagoya.	Philips 6500 454 LP
Concierto de Aranjuez, Fantasía para un Gentilhombre – Eduardo Fernández.	Decca 417 199-1 LP
Concierto de Aranjuez – Narciso Yepes.	Decca SPA 233 LP
Conciertos Andaluz and Aranjuez – The Romeros.	Philips SAL 3677 LP
Concierto Madrigal – Angel and Pepe Romero.	Philips 6500 918 LP
Fantasía para un Gentilhombre – Angel Romero.	EMI SD 3415 LP
Concierto para una Fiesta – Pepe Romero.	Philips 11133 CD
Elogio de la Guitarra – Angel Romero.	Angel S 37312 LP
Rodrigo: solo works – Pepe Romero.	Philips 9500-915 LP
Music of Spain Vols. 7 & 8 – Julian Bream.	RCA RI 45548 LP
The Rodrigo Edition (4 CDs).	EMI CS2 7 67435 2 CD
Rodrigo Solo Guitar Works (Vol.1) – Scott Tennant.	GHA 126-026 CD
Shadows and Lights: Joaquín Rodrigo at 90/Concierto de Aranjuez – Pepe Romero.	Video-Philips 070-163-3

SELECTED READING

Joaquín Rodrigo – Federico Sopeña.	Ministry of Education and Science, Madrid 1973
Joaquín Rodrigo: Su vida y su obra – Vicente Vayá Pla.	Real Music, Madrid 1977
Joaquín Rodrigo: Concierto de Aranjuez – Graham Wade.	Mayflower Study Guides, Leeds 1985
Rodrigo, Conciero de Aranjuez and Fantasía para un gentil hombre – Great composers and their music; No. 51.	Marshall Cavendish, London 1985
The Birthplace of Joaquin Rodrigo – Graham Wade.	Classical Guitar, January 1985
Interview.	Classical Guitar, October 1992
Joaquin Rodrigo, 90 Aniversario.	SGA de Espana, Madrid 1992
Hand in Hand with Joaquin Rodrigo. Victoria Kamhi Rodrigo.	LALR Press, Pittsburgh 1992
Joaquin Rodrigo, Catalogo general de obras – Raymond Calcraft.	Ediciones Rodrigo, Madrid 1996
Article.	Classic CD, August 1996
Rodrigo Solo Guitar Works – Graham Wade.	GRM Publications, Leeds 1996

Joaquín Rodrigo's Coat of Arms which was obtained as a result of the title of 'Marqués de los Jardines de Aranjuez' conferred by the King Juan Carlos of Spain to the composer. It is made up of the guitar, solo instrument of the 'Concierto de Aranjuez', above waves of water reflecting Rodrigo's favourite memories of nature, surrounded by the typical Spanish flowers found in the garden of the Palace of Aranjuez, red carnations and roses.

ANTONIO RUIZ-PIPÓ

Born -
Granada, Spain
7 April 1934

Antonio Ruiz-Pipó

Antonio Ruiz-Pipó's father was murdered by the Falangists in 1936. His family moved to Barcelona in 1939. He first studied music whilst at boarding school in Barcelona. There he learned singing and also played the piano. He also studied the guitar for a while but now does not play it. He went on to university, where he studied Gregorian chant, piano, organ, harmony and chamber music. He studied piano with Alicia de Larrocha for four years, and composition with the Catalan composer Manuel Blancafort. During this time he had the opportunity to meet Heitor Villa-Lobos. Ruiz-Pipó became a member of the prestigious 'Manuel de Falla' Composers' Circle of Barcelona.

In 1951 Ruiz-Pipó was awarded a scholarship by the French government to study in Paris at the Ecole Normale de Musique. There he continued his piano studies with Marc Bascouret and Alfred Cortot, composition with Maurice Ohana, and orchestration with Salvador Bacarisse. He won several important composition prizes. As a pianist Antonio Ruiz-Pipó has played with many leading orchestras all over the world. His recordings of all Bizet's piano music won him 'The Bizet Medal'.

Antonio Ruiz-Pipó was first persuaded to compose for the guitar by Narciso Yepes. He came to the notice of guitarists internationally through his very popular composition 'Cancion y Danza'. He has however written many other works for the guitar, including some for two guitars, four guitars, eight guitars, and a quintet for guitar, voice and guitar, guitar and strings, and guitar with large orchestra.

Antonio Ruiz-Pipó now lives in Paris, where he is a professor at the Ecole Normale and at the Conservatoire of Music. He has won several prizes for composition, including the Premio Internacional de Composicion 'Zaragoza' in 1975, and the Premio Nacional Padre Antonio Soler. He is a distinguished member of the Smetana Society of Prague, teaches and gives master classes all over the world, and is a member of the jury for several international music competitions.

SELECTED RECORDINGS
Narciso Yepes -	Spanish Guitar Music
Deutsche Grammophon	DG 139 366 LP

SELECTED MUSIC
Canciónes y Danzas 1, 2 & 3	Ediciones Musicales Madrid
Quatre Chansons et danses	UME
Preludio y Toccata	UME
Hommage à Cabezón	Max Eschig
Hommage à Villa-Lobos for Two Guitars	Bèrben
Tiento por Tiento - Hommage a Mudarra	Bèrben
Nenia - Hommage a Falla	Bèrben
8 Preludios	Bèrben

SELECTED READING
Interview	Guitar International, January 1986
Interview	Classical Guitar, July 1991

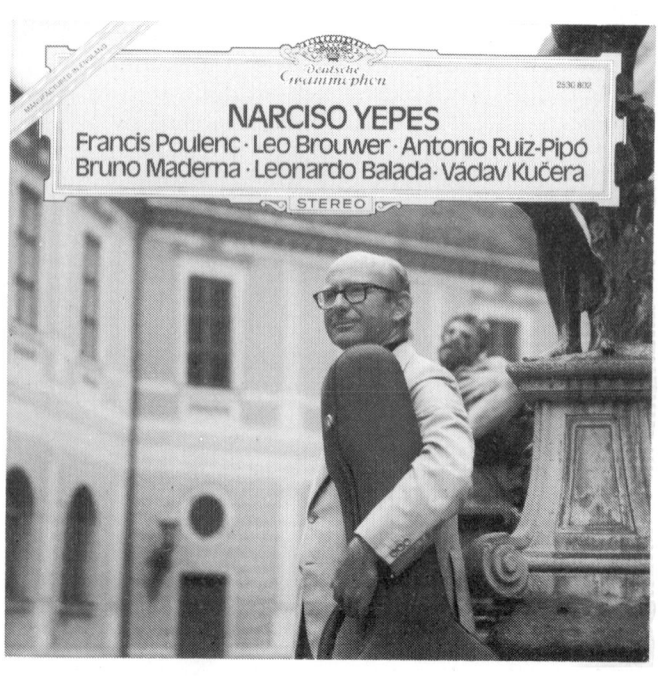

GUIDO SANTORSOLA

Born – Candosa di Puglia, Italy
18 November 1904
Died – Montevideo, Uruguay, 25 September 1994

Guido Santórsola

Guido Santórsola was taken to Brazil with his family at the age of five. There he began to study the violin, and by the time he was nine years old he was already performing in public.

He received his early music education in São Paulo, and studied composition with Agostino Cantu and Lamberto Baldi. He later went to Europe to work in Naples and at Trinity College of Music, London.

In 1931 Santórsola moved to Montevideo, Uruguay, and in 1936 he became a Uruguayan citizen. He performed extensively in string ensembles, both as a soloist with the orchestra and as a conductor. He was the director of the Escuyela Normal de Música in Montevideo. An early interest in the guitar became fully developed when a lasting friendship with Andrés Segovia was made during Segovia's stay in Montevideo during World War II.

Guido Santórsola wrote almost two dozen works for the guitar, and a text on the harmonic principles applied to the guitar. His Concerto for Two Guitars and Orchestra (1966) was dedicated to Sergio and Eduardo Abreu.

SELECTED MUSIC
Chôro No 1 and Valsa Chôro.	CO 245
Giga.	BR 3082
Preludio No 2.	BR 2795
Ringraziamento and Tempo di Minuetto.	CO 242
Sarabanda.	BR 3081
Sonata No 2, Hispanica.	Bèrben
Sonoridades 1971: Four Latin American Pieces.	Bèrben
Sonoridades 1971: Sonata No 4 (Italiana).	Bèrben
Three Airs of Court: Preludio, Aria, Finale (Giga).	CO 219
Concertino for Guitar and Orchestra (Piano reduction).	Southern

SELECTED READING
Article.	Guitar International, September 1989
Appreciation.	Classical Guitar, March 1995

TORU TAKEMITSU

Born – Tokyo, Japan
8 October 1930
Died – Tokyo, Japan, 20 February 1996

Toru Takemitsu

Toru Takemitsu was mainly a self-taught composer, although at the age of eighteen he did study with the Japanese master Kiyose. His music was often a fusion of European and Japanese elements. Using traditional Japanese instruments alongside European orchestral instruments, he had a distinctive style which earned him a reputation as Japan's finest composer in the 1980s and early 1990s.

Takemitsu's first prominent composition for the classical guitar was Folios, written in 1973. Other works for guitar include 12 Songs for Solo Guitar based on the melodies of the Beatles, Gershwin, Arlen and traditional folk songs amongst others. Toward the Sea, a duo for alto flute and guitar, was written in 1981.

Takemitsu often confirmed his admiration for the guitar, and his contribution to the instrument's repertoire is of great importance.

SELECTED MUSIC
Folios for Guitar:	Salabert
Toward the Sea:	Schott (Japan)
All in Twilight: 4 pieces ed. Bream.	Schott (Japan)
12 Songs for Guitar.	ZG
To the Edge of Dream (with orchestra).	Schott (Japan)

SELECTED READING
The Contemporary Guitar: Schneider.	Soundboard, August 1981
Appreciation.	Guitar Review, Spring 1996

SELECTED RECORDING
John Williams plays Takemitsu.	Sony SK46720 CD
Julian Bream – To the Edge of Dream.	EMI CDC 7 54661-2

ALEXANDRE TANSMAN

Born – Lodz, Poland, 12 June 1897

Died – Paris, France

15 November 1986

Alexandre Tansman with Andrés Segovia

Alexandre Tansman came to prominence following a concert of his music in Paris in 1921. It was during his stay in Paris that he met Andrés Segovia. After that time Tansman wrote a number of important works for the guitar.

Towards the end of 1926 some young Polish composers established in Paris the Young Polish Musicians Society. (Musiciens Polonais). Alexandre Tansman was named an honorary member of the Society together with Ignacy Paderewski and Karol Szymanowski In 1927 he went to the USA and appeared as a pianist with the Boston Symphony Orchestra. Following this he performed his works with many other major American orchestras, both as a piano soloist and as a conductor.

Tansman lived and travelled widely in the United States, Europe and Asia. Originally influenced by his fellow countryman Chopin, his compositions reflect the wide experience of his travels together with his own strong lyrical individuality. His works include operas, ballets, orchestral, choral and chamber music as well as concert and solo instrumental music.

In 1952 his composition Cavatina for solo guitar was a prizewinner at the International Music Competition in Siena, Italy.

SELECTED MUSIC

Cavatina.	GA 165
Danza Pomposa.	GA 206
Mazurka.	GA 116
Pezzo in Modo Antico, ed. Gilardino.	Bèrben
Suite in Modo Polonico.	ESC
Twelve Easy Pieces.	ESC
Variations on a Theme of Scriabin.	ESC

SELECTED RECORDINGS

Tansman and Mompou: Andrés Segovia.
    Brunswick AXA 4532 LP
Musique de Cour – for guitar and orchestra:
Sonja Prunnbauer.   Schwann VMS 2062E LP
Musique Française – Alexandre Tansman: Alan Prevost.
    Cybelia CY 857 CD
Tansman Guitar Music: Marc Regnier.
    Marco Polo 8-223690 CD
Recital: Krzysztof Pelech.   Kos Records Kos CD 11

JOAQUIN TURINA

Born – Seville, Spain, 9 December 1882

Died – Madrid, Spain

14 December 1949

Joaquín Turina

Joaquín Turina was one of Spain's most outstanding musicians of the twentieth century. He was not only a composer, but also a fine pianist and conductor. He greatly admired the guitar and wrote several pieces for it, which he dedicated to Andrés Segovia. The best known of these are Fandanguillo, Ráfaga, Sonatina, and Hommage à Tárrega. His best-known chamber work, La Oración del Torero was originally written for four guitars.

SELECTED MUSIC
Fandanguillo, ed. Segovia.	BA 12928 and GA 102
Hommage à Tárrega.	GA 136
Ráfaga.	GA 128
Sacro-Monte, ed. Azpiazu.	Salabert
Sevillana: Fantasia, ed. Segovia.	GA 158
Sonatina (Sonata in D).	GA 132

WILLIAM WALTON

Born – Oldham, England, 20 March 1902

Died – Ischia, Italy

8 March 1983

William Walton

William Walton was originally a chorister at Christ Church, Oxford. He was mainly self-taught as a composer. His talent was first recognized through a performance of a string quartet at an international festival in Salzburg in 1923. Walton was sometimes called the Hindemith of English music, but most authorities now agree that he is a composer in the English tradition established by Elgar.

It was not until he was sixty-nine that Walton completed his first solo work for guitar, the Five Bagatelles. He had written a song cycle for voice and guitar (Anon in Love) in 1959, but his Bagatelles, written for Julian Bream and dedicated to Malcolm Arnold on the occasion of his fiftieth birthday, are regarded as one of the finest additions to the classical guitar repertory.

SELECTED RECORDINGS
Julian Bream '70s.	RCA SB 6876 LP
Dedication: Julian Bream.	RCA RL 25419 LP
Oeuvres: Walton, Constant, Berkeley.	
	Roberto Aussel Mandala 4802 CD

SELECTED READING
Masterworks – Five Bagatelles: Carlos Bonell.	
	Guitar, June 1983
Behind the Façade: Susana Walton.	OUP 1988
Walton's Five Bagatelles: Donley.	
	Classical Guitar, June/July/August 1990

SOME OTHER PROMINENT TWENTIETH CENTURY COMPOSERS WHO ARE NOT GUITARISTS BUT WHO HAVE WRITTEN FOR THE CLASSICAL GUITAR

Amy, Gilbert (1936)
Angerer, Paul (1927)
Apostel, Hans Erich (1901-1972)
Artner, Norbert (1922-1971)
Auric, Georges (1899-1983)

Bacarisse, Salvador (1898-1963)
Bartolozzi, Bruno (1911-1980)
Baur, Jürg (1918)
Berg, Gunnar (1909-1989)
Bettinelli, Bruno (1913)
Bialas, Günther (1907)
Bolcom, William (1938)
Bolling, Claude (1930)
Bondon, Jacques (1927)
Borup-Jørgensen, Axel (1924)
Boulez, Pierre (1925)
Bresgen, Cesar (1913-1988)
Burghauser, Jarmil (1921)
Burkhard, Willy (1900-1955)
Burkhart, Franz (1902)
Bussotti, Sylvano (1931)

Cardew, Cornelius (1936-1981)
Carter, Elliott, (1908)
Chappell, Herbert (1934)
Cerf, Jacques (1932)
Corieliano, John (1929)

David, Johann Nepomuk (1895-1977)
David, Thomas Christian (1925)

Einem, Gottfried von (1918)
Erbse, Heimo (1924)

Farkas, Ferenc (1905)
Feld, Jindrich (1925)
Fheodoroff, Nikolaus (1931)
Foss, Lukas (1922)
Fricker, Peter Racine (1920-1990)

Gefors, Hans (1952)
Genzmer, Harald (1909)
Ghedini, Giorgo Federico (1892-1965)
Gowers, Patrick (1936)
Gray, Steve (1947)
Guarnieri, Camargo M. (1907)

Halffter, Cristobal (1930)
Halffter, Ernesto (1905)
Hallnas, John Hilding (1903-1984)
Harris, Albert (1916)

Hartig, Heinz Friedrich (1907-1969)
Harvey, Richard (1953)
Hasenohrl, Franz (1885-1970)
Haubenstock-Ramati, Roman (1919-1994)
Haug, Hans (1900-1967)
Humel, Gerald (1931)

Ibert, Jacques (1890-1962)

Jelinek, Hanns (1901-1969)
Jolivet, André (1905-1974)

Kagel, Mauricio (1931)
Kelterborn, Rudolf (1931)
Klebe, Giselher (1925)
Kont, Paul (1920)
Kotonski, Wlodzimierz (1925)
Kounadis, Arghyris P. (1924)
Kovats, Barna (1920)
Krenek, Ernst (1900-1991)
Kronsteiner, Joseph (1910)
Kubizek, Augustin (1918)

Lacerda, Osvaldo (1927)
Lampersberg, Gerhard (1928)
Lechthaler, Josef (1891-1948)
Linde, Hans-Martin (1930)

Maderna, Bruno (1920-1973)
Malipiero, Gian Francesco (1882-1973)
Migot, Georges (1891-1976)
Milhaud, Darius (1892-1974)
Miroglio, Frances (1924)
Mittergradnegger, Gunther (1923)
Molleda, José Muñoz
Mompou, Federico (1893-1987)
Morancon, Guy (1927)

Nielsen, Tage (1929)

Pfister, Hugo (1914-1969)
Porrino, Ennio (1910-1959)
Poulenc, Francis (1899-1963)
Previn, André (1929)

Rawsthorne, Alan (1905-1971)
Rebay, Ferdinand (1880-1971)
Reitz, Heiner (1925)
Roussel, Albert (1869-1937)
Ruders, Poul (1949)

Saxton, Robert (1953)

Schibler, Armin (1920-1986)
Schoenberg, Arnold (1874-1951)
Schwantner, Joseph (1943)
Schwertberger, Gerald (1941)
Sculthorpe, Peter (1929)
Searle, Humphrey (1915-1982)
Seiber, Mátyás (1905-1960)
Skorzeny, Fritz (1900-1965)
Sojo, Vicente Emilio (1887-1974)
Stravinsky, Igor (1882-1971)
Surinach, Carlos (1915)
Suter, Robert (1919)

Tippett, Michael (1905)

Uhl, Alfred (1909-1992)

Vlad, Roman (1919)

Webern, Anton (1883-1945)
Weiss, Harald (1949)
Westlake, Nigel (1958)
Wissmer, Pierre (1915)

Zbinden, Julien-François (1917)
Zehm, Friedrich (1923)
Zimmermann, Bernd Alois (1918-1970)

David Russell with Spanish composer Vicente Ascencio

A selection of Classical Guitar magazines. The world's foremost publication devoted to the instrument

THE CLASSICAL GUITAR
ITS MAKERS

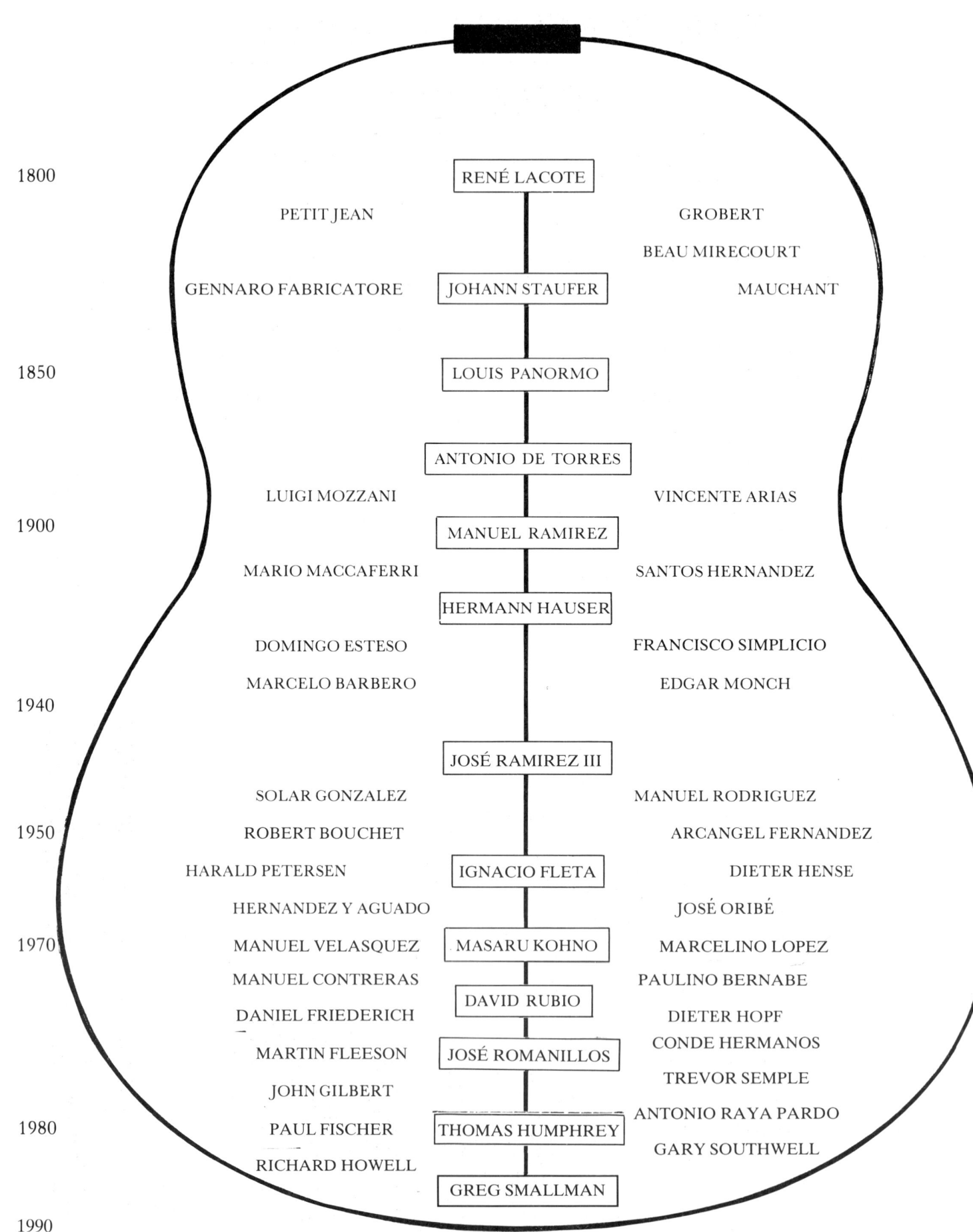

A general chart showing the finest classical guitar makers since 1800

THE CLASSICAL GUITAR SINCE 1800 ITS GUITAR MAKERS

As has already been pointed out, the evolution of the guitar since 1800 shows a parallel development and growth of the guitarist, guitar repertory and the instrument itself. Historically the luthier and the guitarist have always worked closely together to improve the sound and volume of the guitar.

In the nineteenth century Sor worked with Panormo, Carulli with Lacôte, Legnani with Staufer, Madame Sidney Pratten with Panormo, and Arcas and Tárrega with Torres. It was the joint efforts of these great guitar figures that led to the ideas that contributed to the development of the guitar as we know it today.

In the twentieth century Andrés Segovia, over the years, worked with several important guitar makers, such as the Ramírez family, Hauser and Fleta. In more recent times Julian Bream has encouraged David Rubio and José Romanillos. It was with Andrés Segovia's encouragement and advice that the luthier Albert Augustine was to develop the first nylon guitar string, a vital step forward for the classical guitarist in 1948.

This section of the book spotlights the most innovative guitar makers since 1800.

Brian Cohen, a prominent English luthier, in his workshop

STAUFER

Staufer guitar

Johann George Staufer, or Stauffer (26 January 1778 – 24 January 1853), was one of the foremost guitar makers of the nineteenth century. His workshops were in Vienna, and many important guitarists including Regondi, Mertz and Schubert used his guitars. Luigi Legnani also used Staufer's guitars, and suggested several methods of improved construction. Staufer eventually produced large quantities of a guitar bearing the label 'Legnani model'.

Johann Staufer was the inventor of the guitar with a detachable neck, and of the arpeggione. Sometimes called the 'guitare d'amour', the arpeggione (a bowed instrument) was a mixture of the guitar and cello, and first appeared in 1824. Although Schubert was quite taken with the instrument – he wrote a sonata in A minor for it – it did not achieve any further success.

Johann Staufer composed a few pieces for the guitar and was also a publisher of guitar solos.

LACOTE

Lacôte guitar

René-François Lacôte (1785-1855) was born in Mirecourt, France. He made guitars for the most famous players of his day, including Fernando Sor and Carulli.

A writer in the 'Giulianiad' magazine (1833) commented: 'The superiority of Lacôte's guitars consists in their symmetrical proportions; in the quality of the wood; in the mathematical exactness of the frets, neck and head; and in their general workmanship'. On some of his earlier labels Lacôte described himself as a pupil of M.Pone. Later labels read 'Lacôte & Cie' and gave particulars of some of the many medals and decorations that he had won at the great exhibitions.

Lacôte guitars have lute-type fingerboards with top frets let into the table of the guitar. In some, the wood is scalloped out between the frets, and later instruments often have an enclosed machine head. Fine guitars of the Lacôte type are sometimes found without labels; these were probably made by apprentices of Lacôte.

PANORMO

Louis Panormo

Panormo guitars were made by the sons and grandsons of Vincenzo Panormo, who was born at Monreale, Sicily, 30 November 1734.

Vincenzo Panormo was regarded as one of Italy's finest violin makers. He moved to England in 1777 and settled in London with his family. Three of his four sons – Joseph, Louis and George – were to become leading guitar makers.

Joseph Panormo had a workshop in Church Street, Soho. In 1809, Fernando Sor left him his Spanish-made guitar (probably a José Martinez of Málaga) to copy. The result was a blend of Spanish design and Italian craftsmanship. This guitar became the basis of later models to be made by Louis and other members of the Panormo family.

Louis Panormo had a shop at 46 High Street, Bloomsbury, and together with several members of his family developed a prosperous guitar-making business. Louis eventually emigrated to New Zealand, but the business continued under the management of his brother George and nephew George junior. In all, Panormo guitars were made in London for around 70 years. Their output was approximately seven to ten guitars per week for a good portion of this period. The Panormo family offered a selection of good quality instruments, from basic models to high-quality recital instruments. They were used by many of the top players of the day.

SELECTED READING
Louis Panormo. Guitar, June 1975
The Panormo Family of Guitar Makers. Classical Guitar, July 1985
Louis Panormo: The Final Years. Classical Guitar, June 1986

Panormo Guitar

TORRES

Antonio de Torres

Don Antonio de Torres Jurado was born in San Sebastián de Almería, Spain, on 18 June 1817. He died there on 19 November 1892. He is the man to whom we owe the modern concert guitar.

While Torres was working for the guitar maker José Pernas in Granada that he was approached by one of the foremost classical guitarists of the time, Julián Arcas. For some time Arcas had been unhappy with the sound and volume of his guitar, and put several ideas to Torres about improving the instrument.

With Torres' craftsmanship and ingenuity, the proportions of the classical guitar became enlarged from the original nineteenth century small-bodied guitar to the type of guitar we know today. After Arcas, Torres worked with Francisco Tárrega and developed an instrument which has become the basis of today's classical guitars.

Torres made guitars in two distinct periods. The first period lasted from 1850-1869. Then he retired from guitar making to open a china shop. He returned to guitar making in 1880 and continued to construct many fine instruments until his death in 1892. He never signed the labels of his guitars, and only numbered those of the second period.

SELECTED READING
Torres and the First Generation.   Guitar, October 1973
Torres.   Guitar Review No.16, 1954
Antonio de Torres: José Romanillos.
          Element Books, 1988, reprinted Bold Strummer 1996

Torres Guitar

HERNANDEZ

Santos Hernandez

Santos Hernadez was born in 1875 in Madrid. At the age of ten he began to work as an assistant in a business trading in ceremonial dress for the Catholic church. He soon moved on to become an apprentice in the workshop of the well-known guitar maker Valentin Viudes. After a short while he began to study with another prominent guitar maker of the day, Saturnino Rojas. Hernandez then had to go into the army. In 1900 he completed his military duties and set up his own Madrid workshop. Then in 1905, after being recommended by a friend, he went to work for Manuel Ramírez and was soon recognised as the best luthier in Ramírez's famous workshop. It was one of his guitars that was given as a gift in 1916 by Manuel Ramírez to the young Andrés Segovia. Although Santos Hernandez was an excellent classical guitar maker, it was as a maker of flamenco guitars that he is now best known. Many authorities regard him as the most important figure in the development of the modern flamenco guitar. After leaving Ramírez in 1921, Hernandez worked at his own Madrid workshop until his death in 1943.

SELECTED READING
Article   Classical Guitar, July 1991

HAUSER

Hermann Hauser II (right)

Joseph Hauser, in the late nineteenth century, was the first member of the Hauser family to make musical instruments. He was a talented composer and an accomplished zither player. He won many medals and presentations from the German state for his outstanding achievements in music.

It was his son Hermann Hauser (1882-1952) who extended his father's instrument-making profession. He built a vast selection of string instruments including lutes, viols, zithers, violins and guitars. The first guitars he built were similar to the small-bodied mid-nineteenth century French guitars. In the late 1920s Hermann Hauser was fortunate to have Andrés Segovia as a guest in his house. Much impressed with the workmanship of Hauser's guitars, Segovia suggested that Hauser should make a guitar of the same size as his Ramírez. Within a short period of time Hauser had built a guitar of exceptional sound and quality. Segovia was to use this guitar for many years, establishing Hauser as one of the foremost guitar makers of the twentieth century.

Since Hauser's death, his son Hermann Hauser Junior and grandson Hermann Hauser III have carried on the tradition of guitar making. Hauser guitars remain among the most sought-after in the world.

SELECTED READING
Hermann Hauser.   Guitar & Lute, May 1978.

Workshop address:
Hermann Hauser, 8386 Reisbach an der Vils, Bayern,
                                    West Germany.

RAMIREZ

Jose Ramirez III

The Ramírez guitar is one of today's most popular guitars for concert guitarists. Under the management José Ramírez IV, the Ramírez workshops in Madrid employ about seventeen luthiers with several assistants. Their large production is exported all over the world, and is in constant demand.

The Ramírez tradition dates back to the second half of the nineteenth century, when José Ramírez I set up a workshop in Madrid. As a child he had been an apprentice guitar builder to Francisco González. In his Madrid workshop José Ramírez I, now recognized as a master luthier, taught his younger brother, Manuel Ramírez, also Julian Gomez and Enrique Garcia.

It was Manuel Ramírez who gave Andrés Segovia one of their finest guitars as a gift, after hearing him play, when the guitarist was still in his teens and unknown. For many years Segovia, on his concert tours throughout the world, played only the Ramírez guitar. Since that time the name Ramírez has been synonymous with the best in classical guitars.

Over the years the Ramírez workshop has had many apprentices who in turn became great guitar makers. Included are Santos Hernández, Domingo Esteso, Marcelo Barbero, Manuel Rodriguez, Manuel Contreras and Paulino Bernabe.

The Ramírez workshops, now managed by fourth generation members of the Ramírez family, can be considered a vital part in the development of the classical guitar.

SELECTED READING

Article.	Guitar Player, April 1973
Article.	Guitar & Lute, May 1979
Article.	Frets, January 1982
Interview.	Guitar International, August 1984
How the Guitar Sounds: José Ramírez III.	
	Soneto, Madrid 1993

Workshop address:
Calle de la Paz 8, Madrid 28012, Spain.

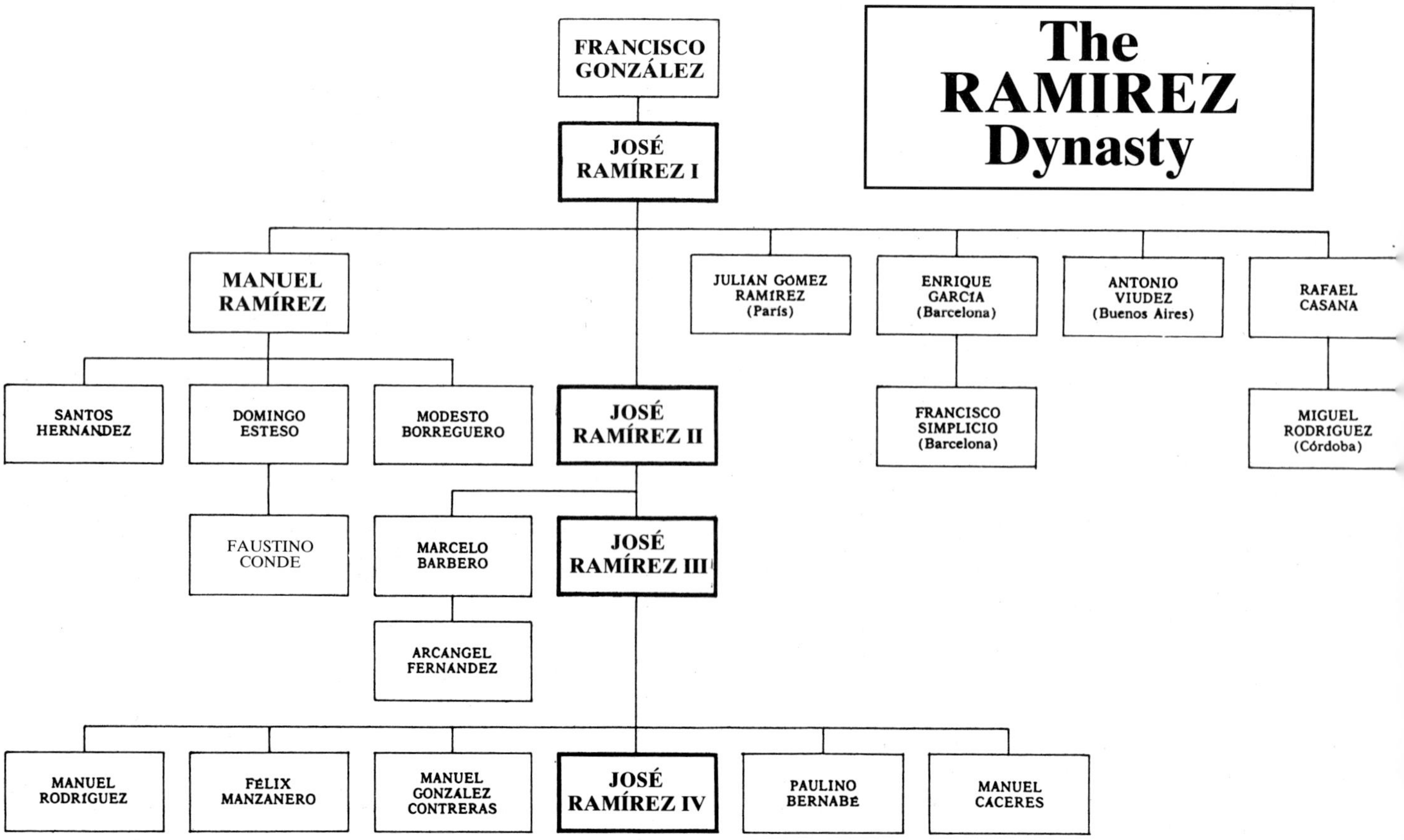

The RAMIREZ Dynasty

FLETA

Ignacio Fleta

Ignacio Fleta, regarded by many as the greatest guitar maker of the twentieth century, was born in Huesca, Spain, on 31 July 1897. He died in Barcelona on 11 August 1977. Ignacio Fleta's father was a joiner, and it was from him that Fleta learned many aspects of the craft. As a youth, he was fascinated by music, and at the age of eight he was able to play the bandurria and the guitar. At the age of thirteen he went to Barcelona and learned the basics of guitar construction from a French Luthier. He worked in the luthier's workshop with his two brothers, and studied violin, cello and bass-viol making as well.

In 1927 Ignacio Fleta opened his own workshop in Barcelona. The first instruments he made were cellos, but soon he was making guitars and violins as well. From 1939 to 1945 he reproduced a collection of old instruments for the musical society 'Ars Musica'. The collection included the Gothic harp, fiddle, lute, vihuela, and other instruments right through to the modern guitar. The brilliance of his construction brought Fleta world-wide fame.

In 1955 Ignacio Fleta heard Andrés Segovia for the first time. He was so impressed that he decided from that moment on that he would build only guitars. In 1957 he built the first of three guitars which Segovia would play in his recitals all over the world. Since that time over 700 guitars have been made in the Fleta workshop, many of them owned by today's foremost guitarists.

Since Ignacio Fleta's death in 1977, his two sons, Francisco (born 22 July 1925) and Gabriel (born 21 December 1929), have carried on the business with equal success.

Workshop address:
Calle de los Angeles 4, Barcelona, Spain.

Fleta guitar

BOUCHET

Robert Bouchet

Robert Bouchet was born on 10 April 1898, and died in 1986. He was trained as a painter in Paris, the city of his birth. Although he played the guitar from 1932, it was not until 1946 that he made his first guitar. After losing his own guitar, he decided to try and make one himself. On his regular visits to the workshop of a friend, a Spanish luthier by the name of Ramírez, Bouchet had observed all the various stages of guitar making. He had always been good at making things, and found that he had no problem in constructing a guitar. Friends were so impressed with his first instrument that Bouchet soon received orders for more. His output was not large, but his reputation grew quickly and many top players came to buy a guitar from him. Included were Ida Presti, Alexandre Lagoya, Emilio Pujol, Oscar Ghiglia, Turibio Santos, Manuel López Ramos and Julian Bream.

After he reached the age of eighty, Robert Bouchet made guitars only rarely. He lived in the countryside on the outskirts of Paris, where he died on 15 August 1986.

SELECTED READING
Robert Bouchet. Guitar, February 1973
Appreciation. Guitar International, November 1986

MASARU KOHNO

Masaru Kohno

Masaru Kohno was born in Mito City, Japan, on 15 August 1926. He graduated from the Tokyo College of Arts and Crafts in 1948, majoring in woodcraft. It was then that he became interested in guitar making, which led him to Spain in 1960. There he spent six months in the Madrid workshops of Arcangel Fernández. On his return to Tokyo, he established his own guitar workshop. Within a short time his exceptional talent was recognized by Japanese guitarists. In 1967, with the award of first prize for guitar making at the Liège Concours National des Guitares, his talent was recognized internationally.

Masaru Kohno has since maintained his reputation as one of the most important of contemporary guitar makers.

Workshop address:
Nishiikebukuro 5-27, Toshimaku, Tokyo, Japan.

RUBIO

David Rubio

David J. Rubio was born in London in 1934. He originally decided to become a doctor, but before he qualified he had already decided that this was not the career for him. He went to Spain to study flamenco guitar, feeling that he would like to be a professional player of the intrument. He settled in Madrid, spending his days practising in the guitar workshop of Sabrinos de Esteso. It was there that he developed an interest in guitar making, and during his three-year stay in Madrid he was able to serve a full apprenticeship as a guitar maker.

In 1961 Rubio moved to New York City and continued to study guitar construction with a maker by the name of Amedeo. In 1963 Amedeo died and Rubio set up his own workshop. He began to build guitars and lutes of exceptional quality, and soon his reputation was such that leading guitarists, including Julian Bream, became his customers.

In 1967 Rubio returned to England and set himself up in Duns Tew, Oxford, as a builder of guitars and lutes. He also began to construct stringed instruments of the Baroque period, including viols, cellos and harpsichords. For many years he concentrated on harpsichords, leaving the construction of guitars to other members of his workshop.

Rubio has recently worked with guitarist Paul Galbraith and developed an eight-string guitar at his Cambridge workshop. Called 'The Brahms Guitar' this new instrument has an extra bass string and an extra treble string, giving the guitarist a much greater range. This extended range facilitates the transcription of works for guitar by composers like Brahms.

SELECTED READING

Article.	Guitar, October 1972
Article.	Guitar, August 1976
Article.	Guitar & Lute, January 1979
Interview.	Classical Guitar, July 1993

Workshop address:
13 St Peter's Street, Cambridge CB3 0BD.

Rubio Guitar

BERNABE

Paulino Bernabe

Paulino Bernabe was born in Madrid on 2 July 1932. At the age of seventeen he began to study the classical guitar with Daniel Fortea, a pupil of the great Tárrega. It was during the four years he spent with Fortea that he developed an interest in constructing guitars.

In 1954 the young guitarist became an apprentice guitar maker to José Ramírez. By 1969 his skills as a luthier were acknowledged with his promotion to workshop manager for the Ramírez company.

In 1970 Bernabe left Ramírez and opened his own workshop at 8 Cuchilleros Street, Madrid. The change gave him the opportunity to introduce new ideas into the construction of his guitars, and soon the Bernabe guitar became one of the most sought-after classical guitars. In 1973 he completed a 10-string guitar for Narciso Yepes, which the guitarist has used since. In 1974 Bernabe received the Gold Medal at the International Crafts Exhibition held in Munich, Germany, for his craftsmanship.

Workshop address:
Cuchilleros 8, Madrid 12, Spain.

CONTRERAS

Manuel Contreras

Born in Madrid in 1926, Manuel Contreras was originally a cabinet-maker. He joined the Ramírez company as a senior journeyman in 1959. In 1962 he left Ramírez and set up his own workshop at Calle Mayor, 80, Madrid.

Contreras then established himself as one of the finest and most innovative guitar makers in Spain. In 1979 he was awarded the Export Award from the Madrid Chamber of Commerce and Industry. A year later he was given an honourable mention by the same body. Other awards, including the Medal of the City of Salon-de-Provence and the Medal of the City of Digne-les-Bains, were to follow. In 1981 Contreras visited Japan as a guest of the Niibori Guitar Academy as a tribute to his craftmanship. In 1987 the Isla de la Francia Guitar Circle presented him with the Order of the Good Rosette in recognition of his work in improving the classical guitar's sonority.

Contreras's most famous innovations were his double-top concert guitar (1974), based on an idea of Celedonio Romero, and the Carlevaro model (1983), based on an original idea of the Uruguayan guitarist Abel Carlevaro.

Manuel Carlevaro died in Madrid, 7 July 1994. His workshop continues under the direction of his son Pablo.

SELECTED READING
Interview.　　　　　　Guitar International, December 1987
Article.　　　　　　　　　Classical Guitar, April 1995

Workshop address:
Calle Mayor 80, Madrid, Spain.

BOLIN

George Bolin

George Bolin was born on the isle of Gotland, Sweden, in 1912. The son of a farmer, his first interest in music was in playing the mandolin, and then the banjo.

He studied as a joiner in Gotland, and then, after gaining his apprentice's diploma, moved to Stockholm, where he worked for one year in the famous Carl Malmsten workshop. After two years working as a joiner Bolin returned to the Carl Malmsten school as a teacher. He remained there for twenty-seven years, for the last three of which he was headmaster. In his early years Bolin retained an interest in music by playing a banjo in a local band.

Bolin began to lose interest in the banjo and built himself a tenor mandola. A student asked him to mend a broken guitar, and soon after, in 1944, he began to construct guitars on a regular basis. His first recognition as a maker of note came when Andrés Segovia bought a guitar from him. After that many leading players purchased his guitars. Bolin was an innovator and he collaborated with Svea Hammarberg, Per-Olof Johnson and other guitarists to develop new ideas in guitar construction. His alto guitars became well known through Göran Söllscher who frequently plays them. Bolin also made octave, third, contra and bass guitars for ensemble use, as well as many fine regular six-string guitars. He also invented 'The Toneboard', an amplifier with natural acoustic sound. This system has been used to amplify the orchestral string sections in some concert halls in Stockholm.

George Bolin died 21 April 1993 in Stockholm, Sweden.

SELECTED READING
Profile	Guitar International April 1987
Profile	Gitarre & Laute 4/1993

FRIEDERICH

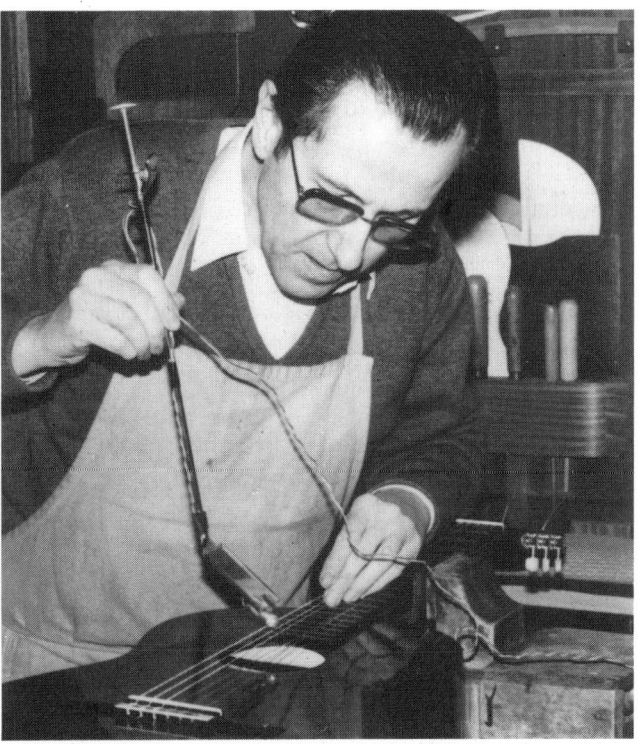
Daniel Friederich

Daniel Friederich was born in Paris, France, in 1932. His family, which originated from Luxembourg, had a long tradition of cabinet making. Friederich continued in the family tradition starting his apprenticeship as a cabinet maker at the age of thirteen and a half. By the time he was eighteen he was a fully qualified cabinet maker. In 1954, after attending a concert given by Ida Presti, he began studying the guitar. His teacher was Christian Aubin. Not being able to afford a good guitar, Friederich decided to make one. With the help of Aubin, and later Robert Bouchet, he made several guitars. He was also given great encouragement by Alexandre Lagoya and Ida Presti. In 1967 Friederich entered the Liège Guitar Making Competition. The jury included Fleta, Bouchet, Alirio Díaz and Konrad Ragossnig. He won the gold medal for the quality of his workmanship, and a silver medal for the sound of his instrument. From that time on, Daniel Friederich has had international recognition for the high quality of his classical guitars.

Friederich continues to experiment with the construction and sound quality of his much sought-after guitars. In 1977 he presented his lecture, 'The History and Function of the Guitar', at the University of Paris. Since 1982 he has been on the jury of the 'Best Craftsmen of France – Stringed Instrument Section' competition.

SELECTED READING
Interview	Guitar, April 1985

MANUEL RODRIGUEZ AND SONS

The pictures below show some of the many stages of the guitar-making process taken in the Madrid workshop of Manuel Rodriguez and Sons.

Manuel Rodriguez was born on October 7, 1926. He began to work in the Ramirez workshop in March, 1939 as an apprentice. After a break of five years to complete his school education the young luthier went back to Ramirez in 1945 and remained there until 1955. Already recognized as one of Madrid's best makers Rodriguez worked from home until 1957 when he established his own workshop in Madrid. In 1959 he decided to emigrate to the USA setting up his workshop in Los Angeles. This was to prove a successful venture and Rodriguez remained there until 1974 when he decided to return to Madrid to once again set up his workshop, with his sons Manuel Junior and Norman, in Madrid at Hortaleza 26 which is still their current Madrid address.

In recent times (1995) the Rodriguez family have built one of the world's finest classical guitar manufacturing complexes in Toledo, Spain. They expect to reach an annual production of 10,000 quality guitars by the year 2000.

SELECTED READING
Interview.   Classical Guitar, December 1994

ROMANILLOS

José Romanillos

José Luis Romanillos Vega was born in Madrid on 17 June 1932. Prior to his coming to England, his only real interest in the guitar was as a player. By profession he was a woodworker, and he became interested in the construction of guitars after he had tried to repair some guitars belonging to friends.

In 1956 he came to London. He could not afford to buy a guitar, so he decided to build one. With the help of a guitarist friend, his first guitar was completed in six months. Encouraged by the reaction of his friends to this first effort, he developed his craft by building more guitars. He returned to Spain for three years in 1964, building several more guitars during this time. On his return to England in 1967, he brought two of these guitars with him. He showed them to Carlos Bonell and Gilbert Biberian, who were both most impressed by his craftsmanship and the fine sound. With this encouragement, Romanillos decided to give up his regular job as a cabinet maker to devote his time to guitar making.

In 1970 Romanillos showed one of his new guitars to Julian Bream, who was so impressed that he helped him to set up a workshop near his home in Semley, Wiltshire. For many years the guitarist showed a great interest in the development of Romanillos's new guitars, playing them in concert and on some of his recordings. Bream also used several of the luthier's replicas of old fretted instruments in Channel 4's television series on the history of the guitar in Spain, Guitarra!

José Romanillos has established himself as one of the great twentieth century luthiers. His instruments are prized by guitarists all over the world. In recent years he has given masterclasses on guitar making in many countries. His book, an important biography of the nineteenth century guitar maker Torres, was published in 1987.

SELECTED READING
Antonio de Torres, Guitar Maker
His Life & Work (José L. Romanillos) Element Books, 1987
Interview. Guitar, December 1972
Interview. Guitar, June 1978
Interview. Guitar, December 1980
Interview. Guitar, December 1981
Interview. Classical Guitar, February, 1986
Interview. Guitar International, March 1987
Interview. Classical Guitar, January 1991

Workshop address:
Madrigal, Barker's Hill, Semley, Shaftesbury, Dorset SP7 9BJ, England.

HOPF

Dieter Hopf

Dieter Hopf was born in Zwote (Klingenthal), East Germany, on 29 May 1936. His family have been violin makers for over three hundred years. In 1949 the family moved to Taunustein/Weben, near Wiesbaden, in West Germany. Here they set up a factory to make cheap guitars, strings and recorders. Dieter Hopf attended a course in violin making at the musical instrument school in Mittenwald. He left there in 1955 and worked for his father for two years. He then went to England to gain experience as an instrument repairer at Selmer's music store in London. In 1958 the young maker returned home with the ambition to make classical guitars which would be accepted internationally as being on the same level as those of Fleta, Ramírez and Kohno.

By 1970. under the direction of Dieter Hopf, the company was well established and successful. Over the years he has achieved his ambition by producing instruments of the highest quality that are now played by many top guitarists throughout the world. His innovations include the 'La Portentosa' model, a large-bodied guitar with a long scale and rosette bridge which help to produce greater volume and clarity of sound.

SELECTED READING
Article. Guitar International, May 1984
Article. Classical Guitar, December 1995

Workshop address:
Platter Strasse 79, D-6204 Taunusstein-Wehen, Germany.

GILBERT

John M. Gilbert

John M. Gilbert (born New York, 8 December 1922) started building guitars as a hobby in 1965. At that time he was working as chief tool engineer for the Hewlett-Packard Company. For a period of nine years he perfected his craft as a luthier and guitar repairer while maintaining his engineering career. In 1974 he turned to guitar making as a full-time job.

Gilbert established himself as an innovative luthier within a relatively short period of time, and is now regarded by many as the USA's finest classical guitar maker. His distinctive guitars are used by many prominent guitarists.

Since 1956 Gilbert has been based in Woodside, California, where he has his workshop. He has now been joined by his son William, another fine guitar maker, who will help maintain the tradition of the Gilbert workshop for many years to come.

Workshop address:
1485 La Honda Road, Woodside, California 94062, USA.

FISCHER

Paul Fischer

Paul Fischer was born in the Isle of Man, England, on 20 August 1941. His first experience as a musical instrument maker came in 1956-1961 when he had a five-year indentured apprenticeship as a harpsichord, clavichord and spinet maker with Robert Goble in Oxford. He also studied at the Oxford College of Technology and City and Guilds of London Institute. After military service, Fischer became the manager of David Rubio's musical instrument studio at Duns Tew, Oxford. During his six-year stay there, he made guitars, lutes, early fretted instruments and harpsicords.

In 1973 Paul Fischer opened his own studio, specializing in the classical guitar and early fretted instruments. Since then he has established himself internationally as one of the world's foremost luthiers. His instruments are often featured in musical instrument exhibitions, and he lectures regularly in the UK and Europe on the craft of instrument making.

SELECTED READING
Interview.   Classical Guitar, November & December 1986
Article.   Classical Guitar, August 1994

Workshop address:
West End Studio, West End, Chipping Norton, Oxfordshire OX7 5EY.

GREG SMALLMAN

Greg Smallman

Greg Smallman was born in Cronulla, New South Wales, Australia, on 19 June 1947. His talents as a guitar maker of unique ability first became known internationally through John Williams, who in recent years has played Smallman's guitars virtually exclusively.

Smallman lives with his family in the rain forest in northern New South Wales, isolated from the world at large as his home and workshop are off the beaten track and he has no telephone. His fine guitars, distinguished by their brilliant sound, volume and ease of playing, are now much sought after by guitarists throughout the world. Smallman's output is very small, usually around four guitars a year, so their exclusivity is guaranteed.

SELECTED READING
Interview.   Guitar International, August 1988.

Workshop address:
c/o P.O. Box 510, Glen Innes 2370, New South Wales, Australia.

HUMPHREY

Tom Humphrey

PHOTO: COLIN COOPER

Thomas Humphrey was born in St Clouds, Minnesota, 13 November 1948. He is the son of the artist Donald Humphrey, and Mary Humphrey, a well-known social advocate.

Humphrey first studied the cello, but he became interested in the guitar and its construction when he moved to New York in 1970. A year later he established his first guitar workshop in New York City. Over the next few years he developed new construction methods to maximise the performance and sound capabilities of the instrument. In 1985 he completed his 'Millenium' model which revolutionised the basic principles of guitar making. Since that time this patented instrument has been used by many world-class performing and recording guitarists. Humphrey, who has the distinction of having been profiled in TIME magazine, continues to make his innovative guitars from his New York City workshop.

SELECTED READING
Interview   Acoustic Guitar Magazine, February 1996
Profile   TIME magazine, 2 July 1990

Workshop address:
37 West 26th Street, New York City, USA

CLASSICAL GUITAR CONSTRUCTION – SELECTED READING

Manual of Guitar Technology: Franz Jahnel.
　　　　　　　　　　　　　　　Das Musikinstrument 1981
Classical Guitar Construction: Irving Sloane.　　Dutton 1966
Guitar Repair: Irving Sloane.　　　　　　　　Dutton 1973
Classical Guitar, Design and Construction: McLeod & Welford.
　　　　　　　　　　　　　　　　　　　　Dryad 1971
Make Your Own Spanish Guitar: A. P. Sharpe.　Clifford Essex 1957
Classic Guitar Making: Arthur E. Overholtzer Brock 1974
　　　　　　　　　　　　　　　　　　　　Williams 1983
The A-Z of Guitar Construction. Guitar Review No. 28, 1965.

Make Your Own Classical Guitar: Stanley Doubtfire. Gollancz 1981
Making Musical Instruments: The Guitar – José Romanillos.
　　　　　　　　　　　　　　　　　　Faber and Faber 1979
The Fine Guitar: José Oribe.　　　　　Vel-Or Publishing 1985
Antonio de Torres: José L. Romanillos.　　Element Books 1987
Guitar Making: Tradition and Technology – Cumpiano/Natelson.
　　　　　　　　　　　　　　　　　　Rosewood Press 1987
The Development of the Modern Guitar – John Huber.
　　　　　　　　　　　　　　　　　　Bold Strummer 1991
Making Master Guitars – Roy Courtnall.　　Hale and Co 1993
Things About The Guitar – José Romanillos III.
　　　　　　　　　　　　　　　　　　Soneto 1992

ALBERT AUGUSTINE

Albert Augustine with Andrés Segovia

Albert Augustine (1900-1967) was the pioneer of the nylon guitar string. As such he may be regarded as one of the most important figures in the evolution of the classical guitar.

It was with the encouragement of Andrés Segovia that Albert Augustine, luthier and patron of the arts, began to research the possibilities of developing a nylon guitar string. Before 1947 guitarists used gut treble strings and metal wound silk floss basses. They were unreliable, difficult to tune, and soon wore out or broke, even after limited use. During and after World War II the supply situation of good strings for all instruments became very difficult. Segovia, together with Albert Augustine, discussed the matter with an executive of the Du Pont Chemical Company, who made available monofilament nylon originally developed for the manufacture of fishing lines. In 1947 Albert Augustine's workshops in New York produced the first commercially available nylon guitar strings. Since that time, the Augustine brand of guitar strings has remained one of the leaders among the many brands of classical guitar strings available today, including Savarez and Concertiste (produced in France) and D'Addario, Aranjuez and La Bella (produced in the USA).

For much of his life Albert Augustine experimented in the building of guitars, and completed several fine instruments before his death in April 1967. His New York workshop, under the supervision of Frank Haselbacher, continues to this day to produce fine classical guitars. The Augustine string business continues to prosper under the management of his widow Rose Augustine (currently the editor of 'Guitar Review').

In recent years the Augustine company has sponsored many classical guitar concert series and festivals, including the Bath Festival in the United Kingdom. This festival now includes the annual Albert Augustine Competition, and this event has given many young guitarists their first opportunity to have their talents heard by a large audience.

Rose Augustine

D'ADDARIO

The D'Addario family business of string making goes back eight generations. They first started making strings in the town of Salle in the province of Pescara, Italy. Charles D'Addario emigrated to the USA in 1909 and continued the family tradition, first by importing and distributing strings and then, in 1916, by making them in a small workshop in Long Island City. At that time the business concentrated on violin strings. John D'Addario joined his father in 1935, and became interested in other aspects of string making. In 1938 they began to make their first steel guitar strings for jazz and western guitars. Their business grew at a rapid rate from then, and after John's son, John Jnr, joined them in the late 1960s they changed their trading name to Darco Music Strings. The company prospered and was bought out by the Martin Guitar Company in 1970. In September 1974 John D'Addario, after leaving the Darco business, was joined by his youngest son James. Together with John Jnr, they began to produce strings again as J. D'Addario & Company Inc. Since that time the D'Addario company has become one of the largest string-making companies in the world, making strings for virtually every stringed instrument. Since 1974 they have maintained a special interest in strings for the classical guitar, working with many of the world's finest players. They have introduced many new manufacturing techniques, including laser technology, which are reflected in their range of Pro Arte classical guitar strings.

The D'Addario family made a further great contribution to the classical guitar in 1981, with the setting up of the D'Addario Foundation. This is a non-profit organization which sponsors an annual concert series in major cities of the USA, giving deserving new classical guitarists a chance to be featured alongside established artists. Janet D'Addario is the Foundation director, and Benjamin Verdery is the artistic director. The D'Addario Foundation's Concert Series has become one of North America's most important events for classical guitarists.

SELECTED READING
Meet the D'Addarios.   Guitar Player, February 1976
The D'Addario Foundation.   Guitar Player, November 1983
Article.   Classical Guitar, August 1995

John Jnr (left) and Jimmy D'Addario

THE CLASSICAL GUITAR
ITS SCHOLARS

THE CLASSICAL GUITAR SINCE 1800

ITS SCHOLARS

Another vital contribution to the evolution of the classical guitar since 1800 has been its numerous scholars, those guitarists who have dedicated themselves to research and education rather than the concert platform.

In the early nineteenth century, François de Fossa, a professional soldier who was also an enthusiastic amateur guitarist and composer, was instrumental in preserving Luigi Boccherini's guitar quintets (written towards the end of the eighteenth century under the patronage of the Marquis de Benavente) for future generations. According to Dionisio Aguado, it was also de Fossa who formulated the rules for the production of artificial harmonics on the guitar.

Since that time there have been many more classical guitarists who have devoted every spare moment to research and to the historical documentation of the classical guitar. The main section of this book has included several classical guitarists and personalities who have made a major contribution to the scholarship of the instrument. Included are Philip Bone, Alexander Bellow, François de Fossa, Domingo Prat and André Verdier. Also included in the main section are contemporary guitarists such as James Tyler and Harvey Hope (early guitar), Simon Wynberg (nineteenth century guitar), all of whom have made and continue to make great contributions in researching the guitar in their particular field.

This section is devoted to some of the other important scholars of recent years. Their enormous contribution to the classical guitar (and that of many other guitar scholars all over the world) is often overlooked by the majority of classical guitar lovers.

RUGGERO CHIESA

Ruggero Chiesa was born in Camogli, Italy, on 1 August 1933. He first studied the guitar with Carlo Palladino in Genoa. He later attended the Accademia Chigiana di Siena where he studied with both Andrés Segovia and Alirio Díaz. He also studied vihuela with Emilio Pujol at Siena.

Ruggero Chiesa

From 1963 Chiesa taught at the G.Verdi Conservatory in Milan. From 1976 he held an annual course on the transcriptions of tablature, as well as diverse seminars on guitar topics, at the Accademia Chigiana di Siena and also at Gargnano. In 1983 he became the director of the Corsi Accademici di Chitarra held annually at Bassano del Grappa (Vicenza), Italy. Many of Chiesa's pupils have won national and international competitions and now enjoy successful careers as concert guitarists. Amongst these are included Emanuele Segre, Massimo Laura, Elena Casoli and Leopoldo Saracino.

Ruggero Chiesa founded in 1972 'Il Fronimo', a prestigious quarterly guitar and lute magazine of which he is still the editor. He was also prominent as an editor of music. He edited more than 150 works of various composers and was the author of several didactic works. Among his many publications are the complete works of Luis Milán, Francesco da Milano and Michelangelo Galilei. Chiesa also edited the complete works for guitar of Nicoló Paganini. Several contemporary composers, including Castelnuovo-Tedesco, Bruno Bettinelli, Franco Donatoni and Aldo Clementi, dedicated works to him. Ruggero Chiesa died on 14 June 1993.

SELECTED READING
Il Fronimo. Issue 1 (1972) to current issue
Interview. Classical Guitar, July 1985
La Chitarra. EDT, Torino 1990

JOHN GAVALL

John Gavall

John Gavall was born in Liverpool, England on 29 January 1919. He was educated at Malvern and earned his M.A. at Peterhouse.

From the early 1950s he was a frequent performer on radio and television in Great Britain, and it was from that time that he became a very active protagonist of the guitar as an ideal instrument for the dissemination of musical knowledge and education.

In 1954 he became a full-time music teacher. Between 1955 and 1962 he was appointed Music Adviser to the West Riding of Yorkshire Education Authority. In 1962 as a guitarist, in competition with such traditional applicants as organists, pianists and conductors, Gavall took over as Senior Music Adviser for all of the thousand or more schools and colleges of the West Riding Education Authority. In this position, he directed the musical activity and teaching for all schools in one of the largest counties of Great Britain. This was the first time that a guitarist had gained such an important position in musical education in Great Britain.

Over the years John Gavall has been responsible for a large number of publications for the guitar. The most important of these is probably his five-volume set Learning Music Through The Guitar, published by Belwin Mills. Gavall wrote this set of books to prove that the guitar had enormous potential for music education and that it should be a serious part of all teacher training.

In 1972 John Gavall was appointed Lecturer in Music at Moray House College in Edinburgh. From that time Moray House offered tuition and harmony through the guitar, and also the techniques of teaching guitar to large groups of adults or college students. Gavall was also one of the first to use closed circuit television in guitar education.

John Gavall has been one of the most important figures in Great Britain for the promotion of the guitar.

ANGELO GILARDINO

Angelo Gilardino

Angelo Gilardino was born in Vercelli, Italy, on 16 November 1941. He studied the guitar, cello and composition with local teachers in Vercelli from an early age. He went on to study harmony and counterpoint with Giuseppe Rosetta at the Viotti Institute in Vercelli. Gilardino also studied musical history, tablature, conducting and accompaniment, and from 1965 was Professor of Guitar at the Viotti Institute. Since 1981 he has been Professor of Guitar at the Vivaldi State Conservatory in Alessandria. He also gives masterclasses and presents seminars for guitar throughout Italy and other parts of Europe.

Now recognised internationally as a musicologist and guitar authority, Gilardino has also had two periods as a concert artist, 1958 to 1968 and 1971 to 1981. His performances were nearly always devoted to twentieth century music, and many well-known composers, including Ascencio, Berkeley, Castelnuovo-Tedesco, Rodrigo, Ruiz-Pipó and Duarte, have dedicated works to him.

In 1968 Gilardino, on the recommendation of Castelnuovo-Tedesco, was appointed editor of modern and contemporary guitar works for the important publishing house Edizioni Musicali Bèrben.

He has held that position to the present day. He is a regular contributor to the Italian guitar magazine, il Fronimo. In 1989 his contribution to Bèrben's two-volume Manuale di storia della chitarra volume 2, La chitarra moderna e contemporanea, was published.

Angelo Gilardino is also a prolific composer for guitar, and has had several works published since 1981.

SELECTED MUSIC
Studi di virtuosita e di trascendenza (5 volumes).	Bèrben
Sonata No.1.	Bèrben
Sonata No.2.	Bèrben
Variazioni sulla Follia.	Bèrben

SELECTED READING
Various Articles.	Il Fronimo
Manuale di storia della chitarra – Volume 2.	Bèrben

SELECTED RECORDING
Gilardino plays Haug, Wissmer, Duarte, Tansman etc.
Bèrben BRMS 0074 LP

FREDERIC V. GRUNFELD

Frederic Grunfeld

Frederic Grunfeld was born in Berlin, Germany, on 2 June 1929 and died in 1987. He was trained in both music and art at the University of Chicago, from where he graduated. He began his career as a critic on the radio in the 1950s when he introduced a new programme entitled 'Music Magazine' on WQXR radio station. Grunfeld was involved in several volumes of Time-Life Great Music Series, and wrote several important music books including The Art and Times of the Guitar (Macmillan), one of the finest general histories of the guitar ever written. By 1971 the fourth edition of the work had been printed. In 1974 Collier Books released a paperback edition, and in 1975 Zen-On Publishers of Tokyo published a Japanese edition. The USA specialist publisher, De Capo Press, published a reprint in paperback in 1989.

SELECTED READING
The Art and Times of The Guitar.
                    Macmillan, New York 1969

THOMAS F. HECK

Thomas F. Heck

Thomas F. Heck was born in Washington, USA, on 10 July 1943. He began to study the classical guitar in Paris, where he lived while his father was stationed for a number of years with the USA State Department. On returning to the United States, Heck entered Notre Dame, where he received his B.A. degree. He went on to spend a year at the Academy of Music in Vienna, following which he entered the graduate programme at Yale University. In 1970, he earned his Ph.D. degree in Music History there.

In recent years Thomas F. Heck has established himself as a foremost historian, teacher and authority of the guitar. He was an editor and contributor of Soundboard magazine, the quarterly magazine published in California devoted to the classical guitar.

SELECTED READING
What is a guitar?   Soundboard No.3, 1976
Giuliani: Ph.D. Dissertation.   Univ. Microfilms 71-76, 249
Articles on Aguado, Carulli, Giuliani, Legnani, Matiegka,
Regondi, Tárrega, Ferranti.   New Grove, 1980
The role of Italy.   Guitar Review No 34, 1971
Mauro Giuliani – Guitarist Composer. Editions Orphee 1995
Article.   Classical Guitar, October 1985

BRIAN HODEL

Brian Hodel

Brian Hodel was born in Beckley, West Virginia, on 21 June 1948 Over a period of years he has established himself as a foremost writer, arranger and perfomer in the area of Brazilian music. After several years of music studies in the USA, where he was a guitar teacher at the University of Washington, he went to Brazil to live, and continued his studies there. He returned to the USA in 1989 and settled in Los Angeles, where he received an MA in music from the University of California in 1990.

Hodel has written several outstanding articles on the guitar music of Brazil and other South American countries for Guitar Review. He has also contributed articles to Classical Guitar magazine. He has edited books of Brazilian music for guitar for Macmillan and Big Three publishers in the USA, and has contributed several original pieces to the 'Modern Times' series published by Chanterelle Verlag in West Germany. In recent times he has devoted more of his time to composing, having written a string qaurtet, a rhapsody for piano, and a song cycle for three voices and chamber orchestra.

SELECTED READING
Brazilian Popular Music and The Guitar – Article.
    Classical Guitar, May/June 1983.
Abel Carlevaro – Article.   Guitar Review, Summer 1985.
Egberto Gismonti – Article.   Guitar Review, Fall 1985.
Astor Piazzolla – Article.   Guitar Review, Winter 1986.
Radamés Gnattali – Article.   Guitar Review, Summer 1986.
Ear Training for Guitarists.   Guitar Review, Winter 1987.
Grosse Fugue Villa-Lobos.   Guitar Review, Fall 1987.
Villa-Lobos and the Guitar.   Guitar Review, Winter 1988.

JOHN HUBER

John Huber

John Huber was born in Mayport, PA, USA, on 2 March 1940. He played the piano and the violin from the age of six. He changed to guitar at the age of fourteen, at which time his musical interest lay in folk music and the blues. He earned a B.A. in Philosophy at the Marietta College in Ohio. During his time there his interest in classical and flamenco guitar began. A self-taught guitarist, he developed a passionate interest in flamenco which encouraged him to go in 1961 to Seville, Spain, where he lived and played among the leading flamenco guitarists of the day, including Antonio Sanlúcar and Melchor de Marchena. Over the next few years he also developed an interest in guitar construction, and spent time extending his knowledge of this skill with Paco Barba in Seville, Manuel Reyes in Córdoba and Bernabe Ferrer in Granada.

In 1965 Huber moved to Stockholm, Sweden, and joined the Levin guitar company as a guitar maker. In 1967 this company was acquired by the C.F.Martin Company, and Huber returned to the USA to work in the Martin repair department. Within a short period of time he was made Director of Research. Further promotion came with his appointment as Director of Sales in Europe. The combination of Huber's multilingual talents with his guitar playing and construction ability made him the ideal choice for this position. In 1973 Huber left the Martin organization and worked for a while with Juan Orozco in the USA and for Dieter Hopf in Germany. In 1976 his growing interest in the construction of both violins and guitars encouraged him to enrol at the Univerity of Uppsala in Sweden, where he gained a Ph.D. in musicology in 1986. He was then awarded several grants from the Swedish Government to research violin construction at the Academy of Music in Stockholm.

John Huber has written three published books on the violin, and will have his book on modern classical guitars published in 1992. He is well known and respected internationally as a leading authority on the guitar.

SELECTED READING
Development of the Modern Guitar.
                                           Bold Strummer 1992

OLIVER HUNT

Oliver Hunt

Oliver Hunt was born on 16 June 1934. He studied the guitar at the Guildhall School of Music in London with Adele Kramer in 1958. He also studied privately with Julian Bream. He continued his musical studies in theory and composition at the Royal Academy of Music with Sir Lennox Berkeley and James Illiff, winning the William Wallace Exhibition for Composition.

Oliver Hunt, who is currently Professor of Guitar at the London College of Music, has composed a wide variety of works including solo works for guitar, piano and organ as well as choral, orchestral and chamber music. A work that attracted considerable attention is his Barber of Baghdad Suite (1976), written for the English guitarist Robert Brightmore. He has also written an excellent text book for guitarists entitled Musicianship and Sight Reading for Guitarists.

SELECTED MUSIC
The Barber of Baghdad.	Revelo-Cornish Music
Leviathan.	Revelo-Cornish Music
Garuda.	Musical New Services
Two White Doves (duet).	Revelo-Cornish Music
Quartet No.1.	Revelo-Cornish Music
Quartet No.2 'The Sun'.	Revelo-Cornish Music

SELECTED READING
Oliver Hunt.   Guitar, March 1977
Analysis: series of articles.
        Classical Guitar, Sep/Oct 1982 to Jan/Feb 1983.
Aural Perception & Training.
        Classical Guitar, Jan/Feb 1984 to May/Jun 1984.

BRIAN JEFFERY

Brian Jeffery

Brian Jeffery was born in London on 13 October 1938. He was educated at Oxford, and holds a doctorate in musicology and French. He has been a lecturer in French at the University of St Andrews, and visiting professor in the Department of French at the University of California, at Berkeley and Santa Barbara. He also lectured at the University of Warwick.

At school Brian Jeffery played both the piano and the cello, but it was while he was at Oxford that he started to play the lute and then the guitar. He has published many scholarly articles, books and reviews in the fields of the Renaissance, literature and music. His thesis at Oxford was on the 16th century composer Anthony Holborne. Jeffery's biography of Fernando Sor, and his complete editions of the guitar works of Sor and Giuliani, have been major contributions to the growing library of books and music of classical guitar interest. He published in 1990 a complete reprint of the first editions of all Beethoven's piano sonatas. All these works, and many more, have been published by Jeffery's own publishing firm, Tecla Editions.

Brian Jeffery has appeared as a recitalist and accompanist on both lute and guitar, although today he no longer performs in concert.

SELECTED MUSIC
The Complete Works for Guitar of Fernando Sor.
Tecla Editions
The Complete Works of Mauro Giuliani. Tecla Editions

SELECTED READING
Fernando Sor: composer and guitarist.
Tecla Editions 1977 and 1995

Fernando Sor: concert performer.
Guitar Review, No.39, 1974
Interview. Guitar Player, July 1979

SELECTED RECORDING
Brian Jeffery presents Fernando Sor.
Hansen Records MM122 LP

MICHAEL MACMEEKEN

Michael Macmeeken

Michael Macmeeken was born in Edinburgh on 26 September 1942. He was a pupil of Regino Sainz de la Maza, graduating at the Madrid Royal Conservatory of Music. He went into publishing, becoming a founding director of Editions Chanterelle, a specialist publisher of classical guitar music. Now called Chanterelle Verlag Heidelberg, the company is based in Germany, where Macmeeken lives. Chanterelle has become one of the most respected and innovative guitar music specialist publishers. The backbone of their catalogue is the collected works of Aguado, Coste, Llobet, Mertz, Paganini, Regondi, Sagreras, Sor and Zani de Ferranti.

FREDERICK NOAD

Frederick Noad

Frederick Noad was born in Blankenberg, Belgium, on 8 August 1929. His parents were British. He studied violin and piano at Wellington College under the direction of Maurice Allen. He took up the classical guitar, and this was to become his favourite instrument. After taking his M.A at Oxford, Noad moved to Los Angeles, California, where he opened a Spanish guitar centre modelled on that opened by Len Williams in London.

Joaquín Rodrigo heard him play in 1961, and immediately recommended him for a scholarship to attend Segovia's masterclass in Santiago de Compostela. This Noad attended in 1962, and in the same year completed his first book, 'Playing The Guitar', for Collier Books, New York. It was an instant success, reaching the paperback best-seller lists. After many reprintings, it is now in its third edition.

On his return to the USA, Noad studied composition privately with Mario Castelnuovo-Tedesco. In 1966 he presented the first of what was to be twenty-six programmes of guitar lessons for the KCET television station in Los Angeles. In 1968 he added a further thirteen lessons to the series. In the same year his new method, Solo Guitar Playing, was published by Macmillan of New York; it is now claimed to be the most widely used classical guitar instruction book in schools and colleges in the USA. During the same period, he went to Europe and Scandinavia to undertake research for a new anthology series, subsequently been published by Ariel Music.

Frederick Noad, who is also an accomplished lute player, has taught guitar at various institutions including the University of California and the California Institute of Arts. In 1974 he was one of the original founders of the Guitar Foundation of America, for which he served as chairman in 1975.

In 1981 Noad presented a new series of video lessons for television, 'The Guitar with Frederick Noad'. It was a great success and was seen on television stations throughout the USA and also in many other countries. More recently, he initiated a series of radio broadcasts on National Public Radio for the G. Schirmer publishing house, entitled 'Overtones' and covering aspects of the music of our time.

SELECTED MUSIC
Solo Guitar Playing Volumes 1 & 2.	Macmillan
The Renaissance Guitar.	Ariel
The Baroque Guitar.	Ariel
The Classical Guitar.	Ariel
The Romantic Guitar.	Ariel

SELECTED RECORDINGS
Guitar for Beginners – Six Tuition Videos.	IMP

SELECTED READING
Interview.	Classical Guitar, November 1993

THEODORE NORMAN

Theodore Norman

Born in Montréal, Canada, on 14 March 1912, Theodore Norman first studied violin with Willy Hess and composition with Adolph Weiss. He played first violin in the Los Angeles Philharmonic Orchestra from 1935 to 1942.

Norman became interested in the guitar while composing his ballet Metamorphosis, in which he used a guitar. After concentrated study with the guitarist Aurio Herrero in Madrid, he wrote ten pieces for guitar in the twelve-tone system, the first of their type to be published. In Europe, where he met leading classical and flamenco guitarists, he gave a concert on French radio of his own compositions and works by other composers.

On his return to the United States, Norman played the guitar part in Pierre Boulez's Le Marteau sans Maître and Schoenberg's Serenade, recording both works for Columbia Records.

Theodore Norman has transcribed and had published hundreds of works of the great classical composers for one and two guitars. He has also developed a unique system for notating flamenco music. He is currently Head of the Guitar Department at UCLA in California.

SELECTED READING
The Art of Theodore Norman.   Guitar Review, Fall 1988

MATANYA OPHEE

Matanya Ophee

Matanya Ophee was born in Jerusalem on 5 June 1932, and began his guitar studies in 1955 with Esther Bromberger, a pupil of Luigi Mozzani. He later studied for two years with Richard Pick in Chicago. Further studies in music theory were taken under Gérard Le Coat at the Conservatoire de Lausanne in Switzerland, and in composition with Eli Yarden in Israel.

Since that time Ophee has lived in the USA, where for many years he has had two succesful parallel careers, one as an airline pilot and the other as a musicologist, guitarist and guitar historian. His many articles have appeared in leading guitar journals throughout the world and in many languages. His research into the repertoire of chamber music with guitar and the history of the guitar in Russia have been notable contributions to public knowledge. He is recognized, among others, for bringing to light the biography and accomplishments of the French nineteenth-century guitarist François de Fossa (1775-1849).

Matanya Ophee established the publishing company Editions Orphée, which is based in Columbus, Ohio, and is recognized internationally as a leading publisher of guitar music and books. In 1989 he retired from aviation, and now devotes his full time to music and the guitar.

SELECTED READING
Luigi Boccherini's Guitar Quintets:
New Evidence (with a biography of François de Fossa):
Ophee.   Editions Orphée, 1981
Article: Chamber Music for Terz-Guitar.
                                              Guitar Review No.42
Article: The History of Apoyando:Another View.
                                              Guitar Review No.51
Article: The First Guitar Concerto and Legends.
                                           Classical Guitar, July 1985
Article: On Primary Sources.   Classical Guitar, July 1986
Article: Some Considerations of
19th Century Guitar Music and its
Performance Practice Today.   Classical Guitar, August 1986

CORAZON OTERO

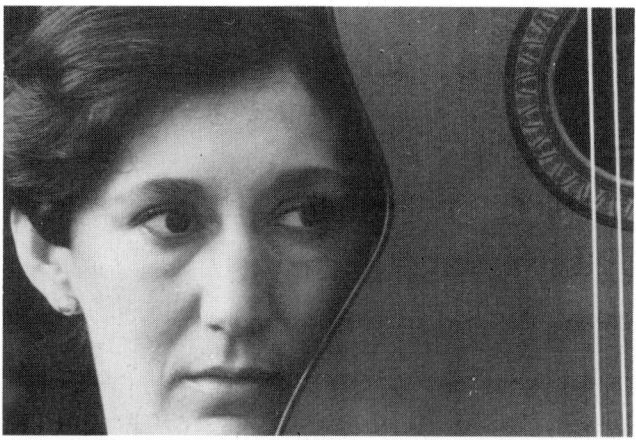

Corazón Otero

Corazón Otero was born in Mexico City, 8 March 1944. She was interested in music from an early age. She began to study the guitar seriously in 1970. Her teachers have included Mario Beltran de Rio and Manuel López Ramos. She has also taken part in masterclasses with Abel Carlevaro, Leo Brouwer and John Williams.

In recent years she has established herself as a major figure in Mexico's classical guitar world, both as a performer and as a scholar. She is a founder of the 'Concurso Internacional de Guitarra Manuel M. Ponce' in Mexico City. Several composers have dedicated works to her, including Alexandre Tansman, Angelo Gilardino, Guido Santórsola and John W. Duarte.

Corazón Otero has made a major contribution to guitar literature with her books on the lives and guitar works of Manuel Ponce, Alexandre Tansman and Mario Castelnuovo-Tedesco.

SELECTED READING
Manuel M. Ponce y la Guitarra. Ediciones Musicales Yolotl,
                                                         Mexico 1980
       (Also available inEnglish and French editions).
Mario Castelnuovo-Tedesco: su vida y su obras para guitarra.
                              Ediciones Musicales Yolotl, Mexico 1987
Alexandre Tansman: su vida y su obras para guitarra.
                              Ediciones Musicales Yolotl, Mexico 1989.

PETER PAFFGEN

Peter Päffgen

Peter Päffgen was born in Düsseldorf, West Germany, on 18 November 1950, and studied music and theatre at university. At the same time he studied lute with Professor Michael Schäffer. He qualified in 1978, earning a Ph.D. with his paper on lute music of the sixteenth century.

In 1979 he began to publish the bi-monthly magazine 'Gitarre & Laute' from Cologne, a well-produced magazine has become the most important German-language publication for classical guitarists in Germany. He has also published several important guitar music works and recordings through his magazine's subsidiary, G & L Publications. In 1988 Päffgen completed his history of the classical guitar, Die Gitarre: Grundzuge ihrer Entwicklung.

SELECTED READING
Gitarre & Laute magazine.   1979 to current issue
Laute und Lautenspiel in der ersten Halfte des 16 Jahrhunderts. Beobachtungen zur Bauweise und Spieltechnik.
                                        Regensberg 1979
Die Gitarre: Grundzuge ihrer Entwicklung.
                                        Schott, Mainz, 1988

JOZEF POWROZNIAK

Jozef Powrozniak

Jozef Powrozniak was born in Staniatki on 4 December 1902. For many years he was Poland's foremost guitar historian and a leading teacher of the instrument. He studied music at the Conservatory of Music in Kraków from 1923 to 1925, and at the Institute of Music in Kraków from 1926 toi 1929. Over the years he wrote many publications for the classical guitar, including transcriptions and methods. It has been estimated that over ninety per cent of Polish classical guitar publications have been written or edited by him.

From 1929 Powrozniak taught at the State Academy in Chorzow. He was the Director of Music at the Music Lyceum in Katowice (1949-1951), and Rector of the State Academy of Music in Katowice from 1951 to 1963, and again from 1972 to 1975. He died in Katowice on 10 July 1989.

SELECTED READING
Gitarren-Lexicon (German edition).
                                Verlag Neue Musik, Berlin, DDR

RONALD C. PURCELL

Ronald Purcell

Ronald Charles Purcell was born on 5 October 1932 in San Jose, California, USA. He first began to play the guitar at the age of seven, but it was not until he was in Europe at the age of eighteen that he discovered the classical guitar. He started an intense study of the instrument, and among his teachers over the next few years were several notable guitarists including Andrés Segovia, Emilio Pujol, Alirio D,az and Oscar Ghiglia.

Purcell studied at the Free University of Berlin and the Los Angeles Conservatory of Music, where he received his B.M. degree in composition in 1961. He was a composition student of Mario Castelnuovo-Tedesco for a number of years, and he also studied with the noted musicologist of Hispanic music, Mario Santiago Kastner. Ronald Purcell is the author of a book devoted to Segovia's contribution to the guitar, and of a discography of lute and guitar records. He is a regular contributor of articles to guitar magazines including Soundboard. He was appointed President of the American Guitar Society, and he was also the first President of the Guitar Foundation of America, which was founded in 1973. Since 1975 he has acted as the guitar consultant for the publishers Belwin Mills, and has completed more than thirty-five music publications for guitar.

Ronald Purcell is one of the USA's most highly regarded guitar authorities. He currently teaches guitar, lute, vihuela and other courses at the California State University at Northridge.

HECTOR QUINE

Hector Quine

Hector Quine was born in London on 30 December 1926. He received his general education at Hextable College in Kent. He initially studied music privately with Penelope Englehart. Quine, whose principal instrument is the guitar, was appointed Professor of the Guitar at Trinity College of Music in London in 1958. The following year he was Professor at the Royal Academy of Music in London, and from 1966-1980 he was Professor at the Guildhall School of Music in London. From 1954 he was principal guitarist at the Royal Opera House, London.

Hector Quine is highly regarded in Great Britain as a leading teacher and editor of guitar music. For many years he has edited most of the guitar works for Oxford University Press. His works include some studies and exercises for the guitar composed jointly with Stephen Dodgson, the well-known English composer.

SELECTED READING
Interview.   Guitar International,
Interview.   Classical Guitar, August 1990

AARON SHEARER

Aaron Shearer

Aaron Shearer was born in Anatone, Washington, USA, on 6 September 1919. His first musical instrument was the harmonica, which he began to play at the age of six. Three years later he took up the guitar. His first interest was hillbilly music but he eventually developed an interest in both classical and jazz guitar styles.

During the 1940s Shearer gave classical recitals but spent most of his time playing jazz in nightclubs in the north west and Los Angeles. In 1949 he suffered a severe case of tendinitis which virtually ended his hopes of a professional playing career. It was then that he decided to embark upon a teaching career.

On the recommendation of Andrés Segovia, Shearer moved to Washington DC to study with Sophocles Papas. He soon joined, with Papas, the faculty of Washington's American University, founding what is claimed to be the first degree course for guitar in the USA. In the mid-1960s Aaron Shearer became a faculty member of the Peabody Conservatory in Maryland, starting the first guitar degree programme there. Since 1981 he has been director of the guitar programme at the North Carolina School of Arts in Winston-Salem. It was in 1959 that Shearer published his first teaching method, which eventually developed into six volumes. It was highly acclaimed, and has been in publication (Belwin Mills) ever since. He has recently completed a new series of method books (Mel Bay) which he believes are much more comprehensive than the original method. Among his many former pupils are some of the best guitarists of the nineties, including Manuel Barrueco, Ricardo Cobo, David Starobin and David Tanenbaum.

SELECTED READING
Interview.   Guitar Player, July 1989

SELECTED MUSIC
Classic Guitar Technique.   Belwin Mills
Learning the Classic Guitar. (3 Vols).   Mel Bay Publications

RICHARD STOVER

Richard Stover

Richard Stover was born in Clinton, Iowa, USA, on 11 September 1945. He has been one of the major figures in the rediscovery of most of the guitar works of Agustín Barrios Mangoré.

Stover was brought up in California. He began to study the guitar when he was an exchange student in Costa Rica. On his return to the United States he studied with Japanese guitarist Ako Ito in San Francisco.

In 1966 he travelled to Spain, where he studied with José Tomás at Santiago de Compostela. In 1966-1967 he studied Spanish literature and poetry at the Faculty of Philosophy and Letters at the University of Madrid. During this time he furthered his guitar studies with Jorge Fresno.

In 1967 he travelled throughout Argentina for over a year. On his return to the United States of America he continued his guitar studies at various guitar courses for a period of a few years. In 1969 he studied with Manuel López Ramos, in 1970 with Rey de la Torre, and in 1978 with Leo Brouwer. In 1975, he earned his Bachelor of Arts degree, with an independent major in Latin American Ethnomusicology, at the University of California in Santa Cruz.

Between 1975-1979 Stover was Associate in Music at the University of California, Santa Cruz. At the same time he was a Visiting Lecturer at the Merrill College, UCSC.

Richard Stover founded his own publishing firm, Gringo Publications, some years ago. Through this he edited a large number of compositions for the guitar by a diversity of composers from both South and North America.

He is also a regular broadcaster, author of many articles for guitar magazines, and has appeared in concert in most parts of the North American continent both as a soloist and with his ensemble Los Gringos. He has recently formed a recording company, El Maestro, which has among its releases several important albums including collections of the original recordings of Barrios and Miguel Llobet.

In 1990 Stover was awarded a Fulbright Fellowship to research the life and music of Agustín Barrios Mangoré. He currently lives in Puerto Rico.

SELECTED READING
Six Silver Moonbeams – Biography of Barrios – Richard Stover.   Querico USA 1992
IberoAmerican Guitar Series.
                              Classical Guitar 1994-96

SELECTED MUSIC
Barrios Guitar Works.	Belwin Mills
Barrios Guitar Works.	Querico
Barrios Guitar Works.	Mel Bay Publications

GRAHAM WADE

Graham Wade

Graham Wade was born in Coventry, England, on 18 January 1940. He began playing the guitar in 1953 after first studying the piano. He was educated at Cambridge University, and is a fellow of Trinity College of Music, London. His first teachers included Jerzy Jezewski and Julian Byzantine.

Wade is known internationally as a writer for the guitar. His books have proved important additions to the growing library of guitar literature. His two-volume Guitar Tutor, with recorded cassettes, published by International Correspondence Schools, has sold in fifty countries since 1974. He has contributed many articles for important music periodicals including Classical Guitar, Guitar Review and Music and Musicians, and he is a contributor to the New Grove Dictionary of Musical Instruments. Wade also provided background research for Julian Bream's important television series Guitarra!, and has written sleeve notes for several leading record companies.

Graham Wade ran his own guitar summer school in Lincolnshire for several years, and has tutored and lectured at many others throughout the world, including the Segovia Masterclass at USCLA in 1986.

For many years he was Professor of Guitar at the City of Leeds College of Music, and Guitar Tutor for the University of Leeds.

SELECTED READING
Traditions of the Classical Guitar.   John Calder, 1980
Segovia: A Celebration of the Man and his Music.
                                            Allison & Busby, 1983
The Guitarist's Guide to Bach.   Wise Owl, 1985
Rodrigo and the Concierto de Aranjuez.   Mayflower, 1985
Villa-Lobos and the Guitar – Turibio Santos (Translation by Graham Wade with Victoria Forde).   Wise Owl, 1985
Maestro Segovia.   Robson Books, 1986
Interview.   Classical Guitar, November 1988
Rodrigo Solo Guitar Works.   GSM 1996
A New Look at Segovia, His Life, His Music.   Mel Bay 1996

JOSEF ZUTH

Josef Zuth

Josef Zuth was born in Fischern, near Karlsbad, Germany on 24 November 1879. He began to study the guitar and mandolin whilst he was employed as a civil servant in Vienna at the beginning of this century. He first studied under J. Krempl in 1908 and then went on to study with Dr. Richard Batka at the university in Vienna. He made such progress that he was appointed professor of guitar in the Volkshochule, Urania, Vienna in 1918. Amongst his pupils was the prominent Austrian guitarist, Luise Walker. In 1919 Zuth graduated as a Doctor of Philosophy with his thesis on Simon Molitor (1766-1848), the well known Austrian guitarist.

In 1921 Zuth began to edit the guitar magazine, Zeitschrift fur die Gitarre. This was published by Anton Goll who had also published Zuth's thesis on Simon Molitor. In 1928 Zuth began to make regular contributions to other music journals published in Vienna. In 1928 he began to edit for Anton Goll the series Musik im Haus which included many studies on the guitar and its repertoire. In 1928 Zuth's Handbuch der Laute und Gitarre was published. This book was made up of biographies of well-known guitarists and lutenists. Zuth died in Vienna, 3 August 1932.

SELECTED READING
Simon Molitor, Viennese Guitarist and Composer
                                        Anton Goll, Vienna 1919
Handbuch der Laute und Gitarre   Anton Goll, Vienna 1928

THE FLAMENCO GUITAR

La Zambra Gitana, 1890

THE FLAMENCO GUITAR

The first edition of this book did not include a chapter on the flamenco guitar. This was a conscious decision, for at the time I felt that flamenco was a separate art form, well dealt with in several books covering all the various aspects of this exciting music. I now respect the opinion that there is a place in this book on the classical guitar for a brief chapter on the great flamenco guitar virtuosos. These virtuosos have over the years borrowed from and extended classical guitar techniques in order to develop their own special art, and in turn they have influenced both the music and technique of the modern classical guitar. This chapter is therefore intended as a guide to interested readers to extend their knowledge and appreciation of flamenco. In particular the selected reading, music and recording lists at the end of this chapter are an excellent guide for further information on the best of flamenco and its guitarists.

Flamenco, as we know it today, is not a particularly old art form. Its origins nevertheless do go back to the time when Southern Spain was occupied by the Moors. After the Moors were expelled from Spain by Ferdinand and Isabella in 1492, nomadic bands of Gypsies were forced by a royal edict to settle in Andalusia. Over the next two hundred years these Gypsies developed their own form of music and dance, absorbing aspects of Arab, Christian, Jewish and Spanish folk music into their own traditions. Many historians agree that the original forms of flamenco were sung without instrumental accompaniment but the guitar, the national and most popular instrument of Spain, became an integral part of flamenco. Flamenco as we know it today originated about two hundred years ago, with the guitar acting as an accompaniment instrument only. Over the years brief solo spots for the guitarists became extended as their virtuosity grew. The first great soloist of which we have recorded examples was Ramón Montoya (1880-1949). He was influenced by Patino (1830-1900), Paco Lucena (1859-1898) and Javier Molina (1868-1956), all virtuosos in their own right. But it is Ramón Montoya who is regarded by most aficionados as the father of the solo flamenco guitar, and it is his virtuosic style that has been a source of inspiration to all flamenco guitarists of the twentieth century.

The guitar used by flamenco guitarists is in general appearance not very different from the classical guitar. The size and shape are similar, but it does have a bright, loud and cutting sound, very different from that of the instrument used by classical guitarists. This unique sound is due to its light construction, with a thin spruce top and back and sides of cypress. The flamenco guitar is also fitted with tapping plates (golpeadores) to protect the spruce top from the vigorous finger tapping of the player. Traditionally the flamenco guitar also had distinctive pegs of ebony or rosewood for tightening the strings, instead of the metal machine heads used on the classical guitar. In recent years several prominent flamenco guitarists have begun to use instruments with the dark coloured palo santo wood, instead of cypress, for the back and sides. Such an instrument, with its distinctive sound, is known as a 'guitarra negra'.

The origin of the word "Flamenco" has been the cause of much debate over the years. Some authorities claim that it is derived from the Arabic "felagmengu" meaning fugitive peasant. Other authorities believe it is derived from the Arabic "felah men ikum" which means "songs of the labourers". This refers to the menial work given to poor uneducated people.

Paco Peña's Flamenco Dance Company

RAMON MONTOYA

Born – RAMON MONTOYA SALAZAR

Madrid, Spain, 2 November 1880

Died – Madrid, 20 July 1949

Ramón Montoya

Ramón Montoya was an exceptional guitarist. A master of his instrument, he is regarded as being responsible for incorporating the tremolo and arpeggios into flamenco guitar technique. He introduced the Rondeña as a solo guitar work and created many falsetas which are still played by flamenco guitarists. His artistry was equal both as a soloist and as an accompanist. He performed on an international basis with singers Antonio Chacon and Aurelio Selle, and with dancers La Joselito and Antonia Merce ('La Argentinita'). In recognition of his great contribution to flamenco, he was known as Don Ramón Montoya.

SELECTED RECORDINGS
Ramón Montoya and Manolo de Huelva.
                                  Dial Discos 54 9317-18 LP
Flamenquistas   Vol.2. Stinson SLPS 34 LP
Ramón Montoya.   Chant du Monde LDX 274879 CD
Ramón Montoya – 1910-1920.   FODS SE-70 7022 CD

SELECTED MUSIC
Arte Clasico Flamenco – Ramon Montoya.   AFFEDIS

MANOLO de HUELVA

Born – MANUEL GOMEZ VELEZ

Rio Tinto, Spain, 16 November 1892

Died – Seville, Spain, 12 May 1976

Manolo de Huelva

Manolo de Huelva was a contemporary of Ramón Montoya, but unlike Montoya was a somewhat introverted and secretive character. His great artistry was recognized by his contemporaries, but there are only a few recorded examples of his work. Huelva preferred to keep the secrets of his artistry as both soloist and accompanist to himself, so that his impact on flamenco guitar was very limited in comparison to Montoya's. Yet aficionados who heard both players play 'live' regard him as Montoya's equal.

SELECTED RECORDING
Ramón Montoya & Manolo de Huelva.
                                  Dial Discos 54 9317-18 LP

NIÑO RICARDO

Born – MANUEL SERRAPI SANCHEZ

Seville, Spain, 1 July 1904

Died – Seville, 14 April 1972

Niño Ricardo

Niño Ricardo was taught to play the guitar by his father at an early age. He soon showed great talent, and as a teenager was touring the Spanish bullrings in a flamenco show with Ramón Montoya and La Niña de Los Peines. Ricardo was greatly influenced by his teacher Javier Molina. A great accompanist and soloist, Ricardo introduced new chords and harmonies into the flamenco guitar repertoire, so extending the pioneering work of Ramón Montoya. He also introduced a more aggressive approach to soloing which was emphasized by his re-introduction of the dissonant sounds of the Arabic scales. His style became, and remains today, greatly admired by lovers of flamenco all over the world. Niño Ricardo was also a talented and artistic painter.

SELECTED RECORDINGS

Flamenquistas Vol.2.	Stinson SLPS 34 LP
Toques Flamencos:	Niño Ricardo. Clave 18-1151 LP
Niño Ricardo.	Chant du Monde LDX 4339 CD
Niño Ricardo – 1940-1950.	FODS SE-70 7023 CD

MELCHOR DE MARCHENA

Born – MELCHOR GIMENEZ TORRES

Born – Marchena (Seville), Spain, 6 Januar 1907

Died – Seville, 12 March 1980

Melchor de Marchena

Melchor de Marchena was regarded as one of the greatest accompanists for flamenco singers. Throughout his career he was constantly in demand from the finest singers of the day, including Pepe Pinto, Niña de los Peines and Manolo Caracol.

SELECTED RECORDING

Melchor de Marchena.	Hispavox 53040 32581 LP

SABICAS

Born – AGUSTIN CASTELLON CAMPOS

Pamplona, Spain, 15 March 1912

Died – New York, USA, 1 April 1990

Sabicas

By the time he was thirteen Sabicas had already earned himself a high reputation. His talent was quickly recognised by Ramón Montoya and others. Over the years he was to extend and enrich the new flamenco guitar techniques introduced by Montoya and Ricardo. He became a world-famous artist, accompanying the great flamenco names of the day, including Carmen Amaya. At the same time he established himself as one of the great flamenco soloists of all time, inspiring through his many recordings and live performances generations of guitarists right up to the present day. He lived for many years in New York, where he died in 1990.

SELECTED MUSIC
The Flamenco Art of Sabicas.   Hansen

SELECTED RECORDINGS
Sabicas et Mario Escudero.	Barclay 920 176 LP
Flamenco Concerto/Torroba.	Erato EFM 8080 LP
Day of the Bullfight.	ABC Westminster WG 1009 LP
Sabicas.	Hallmark HM 616 LP
Flamenco Fantasy.	MFP 5174 LP
Sabicas.	Polydor 236 561 LP
Sabicas – 1930-1940 (3 Vols).	FODS SE-70 7019/7037/7038
Sabicas.	Chant du Monde LDX 274935 CD
Sabicas – Performance Video.	Alegrias Productions

CARLOS MONTOYA

Born – Madrid, Spain, 13 December 1903

Died – Wainscott, Long Island, New York, USA

3 March 1993

Carlos Montoya

Although Carlos Montoya was Ramón Montoya's nephew, his artistry has in the main been ignored by serious flamenco aficionados. This is despite the fact that he worked with many of the legends of flamenco, including Carmen Amaya, Pilar Lopez and La Argentinita. Over the years he developed his own brilliant style, but for many flamencologists it smacked of showmanship and lacked authenticity. In 1940 Carlos Montoya married and settled in the USA. Within a few years he became a major recording artist and an international concert artist. His association in 1955 with the dancer Vicente Escudero was a great success.

Despite any reservations about the authenticity of Carlos Montoya's music, few guitarists have done as much to make people around the world aware of flamenco music.

SELECTED RECORDINGS
Flamenco Fire.	HMV CLP 1177 LP
Adventures in Flamenco.	HMV CLP 1876 LP
Aires Flamenco.	Musidisc CV 1017 LP
Flamenco Holiday.	Everest 2210 LP
Recital de Guitare Espagnole.	Musidisc CV 901 LP
Malagueña.	RCA Victor LSP 2380 LP
Suite Flamenca.	United Artists SULP 1224 LP
Carlos Montoya.	Vox ACD 8063

MARIO ESCUDERO

Born –

Alicante, Spain

11 October 1928

Mario Escudero

Mario Escudero is of Castilian and Gypsy descent. He made his professional debut in concert with Maurice Chevalier at the Cinema Galia in Bordeaux, France. At the age of fourteen he earned the post of main guitarist with the Vicente Escudero Spanish Dance Company on a European concert tour. He has also toured with Carmen Amaya, Antonio, José Greco and Rosario. In the 1950s he decided to make his home in the USA. He soon became a regular artist on both radio and television and made several recordings. In 1965 he returned to Seville, Spain, to live and work there, although he also continues to teach and play in the USA.

SELECTED MUSIC
The Flamenco Art of Escudero.   Hansen

SELECTED RECORDINGS
Mario Escudero.	ABC 396 LP
Escudero at El Poche.	ABC 492 LP
Classical Flamenco Guitar.	WRC ST 1028 LP
Sabicas et Mario Escudero.	Barclay 920 176 LP

PEPE MARTINEZ

Born –

Macarena, Seville, Spain, 1923

Died – Seville, 18 September 1985

Pepe Martínez

Pepe Martínez was probably the last direct link with Ramón Montoya. He began his professional career as an accompanist in his teens. It was during this time that he met and played with Montoya. Over the years he accompanied top flamenco artists including Manuel Vallejo, Pepe Marchena, Juanito Valderrama, Niña de los Peines and many others. From his mid-thirties he concentrated on a highly successful solo career. From 1959 he began an annual concert tour every autumn of Great Britain. With the help of Ivor Mairants he made two LP recordings for the Fontana label in London; these were to further his international career.

SELECTED RECORDINGS
The Lyrical Guitar of Pepe Martínez.	Fontana TL 5207 LP
Pepe Martínez.	Decca SA C7811 LP
Alegrías Flamencas.	Concert Hall SVSC 2456 LP
Pepe Martínez.	Mandala 4865 CD

SELECTED MUSIC
Pepe Martinez Solos.   Schott

MANUEL CANO

Born –

Granada, Spain, 23 February 1926

Died – Granada, 12 January 1990

Manuel Cano

Manuel Cano began to play the guitar at the age of eight. During his youth in Madrid, he studied flamenco and classical guitar with some of the leading guitarists there. He decided to study the traditions of music and flamenco, and moved to Andalusia. In 1959 he recorded his first LP, called 'Suite Granadina y Flamenco Clásico'. Its success led to his first concert appearance in 1960 in Seville, then another in Granada. In 1961 he appeared in the Curso Internacional de Extranjero in Granada, which was to lead to further concert engagements including several in France. From that time Cano led a successful career as a concert and recording artist, appearing many times on television and radio.

SELECTED RECORDINGS
Evocation of Ramón Montoya.
                    Musical Heritage MHS 1154 LP
Manuel Cano: Motivos Andaluces/Semblanzas Flamencas.
                    RCA RPL-8180 LP

JUAN SERRANO

Born –

Córdoba, Spain

1 January 1934

Juan Serrano

Juan Serrano learned to play the guitar at the age of nine from his father, Antonio del Lunar, who was a well-known guitarist in Córdoba. In 1952 he moved to Madrid to play in the best flamenco night-clubs.

It was here that he met both Manolo de Huelva and Melchor de Marchena. He was soon recognized as one of the best accompanists of the time, and made several recordings with top singers and dancers. But he decided that he would rather have a career as a soloist and, during a visit to the USA with a dance company in 1962, he realized that there was more opportunity to fulfil his ambition there. He settled in New York in 1963, since when he has led a succesful concert, recording and teaching career.

SELECTED RECORDINGS
La Virtuosa Guitarra.	Philips BBE 12433 LP
Flamenco Fenómeno.	Polydor 236 569 LP
Sabor Flamenco.	Concord CCD-4490
Flamenco Tuition Video.	Mel Bay Publications

SELECTED MUSIC
Flamenco Guitar Method.	Mel Bay Publications
Flamenco Guitar Solos.	Mel Bay Publications
Flamenco Concert Selection.	Mel Bay Publications
Sabor Flamenco.	Mel Bay Publications

PACO PEÑA

Born –

Córdoba, Spain

1 June 1942

Paco Peña

Paco Peña learned to play the guitar from an early age. At the age of twelve he began his professional career as an accompanist with various flamenco companies in Spain. After touring the United Kingdom with one of these companies in 1963, he decided to divide his time between London and Spain. In 1966 he settled in London, embarking on a highly successful career as a concert and recording artist, with many television and radio appearances. Since 1980 he has held an annual international festival of guitar in Córdoba, where he now also has a home. His Spanish Dance Company has for many years enjoyed great popularity, both in the United Kingdom and other countries. Although Peña is a flamenco guitarist following in the traditions of Montoya and Ricardo, he continues to extend the boundaries of the audience for flamenco by his long association with the classical guitarist John Williams, and more recently with the Argentinian guitarist Eduardo Falú, the Chilean group Inti-Illimani and others.

SELECTED RECORDINGS
Fabulous Flamenco.	Decca PFS 4334 LP
The Art of Flamenco Guitar.	Decca PFS 4270 LP
La Gitarra Flamenco.	Decca PFS 4419 LP
Paco Peña Live in London.	Decca MOR 524 LP
Inti-Illimani: Fragments of a Dream.	CBS MK 44574 CD
Music of Montoya & Ricardo.	Nimbus NI 5093 CD
Azahara.	Nimbus NI 5116 CD
Encuentro with Eduardo Falú.	Nimbus NI 5196 CD
Misa Flamenca.	Nimbus NI 5288 CD

SELECTED MUSIC
Toques Flamenco.	Music Sales

ANDRÉS BATISTA

Born –

Barcelona, Spain

12 October 1939

Andrés Batista

Andrés Batista studied classical guitar from the age of ten with Antonio Francisco Serra, and flamenco guitar with Miguel Borrull Jnr. Over the years he has accompanied many of the top figures in flamenco including Carmen Amaya, Vicente Escudero and Maria Marquez. Since 1960 he has been a member of the Spanish Society of Authors and has made twelve recordings. He has received many awards, including a gold record from the radio station 'The Voice of Madrid'. He lives in Madrid, combining a career as a composer, guitarist and teacher.

SELECTED RECORDING
Guitarra Flamenca: Andres Batista.	EMI PCS 7028 LP

SELECTED MUSIC
Flamenco Guitar Method.	UME
Flamenco Studies Vols.1 and 2.	UME
Manual Flamenco.	Batista, Madrid

SELECTED READING
Interview.	Guitar International, February 1989
Interview.	Classical Guitar, July 1995

PACO DE LUCIA

Born – FRANCISCO SANCHEZ PECINO

Algeciras, Spain

21 December 1947

SELECTED RECORDINGS
Recital de Guitarra Paco de Lucia.	Philips 63 28 036 LP
El Duende Flamenco.	Philips 63 28 061 LP
Almoraima.	Philips 63 28 199 LP
Paco de Lucia interpreta Manuel de Falla.	Philips 91 13 008 LP
Garcia Lorca: Douze Chansons pour 2 Guitares.	Philips 6599 856 LP
Entre Dos Aguas.	Philips 814 106-2 CD
Concierto de Aranjuez.	Philips 510 301-2 CD
Siroco.	Merway 830 913-2 CD
Paco de Lucia Sextet Live.	Philips 822 540-2 CD
Solo Quiero Caminar.	Philips 810 009-2 CD

SELECTED READING
Article.	Guitar International, Aug/Sept/Oct 1989
Interview.	Classical Guitar, December 1992
Interview.	Classical Guitar, November 1995
Paco de Lucia – A New Tradition – Paco Sevilla.	Sevilla Press 1995
Paco de Lucia and Family – Donn E. Pohren.	Society Spanish Studies 1992
Interview.	Classical Guitar, April 1996

SELECTED MUSIC
Lo Mejor de Paco de Lucia. Canciones del Mundo (Warner)
La Guittara de Paco de Lucia. Seemsa

Paco de Lucia

Paco de Lucia is generally regarded as the dominant flamenco figure of the sixties, seventies and eighties. Born into a flamenco family, Lucia began to play the guitar at the age of seven. His father, Antonio Sanchez Pecino, was a semi-professional guitarist who recognized his son's natural talents. He ensured that his son spent all his spare hours practising and developing one of the greatest flamenco guitar techniques the world has yet seen. Lucia began his professional career by appearing in a guitar duo with his brother Ramón. He also appeared with his brother Pepe, a singer, in a duo called Los Chiquitos de Algeciras. This duo entered the Jerez Concurso in 1962 and both young brothers won important awards. Success followed success, and over the years Paco de Lucia has become a major international star with a huge following. He became a major innovator in the world of flamenco by introducing Latin American and jazz harmonies into flamenco, and in so doing influenced a whole new generation of young flamenco guitarists. His television and concert appearances all over the world with jazz/rock guitarists John McLaughlin, Larry Coryell and Al Di Meola have given flamenco a wide international audience. A prolific recording artist, Paco de Lucia is sure to be the major figure in flamenco for many years to come.

MANOLO SANLUCAR

Born – MANUEL MUNOZ

Sanlúcar de Barrameda, Spain

24 November 1943

Manolo Sanlúcar

Manolo Sanlúcar first learnt the guitar with his father. By the time he was thirteen he was already serving his apprenticeship, accompanying singers that included Pepe Pinto, Antonio Canillas, La Paquera and others. As his career developed, the young guitarist decided to become a soloist. In 1972 he won the prestigious guitar prize of the Jerez Catedra de Flamencologia. He had already made some recordings, but with this competition success he soon earned a recording contract with CBS and later with RCA. Since that time Sanlucar has become established as one of the best of the new breed of flamenco guitarists. Like Paco de Lucia, he has introduced other music forms, including jazz, into his flamenco style.

Sanlúcar has recorded a concerto for flamenco guitar and orchestra on the RCA label. Since 1981 he has recorded for the Philips label.

SELECTED RECORDINGS
Sentimiento.	CBS NL 35413 LP
Manolo Sanlúcar: Flamenco.	CBS 73488 LP
Fantasía para guitarra y orquesta.	RCA PL 35172 LP
Azahares.	RCA PL 35350 LP

SERRANITO

Born –

VICTOR LUIS MONGE FERNANDEZ

Madrid, Spain, 16 July 1942

Serranito

Serranito first studied the guitar with his father. By the age of ten he had already made some public performances, and at eighteen was recognized as a talented guitarist. In 1968 he made his first solo recording, and a successful European concert tour followed in 1970. In 1971 he had two major competition successes, the 'Premio Nacional de Guitarra Flamenca' of the Catedra de Flamencologia de Jerez, and the 'Primer premio Guitarra Flamenca de Concierto'. Serranito won the latter at the fifth Concurso Nacional de Arte Flamenco held in Córdoba. Since these achievements he has enjoyed fame both in Spain and abroad as one of the finest flamenco guitarists of the day.

SELECTED RECORDINGS
El Flamenco en La Guitarra de Serranito.	Hispavox HH 10-251 LP
Victor Monge: 'Serranito'.	Decca PFS-R 4415 LP
Virtuosismo Flamenco.	Hispavox HH 10-349 LP
Victor Monge: 'Serranito'.	Columbia TXS 3217 LP
Tensión de Sonoridades para dos Guitarras.	Hispavox HH 10-300 LP
Ecos del Guadal Guadalquivir.	Vic Blan CD001

THE FLAMENCO GUITAR

Selected Reading

Arte y Artistas Flamencos – Fernando el de Triana – Editoriales Andaluzas Unidas SA, 1935
Lives & Legends of Flamenco: Donn E. Pohren – Society of Spanish Studies, 1964
The Flamenco Guitar: David George – Society of Spanish Studies, 1971
The Art of Flamenco: Donn E. Pohren – Society of Spanish Studies, 1972
A Way of Life: Donn E. Pohren – Society of Spanish Studies, 1980
The Flamencos of Cadiz Bay: Gerald Howson – Hutchinson, 1965. Bold Strummer, 1995
Manuel Flamenco: Andrés Batista – Batista, Madrid, 1985
Flamenco, Kunst Zwischen Gestern Und Morgen: Anja Vollhardt – Weingarten, 1988
Flamenco, Body and Soul: An Aficionado's Introduction; Serrano/Elgorriaga – Fresno, California, 1990, State University
The Wind Cried Paul Hecht: Bold Strummer, 1995

Selected Music and Methods

El Arte Flamenco de la Guitarra: Juan Martín – UMP
Metodo de Guitarra Flamenca: Andrés Batista – UME
Flamenco Guitar Method: Ivor Mairants – Music Sales
The Exciting Sound of Flamenco: Juan Martín (2 Vols.) – UMP
Authentic Flamenco Guitar Transcriptions (4 Vols.) – Gendai Guitar
Andalucian Suite (Vol.1): Juan Martin – IMP
La Zarzamora – Gendai Guitar
Pasion Flamenca – Gendai Guitar
Anthology Flamenco Falsetas – Mitchell: Bold Strummer
La Guitarra Flamenca – Juan Grecos – UME
Keys to Flamenco (Vols. 1 and 2) – Koster – AIG

Selected Videos

Flamenco! Carlos Saura: Juan Lebron Productions 11411
Juan Martin Flamenco Tuition – 3 Videos: Flamencovision/Warner

THE CLASSICAL GUITAR

ITS PLAYERS AND ITS PERSONALITIES SINCE 1800

INDEX

MIGUEL ABLONIZ (1917-) 23	ALIRIO DIAZ (1923-) 83
SERGIO ABREU (1948-) 24	SIMON DINNIGAN (1968-) 84
MARIO ABRIL (1940-) 24	MICHEL DINTRICH (1933-) 84
DIONISIO AGUADO (1784-1849) 25	CARLO DOMENICONI (1947-) 85
MIGUEL ALCAZAR (1942-) 26	JOHN W. DUARTE (1919-) 86
LAURINDO ALMEIDA (1917-) 28	ARNAUD DUMOND (1950-) 87
MARIA LUISA ANIDO (1907-) 30	ROLAND DYENS (1955-) 87
WILFRID APPLEBY (1892-1987) 31	
JULIAN ARCAS (1832-1882) 32	HERBERT J. ELLIS (1865-1903) 88
ALICE ARTZT (1943-) 33	MARGARTA ESCARPA (1964-) 89
ROBERTO AUSSEL (1954-) 33	GABRIEL ESTARELLAS (1952-) 89
JOSÉ DE AZPIAZU (1912-1986) 34	REINBERT EVERS (1949-) 90
CRISTINA AZUMA (1964-) 35	
	EDUARDO FALU (1923-) 91
CARLOS BARBOSA LIMA (1944-) 36	DIMITRI FAMPAS (1921-) 92
AGUSTIN BARRIOS MANGORÉ (1885-1944) 38	EDUARDO FERNANDEZ (1952-) 93
MANUEL BARRUECO (1952-) 40	ZANI DE FERRANTI (1801-1878) 94
RENÉ BARTOLI (1941-) 42	ELIOT FISK (1955-) 95
WILLIAM A. BAY (1945-) 42	ABEL FLEURY (1903-1958) 96
SIEGFRIED BEHREND (1933-1990) 43	WILLIAM FODEN (1860-1947) 97
PAULO BELLINATI (1950-) 44	DANIEL FORTEA (1878-1953) 98
ALEXANDER BELLOW (1912-1976) 45	FRANÇOIS DE FOSSA (1775-1849) 98
BALTAZAR BENITEZ (1944-) 46	ALEXANDER FRAUCHI (1954-) 99
DANIEL BENKÖ (1947-) 46	JOAQUIM FREIRE (1956-) 100
MATS BERSTROM (1961-) 47	SHIN-ICHI FUKUDA (1955-) 101
HECTOR BERLIOZ (1803-1869) 48	
GILBERT BIBERIAN (1944-) 49	PAUL GALBRAITH (1964-) 102
VAHDAH OLCOTT BICKFORD (1885-1980) 50	JOSE MARIA GALLARDO DEL REY (1961-) 103
ERNESTO BITETTI (1943-) 51	GERALD GARCIA (1949-) 104
VLADISLAV BLAHA (1957-) 52	HECTOR GARCIA (1930-) 104
DIEGO BLANCO (1951-) 52	OSCAR GHIGLIA (1938-) 105
VLADIMIR BOBRI (1898-1986) 53	ANTHEA GIFFORD (1949-) 106
DUSAN BOGDANOVIC (1955-) 54	MIGUEL ANGEL GIROLLET (1947-1996) 106
PHILIP J. BONE (1873-1964) 55	MAURO GIULIANI (1778-1829) 108
CARLOS BONELL (1949-) 56	VICENTE GOMEZ (1911-) 110
REMI BOUCHER (1964-) 57	JOSÉ LUIS GONZALEZ (1932-) 110
LIONA BOYD (1952-) 58	PAUL GREGORY (1956-) 111
FREDERICK BRAND (1806-1874) 59	SLAVA GRIGORYAN (1976-) 112
ARNE BRATTLAND (1955-) 59	DAVID GRIMES (1940-) 112
JULIAN BREAM (1933-) 60	STEFANO GRONDONA (1958-) 113
ROBERT BRIGHTMORE (1949-) 63	MARIA ESTHER GUZMAN (1960-) 114
LEO BROUWER (1939-) 64	
JULIAN BYZANTINE (1945-) 66	FRANZ HALASZ (1964-) 114
	OLE HALÉN (1944-) 115
OSCAR CACERES (1928-) 67	NICOLA HALL (1969-) 115
BARTOLEME CALATAYUD (1882-1973) 68	FREDERICK HAND (1947-) 116
MATTEO CARCASSI (1792-1853) 69	JOSEP HENRIQUEZ (1951-) 117
JORGE CARDOSO (1949-) 70	JOSEF HOLECEK (1939-) 117
ABEL CARLEVARO (1918-) 71	JUSTIN HOLLAND (1819-1887) 118
FERDINANDO CARULLI (1770-1841) 71	JOHN HOLMQUIST (1955-) 119
LEIF CHRISTENSEN (1950-1988) 72	HARVEY HOPE (1943-) 120
GEORGE CLINTON (1931-1991) 73	TILMAN HOPPSTOCK (1961-) 121
RICARDO COBO (1963-) 74	DON A. F. HUERTA (1804-1875) 122
OLGA COELHO (1909-) 75	
COLIN COOPER (1926-) 76	MINORU INAGAKI (1958-) 123
ERNESTO CORDERO (1946-) 77	EDUARDO ISAAC (1956-) 123
IRMA COSTANZO (1937-) 78	SHARON ISBIN (1956-) 124
NAPOLÉON COSTE (1805-1883) 79	ALEXANDER IVANOV-KRAMSKOY
COSTAS COTSIOLIS (1957-) 80	(1912-1973) 125
	RICARDO FERNANDEZ IZNAOLA (1949-) 125
BETHO DAVEZAC (1938-) 81	
ANIELLO DESIDERIO (1971-) 81	PER OLOF JOHNSON (1928-) 126
ANTON DIABELLI (1781-1858) 82	JEAN PIERRE JUMEZ (1943-) 127

DEAN KAMEI (1950-)	128
MARIA KÄMMERLING (1946-)	128
WILLIAM KANENGISER (1959-)	130
HUBERT KÄPPEL (1951-)	131
ELI KASSNER (1924-)	131
MARCELO KAYATH (1964-)	132
CHRIS KILVINGTON (1944-)	133
HORST KLEE (1952-)	134
FRANCIS KLEYNJANS (1951-)	145
TIMO KORHONEN (1964-)	135
NIKITA KOSHKIN (1956-)	136
ELEFTHERIA KOTZIA (1957-)	137
NORBERT KRAFT (1950-)	138
ALEXANDRE LAGOYA (1929-)	139
ROBERTO LARA (1927-1988)	140
ANTONIO LAURO (1917- 1986)	141
JONATHAN LEATHWOOD (1970-)	142
LUIGI LEGNANI (1790-1877)	143
DAVID LEISNER (1953-)	144
PHILIPPE LEMAIGRE (1950-)	144
WOLFGANG LENDLE (1948-)	145
WULFIN LIESKE (1956-)	146
DAGOBERTO LINHARES (1953-)	147
MIGUEL LLOBET (1878-1928)	148
MICHAEL LORIMER (1946-)	149
GUY LUKOWSKI (1942-)	149
VINCENZO MACALUSO (1941-)	150
MARIO MACCAFERRI (1992-)	152
IVOR MAIRANTS (1908-)	154
DEBORAH MARIOTTI (1959-)	155
BARRY MASON (1947-)	156
AKINOBU MATSUDA (1933-)	157
SUSANNE MEBES (1960-)	158
DOMINGO MERCADO (1919-1994)	158
JOHANN KASPAR MERTZ (1806-1856)	159
VLADIMIR MIKULKA (1950-)	160
JOHN MILLS (1947-)	160
SIMON MOLITOR (1766-1848)	161
JORGE MOREL (1931-)	162
ALFONSO MORENO (1950-)	164
LUIGI MOZZANI (1869-1943)	164
THOMAS MÜLLER-PERING (1958-)	165
MARTIN MYSLIVECEK (1950-)	166
SANTIAGO NAVASCUES (1933-)	167
MICHAEL NEWMAN (1957-)	167
DOUGLAS NIEDT (1952-)	168
KAARE NORGE (1963-)	169
NIGEL NORTH (1954-)	169
CRAIG OGDEN (1967-)	170
STEIN-ERIK OLSEN (1953-)	171
JORGE ORAISON (1946-)	171
JESUS ORTEGA (1935-)	172
JULIO MARTINEZ OYANGUREN (1905-1973)	172
IVAN PADOVEC (1800-1873)	173
NICOLO PAGANINI (1782-1840)	174
SOPHOCLES PAPAS (1893-1986)	175
CHRISTOPHER PARKENING (1947-)	176
MARIO PARODI (1917-1970)	177
CARLOS PAYES (1944-)	178
STEPHEN FUNK PEARSON (1950-)	179
KRZYSZTOF PELECH (1970-)	180
BORIS A. PEROTT (1882-1958)	181
RICHARD PICK (1915-)	182
ALVARO PIERRI (1953-)	182
BARBARA POLASEK (1939-)	183
ALBERTO PONCE (1935-)	184
DOMINGO PRAT (1886-1944)	184
MADAME SIDNEY PRATTEN (1821-1895)	186
IDA PRESTI (1924-1967)	187
SONJA PRUNNBAUER (1948-)	188
EMILIO PUJOL (1886-1980)	189
IVAN PUTILIN (1909-)	190
RAFAEL RABELLO (1962-)	190
KONRAD RAGOSSNIG (1932-)	191
STEPAN RAK (1945-)	192
ALEXANDER-SERGEI RAMIREZ (1962-)	193
MANUEL LOPEZ RAMOS (1929-)	194
GIULIO REGONDI (1822-1872)	194
IGNACIO RODES (1961-)	196
ISTVAN RÖMER (1962-)	196
ANGEL ROMERO (1946-)	197
CELEDONIO ROMERO (1913-1996)	198
PEPE ROMERO (1944-)	199
DAVID RUSSELL (1953-)	200
MICHEL SADANOWSKY (1950-)	202
EDUARDO SAINZ DE LA MAZA (1903-1982)	202
REGINO SAINZ DE LA MAZA (1896-1981)	203
GEORGE SAKELLARIOU (1944-)	204
MARCO DE SANTI (1957-)	204
TURIBIO SANTOS (1943-)	205
MARIA LIVIA SÃO MARCOS (1942-)	206
TADASHI SASAKI (1943-)	207
JUKKA SAVIJOKI (1952-)	207
RICHARD SAVINO (1956-)	208
ISAIAS SAVIO (1902-1977)	209
KARL SCHEIT (1909-1993)	210
STEPHAN SCHMIDT (1967-)	211
JOHN SCHNEIDER (1950-)	212
FRANZ SCHUBERT (1797-1828)	213
ANDRÉS SEGOVIA (1893-1987)	214
EMANUELLE SEGRE (1965-)	217
PETER SENSIER (1918-1977)	218
ERNEST SHAND (1868-1924)	219
MARIA ISABEL SIEWERS (1950-)	219
SEPPO SIIRALA (1952-)	220
RONOEL SIMÕES (1919-)	220
PER SKARENG (1959-)	221
NEIL SMITH (1945-)	221
REGINALD SMITH BRINDLE (1917-)	222
RAPHAELLA SMITS (1957-)	222
MARCO SOCIAS (1966-)	223
MAREK SOKOLOWSKI (1818-1883)	224
GÖRAN SÖLLSCHER (1955-)	225
FERNANDO SOR (1778-1839)	226
ROBERT SPENCER (1932-)	228
DAVID STAROBIN (1951-)	229
PAVEL STEIDL (1961-)	230
ERIK STENSTADVOLD (1948-)	231
ICHIRO SUZUKI (1948-)	231
LASZLO SZENDREY-KARPER (1932-1991)	232
DAVID TANENBAUM (1956-)	233
RENATO TARRAGO (1927-)	234
FRANCISCO TARREGA (1854-1909)	236
SCOTT TENNANT (1962-)	239
MILAN TESAR (1938-)	239
JOSÉ TOMAS (1934-)	240
REY DE LA TORRE (1917-1994)	241
MICHAEL TRÖSTER (1956-)	242
JAMES TYLER (1940-)	242
TERRY USHER (1909-1969)	243
ALBERT VALDES BLAIN (1921-)	244
ROLAND VALDES BLAIN (1922-)	244
BENJAMIN VERDERY (1955-)	245
ANDRÉ VERDIER (1886-1957)	245
ROBERT VIDAL (1925-)	246
HEITOR VILLA-LOBOS (1887-1959)	248
LUISE WALKER (1910-)	251
TIMOTHY WALKER (1943-)	251
BUNYAN WEBB (1936-1978)	252
CARL MARIA VON WEBER (1786-1826)	253
JOHN WILLIAMS (1941-)	254
LEN WILLIAMS (1910-1987)	257
LEO WITOSZYNSKYJ (1941-)	258
SIMON WYNBERG (1955-)	259
KAZUHITO YAMASHITA (1961-)	260
NARCISO YEPES (1927-)	261
ANDREW YORK (1958-)	262
FABIO ZANON (1966-)	263
LUIS ZEA (1953-)	264
MILAN ZELENKA (1939-)	265
FREDERIC ZIGANTE (1961-)	266

ITS DUOS, TRIOS, QUARTETS & MORE

SERGIO & EDUARDO ABREU	270
ILSE & NICOLAS ALFONSO	270
AMADEUS DUO	271
ASSAD BROTHERS	272
CASTELLANI-ANDRIACCIO DUO	273
DORIGNY/ITO DUO	273
DUO BATENDO	274
DUO SONARE	274
EVANGELOS & LISA	275
GARAU-MILLET DUO	276
GRONINGER DUO	276
HILL-WILTSCHINSKY DUO	277
MONTES-KIRCHER DUO	277
POMPONIO-ZARATE DUO	278
AMSTERDAM GUITAR TRIO	279
FALLA TRIO	280
PRO ARTE TRIO	280
TRIO CONCENTUS	281
ZAGREB GUITAR TRIO	281
AIGHETTA GUITAR QUARTET	282
ENGLISH GUITAR QUARTET	282
LOS ANGELES GUITAR QUARTET	283
PRAGUE GUITAR QUARTET	284
ROMERO FAMILY QUARTET	285
NIIBORI GUITAR ENSEMBLE AND ORCHESTRA	286

ITS COMPOSERS

ANTON GARCIA ABRIL (1933-)	296
MALCOLM ARNOLD (1921-)	297
VICENTE ASENCIO (1908-1979)	298
RICHARD RODNEY BENNETT (1936-)	299
LENNOX BERKELEY (1903-1989)	299
BENJAMIN BRITTEN (1913-1976)	300
MARIO CASTELNUOVO-TEDESCO (1895-1968)	301
PETER MAXWELL DAVIES (1934-)	303
STEPHEN DODGSON (1924-)	304
MANUEL DE FALLA (1876-1946)	305
ALBERTO GINASTERA (1919-1983)	306
RADAMÉS GNATALLI (1906-1988)	306
CARLOS GUASTAVINO (1912-)	307
HANS WERNER HENZE (1926-)	307
ANTONIO JOSÉ (1902-1936)	308
VACLAV KUCERA (1924-)	309
FRANK MARTIN (1890-1974)	309
FRANCISCO MIGNONE (1897-1986)	310
FEDERICO MORENO TORROBA (1891-1981)	311
MARCOS NOBRE (1939-)	312
JANA OBROVSKA (1930-1987)	313
MAURICE OHANA (1914-1992)	314
GOFFREDO PETRASSI (1904-)	314
ASTOR PIAZZOLLA (1921-1992)	315
MANUEL PONCE (1886-1948)	316
JOAQUIN RODRIGO (1901-)	318
ANTONIO RUIZ-PIPO (1934-)	320
GUIDO SANTORSOLA (1904-1994)	321
TORU TAKEMITSU (1930-1996)	321
ALEXANDER TANSMAN (1897-1986)	322
JOAQUIN TURINA (1882-1949)	323
WILLIAM WALTON (1902-1983)	323

ITS GUITAR MAKERS

STAUFER (1778-1853)	330
LACOTE (1785-1855)	330
PANORMO FAMILY	331
TORRES (1817-1892)	332
HERNANDEZ (1875-1943)	333
HAUSER (1882-1952)	333
RAMIREZ FAMILY	334
FLETA (1897-1977)	335
BOUCHET (1898-1986)	336
KOHNO (1912-)	336
RUBIO (1934-)	337
BERNABE (1932)	338
CONTRERAS (1926-)	338
BOLIN (1912-1993)	339
FRIEDERICH (1932-)	339
MANUEL RODRIGUEZ AND SONS	340
ROMANILLOS (1932-)	341
HOPF (1936-)	342
GILBERT (1922-)	342
FISCHER (1941-)	343
GREG SMALLMAN (1947-)	343
HUMPHREY (1948-)	344
ALBERT AUGUSTINE (1900-1967)	345
D'ADDARIO	346

ITS SCHOLARS

RUGGERO CHIESA (1933-1993)	348
JOHN GAVALL (1919-)	349
ANGELO GILARDINO (1943-)	350
FREDERIC V. GRUNFELD (1929-1987)	351
THOMAS F. HECK (1943-)	351
BRIAN HODEL (1948-)	352
JOHN HUBER (1940-)	352
OLIVER HUNT (1934-)	353
BRIAN JEFFERY (1938-)	354
MICHAEL MACMEEKEN (1942-)	354
FREDERICK NOAD (1929-)	355
THEODORE NORMAN (1912-)	356
MATANYA OPHEE (1932-)	356
CORAZON OTERO (1944-)	357
PETER PAFFGEN (1950-)	358
JOSEF POWROZNIAK (1902-1989)	358
RONALD PURCELL (1932-)	359
HECTOR QUINE (1926-)	359
AARON SHEARER (1919-)	360
RICHARD STOVER (1945-)	361
GRAHAM WADE (1940-)	362
JOSEF ZUTH (1879-1932)	362

THE FLAMENCO GUITAR

RAMON MONTOYA (1880-1949)	366
MANOLO DE HUELVA (1892-1976)	366
NIÑO RICARDO (1904-1972)	367
MELCHOR DE MARCHENA (1907-1980)	367
SABICAS (1912-1990)	368
CARLOS MONTOYA (1903-1993)	368
MARIO ESCUDERO (1928-)	369
PEPE MARTINEZ (1923-1985)	369
MANUEL CANO (1926-1990)	370
JUAN SERRANO (1936-)	370
PACO PEÑA (1942-)	371
ANDRÉS BATISTA (1939-)	371
PACO DE LUCIA (1947-)	372
MANOLO SANLUCAR (1943-)	373
SERRANITO (1942-)	373

SOURCES OF INFORMATION AND SUPPLIES

GUITAR MAGAZINES

Acoustic Guitar,
412 Red Hill Avenue #15,
San Anselmo,
California 94960,
USA

Classical Guitar,
Olsover House,
43 Sackville Road,
Newcastle upon Tyne,
NE6 5TA,
UK

Il Fronimo,
Edizioni Zerboni,
Via M. F. Quintiliano 40,
20138 Milano,
Italy

Gendai Guitar,
1-11 Chihay-cho,
Ikebukuro,
Toshima-ku,
Tokyo,
Japan

Gitarr och Luta,
c/o Erik Mollerström,
Ostermalmsgaten 5,
S-114 4 Stockholm,
Sweden

Gitarre & Laute,
Postfach 410408,
5000 Köln,
W. Germany

American Luthier
Guild of American Luthiers,
8222 S. Park Place,
Tacoma,
WA 98408, USA

Fingerstyle Guitar
3645 Jeannine Drive,
Suite 208,
Colorado Springs,
CO 80917
USA

Staccato
Akazienweg 57,
50827 Koln,
Germany

Guitar Maker,
Association String Instrument Artisans,
PO Box 341,
Paul Smiths,
NY 12970-0341

Guitar Player,
411 Borel Avenue #100,
San Mateo,
CA 94402,
USA

Guitar Review,
40 W. 25th Street,
New York
NY 10010,
USA

European Guitar Teachers Association
Guitar Journal,
52 Ashurst Road,
Cockfosters,
Herts, EN4 9LF,
UK

Les Cahiers de la Guitarre,
BP83,
94472 Boissy-St-Lèger,
Cedex,
Paris,
France

Musikblatt,
Tannenweg 14,
3400 Göttingen,
W. Germany

Soundboard (GFA),
PO Box 878,
Claremont,
CA 91711,
USA

RETAIL SUPPLIERS OF CLASSICAL GUITARS, BOOKS, RECORDS, MUSIC

GREAT BRITAIN

Blackwells Music Shop,
38 Holywell Street,
Oxford
OX1 3SW
Books/music

Bristol Spanish Guitar Centre,
429 Gloucester Road, Horfield,
Bristol BS7 8TZ
Guitars/music/books/recordings

Chappells,
New Bond Street,
London WC1
Guitars/music/books

Raymond Ursell,
48 Station Road,
North Hykeham,
Lincoln LN6 9AQ
Guitars

Forsyths,
126 Deansgate,
Manchester M3 2GR
Guitars/music/books/recordings

W. & G. Foyle Ltd,
119-125 Charing Cross Road,
London WC2
Books/music/recordings

Classical Guitar Centre Ltd.
51A St Mary's Road,
Bearwood,
West Midlands
B67 5DH
Guitars/music/books/recordings

HMV Record Shop,
150 & 363 Oxford Street,
London WC1
Specialist recordings

London Guitar Studio,
62 Duke St,
London W1M 5DS
Guitars/music/books/recordings

Ashley Mark Publishing Company
Olsover House,
43 Sackville Road,
Newcastle upon Tyne
NE6 5TA
Mail order only/music/books/ recordings

Ivor Mairants Musicentre,
56 Rathbone Place,
London W1P 1AB
Guitars/music/books/recordings

May & May,
Arundell House,
Tisbury,
Salisbury SP3 6QU
Mail order. New, secondhand and rare books on music.

Nottingham Spanish Guitar Centre,
44 Nottingham Road,
New Basford,
Nottingham
NG7 7AE
Guitars/music/books/recordings

Spanish Guitar Centre,
36 Cranbourn Street,
London WC2 7AD
Guitars/music/books/recordings

Tower Records,
1 Piccadilly Circus,
London W1
Specialist recordings

J.G.Windows Ltd,
1-7 Central Arcade,
Newcastle upon Tyne
NE1
Guitars/music/books/recordings

UNITED STATES OF AMERICA

Barnes & Noble,
128 5th Avenue,
New York
Books/music

The Bold Strummer,
1 Webb Road,
Westport, CT 06880
Mail order – books/music

Jack Cecchini Guitar Studios,
5344 N. Magnolia,
Chicago,
Illinois
Guitars/music/books

Guitar Studio,
1433 Clement Street,
San Francisco,
CA 94118
Guitars/books/music/recordings

Editions Orphée Inc.,
1240 Clubview Bvd, North Columbus,
Ohio 43235-1226
Mail order – books/music/recordings

Joseph Patelson Music House,
160 West 56th Street,
New York NY 10019
Books/music/recordings

Beverly Maher,
The Guitar Salon,
New York,
Fax: (212) 367 9767
Guitars

Luthier Music Corporation,
341 West 44th Street,
New York NY 10036
Guitars/music/books/recordings

Tower Records,
at Lincoln Centre and Greenwich
Village, New York and in most
USA cities
Recordings/books/magazines

Guitar Salon International,
3100 Donald Douglas Loop No,
Santa Monica,
CA 90405,
USA
Guitars

R. E. Bruné,
800 Greenwood Street,
Evanston,
Illinois 60201
Guitars

CANADA

Eli Kassner Guitar Academy,
19 Belmont Street,
Toronto
Guitars/music/books

FRANCE

FNAC. Several stores in Paris including
Rue de Rennes and Les Halles Forum
Centre
Recordings/books

La Guitarreria,
5 Rue d'Edimbourg,
75008 Paris
Guitars/music/books

L'Atelier,
5 Rue d'Edimbourg,
75008 Paris
Music/recordings

La Libraire Musicale de Paris,
68 bis Rue Réaumur, 75003
Paris
Books/music

BELGIUM

Uni-Sound BVBA,
St Jacobstraat 13,
8000 Bruges
Books/music/recordings

GERMANY

Chanterelle Verlag,
Postfach 103909,
D-6900 Heidelberg
Mail order – books/music/recordings

Steinway House,
Colonnaden 29,
2000 Hamburg
Guitars/music/books/recordings

Heiner Viertmann,
Beethovenstrasse 27,
Postfach 260128,
5000 Köln 1
Guitars/music/books/recordings

ITALY

Hortus Musicus,
Viale Liegi 7,
Rome 00198
Music/books/recordings

G.Ricordi & Co.,
Via Salomone 77,
Milan
Guitars/music/books/recordings

SPAIN

Bowden Music,
Calle Huerto de Torella 13,
Palma de Mallorca
Guitars/music/books/recordings

Casa Luthier,
Balmes 77, 08007
Barcelona
Guitars/music/books/recordings

Manuel Rodríguez,
Hortaleza 26,
Madrid 28004
Guitars/music/books/recordings

JAPAN

ARP International,
2-24-13 Kamisaginomiya,
Nakano-ku,
Tokyo 165
Music/books/recordings

Yamaha Music Store,
Central Ginza, Tokyo
and branches throughout Japan
Guitars/music/books/recordings

Casa de la Guitarra SA,
Shimo-Ochiai 3-17-49,
Shinjuku-Ku,
Tokyo 161
Guitars/music/books/recordings

NETHERLANDS

Broekmans & Van Poppel,
Baerlestraat, 92-04,
Amsterdam Z
Books/music

La Guitarra Buena,
Reestraat 14,
1016 DN Amsterdam
Guitars/music/books/recordings

SWEDEN

Gitarren AB,
Skanstorget 10,
Gothenburg
Guitars/music/books/recordings

Musikerma Evert Ahlander,
Box 184,
Bondegatan 20,
S 561 23 Huskvarna

SWITZERLAND

Aux Gitarres,
Theatrestrasse 7/3,
CH-4051 Basel
Guitars/music/books

Music Hug,
Limmatquai 26-28,
8001 Zürich
Guitars/music/books/recordings